# ECHOES OF THE MOST HOLY

# ECHOES OF THE MOST HOLY

## The Day of Atonement in the Book of Revelation

André Reis

*Foreword* by Steven Thompson

WIPF & STOCK · Eugene, Oregon

ECHOES OF THE MOST HOLY
The Day of Atonement in the Book of Revelation



Wipf and Stock
An Imprint of Wipf and Stock Publishers
199 W. 8th Ave., Suite 3
Eugene, OR 97401

www.wipfandstock.com

PAPERBACK ISBN: 978-1-6667-3618-2
HARDCOVER ISBN: 978-1-6667-9418-2
EBOOK ISBN: 978-1-6667-9419-9

*Cataloguing-in-Publication data:*

Names: Reis, André.
Title: Echoes of the most holy: the Day of Atonement in the book of Revelation
/André Reis.
Description: Eugene, OR: Wipf and Stock, 2022 | Includes bibliographical references. Identifiers: ISBN 978-1-6667-3618-2 (paperback) | ISBN 978-1-6667-9418-2 (hardcover) |
ISBN 978-1-6667-9419-9 (ebook)
Subjects: LCSH: New Testament | Book of Revelation | Biblical Intertextuality
Classification: LCC BS2825.52 C8 2022 (print) | LCC BS2825.52 (ebook)

To Francini, Pam, Chloe & Mckayla

ἡ ἀγάπη οὐδέποτε πίπτει
εἴτε δὲ προφητεῖαι, καταργηθήσονται
εἴτε γλῶσσαι, παύσονται
εἴτε γνῶσις, καταργηθήσεται

1 Corinthians 13:8

# CONTENTS

ABBREVIATIONS i
FOREWORD vii
ACNOWLEDGMENTS ix
PREFACE xi

Introduction: TOWARD AN INTERTEXTUAL READING OF REVELATION 1

The Research Question 5
Biblical Intertextuality: An Overview 7
Reading Revelation Intertextually 13
General Assumptions About Revelation 21
*Authorship* 22
*Date of Composition* 22
*Literary Genre* 23
Conclusion 24

1. THE DAY OF ATONEMENT IN THE OLD TESTAMENT 25

The Theology of Levitical Rituals 25
*God Abides in the Sanctuary* 28
*Defiling the Sanctuary Jeopardizes the Covenant* 28
*Cleansing the Sanctuary: The Meaning of Kipper* 30
The Origins of the Day of Atonement in Israel 33
*The Day of Atonement in the Israelite Calendar* 35

The Rituals of Yom Kippur 35
*Blowing the Šôpar* 38
*Israel's Role* 38
*The High Priest's Role* 40
*God's Role* 41
*Ritual Ablutions* 42
*The High Priest's Clothing* 43
*The Sacrificial Animals* 44
*Casting Lots for the Two Goats* 44
*The First Purification of the Most Holy Place: The Sacrifice for the High Priest and His Household* 45
*The Offer Incense* 46
*The First Purification of the Holy Place: The Altar of Incense* 47
*The First Purification of the Outer Altar* 48
*The Second Purification of the Most Holy Place: The Sacrifice for the People* 49
*The Second Purification of the Holy Place* 49
*The Second Purification of the Outer Altar* 49
*The Rite of the "Goat for Azazel"* 49
*Confession of Sin over the "Goat for Azazel"* 50
*The Meaning of laʿazāʾzēl* 52
*The Burnt Offerings* 56
*Atoning Intentional vs. Unintentional Sins* 57
The Day of Atonement Covenant Lawsuit 58
Conclusion 58

Excursus: The Origins of the Israelite Elimination Ritual in Its Ancient Near East Context 59

*The Greek Pharmakos Rites and the Ritual of the "Goat for Azazel"* 60
More on the Meaning of *laʿazāʾzēl* 62
Alternative Views on the Meaning of *laʿazāʾzēl* 64
*Azazel as the Goat's Function* 64

*Azazel as the Place Where the Goat is Dispatched* 65
*Azazel as "Removal"* 66
*Azazel as "On Behalf of Azazel"* 67
*Azazel as the "Wrath of God"* 67
Conclusion 68

2. THE DAY OF ATONEMENT IN SECOND TEMPLE LITERATURE 69

The Day of Atonement in the Book of Jubilees 70
The Day of Atonement in the Apocalypse of Abraham 72
Azazel in 1 Enoch 75
The Day of Atonement in Philo 76
The Day of Atonement in Josephus 77
Conclusion 78

3. THE DAY OF ATONEMENT IN THE NEW TESTAMENT 79

The Jewish Feasts in Nascent Christianity 79
The Day of Atonement in the New Testament 81
The Day of Atonement in the Gospels 83
*"My Blood Poured Out for Many"* 83
*The Release of Barabbas* 83
*Jesus' Humiliation* 85
*The Veil of the Temple* 86
*Jesus as a High Priest in the Gospel of John* 88
The Day of Atonement in Acts and the Epistles 89
*The Day of Atonement in the Letters of Paul* 90
*Did the "Goat for Azazel" Prefigure Christ?* 92
*The Day of Atonement in the Epistle to the Hebrews* 94
*"Within the Veil": Day of Atonement or Inauguration?* 98
The Expression *Peri Hamartias* in the New Testament 105
Atonement in the New Testament:
The Meaning of *Hilaskesthai* 110
Conclusion 115

4. THE DAY OF ATONEMENT IN THE BOOK OF REVELATION 117

John's Allusive Method 117

The Day of Atonement in Revelation: An Overview 119

Revelation 1: Jesus as Heavenly High Priest 121
*Atoning Blood in Revelation 1* 121
*"A Loud Voice as a Trumpet"* 122
*Jesus' High-Priestly Attire* 125
*Podērēs in the Epistle of Barnabas* 131
*Jesus Golden Sash* 131
*The Day of Atonement as Validation of Jesus' High Priesthood* 132

Revelation 2 & 3: The Day of Atonement as Precursor to the Letters to the Churches of Asia 133
*Jesus' High-Priestly Intercession Portrayed* 136

Revelation 4 & 5: The Heavenly Throne Room and the Slaughtered Lamb 138
*The Slaughtered Lamb Offered Inside the Heavenly Most Holy Place* 139
*The High-Priestly Elders* 141
*The Offer of Incense in the Heavenly Most Holy Place* 142
*Day of Atonement or Inauguration?* 143

Revelation 6: The Souls Under the Altar of Incense 145

Revelation 7 & 14: The Priestly 144,000 147
*Cultic Purity Instead of Forgiveness* 150
*Casting Lots Over Humankind: The Three Angels* 151

Revelation 8: The Seventh Seal and the Angel with the Golden Censer 152

Revelation 9: The Golden Altar of Incense and Defiant Humanity 159

Revelation 11: Measuring the Temple, the Altar, and the Ark of the Covenant 162

Revelation 15: The Opening of the Heavenly Most Holy Place 165
Revelation 17: The Harlot, the Beast, and the "Goat for Azazel" 167
Revelation 18: Babylon as an Eschatological *Pharmakos* 171
Revelation 19: Jesus, the High-Priestly Warrior 172
Revelation 12 & 20: The Judgment of the Dragon 174
*Azazel in the Book of Enoch and Revelation* 177
Revelation 21: The High-Priestly New Jerusalem 185
Revelation 20 and 22: Eschatological Retribution for the Wicked 187
Conclusion 191

SUMMARY AND CONCLUSION 193

BIBLIOGRAPHY 199

# ABBREVIATIONS

| | |
|---|---|
| *AAA* | Annals of Archaeology and Anthropology |
| *AASS* | *Asia Adventist Seminary Studies* |
| AB | The Anchor Bible |
| *ABR* | *Australian Biblical Review* |
| ABRL | Anchor Bible Reference Library |
| ANE | Ancient Near East |
| *ANRW* | *Aufstieg und Niedergang der römischen Welt*. 107 vols. Edited by Wolfgang Haase. Berlin: de Gruyter, 1972– |
| *Ant.* | *Antiquities* (by Josephus) |
| AOTC | Apollos Old Testament Commentary |
| AUSDDS | Andrews University Seminary Doctoral Dissertation Series |
| *Aug* | *Augustinianum* |
| *AUSS* | *Andrews University Seminary Studies* |
| AYB | The Anchor Yale Bible |
| *AYBD* | *The Anchor Yale Bible Dictionary*. 6 vols. Edited by David Noel Freedman. New York: Doubleday, 1992 |
| b. | Talmud (Babylonian) |
| BBRSup | Bulletin for Biblical Research Supplements |
| BCE | Before the Christian Era |
| BDAG | Walter Bauer, Frederick W. Danker, William F. Arndt and F. Wilbur Gingrich. *A Greek-English Lexicon of the New Testament and other Early Christian Literature*. 3rd ed. Chicago: Chicago University Press, 2000 |
| BDB | *Enhanced Brown-Driver-Briggs Hebrew and English Lexicon*. Oxford: Clarendon, 1977 |
| BECNT | Baker Exegetical Commentary on the New Testament |
| *Bib* | *Biblica* |

| | |
|---|---|
| *BibInt* | *Biblical Interpretation* |
| *BibR* | *Biblical Research* |
| *BibSac* | *Bibliotheca Sacra* |
| BIS | Biblical Interpretation Series |
| BFCT | Beiträge zur Förderung christlicher Theologie |
| BJS | Brown Jewish Studies |
| *BN* | *Biblische Notizen* |
| BNTC | Black's New Testament Commentaries |
| BRS | The Biblical Resource Series |
| *BTB* | *Biblical Theology Bulletin* |
| BTCB | Brazos Theological Commentary on the Bible |
| *BVC* | *Bible et Vie Chrétienne* |
| BZAW | Beihefte zur Zeitschrift für die alttestamentliche Wissenschaft |
| *BW* | *The Biblical World* |
| BZNW | Beihefte zur Zeitschrift für die neutestamentliche Wissenschaft und die Kunde der älteren Kirche |
| CC | Continental Commentary |
| CE | Christian Era |
| *CBQ* | *Catholic Biblical Quarterly* |
| *CH* | *Church History* |
| ConNT | Coniectanea neotestamentica or Coniectanea biblica: New Testament Series |
| *CTR* | *Criswell Theological Review* |
| CRINT | Compendia Rerum Iudaicarum ad Novum Testamentum |
| DARCOM | Daniel and Revelation Committee Series |
| *DDD* | *Dictionary of Deities and Demons.* Edited by Karel van der Toorn, Bob Becking and Peter W. van der Horst. Grand Rapids: Eerdmans, 1999 |
| *DSSR* | *The Dead Sea Scrolls Reader.* 6 vols. Edited by Donald W. Parry and Emanuel Tov. Leiden: Brill, 2004–2005 |
| *EI* | *Eretz Israel* |
| *EncJud* | *Encyclopaedia Judaica.* 16 vols. Edited by Cecil Roth and Geoffrey Wigoder. Jerusalem: Keter, 1972 |
| *EQ* | *The Evangelical Quarterly* |
| EUS | European University Studies |
| *ExAud* | *Ex Auditu* |
| *ExpTim* | *Expository Times* |

| | |
|---|---|
| FAT | Forschungen zum Alten Testament |
| *FF* | *Forschungen und Fortschritte* |
| FIOTL | The Formation and Interpretation of Old Testament Literature |
| *GOTR* | *Greek Orthodox Theological Review* |
| *HALOT* | Koehler, L., W. Baumgartner, and J. J. Stamm. *The Hebrew and Aramaic Lexicon of the Old Testament*. 5 vols. Translated and edited under the supervision of M. E. J. Richardson. Leiden: Brill, 1994–2000 |
| HBS | Herders Biblische Studien |
| HCOT | Historical Commentary on the Old Testament |
| *HeytJ* | *Heythrop Journal* |
| *HTR* | *Harvard Theological Review* |
| *IBS* | *Irish Biblical Studies* |
| ICC | International Critical Commentary |
| *IDB* | *The Interpreter's Dictionary of the Bible*. 4 vols. Edited by G. A. Buttrick. Nashville, 1962 |
| *IDBSup* | *The Interpreter's Dictionary of the Bible Supplementary Volume*. Edited by Keith Crim and Victor Paul Furnish. Nashville: Abingdon, 1976 |
| *Int* | *Interpretation* |
| *ISBE* | *International Standard Bible Encyclopedia*. 4 vols. Rev. ed. Edited by G. W. Bromiley et al. Grand Rapids: Eerdmans, 1979–1988 |
| *JAOS* | *Journal of the American Oriental Society* |
| *JAMS* | *Journal of the American Musicological Society* |
| *JATS* | *Journal of the Adventist Theological Society* |
| *JBL* | *Journal of Biblical Literature* |
| *JETS* | *Journal of the Evangelical Theological Society* |
| *JECH* | *Journal of Early Christian History* |
| *JHS* | *The Journal of Hebrew Scriptures* |
| *JNES* | *Journal of Near Eastern Studies* |
| *JQR* | *The Jewish Quarterly Review* |
| *JR* | *Journal of Religion* |
| *JSJ* | *Journal for the Study of Judaism* |
| *JSNT* | *Journal for the Study of the New Testament* |
| JSNTSup | Journal for the Study of the New Testament Supplement Series |
| *JSOT* | *Journal for the Study of the Old Testament* |
| JSOTSup | Journal for the Study of the Old Testament Supplement Series |

| | |
|---|---|
| *JSPS* | *Journal for the Study of the Pseudepigrapha* |
| JSPSup | Journal for the Study of the Pseudepigrapha Supplement Series |
| *JSS* | *Journal of Semitic Studies* |
| *JTS* | *Journal for Theological Studies* |
| KEK | Kritisch-exegetischer Kommentar über das Neue Testament |
| *KuD* | *Kerygma und Dogma* |
| *Lat* | *Lateranum* |
| LBC | Layman's Bible Commentary |
| LHBOTS | Library of Hebrew Bible/Old Testament Studies |
| LNTS | Library of New Testament Studies |
| *LOEB* | *Josephus. With An English Translation by H. St. J. Thackeray.* The Loeb Classical Library. 9 vols. Edited by T. E. Page et al. Cambridge: Harvard University Press, 1961 |
| *LS* | *Letter and Spirit* |
| LXX | *Septuaginta.* Edited by Alfred Rahlfs. Stuttgart: Deutsche Bibelgesellschaft, 1979 |
| m. | Mishnah |
| *MelT* | *Melita Theologica* |
| MT | Masoretic Text of the Hebrew Bible |
| *MTZ* | *Münchener Theologische Zeitschrift* |
| *NA*$^{28}$ | Novum Testamentum Graece. 28th rev. ed. Edited by E. Nestle, K. Barbara Aland et al. Stuttgart: Deutsche Bibelgesellschaft, 2012 |
| NAC | The New American Commentary |
| NASB | New American Standard Bible |
| NBL | Neues Bibellexikon |
| *Neo* | *Neotestamentica* |
| NES | Near Eastern Studies |
| NICNT | New International Commentary on the New Testament |
| *NIDNTT* | *The New International Dictionary of New Testament Theology.* 4 vols. Edited by Colin Brown. Grand Rapids: Zondervan, 1975 |
| NIGTC | New International Greek Testament Commentary |
| NIV | New International Version |
| NIVAC | The New International Version Application Commentary |
| NKJV | New King James Version |
| *NovT* | *Novum Testamentum* |
| NRSV | New Revised Standard Version |

| | |
|---|---|
| NT | New Testament |
| NTA | Neuetestamentliche Abhandlungen |
| NTC | New Testament Commentary |
| NTL | New Testament Library |
| NTM | New Testament Monographs |
| *NTS* | *New Testament Studies* |
| OT | Old Testament |
| *OTP* | *Old Testament Pseudepigrapha.* 2 vols. Edited by James H. Charlesworth. Peabody: Hendrickson, 2010 |
| OSt | Oudtestamentische Studiën |
| PC | The Pulpit Commentary |
| PCNT | Paideia Commentary on the New Testament |
| PNTC | Pelican New Testament Commentaries |
| *POT* | *Pseudepigrapha of the Old Testament.* 2 vols. Edited by R. H. Charles. Bellingham: Logos, 2004 |
| PVTG | Pseudepigrapha Veteris Testamenti Graece. 6 vols. Edited by A. M. Denis and M. De Jonge. Leiden: Brill, 1970 |
| *RB* | *Revue Biblique* |
| *ResQ* | *Restoration Quarterly* |
| *RRJ* | *The Review of Rabbinic Judaism* |
| *RSR* | *Religious Studies Review* |
| *SA* | *Studia Antiqua* |
| SAOC | Studies in Ancient Oriental Civilizations |
| SBB | Stuttgarter Biblische Beiträge |
| SBLDS | Society of Biblical Literature Dissertation Series |
| SBLSP | Society of Biblical Literature Seminar Papers |
| SBT | Studies in Biblical Theology |
| SCL | Sather Classical Lectures |
| *SEL* | *Studi Epigrafici e Linguistici sul Vicino Oriente Antico* |
| SHR | Studies in the History of Religions |
| SJLA | Studies in Judaism and Late Antiquity |
| *SJOT* | *Scandinavian Journal of the Old Testament* |
| SNTSMS | Society for New Testament Studies Monograph Series |
| SP | Sacra Pagina |
| *ST* | *Studia Theologica* |
| STDJ | Studies on the Texts of the Desert of Judah |
| SUNT | Studien zur Umwelt des Neuen Testaments |
| SVTP | Studia in Veteris Testamenti Pseudepigrapha |

| | |
|---|---|
| TBN | Themes in Biblical Narrative |
| TCSt | Text-Critical Studies |
| *TDNT* | *Theological Dictionary of the New Testament*. 10 vols. Edited by Gerhard Kittel, and Gerhard Friedrich. Translated by Geoffrey W. Bromiley. Grand Rapids: Eerdmans, 1964– |
| *TDOT* | *Theological Dictionary of the Old Testament*. 15 vols. Edited by G. Johannes Botterweck, Helmer Ringgren, and Heinz-Josef Fabry. Translated by John T. Willis, Geoffrey W. Bromiley, David E. Green, and Douglas W. Stott. Grand Rapids: Eerdmans, 1974–2006 |
| *Them* | *Themelios* |
| TOTC | Tyndale Old Testament Commentary |
| *TS* | *Theological Studies* |
| TSAJ | Texts and Studies in Ancient Judaism |
| *TWOT* | *Theological Wordbook of the Old Testament*. 2 vols. Edited by Robert L. Harris and Gleason L. Archer Jr. Chicago: Moody, 1980 |
| *TynBul* | *Tyndale Bulletin* |
| TNTC | Tyndale New Testament Commentaries |
| *UBS*[5] | *The Greek New Testament*. 5th rev. ed. Edited by Barbara Aland et al. Stuttgart: Deutsche Bibelgesellschaft, 2014 |
| *UF* | *Ugarit Forschungen* |
| *VE* | *Vox Evangelica* |
| *VT* | *Vetus Testamentum* |
| VTSup | Supplements to Vetus Testamentum |
| WBC | Word Biblical Commentary |
| WMANT | Wissenschaftliche Monographien zum Alten und Neuen Testament |
| *WTJ* | *Westminster Theological Journal* |
| WUNT | Wissenschaftliche Untersuchungen zum Neuen Testament |
| *WW* | *Word and World* |
| y. | Talmud (Jerusalem) |
| *ZAW* | *Zeitschrift für die alttestamentliche Wissenschaft* |
| ZCS | Zondervan Commentary Series |
| *ZNW* | *Zeitschrift für die neutestamentliche Wissenschaft* |

# FOREWORD

During the earliest phase of the Christian movement, nearly every convert was Jewish, formed from before birth by Jewish custom and worship, and informed by ongoing exposure to the Hebrew Scriptures. This closely guarded spiritual heritage included careful observance of significant events in Jewish life. Jews joining nascent Christianity brought this rich heritage to their newfound faith, including knowledge of their sacred texts and religious celebrations, especially that most solemn one, the Day of Atonement.

In this detailed study titled *Echoes of the Most Holy: The Day of Atonement in the Book of Revelation*, André Reis attunes his readers to "hear" what he appropriately terms "allusions" and "echoes" of the Day of Atonement in various parts of the New Testament, with particular focus on the book of Revelation, which contains the greatest concentration of a wide range of Hebraic-Jewish "echoes." To this end, Reis applies a coherent, overarching hermeneutical method to identify intertextual markers of the Day of Atonement in Scripture, analyzing the evidence with depth and care and reaching convincing conclusions. His novel use of what might be called "scaled ratings" of intertextual echoes, which he uses to gauge the plausibility of his findings in Revelation, is another strength of his work. Such self-critical check averts binary "right-or-wrong" responses and helps carry his readers further along in considering the validity of his intertextual reading of Revelation. His findings significantly contribute to the growing awareness of the Hebraic religious, cultural, literary, and historical context of Revelation's language and imagery.

It was my privilege to work with André as one of his supervisors as he prepared the dissertation which lies behind this work, and I am grateful for its wider availability now in published form.

*Steven Thompson*
Supervisor of Higher Degrees by Research (retired)
Avondale University, Australia

# ACKNOWLEDGMENTS

It is gratifying to come to the end of a journey that started over a decade ago. As I look back, I'm reminded of the important contribution of key players who made this book possible.

I am grateful for my mother Jandira (*in memoriam*), who taught me to love God and Scripture. A model missionary who never traveled to far-off lands, she spoke vibrantly of her eternal hope to all she encountered. We'll meet again in the resurrection of the just.

I am grateful to Avondale University for recognizing the importance of this research, for affording me complete academic freedom, and for offering me a generous scholarship. Thanks go to Avondale's staff, librarians, and administrators, who provided key support.

I also thank Dr. Steven Thompson for his mentorship during most of the writing process, for taking an active part in the revision process, and for writing the Foreword. I will always cherish your gracious invitation to work with you at Avondale University back in 2010. Our collaboration was highly successful, and I'm grateful for the opportunity.

I am thankful to Dr. David Tasker and Dr. Wendy Jackson for your expertise in the very last stages of the dissertation.

I'd like to thank the ordained minister and New Testament scholar Kendra Haloviak for the significant contributions made during the dissertation acceptance process, not only in terms of the technical presentation but also by suggesting important nuances in the biblical text that I had overlooked.

I also thank Dr. Norm Young for his invaluable input on the final draft. I never cease to be amazed by your vast scholarship and ability to put theological thoughts to words.

I am eternally grateful to my wife Francini and my daughters Pam, Chloe, and Mckayla for their patience, support, and love support throughout the long years of this writing project. Sharing life with you is a blessing and a joy. I love you more than anything in this world.

I thank my extended family and friends for the support you provided to press on. You have always believed in me. Thank you!

I also thank the editorial team at Wipf & Stock, particularly Matt Wimer, George Callihan, Kara Barlow, and Shannon Carter, for their expert collaboration and professionalism in getting this book published.

Lastly, I give God thanks, "praise and honor and glory and power" for the grace given me to complete this journey and allowing me to discover new depths of truth emanating from his divine mind.

Soli Deo Gloria

# PREFACE

The impetus for the dissertation from which this book is derived can be traced back to my experience growing up in an apocalyptic Protestant denomination in nineteen-eighties Brazil. When the dilapidated edifice of my country's military dictatorship came crashing down in 1985, the event renewed my faith community's hope that liberty of expression meant we could preach our version of the Gospel to "all the world" to accelerate the fulfillment of prophecy. My country's lingering social and economic turmoil mirrored global realities, confirming our preordained eschatological scenarios and timelines—affirmed by our very own prophet—signaling the need for a more aggressive push to "finish the work," even if we knew that this would result in our persecution as a prophetic eschatological remnant.

My world changed with the drowning of my older brother at the age of 13 in 1983 and the sudden passing of my father (in his mid-forties) in 1986. Our unimaginable loss heightened my mother's interest in the end times, which had laid dormant under the pressures of raising a family. I began hearing about her hope of seeing my brother and dad again at Jesus' soon coming. The death of loved ones has a way of focusing one's spiritual lenses.

In 1989 my church engaged in soft date-setting for the end by launching the "1,000 Days of Harvest" evangelistic campaign, as if heaven's calendar ran on the earthly. It was around that time, at the age of fifteen, that I became a reluctant preacher, delivering my first sermon in the dorm's chapel in which I nervously tried to explain (for a brief three minutes or so) that the recent opening up of the Soviet Union (I even used the word *perestroika!*) was a metaphor for the brief period of grace that remained before its door was shut, triggering the end of the world. I was sure I would not be on earth to see the end of the decade, much less the century.

When the end of all things overshot the turbulent nineteen-eighties, prophetic disconfirmation tacitly postponed it to the new decade. It was in the maelstrom of the global geopolitical and religious turmoil that fed the apocalyptic fervor of my faith community in the early nineties that I came of age and entered my denomination's theological seminary. I did well academically and even wrote a couple of essays for the church's magazine. I graduated at the top of my class, having just turned 21, and with a bright denominational future. I was certain I was part of a privileged last generation of pastors that would "finish the work" by sheer effort and a life of sinless perfection.

After a brief experience as a youth pastor, I emigrated to the United States, searching for new vistas, especially academic ones. Less than a year later, I was accepted for the MDiv program at Andrews University, my denomination's flagship educational institution in southwest Michigan. While there, I took a detour and started an M.A. in Music which I later finished at Longy School of Music in Boston. During this sabbatical from theology, I got married, raised a family, and started a business, intent on just relishing life for a while. The pressure to perform under unrelenting eschatological expectations eventually necessitates a release.

The catalyst in the quest that gave birth to this book was my mother's unexpected passing in 2009. I was despondent and confused. I was sure—almost like a familial prophecy—that she, a passionate and beloved Bible worker, would be alive to see Jesus return. I was also bewildered that, after decades in the church, she had not yet reached the sinless perfection expected of the remnant before the close of probation. Her terminal disease and my ensuing grief forced me to go back to Scripture, searching for answers.

After a year of study and reflection, I realized that the mixture of sectarian eschatology and perfectionism that my church had steadily fed me had resulted in a toxic theology that clouded my understanding of salvation by faith through God's grace alone and distorted my views on eschatology.[1] In early 2010, I applied to the newly-minted PhD program at Avondale University and was accepted, studying under the tutelage of Dr. Steve Thompson. The topic of my research: the book of Revelation. I had come across Dr. Thompson's work through his book *Apocalypse and Semitic Syntax* (Cambridge, 1985) and only learned later that he was a lecturer at one of my denomination's universities. I was excited and ready to contribute.

What began as a journey of personal reflection about the end of life and the end of the world (related realities during my time of grief) turned into a doctoral degree and the book that you now hold in your hands. The forma-

1. See my article "Robert Sloan Donnell: From Righteousness by Faith to Sinless Perfection," where I discuss the origins of these views.

tive years in my faith community shaped my Christian journey and continue to inform my reading of Scripture and spiritual disciplines, even if I no longer hold to the exuberant apocalypticism and perfectionism of my younger years. I have, however, intentionally preserved my belief in the "blessed hope" of the Second Advent of Christ that sprung my denomination into existence and still gives it momentum, although I may disagree with its hermeneutic of the end time. I engage a few of the problems in specific sections throughout the book.

At the outset of my studies, I realized that the way I had read Revelation within the sectarian confines of my denomination would have to be largely abandoned and replaced by a hermeneutical strategy that does justice to Revelation's literary and theological complexities, especially the way John interacted with the Hebrew Scriptures and its rich traditions. The facile, self-serving answers I had been given would no longer do.

I also realized that, notwithstanding the scholarly interest in John's use of Jewish-Feast imagery, little attention had been paid to the Day of Atonement's intersection with Revelation, arguably the book of the New Testament most dependent on the Hebrew Scriptures. This was a surprising discovery since the Day of Atonement is a fascinating source of theological themes and imagery. In consultation with Dr. Thompson, we agreed that the Day of Atonement would be a promising case study of intertextuality in Revelation. Unsurprisingly, my choice of subject also intersected with my religious journey; since the early days of my church, the Day of Atonement has filled its proselytism with apocalyptic urgency and corporate significance.

What was the Day of Atonement? Prescribed in Leviticus 16, the Day of Atonement—or Yom Kippur—was a day of rest, penitence, and purification for Israelites of loyal character and the renewal of God's covenant with Israel. On this solemn Jewish feast, which took place once a year, sins and impurities incurred by the Israelites throughout the year and accumulated in the tabernacle were removed from it by daubing and sprinkling sacrificial blood to its altars and compartments and transferred by the high priest's confession onto the "goat for Azazel," which carried them to the desert. Israel was thus rendered "clean before the LORD" (Lev 16:30), ensuring that God would continue to dwell in their midst. As it became ingrained in the veil of Jewish consciousness, the Day of Atonement underwent a "process of abstraction" during Second Temple times, when the Most Holy Place lay devoid of the ark of the covenant and its mercy seat. Continuing to reverberate in the Jewish *imaginaire* during this period—as seen in its impact on Second

Temple pseudepigraphal literature, where demonic Azazel plays a significant eschatological role—the Day of Atonement arrived in the New Testament, as its writers read Jesus back into the Day of Atonement, generating irresistible imagery which they used to proclaim Jesus Christ's atoning death and heavenly intercession on behalf of believers. After the temple's destruction in 70 CE, the Day of Atonement moved from the concrete to the metaphorical realm as Jews, even in the absence of its potent rituals, continue to engage in the spiritual rituals of "fasting, acts of self-denial and abstention from work."[2]

What emerges from the intertextual "close reading" method utilized here is a clear picture of how John wove Jesus back into the Levitical Day of Atonement, as seen in its colorful presence in the tapestry of Revelation. In the book's very first chapter, Jesus Christ is introduced as heavenly high priest, seen wearing Day-of-Atonement clothing and offering his atoning blood inside the sanctuary. John's visions then move to that great Levitical *Leitmotif* of *holiness* vs. *uncleanness* that suffused the Day of Atonement's rituals and makes up the hortatory framework in the letters to the seven churches of Asia Minor (Rev 2–3). In Revelation 4–5, the Day-of-Atonement blood of the Lamb offered inside heaven's Most Holy Place, God's throne room, makes Jesus worthy to judge and reign on the universe's throne. This same atoning blood whitens the saints' robes, paving the way for the harvest of the earth (Rev 7 & 14). Whereas intercession at the altar of incense (Rev 8–9) protects the followers of the Lamb, its cessation unleashes judgment on defiant humankind (Rev 6, 15 & 16). The ritual of the "goat for Azazel" provides the motif of eschatological judgment decreed on the dragon and his minions, leading up to the final eradication of sin (Rev 17–20). Lastly, the New Jerusalem's descent (Rev 21–22)—whose cubic shape mirrors the earthly Most Holy Place—inaugurates the new earth free from sin where, like the high priest on the Day of Atonement, "his servants will worship him," dressed in white to "reign for ever and ever" with God and the Lamb (Rev 22:3, 5).

This study is structured as follows. The Introduction titled "Toward An Intertextual Reading of Revelation," presents the general issues pertaining to the study of Revelation, including its relationship to the Old Testament, intertextual theory, and general assumptions about the book's composition. The Introduction sets up the intertextual, "close reading" approach used in the book. Chapter 1, "The Day of Atonement in the Old Testament," explores the Day of Atonement's rituals as found in the Pentateuch. The Excursus at

2. Hieke, "Participation and Abstraction," 157.

the end of chapter 1 surveys the origins of the Israelite elimination rite in its ANE context. Chapter 2, titled "The Day of Atonement in Second Temple Literature," explores how the Day of Atonement percolated through Second Temple Jewish pseudepigraphal literature, affording vivid imagery in that body of literature. The Excursus at the end of this chapter explores the Ancient Near East origins of Israel's elimination rite of the live goat. Chapter 3 title, "The Day of Atonement in the New Testament," looks at how the New Testament writers engaged in the figurative interpretation of the Hebrew Bible and read Jesus Christ back into it. This included drawing on the Day of Atonement language and imagery. Chapter 4, titled "The Day of Atonement in the Book of Revelation," analyzes John's Christological exegesis of the Hebrew Bible and how, through what Richard Hays calls the "conversion of the imagination," John read Jesus back into the Levitical Day of Atonement. The Summary and Conclusion surveys the salient points of this research.

Ultimately, the guiding question of this study is, *Does John still speak?* As I write this, Russia has begun invading Ukraine, and eschatological conspiracy theories are already popping up. Are we willing to listen to John's voice as it echoes in Revelation? If he were here, he would point to Revelation's last chapter and exclaim: "God is in control! He wins at the end!" There is no need to fear unless we ignore the echoes of what God has done in the past.

This volume represents a milestone in an academic journey that began exactly thirty years ago when I entered the seminary in February 1992. Still, it echoes earlier events, starting with my mother's first exposure to the Second Coming of Jesus in the late nineteen-fifties, our family's encounters with death, my spiritual experiences in our small congregation in southern Brazil, and the apocalyptic, perfectionistic fever that consumed my earlier years. In many ways, writing it was a cathartic religious experience grounded in sacred Scripture, aided by the Holy Spirit, tempered by the rigors of academia, and seasoned with the humility that comes with age.

The reflections contained here represent my modest attempt to add my voice to the chorus of theological voices speaking today. I hope that the approach and conclusions offered here will be helpful to all who seek to engage the book of Revelation creatively and responsibly.

André Reis<br>Orlando, Florida<br>February 2022

## INTRODUCTION

# TOWARD AN INTERTEXTUAL READING OF REVELATION

IT IS A DAUNTING TASK to write a book on Revelation. French philosopher turned Bible commentator Jacques Ellul lamented the task as "frightfully ambitious, dreadful and unwelcome."[1] Considering the staggering number of books about Revelation in circulation, his question *"que prétendrions-nous ajouter?"* seems ever more fitting.[2] Ellul's frustration reveals the challenges of grappling with this ancient text and the irresistible allure it exerts on those who venture in. From time immemorial, Revelation has mesmerized readers of every stripe, from peasants to kings, from the illiterate to philosophers.

Like the mythological lake of Narcissus, Revelation has enticed readers to look into its waters; many have only seen their own image reflected.[3] Revelation, with its glorious, cryptic, and at times grotesque images, has fallen prey to "event substitution" by those seeking to advance their preconceived ideas about the "apocalypse."[4] Not surprisingly, the book has yielded a plethora of wild, irresponsible interpretations and become "the paradise of fanatics and sectarians," observed Caird.[5] That is why Chesterton's witty observation, "Though St. John the Evangelist saw many strange monsters in his vision, he saw no creature so wild as one of his own commentators," keeps reappearing.[6] "Wherever the book of Revelation shows up," writes another, "trouble is not far behind" because of its ability to create "the intolerable tension be-

1. Ellul, *L'Apocalypse*, 17.
2. "What can we pretend to add?"
3. See Mills, *Approaching*, 108; Barr, "Waiting," 101–112.
4. See Ezell, *Revelations*, 16–19.
5. Caird, *Revelation*, 2; Nusca, *The Christ*; Gorman, *Reading Revelation Responsibly*, xi–xvii.
6. Chesterton, *Orthodoxy*, 29.

tween reality and hopeful faith."[7] The enduring power of this ancient text has not only afforded hope to believers but also managed to turn it into "the most dangerous book in the history of Christendom."[8] As I have previously observed, the history of religion reveals that the "complex religious-political-social phenomenon" that we call "apocalypticism" is capable of "symbiotically assimilating and tinging the times in which the apocalypticists live."[9] Under this prism, it is not surprising that popular readings of Revelation have ranged from the literal to the allegorical, stemming from the expositor's preconceived ideas of what the book means.

The interpretive exuberance that sees ancient prophetic oracles as mirrors of one's own times is as old as the Judean community of the dry hills of Qumran, an apocalyptic sect active around the turn of the first century BCE which saw themselves as the fulfillment of Daniel's prophecies. Later, the Montanists (2nd century CE), also known as the New Prophecy sect, believed that the New Jerusalem would descend on their cities, Peruza and Tymion.[10] Likewise, Islam, birthed into the mire of the interlocking religious cultures of Late Antiquity Byzantium, was swept up by the apocalyptic fervor of Christianity, Judaism, and Zoroastrianism raging in the 6–7th centuries CE. Daniel and Revelation also provided the rationale for the First and Second Crusades. A few centuries later, the beasts of Revelation 13 provided Luther the ammunition to attack the medieval Papacy.

The same phenomenon resurfaced in antebellum America as reflected in the eagerness with which Protestants in the United States embraced the Second Great Awakening's millennial fervor, which spawned several apocalyptic sects still active today. One such preacher was William Miller (1782–1849), who predicted the end of the world for 1844. In 1863, his disappointed followers founded the Seventh-day Adventist church, whose members see themselves as part of prophetic "Laodicea." They see the church's existence as the direct fulfillment of Daniel and Revelation's prophecies.[11]

In 1993, David Koresh, the leader of the Branch Davidians—a militant offshoot of Seventh-day Adventism—saw in Revelation's symbols "a picture

7. Maier, *Apocalypse Recalled*, 1; see Collins, *Crisis and Catharsis*, 141.

8. Johns, *Lamb Christology*, 5.

9. Reis, Review of *Apocalypse of Empire*, 242; Reis, *Review of Nebuchadnezzar's Dream*.

10. Paulien, "Dreading," 7. See also Tabberne, *Prophets*, 15–16, 20.

11. See Arasola, *The End of Historicism*; Gaustad, *The Rise of Adventism*; Surridge, "Seventh-day Adventism: Self-Appointed Laodicea," 21–42;

of his own apocalyptic world and in its words, he found the voice of God."[12] The problem with Koresh, as Adventist scholar Kendra Haloviak perceptively observed, was not only ethical but also hermeneutical, for he saw in Revelation "a code that anticipates a single, consistent, and final meaning," one that Koresh was more to than happy to decode on his own and foist upon his unsuspecting followers.[13]

The late 19th century saw a renaissance of scholarly interest in tackling Revelation's Gordian Knot by reading it as serious literature. The book's sources came into sharper focus early on, beginning with its relationship to the Old Testament (OT),[14] followed by Second Temple Jewish apocalyptic literature,[15] and the more recent interest in the socio-political *milieu* of first-century Christianity—its *Sitz im Leben*.[16] Exegetes of Revelation today stand on the shoulders of many who have attempted to tame its literary beasts, as evidenced in the vast array of hermeneutical approaches ranging from literary criticism,[17] reader-response criticism,[18] rhetoric analysis,[19] sociology,[20] anthropology,[21] politics,[22] feminism,[23] pastoral approaches,[24] narrative-critical theory,[25] the grammatical-historical method,[26] preterist-idealist,[27] and the historicist camp.[28]

In this volume, we embark on a quest that will take us through the confluence of two thematic streams: Israel's Scriptures and traditions and their encounter with Jesus Christ (the "Christ event"). Vital to this theological convergence are the rich tributaries of Second Temple Jewish literature, which

12. Newport, *Apocalypse*, 2.

13. Haloviak, *Worlds at War*, 3.

14. See Brodie, *The Revelation*; Charles, *Studies*; Charles, *A Critical*; Swete, *The Apocalypse*.

15. See Collins, *The Apocalyptic Imagination*; Collins, "Eschatological Dynamics," 69–89.

16. Aune, *Revelation 1–5; 6–16; 17–22.*

17. See Ford, *Revelation*.

18. Moyise, *The Old Testament in the Book of Revelation*, 138.

19. Fiorenza, *Revelation: Justice and Judgment*.

20. Thompson, *The Book of Revelation*.

21. Collins, *Crisis and Catharsis*.

22. Kraybill, *Apocalypse and Allegiance*; Friesen, *Imperial Cults*.

23. Pippin, *Death and Desire*.

24. Talbert, *The Apocalypse*; Hahn, "Die Offenbarung."

25. Resseguie, *Revelation Unsealed*.

26. Beale, *Revelation*.

27. Noë, "An Exegetical Basis."

28. See Mounce, *Revelation*, 24–27 for a helpful summary of the various schools of interpretation of Revelation. See also Böcher, "Die Johannes-Apokalypse"; Strand, *Interpreting*.

provide essential commentary and reflection on OT traditions, thus becoming a relevant source of language and imagery for the New Testament (NT) authors. Foundational to the approach offered here is the assumption that John was a first-century Christian prophet whose faith community had deep ties to first-century Judaism. As Charles realized long ago, in Revelation, we find "unadulterated Judaism ... a Semitic philosophy of religion"[29] written by a "Palestinian Jew who emigrated to Asia Minor" likely part of a prophetic guild.[30] As such, John of Patmos knew the Jewish Scriptures in Hebrew and Greek, although his command of Greek was probably lacking, as seen in the many solecisms found in the book.[31]

Few would question John's Jewish background, but *how* did John understand the Hebrew Bible in relation to his office as a Christian prophet? According to Collins, John operated from a "massive assumption of continuity," a "failure to distinguish an old and a new Israel."[32] Thus, reading Revelation with an eye to the OT is "an important way of doing justice to its complexity," writes Moyise.[33] In Revelation, Bauckham posits, "God's redemptive acts in the future are portrayed on the model of his past acts," revealed in the Hebrew canon.[34] The birth of Christianity, Farrer suggests, engendered a "rebirth of images" from the OT that were "reborn with Christ."[35]

Readers of Revelation today quickly realize how the deep waters of the OT meet the mighty waves of "the event Christ" in the text, overwhelming both author and reader and filling Revelation's literary ocean with life. As a Jewish convert to Christianity, John was predisposed to revisit Israel's sacred texts and traditions, reading Jesus back into them. These critical hermeneutical assumptions will help us unpack the book's rhetorical appeal arising out of the shared experiences of the author and his readers.[36]

29. Charles, *Studies*, 347, 144.

30. Charles, *Revelation*, xxxviii; see Collins, *Crisis*, 46–50; Aune, *Revelation* 1–5, l. See "prophets" in Revelation 10:7; 11:10, 18; 16:6; 18:20, 24; 22:6, 9. See Hill, "Prophecy and Prophets," 406–11; Aune, "The Prophetic Circle," 103–115.

31. Tenney, *Interpreting*, 26.

32. Collins, *Crisis*, 46–47; see Collins, "Insiders," 208; Ben Ezra, *The Impact*, 2; Lindars, "The Place," 59–66.

33. Moyise, *The Old Testament in the Book of Revelation*, 138.

34. Bauckham, *The Climax*, xi, 201. See Fransen, "Cahier," 67; Beale, "Revelation," 333.

35. Farrer, *A Rebirth of Images*, 14, 15.

36. Barr, "The Apocalypse," 41. See Fiorenza, *Revelation*, 187–99; Hanson, *The Dawn*, 434.

## The Research Question

As a case study of the intersection between the book of Revelation and the Hebrew Scriptures—including later pseudepigraphic works—we begin with the working assumption that the Levitical Day of Atonement (DA) played a role in early Christianity's theological formation. This volume embarks on an intra-biblical, intertextual "close reading" of Revelation, focusing on how the DA as prescribed in the Pentateuch and celebrated in ancient Israel was understood by the author of Revelation as he sought continuity between Jesus and Israel's history. This study focuses on John's interest in three aspects of the DA:

(1) *language* (e.g., Lev 16; 23:26–32; Num 29:7–11);[37]
(2) *imagery*: e.g., the high priest, the Most Holy Place, incense, Azazel;
(3) *themes:* e.g., holiness vs. impurity, covenantal preservation, judgment.

Considering John's frequent *allusions* to the Hebrew cultus, Piper argued in the early fifties that John's visions "are presented within a framework of liturgical activities" connected to the tabernacle. A few years later, Shepherd argued that Revelation "follows the order of the Church's Paschal liturgy."[38] Regarding the DA in the NT, one should mention Young's seminal doctoral dissertation in the early seventies titled "The Impact of the Jewish Day of Atonement Upon the Thought of the New Testament." As Young contended: "By the time of the NT, the DA had become the holy day *par excellence* in the contemporary Jewish liturgy."[39] Following Young, Ben Ezra's doctoral dissertation presented an extensive treatment of the reception of the DA in early Christianity. Ben Ezra concludes that "Christian atonement theology and its festal calendar … emerged under the influence of Yom Kippur."[40]

Nevertheless, even though the presence of the Jewish feasts in Revelation has received several scholarly treatments,[41] the DA has been largely bypassed. Except for the *allusion* to Leviticus 16:12 in Revelation 8:5—recognized by *NA*$^{28}$ and *UBS*$^{5}$—Leviticus 16 is not listed as a source of actual quotations in Revelation, and scholars have only sporadically hinted at the

37. See also Exod 26:33; 30:10.
38. Piper, "The Apocalypse," 10; Shepherd, *The Paschal Liturgy*, 77. See Guilding, *The Fourth Gospel*.
39. Young, "The Impact," 11.
40. Ben Ezra, *The Impact*, 2.
41. E.g., Stramara, *God's Timetable;* Ulfgard, *Feast and Future*.

possibility of *allusions* and *echoes* in Revelation.[42] In 1984, Strand argued that the measuring "of the priests themselves, the sanctuary, the altar, and the congregation" in Leviticus 16 is the background for Revelation 11.[43] Paulien sees the DA in several passages in Revelation: (1) the grape harvest (14:7); (2) the division of people in Revelation in two groups—servants of God and the servants of the "counterfeit trinity (dragon, beast, and false prophet)"; and (3) the section on the trumpets as "strongly supportive of an association with the cultic activities of Yom Kippur."[44] In his three-volume commentary on Revelation, Aune mentions the DA five times, and the equally exhaustive commentary by Beale sees it in four passages (6:9; 8:4; 11:19; 12:10).[45]

Barker is perhaps the only recent commentator to consider the presence of the DA in Revelation on a large scale (mentioned sixty times in her commentary). Barker sees the DA as early as Revelation 1 in the depiction of Jesus as the "great high priest" and the seven trumpets as "the trumpets of the Day of Atonement."[46] Barker's references to the DA are extensive, but in most cases, she merely states a connection without engaging the textual evidence, signaling the need for a more detailed analysis.[47] Lastly, none of the contributors to Brill's tome titled *The Day of Atonement* (2012) so much as allude to the book of Revelation.[48] Likewise, the DA is absent in *The Oxford Handbook of the Book of Revelation* (2020).[49]

The preceding discussion reveals that scholarship has only partially, if at all, dealt with the presence of the DA in Revelation, and the few scattered mentions have lacked scope and a consistent hermeneutical method. Such deficiency creates a lacuna in biblical studies that this book seeks to fill.

42. *NA*[28], 841; *UBS*[5], 867.

43. Strand, "An Overlooked," 322. See Aune, *Revelation 6–16*, 604; Mot, "The Measurement," 229–248. Incidentally, the DA often surfaces in works of popular theology; see Priest, *Rending the Curtain*, offering an eight-week Bible study on the meaning of the cross of Christ based on the Day of Atonement, in which Revelation figures prominently. See also England, *The Day of Atonement*.

44. Paulien, "The Role," 253, 256.

45. Aune, *Revelation 1–5*, 293; Beale, *Revelation*, 619, 660.

46. Barker, *Revelation*, 4, 196. See also Barker, *Temple Themes*; Campbell, *"Findings"*; Campbell, *Reading Revelation*, 251.

47. See Stevenson, *Power and Place*, 31, 138, which leaves the DA largely untouched.

48. Hieke and Niklas, *The Day of Atonement*.

49. Koester, *The Oxford Handbook*. As another example of oversight, deSilva's *Discovering Revelation* (2021) does not so much as mention the word "atonement" and cognates, as if this concept was absent from the text of Revelation.

## Biblical Intertextuality: An Overview

In the remainder of this Introduction, a discussion of the exegetical method used lays the foundation for our exploration. The heuristic questions guiding this study are: As one of the most important festivals of the tabernacle service, what was the DA? What rituals did it entail? How did the DA come to be understood in Second Temple Judaism and early Christianity? How did this influence John's understanding? How and where did he incorporate the language and imagery of the DA in his revelation of Jesus Christ?

The exegetical task proposed so far intersects with the concept of "intertextuality," which occurs when material taken from other texts intersects with another. The term "intertextuality" was coined by Bulgarian-French philosopher Julia Kristeva in 1969 as a reader manifesto against rigid authorial intention and meaning.[50] Kristeva thought every text was an "*intertextualité*," a "mosaic of quotations" that is both influenced by and an influencer of other texts.[51] Kristeva was influenced by Russian philosopher Mikhael Bakhtin (1895–1975), who contended that "the word lives, as it were, on the boundary between its own context and another, alien context."[52]

The influence of intertextuality in biblical studies began in the mid-nineteen-eighties through Fishbane and Hays.[53] Fishbane's work on Jewish exegesis sought to establish a vector of inner-biblical *allusions* framed by the historic-literary traditions of the Hebrew canon. As he later defined intertextuality: "Materials are always moving from one setting to another, being joined to different genres, and resulting in new redactional units for instruction."[54] He proposed four classes of intertextual *allusions* in the OT: scribal, legal, aggadic, and mantological, followed by a method to recognize "multiple and sustained lexical linkages between two texts."[55] Similarly, Hays argued that Scripture "continues to speak in and through later texts that both depend on and transform" the precursor texts.[56] Hays points out that Paul's dependence on "Israel's Scripture" is a dominant motif in his epistles, which should be read against the background of "inner-biblical exegesis" of the

50. Kristeva, *Sèméiotiké*. See Kristeva, "Word, Dialogue and Novel," 36; Culler, *The Pursuit*, 100–101; Vorster, "Intertextuality."

51. Kristeva, *Desire*, 36, 66.

52. Bakhtin, "Discourse," 498.

53. Fishbane, "Revelation," 343–361, Fishbane, *Biblical Interpretation*; Hays, *Echoes*.

54. Fishbane, "The Hebrew Bible," 25.

55. Fishbane, *Biblical Interpretation*, 281.

56. Hays, *Echoes*, 14.

Judeo-Christian tradition.[57] Paul was highly sensitive to the "internal resonances of the biblical text."[58] Hays follows Hollander's definition of *echo* as an *allusion* to a secondary text occurring within a "cave of resonant signification ... while forming echoes that transform their words in new acoustical environments."[59] "Sometimes," observes Hays, "the echo will be so loud that only the dullest" reader would miss it.[60] The task of textual criticism concerning *echoes* is: "(a) to call attention to them so that others hear them; (b) to give an account of the distortions and new figuration that they generate."[61]

Jesus and his followers operated within the "symbolic world shaped by the Old Testament," a religious landscape punctuated by the realization of God's promises to Israel as recorded in the Hebrew Scriptures and enacted in the typology of the sanctuary rituals and feasts.[62] Philip's affirmation to Nathanael: "We have found him about whom Moses in the law and also the prophets wrote, Jesus son of Joseph from Nazareth" (John 1:45) encapsulates the early Christians' understanding of who Jesus was and what he had accomplished. Embodying what Hays calls a retrospective "figural christological reading" of the Hebrew Scriptures and its traditions and through a "conversion of the imagination," the NT writers reread them in light of Jesus' life, death, resurrection, and exaltation, detecting and amplifying a multiplicity of intertextual signals radiating from their sacred texts and collective experiences, and reading Jesus Christ back into them.[63] As defined by Auerbach, a "figural interpretation"

> establishes a connection between two events or persons in such a way that the first signifies not only itself but also the second, while the second involves or fulfills the first. The two poles of a figure are separated in time, but both, being real events or persons, are within temporality. They are both contained in the flowing stream which is historical life, and only the comprehension, the *intellectus spiritualis*, of their interdependence is a spiritual act.[64]

57. Hays, *Echoes*, 14.
58. Hays, *Echoes*, 21.
59. Hollander, *The Figure of Echo*, 64, 19.
60. Hollander, *The Figure of Echo*, 29.
61. Hollander, *The Figure of Echo*, 19.
62. Hays, *Echoes of Scripture in the Gospels*, 10.
63. See Hays, *Reading Backwards*, 94; Hays, *Echoes of Scripture in the Gospels*, 2.
64. Auerbach, *Mimesis*, 73.

Such "figural interpretation" does not mean that the OT "authors—or the characters they narrate—were conscious of predicting or anticipating Christ," Hays explains as he seeks to distinguish *predictions* from *prefigurations*. Discerning a "figural correspondence" is only possible after the second event being prefigured has occurred, at which point "the semantic force of the figure flows both ways, as the second event receives deeper significance from the first." This was a "process of reading backwards in light of new revelatory events," Hays continues.[65] By evoking Israel's Scriptures in their witness to Jesus Christ via figural interpretations, the NT authors maintain theological coherence within their narrative, setting forth "the unity of the canon as a single cumulative and complex pattern of meaning," explains Frei.[66]

Hays also highlights the importance of typology within this figurative matrix. "Typology," he explains, "forges imaginative correlations of events within a narrative sequence," which may or not be historic but can be understood by ideal readers as meaningful to their respective community.[67] In addition, as Manning put it, "typology is a repeatable mode of interpretation that can be shared by a community that agrees on the *status* of the types and antitypes as divine interventions."[68] Further, Stökl warns against mixing *allegorical* with *typological* exegesis because "while allegory seeks to reveal deeper wisdom by translating concrete images to an ideal realm, typology connects textual images of a canon to events in history."[69]

Based on these intertextual premises and focusing on the letters of Paul, Hays proposes five possible sources of *echoes*: (1) Paul's mind; (2) his original readers; (3) the text itself; (4) a contemporary act of reading; and (5) an interpretive community.[70] Building on Hays's work, Porter has proposed five categories of "extratextual" references in the NT's text: (1) *formulaic quotations*; (2) *direct quotations*; (3) *paraphrases*; (4) *allusions*; and (5) *echoes*.[71] An *allusion*, he suggests, is "a figure of speech that makes indirect extratextual references," pulling external players into the text.[72] To be effective, an *allusion*

65. Hays, *Echoes of Scripture in the Gospels*, 3–4, 5.

66. Frei, *The Eclipse*, 33.

67. Hays, *Echoes*, 161.

68. Manning, *Echoes of a Prophet*, 16. He continues: "Christians who believe that the same God worked both in the Passover and in the Cross could independently observe the typological connections between the two."

69. Stökl, "The Christian Exegesis," 213

70. Stökl, "The Christian Exegesis," 26.

71. Porter, "Further Comments," 98–110.

72. Porter, "Allusions and Echoes," 30, 40.

must meet three criteria: (1) it must be intentional; (2) it must come from a "common pool of shared knowledge" (both author and reader can "grasp" it); and (3) it is functional, addressing a "particular literary problem."[73] An *echo*, Porter explains, "is reserved for language that is thematically related to a more general notion or concept."[74]

As seems evident from the many definitions, the dividing line between *allusions* and *echoes* can be easily blurred (e.g., Hays speaks of "allusive echoes") because gauging whether an *allusion* is "intentional," or demonstrates a shared "awareness" by the author and readers cannot be adequately measured by readers today.[75] We can only probe allusive activity in the NT in relation to the authors' evocations of Scripture and its functionality within the four corners of the received text.

Despite the apparent consensus on the role that intertextuality plays in biblical literature, its embrace by the field of biblical studies was not without objections. Hatina, for example, offered incisive criticism of the term's use in biblical hermeneutics because it is inextricably linked to a "political agenda" bent on subverting "the traditional approaches [to exegesis] by undermining the idea of a unified and accumulative sense."[76] For example, he suggests that had Hays omitted the term "intertextuality" altogether, his contribution to the discussion would not be at all impaired.[77] He points out the "irony" that, although the "context" in which a text arises is central to historical criticism, adopters of intertextuality have tended to ignore the very context in which intertextuality arose: the political and ideological framework of European post-structuralism. Such an agenda displaces "traditional structures" and reduces the relationship between readers and authors as "a struggle for power and authority" to the detriment of "meaning, centrality and reference."[78] Intertextuality is "inimical" to traditional hermeneutics, Hatina contends, because it makes language "nebulous, arbitrary," opening the way to "infinite interpretations." Hatina is concerned that "traditional hermeneutics," which

73. Porter, "Allusions and Echoes," 36.

74. Porter, "Allusions and Echoes," 39, 40.

75. Paulien, *Decoding*, 40, suggests that an echo "was in the air of the environment in which the author lived."

76. Hatina, "Intertextuality," 30. Hatina defines the premises of traditional hermeneutics thus: "(1) the potential of language to create stable meaning; (2) the existence of meaning within established forms; (3) the artist's control of meaning; (4) a work's closure; and (5) the ancillary activity of criticism as separate from literature."

77. Hatina, "Intertextuality," 36.

78. Hatina, "Intertextuality," 36.

works from a "work (and author-) oriented perspective," is destabilized by a deconstructive approach in which the "denial of an ultimate referent immediately leads to the instability of texts" and "reader-created" meaning.[79] The reader's role in traditional intertextuality "creates immediate discord with the historical critic who focuses on the author and written text."[80] Ultimately, Hatina sought to preserve the biblical authors as the final authority in creating meaning; whatever "intertextuality" exists in the text, it does so within the confines of stable, discoverable meaning found in the biblical canon.

Following Hatina's prescient caveats, this study will seek to preserve John's authority to create stable, discoverable meaning, even if it adopts a nuanced view of the term "intertextuality" and employs its tools carefully.[81] In this study, the vector of intertextuality between the OT and Revelation will be established by carefully surveying shared language found in Revelation via the Greek text of the LXX and the Hebrew OT in order to approximate authorial intention. This philological method will help unpack the consistency of use of specific terms, variations in translation, and their significance in each respective context.

Due to differing methodologies used to address the use of the OT in the NT, as exemplified by the previous discussion, scholars continue to seek consensus on a methodology to assess John's allusive method. Paulien, for example, has proposed three primary criteria for "accumulating internal evidence" of intertextuality between two texts: (1) verbal parallels: two or more words of significant, shared importance between texts; (2) thematic parallels: similarity of thought and theme; and (3) structural parallels: themes

79. Hatina, "Intertextuality," 30. Hatina defines the main premises of traditional hermeneutics thus: "(1) the potential of language to create stable meaning; (2) the existence of meaning within established forms; (3) the artist's control of meaning; (4) a work's closure and (5) the ancillary activity of criticism as separate from literature." The premises of intertextuality that are "inimical" to traditional hermeneutics: "(1) language is not a medium of thought or a tool for communication; it is nebulous, arbitrary and leads to infinite interpretations; (2) all texts—having no closure, resolution and self-sufficiency—refer endlessly to other texts; (3) the author is never in control over the meaning of the text; (4) meaning is supplanted by the idea of signification, whereby the signifier remains without a corresponding signified; (5) criticism is part of the text and contributes to the creation of meaning; (6) disciplinary boundaries are discarded, leaving all disciplines as part of the discursive environment and ultimately inseparable from literature; and (7) the rules of reason and identity are replaced by the notion of "contradiction" which refers to the fallacy of identity—that the concept does not exhaust the thing conceived. (Hatina, "Intertextuality," 32).

80. Hatina, "Intertextuality," 35. Hatina proposes that the reader's role is "limited only to self-analysis ... as one who participates in the tradition."

81. See Rothstein, "Diversity and Change;" Oropeza and Moyise, *Exploring Intertextuality*, xvii; Miscall, "Isaiah," 44. For an extended discussion, see Hubbard Jr., "Reading," 125–139.

or words used in the same order.[82] In turn, Leonard proposes no less than eight philological markers of "shared language" that can be used to identify intertextual dependence:

(1) Shared language is foremost in establishing a textual connection.

(2) Shared language is more important than non-shared language, which indicates the direction and strength of the "vector of allusion."[83]

(3) Shared language that is rare or distinctive suggests a more robust connection than widely used language.

(4) Shared phrases suggest a stronger connection than individual shared terms.

(5) The accumulation of shared language suggests a stronger connection than a single shared term or phrase.

(6) Shared language in similar contexts suggests a stronger connection than shared language alone.

(7) Shared language need not be accompanied by shared ideology to establish a connection.

(8) Shared language need not be accompanied by shared form to establish a connection.[84]

In addition to Leonard's helpful guidelines, Hays' comprehensive method of identifying *allusions* and *echoes* of Scripture in the letters of Paul is helpful to our study since Paul and John operated within similar religious environments. Hays proposes seven tests to ascertain the validity of *echoes*:

(1) *Availability*: Was the *echo* familiar/available to the author and original readers?

(2) *Volume*: How distinctive (loud) is it?

(3) *Recurrence*: How often does the *echo* appear in the new work?

(4) *Thematic coherence*: Does the *echo* "fit" the context of the new work?

(5) *Historical plausibility*: How likely was the author to know and use the material in the new work?

(6) *History of interpretation*: Have others heard the same *echoes*?

(7) *Satisfaction*: Does the *echo* help clarify the passage's meaning?

82. Paulien, "Elusive Allusions," 41. See also Paulien, "Criteria"; Paulien, "New Testament Use of the Old Testament," 29–49.

83. Eslinger, "Inner-Biblical Exegesis," 52.

84. Leonard, "Identifying," 241–265.

In sum, intertextual theory has enlarged the hermeneutical horizons of biblical studies, affording exegetes indispensable tools for reading and interpreting the book of Revelation. To end this Introduction, below we review three general assumptions about the composition of the book of Revelation.

## Reading Revelation Intertextually

Establishing John's dependence on the OT—and other intertexts—necessitates a coherent method to identify the source of his ideas. As Strand once suggested, "the very multiplicity of the background images [in Revelation] suggests, too, that the new image transcends the background entities or events."[85] Bandy sees three textual layers in Revelation: the *surface layer*, the layer of intertextual connections with the OT, and the *intratextual layer*, which pertains to how John creates a web of internal *allusions* and motif cross-references.[86] This trait reflects a broader characteristic of the NT's allusive method, which, according to Dimant, can be either "expositional," i.e., often carrying an actual quotation, or "compositional," in which the source of dependence is masked.[87] Paulien points out how John's use of the OT is *compositional* because, although he never directly quotes the OT, he intentionally draws on specific ideas in the OT rather than simply throwing ideas around.[88] John's intentionality, Paulien contends, allows the alluded text to be "fully understood in the light of its context within the original work."[89] As Metzger argued, John appeals "primarily to our imagination—not, however, a freewheeling imagination, but a disciplined imagination."[90] But more than just discipline, more than other NT writings, reading Revelation requires a "conversion of the imagination," to see Christ prefigured there.[91]

Scholars have also pointed out the importance of identifying the "ideal reader" of Revelation. This ideal reader was someone who was likely part of a "specific subgroup of Jewish Christians" familiar with the Hebrew cultus,

85. Strand, "An Overlooked," 319.
86. Bandy, "The Layers."
87. Dimant, "Use and Interpretation," 381.
88. Paulien, "The Role," 263.
89. Paulien, *Decoding*, 39.
90. Metzger, *Breaking the Code*, 11.
91. Hays, *Conversion of the Imagination*, 5–6.

who could quickly pick up the *allusions* and *echoes*.[92] This "revelation" of Revelation's ideal reader could help us focus on "*how* the text means" as opposed to "monologic readings that claim to uncover *what* the text means," as Haloviak has suggested.[93] Accepting that Revelation has intended *meanings* and ideal *readers* constitutes a vital interpretive control.[94]

John's vast use of the Jewish Scriptures is beyond parrying, but what text of the OT did John use?[95] Despite the evident influence of the Septuagint (LXX) on the book, it seems clear that Revelation underwent heavy Semitic influence stemming either from OT Hebrew or first-century Aramaic.[96] As Charles observed, "the chief Hebraisms in the Apocalypse ... are sufficient to prove that it is more Hebraic than the LXX itself," and that the Greek "needs at times to be translated into Hebrew in order to discover its meaning."[97]

In a monograph solely dedicated to this aspect of Revelation, Thompson argued that "biblical Hebrew was a model for the Seer" and that "the Greek was little more than a membrane, stretched tightly over a Semitic framework."[98] Aune calls this phenomenon "bilingual interference": John used the LXX but at times attempted to translate the original Hebrew OT into Greek, leading to unusual constructions.[99] Significantly, Beale suggests that this peculiarity is designed to point readers to specific OT backgrounds.[100]

As is evident in the hundreds of *allusions* to the OT in Revelation, John was the foremost NT author to "search the Scriptures" for what "Moses wrote about me," because "they testify of me" (John 5:39, 46). As such, Revelation has Gospel-like qualities, for it is not only forward-looking "prophecy," but also backward-looking *witness*. As an experienced cartographer, John trav-

92. Gilchrest, *Revelation 21–22*, 3–9, 21–22. Bauckham, *The Theology*, 14. See also Barr, "The Story," 23. Suleiman, "Introduction," suggests the following types of readers of any given text: actual reader, ideal reader, mock reader, implied reader, informed reader.

93. Haloviak, *Worlds at War*, 10.

94. Paulien, "The Role," 263–4. Mathewson, *A New Heaven*, 31, argues that Revelation's ideal reader knows the fundamental relationship between new and old meanings.

95. Charles, *Revelation*, I:lxvi; Swete, *The Apocalypse*, cl, clv.

96. See Glassius, *Philologiae Sacrae*. See also Pfochen's *Diatribe de Linguae Graecae*, who argued that the NT reflects "pure Greek." See also Winer, *Grammatik*; Deissmann, *Bible Studies*; Voelz, "The Language"; Wilcox, "Semitisms."

97. Charles, *Revelation*, cxliv.

98. Thompson, *Apocalypse*, 1, 108. For counterpoints to Thompson, see Porter, "The Language of the Apocalypse"; Lindars, Review of *The Apocalypse and Semitic Syntax*. More broadly on the question of the Semitic context of Scripture as a whole, see Evans, "Barnabas Lindars."

99. Aune, *Revelation 1–5*, cxcix.

100. Beale, "Solecisms." See also Laughlin, *The Solecisms*; Trudinger, " 'O AMHN'."

eled through the holy grounds of the Hebrew Scriptures with a "Christological map," continuously setting up signposts and milestones along the way to help those behind him find Jesus Christ there.

An example of how John engages in a "figural christological reading" of the OT are the symbols "lion" and "lamb" in Revelation 5:5–6:

> [5]Then one of the elders said to me, "Do not weep. See, the Lion of the tribe of Judah, the Root of David, has conquered, so that he can open the scroll and its seven seals." [6]Then I saw between the throne and the four living creatures and among the elders a Lamb standing as if it had been slaughtered, having seven horns and seven eyes, which are the seven spirits of God sent out into all the earth.

What we see in this passage is not a chimera, an amalgam of two animals into one, but both are drawn from distinct OT contexts, and the imagery remains unchanged, forming a "juxtaposition" of symbols reflecting a "dialogical intertextuality," where "the alluded text adds a 'voice' to the alluding text so that the reader is forced to configure multiple voices."[101] The phrase "Lion of the tribe of Judah" alludes to Jacob's deathbed speech about Judah, and "lion" describes God.[102] In turn, the imagery of a lamb comes from several moments in Israel's life: the missing lamb of mount Moriah (Gen 22:8), the Passover lamb (Exod 12:7), the daily sacrifice of two lambs as part of the *tāmîd* (Exod 29:38), the messianic oracle of Isaiah 53:7, and at least two sources from Jewish literature which describe the Messiah as a horned lamb (1 Enoch 90; Testament of Joseph 19).

Yet another layer of "Christological exegesis" can be detected in Revelation 5: the chapter's cultic setting reveals that by expanding the general typology of a sacrificial lamb to a lamb offered inside God's throne room, its Most Holy Place, John creates a composite figure of a sacrifice whose atoning blood was offered inside the Most Holy Place of the sanctuary on the DA, forming a dominating *allusion* to the DA. This main *allusion* propagates within a chamber of thematic resonance alongside other *allusions* and *echoes,* such as the imagery of incense offered inside the heavenly Most Holy Place by the high-priestly elders and supporting cultic *echoes,* which accentuate both the dominating *allusion* as well as each other (see pages 140–1).

101. Moyise, "Dialogical," 1, 8. See Murphy, *Fallen,* 193.

102. E.g., Gen 49:9; Job 10:6; Isa 31:4; Jer 50:44; Hos 5:14.

The cumulative effect of all these intertextual reverberations of precursor texts, ideas, sounds, and images in Revelation explored above is the poetic device called *metalepsis* through which an *allusion* or *echo* of a precursor text can only be fully understood by "recovering the original context from which the fragmentary *echo* came, and then reading the two texts in dialogical juxtaposition," Hays explains.[103] More than any other NT writing, Revelation fits Kristeva's "mosaic of quotations" formula: an image retrieved from the OT receives a designated place in the fresco that forms the book, adding nuances to the palette. Elements taken from the OT continue to speak in their new context, allowing John to give them a new voice without negating the former. Like an autostereogram, Revelation's array of images coalesce to form a 3-D image that jumps from the page: a portrait of Jesus Christ.[104]

The previous discussion sought to build a baseline understanding of Revelation's literary characteristics and intertextual engagement with the OT. Below two representative views of the use of the OT in Revelation as proposed by Beale and Moyise are reviewed.[105]

Building on the early 20th-century work of Schlatter, Beale has made a significant contribution to the study of the use of the OT in the NT.[106] Beginning with his 1980 dissertation on the use of Daniel in Revelation followed by his definitive work titled *John's Use of the Old Testament in Revelation*, Beale's working premise is that "John is following others before him ... who reinterpreted earlier Old Testament prophecies and updated them for their own time."[107] As such, Revelation is an elaborate literary work that "is not the result of a mere recording of the actual visions ... but also a result of subsequent reflection on the OT during the writing down of the vision," showing an intention to develop themes from the OT freely and creatively. Themes and keywords from the OT are linked and combined by John and

103. Hays, *Echoes of Scripture in the Gospels*, 11.

104. Notwithstanding the continuous debate, John's allusive method remains *elusive*, prompting Osborne to conclude that the "definitive work on the use of the Old Testament in the Apocalypse is yet to be written. "Osborne, *Revelation*, 2. The representative works on intertextual theory as applied to Revelation are those by Beale, Dumbrell, Vogelgesang, Bauckham, Paulien, Fekkes, Ruiz, Moyise, Porter, Gundry, and Kowalski, listed here: Beale, *John's Use*, 13–59; Beale, *Right Doctrine*; Dumbrell, *The End of the Beginning*; Vogelgesang, "The Interpretation"; Bauckham, *The Climax*; Paulien, *Decoding*; Fekkes, *Isaiah and Prophetic Traditions*; Ruiz, *Ezekiel*; Moyise, *The Old Testament in the Book of Revelation*; Porter, *Hearing*; Gundry, *Three Views*; Kowalski, *Die Rezeption*.

105. Beale, *John's Use*, 23; Moyise, *The Old Testament in the Book of Revelation*.

106. Schlatter, *Das Alte Testament*. See Jenkins, *The Old Testament*; Rissi, *Time and History*, 18.

107. Beale, *John's Use*, 23; Beale, *Handbook*.

"colored both unconsciously and consciously by the traditions which had exerted a formative influence on the author's thinking." Such use of the OT was intentional and effective for his readers.[108]

Beale proposes the terms "influence" or "inner-biblical allusions" to describe John's use of the OT.[109] Such inner-biblical vector of literary dependence, he explains, comes in the form of (1) *clear allusion:* the verbal parallel is almost identical to the OT source and has the same meaning and authorial intention as no other source; (2) *probable allusion:* the idea or structure is the same as the potential OT source; or (3) *possible allusion:* verbal and thematic parallels are not exact but similar to the potential OT passage.[110] Similar to Hays' "availability" test seen above, Beale posits that the validity of an *allusion* is determined by establishing that an author "could have had familiarity" with a specific text from which an *allusion* may be derived.[111] John also reveals "varying degrees of awareness of literary context," with a preference for more generalized "literary and thematic contexts."[112] Beale suggests three additional criteria for the interpretation of OT symbols: (1) how a symbol is used in the OT source; (2) how a symbol is used in the Jewish interpretive tradition; and (3) how a symbol is used in the immediate NT context. Failure to respect these criteria may result in a Pandora's Box of interpretations disconnected from the OT source, he warns.[113]

Beale's understanding of John's use of the OT in Revelation aligns with the approach used in this study. For example, when commenting on OT eschatology as it intersects with the book of Revelation, Beale offers two helpful observations: (1) OT patterns of fulfillment provide templates for future eschatological fulfillments; (2) OT eschatological prototypes are lenses through which present fulfillments are to be understood.[114] Although it is not possible to say precisely how John uses these OT eschatological prototypes due to uncertainty as to when they are a "means" or the "object" of interpretation, there is an interplay between them. Beale argues that changes in "application" of a particular OT text do not necessarily mean "disregard" for

108. Beale, *John's Use*, 66.

109. See Beale, *Handbook*, 51–52; see Moyise, "Intertextuality," 16. For an example of a deconstructive approach, see Royalty, "Don't Touch *This* Book."

110. Beale, *John's Use*, 62.

111. Beale, *John's Use*, 20.

112. Beale, *John's Use*, 74.

113. Beale, *John's Use*, 20–21.

114. Beale, *John's Use*, 79.

the original OT context and authorial intention.[115] He thinks that John may be engaging in "escalated analogy," "interpretative distillation," "interpretative expansions," and even "change of application," which require a broader theological construct to be adequately understood.[116] John's Semitic, paratactic thinking seems to allow two ideas (at times contradictory) to stand side by side more readily than does our modern mind.[117] For example, John's *allusion* to Ezekiel 40 in Revelation 21–22 adds a new application to the ancient prophecy: there is no temple in the New Jerusalem; the city is a temple.[118]

Perhaps Beale's most helpful contribution is the concept of "presuppositional lenses" employed to understand how a potential OT type meets its fulfillment in Revelation.[119] These are bifocal, bi-directional lenses, for "the Old Testament interprets the New Testament, and the New Testament interprets the Old Testament"—even if the OT contexts more often than not have a local application that is only *typologically* applied to NT contexts.[120]

Throughout his published works, Beale offers detailed exegesis that illuminates his approach. At bottom, not unlike Hatina, Beale operates from an assumption of determinate authorial intention in the OT, one that John seeks to respect and build on. Ultimately, Beale's approach seeks to prevent detaching OT typology from its contextual moorings, causing it to wander in a landscape of disjointed, contradictory readings.

In contrast to Beale's approach, Moyise has sought to apply reader-response criticism to Revelation by contending that "[a]ny description of John's use of Scripture must do justice to both the continuities and the discontinuities."[121] Moyise operates under the premise that "emphasis on the author's intention has been largely abandoned in New Testament studies and replaced by a focus either on the text itself or on the role of the reader."[122] A text such as Revelation "can only be understood as part of a web or matrix of other texts, themselves only to be understood in the light of other texts," he writes.[123] Similarly to Beale, he defines intertextuality as a dynamic through which "the Old Testament reflects on the New Testament context, even as the

115. Beale, *John's Use*, 73. See Vos, *The Synoptic Traditions*, 21–37, 41.
116. Beale, *John's Use*, 73, 78–79.
117. Beale, *John's Use*, 48.
118. Beale, *Revelation*, 1061–1062.
119. Beale, *John's Use*, 48.
120. Beale, *John's Use*, 48.
121. Moyise, *The Old Testament in the Book of Revelation*, 22.
122. Moyise, *The Old Testament in the Book of Revelation*, 142.
123. Moyise, "Dialogical," 3.

New Testament context absorbs and changes the Old Testament allusion."[124] This dynamic, however, results in less continuous readings than those of Beale because the key to interpretation comes "from two separate sources," and "the new work forces new meanings from the source text."[125] John's use of the OT creates "inviting connections," he posits, which the reader must negotiate and sometimes leave unresolved.[126] In the case of the use of Ezekiel's temple by John (Rev 21:22), Moyise argues that it is a "denial" of its meaning in Ezekiel 40: "[E]ven when a source is negated, its 'voice' is not completely silenced and can bring associations and connotations that contribute to the interpretation of the text."[127]

For example, Moyise argues that the OT Lion-Lamb imagery analyzed previously finds no resolution in Revelation. He contends that interpretive tensions must remain for two reasons: (1) we do not have access to the author's mind; (2) reader response is not measurable.[128] Therefore, each reader decides how to solve this tension, which leads Moyise to conclude that "by utilizing past texts, the author has produced a fresh composition which invites the reader to participate and create meaning."[129] Moyise also suggests that contradictory readings indicate that either the text's meaning is not recoverable or that multiple interpretations are "complementary."[130]

Their choice of analogies illustrates the contrast between Beale's and Moyise's views. Beale compares the use of the OT in the NT to a fruit that maintains its qualities when placed in a basket, while Moyise prefers the analogy of a fruit salad, where fruits become inseparable from the whole. Thus, while not denying that the OT finds itself in a new environment in the NT, they disagree on *how* this dynamic occurs. Beale contends that Revelation's *allusions* to the OT are bound to their original contexts and original OT authorial intention but receive new "significance" in light of "the Christ

124. Moyise, *The Old Testament in the Book of Revelation*, 19. See also Punt, "Inhabiting," 207–24, who compares the process of writing to creating a "palimpsest" with traces of old, partially erased texts still visible in the new text.

125. Moyise, *The Old Testament in the Book of Revelation*, 111, 19.

126. Moyise, *The Old Testament in the Book of Revelation*, 43.

127. Moyise, "Dialogical Intertextuality," 6–7.

128. Moyise, *The Old Testament in the Book of Revelation*, 43, 132.

129. Moyise, *The Old Testament in the Book of Revelation*, 142. With a similar perspective, cultural historian Timothy Beal claims that "the 'book' of Revelation is not a self-evident, original literary thing created once and for all in the past and then incarnated in various interpretations throughout history. It constantly changes, forever being made and remade in different cultural productions of meaning" (*The Book of Revelation*, 5).

130. Moyise, *The Old Testament in the Book of Revelation*, 53.

event." In turn, Moyise argues that John's use of the OT often subverts its original context, inviting the reader's involvement in recreating meaning. For Beale, "the Christ event" illuminates the OT context and gives it renewed significance which expands the original meaning, while Moyise argues that the new context breaks with the previous meaning requiring a new one.[131]

Beale contends that Moyise is redressing old traditional hermeneutical approaches to Revelation with new terminology (reader-response theory) and see as problematic Moyise's contention that all *allusions* to the OT in the NT are taken out of context.[132] Thus, while Beale seeks to maintain continuity between the OT and the NT, Moyise highlights their discontinuities.[133] Moyise seems more interested in the literary phenomenon created by John's inner-biblical *allusions*, while Beale is concerned with maintaining authorial intention and the typological unity of Scripture.

The above discussion highlights how scholars can differ in understanding John's use of the OT in Revelation. Notwithstanding their diverging views, it is undeniable that their conversation and rich analogies have enhanced our understanding of the possibilities of intertextual theory in biblical studies. Paulien suggested that Beale and Moyise could be right in what they affirm but wrong in what they deny.[134] Thus, we could agree with Beale that, by depending on the OT, John could not simply dismiss the original OT context of the prefigurations he evokes but interprets them retrospectively in light of Christ. Thus, the OT meaning of a particular image remains the anchor for new typological readings in light of "the Christ event."

Conversely, and in agreement with Moyise, it seems inevitable that the modern-day reader has a vital role in the process of reading and creating meaning in Revelation because we no longer have access to John's mind. Perhaps John could agree with both scholars; even as Revelation is rooted in past divine encounters, the text forces the reader to reflect on a novel theological matrix that overwhelms preconceived notions about the Messiah, Jesus, God, and the earthly and heavenly realms. Perhaps, rather than applying an "either-or" approach to Revelation's use of the OT, exegetes should strive towards a hermeneutical strategy that seeks a "both-and" approach; rather

131. Moyise, *The Old Testament in the Book of Revelation*, 19.

132. Beale, *John's Use*, 41; Moyise, *The Old Testament in the Book of Revelation*, 9–20, 112–13.

133. Beale, *John's Use*, 52.

134. The *repartée* was at one point moderated by Paulien in "Dreading," 5–22. Beale responded in "A Response," while Moyise responded in the same issue in Moyise, "Authorial Intention." See also Beale, "Questions," 151–180. See also Moyise, "Recent Developments."

than restricting the meaning of Revelation, one should be open to an ever-receding horizon of meanings.

In sum, as explored so far, three main types of intertextual dependence of the OT in the NT have been proposed:

(1) *quotation:* when the author "clearly indicates that the words that follow are not his or her own but are taken from another source";[135]
(2) *allusion:* when the author "was consciously referring to previous literature," although no credit is given;[136]
(3) *echo:* a non-lexical *thematic allusion* to a text, idea, or imagery.[137]

As far as *quotations* go, there are none in Revelation; allusive activity in the book occurs in the form of *allusions* and *echoes.* Our assessment of the presence of *allusions* and *echoes* of the DA in Revelation will build on four of Hays' seven tests presented above: *availability, volume, thematic coherence,* and *historical plausibility.*

As far as *availability* and *historical plausibility* tests go, it is assumed that the original readers of Revelation were familiar with the DA's language, imagery, and theological themes. More specifically, to the *volume* criterion, *echoes* of the DA in Revelation receive three loudness settings: *soft, medium loud,* and *loud.* In turn, an *echo's* loudness is measured by at least two factors: (1) its original OT context; (2) its thematic reverberation in the respective passage in Revelation. Because an *echo's* loudness goes in tandem with Hays' *thematic coherence* test, the assessment of allusive activity appears in the form of a table at the end of each passage in Revelation, listing the allusive type (*allusion* or *echo*), its strength or *volume,* and the context's *thematic coherence.*[138]

## General Assumptions About Revelation

As the previous discussion laid the preliminary hermeneutical groundwork for this study, this section offers a brief overview of three general assumptions about Revelation: authorship, date of composition, and genre.

135. Moyise, "Quotations," 15.
136. Paulien, "Elusive Allusions," 40–41.
137. Hollander, *The Figure of Echo,* 64.
138. Hays, *Echoes,* 29–32.

## *Authorship*

Several 'Johns' have been proposed as potential authors of Revelation: (1) John, the Apostle; (2) John, the "Elder"; (3) John, the Baptizer; (4) John Mark; (5) Cerinthus; and (6) an unknown John. The view of the authorship of Revelation by the Apostle John has the support of church tradition, starting with Justin Martyr (*Dialogues with Trypho* 81.4) and Irenaeus (*Adversus Haereses* 30). Many scholars, however, remain unconvinced of this hypothesis, mostly on philological grounds: the fourth Gospel and Revelation were not written by the same person, or, at least, not by the same hand.[139] Pierre Prigent argued that both the Gospel of John and Revelation come from the same "milieux," and the only element that separates them is "le genre literaire."[140] Otto Böcher agrees while seeing clear "parallels" between Revelation and the Fourth Gospel because the "Bildmaterial" of both books is "identisch."[141] Influential NT scholar George Ladd argued in favor of John, the Apostle as the author while a disciple wrote the Gospel.[142] In a recent monograph, Breu analyzed Revelation's authorship based on postmodern theories of authorship that are less concerned with "biographical interpretation" and "authorial intention" than the rhetorical *Funktion* of an author's name within the text. Both the author's "presence" and his "absence" become devices to drive home the message.[143]

In sum, the Apostle John's authorship continues to be held by most commentators, and it is probably on target,[144] even though I take no firm position on the author's identity because it is not decisive for the book's interpretation.

## *Date of Composition*

Although the most popular date for the composition of Revelation is about 95 CE, that date has not been unassailable.[145] Sweet thinks that an earlier date "*may* be right, but the internal evidence is not sufficient to outweigh the firm tradition stemming from Irenaeus" of a Domitianic date.[146] Howev-

139. See Mounce, *Revelation*, 8–15, for a concise discussion on the authorship of Revelation.

140. Prigent, *Flash sur l'Apocalypse*, 13.

141. Böcher, "Das Verhältnis," 291, 295–301. See also Brown, *An Introduction*, 804.

142. Ladd, *Revelation*, xxx–xxxvii.

143. Breu, *Autorschaft*, 4.

144. Mounce, *Revelation*, 12–15; Beale, *Revelation*, 34–36; Kistemaker, *Revelation*, 26; Osborne, *Revelation*, 2–6.

145. See Robinson, *Redating*, 221–253.

146. Sweet, *Revelation*, 27.

er, a pre-70 CE composition date has become more visible recently because of internal evidence, while at least one author places it ca. 110–130 CE.[147] Revelation's assumed "ideal readers" revealed in the book's deep engagement with Jewish themes supports the early date. John Marshall calls the designation of Revelation as "Christian" as an obstacle to historical-critical interpretation and argues that "Rev 17:9–11 suggests strongly that the vision narrative is set in the period between June 68 and April 70 CE."[148] John's Jewish background and dependence on the OT, especially his emphasis on the Hebrew cultus, may imply a date closer to Christianity's Jewish roots, possibly even before 70 CE.[149]

### *Literary Genre*

Although John's Apocalypse gave birth to the *apocalyptic* genre, attempts to lock Revelation into a single genre of "Christian apocalyptic" in the style of contemporaneous Jewish apocalypses have met an impasse.[150] For one, Revelation is not anonymous, a common trait of Jewish apocalypses. Further, scholars have placed the book into several categories of genre, such as " mixed genre,"[151] "epistle," "revelation," "prophecy," and even "parable."[152] The book's multifaceted literary features prompted Aune to call it "an anomaly" vis à vis other Christian apocalypses such as The Shepherd of Hermas, the Apocalypse of Peter, and the Apocalypse of Paul.[153]

The working definition of an apocalypse adopted by academia was initially proposed in 1979 by Collins et al.:

147. Smalley, *Revelation*, 2–3, argues for Johannine authorship and a pre-70 CE dating of Revelation. See also Rojas-Flores, "The Book of Revelation," 375–392; Bell, "Date," 93–102; Wilson, "The Problem," 587–605; Gentry, *Before Jerusalem Fell*; Moberly, "When Was Revelation," 376–393; Slater, "Dating," 252–258; Wilson, "The Early Christians," 163–93; Sturdy, *Redrawing*, 81–82.

148. Marshall, *Parables*, 4–5, 92. For a discussion of Revelation in relationship with other Jewish apocalypses, see Aune, "The Apocalypse of John and Palestinian Jewish Apocalyptic," 1–33.

149. Bebis, "Influence of Jewish Worship," 138, has proposed that the book's Jewish themes and Christological focus could have provided the ideal liturgical bridge between Judaism and early Christianity.

150. For a representative sample of studies on the genre of the Apocalypse, see Mazzaferri, *The Genre*; Aune, "The Apocalypse and the Problem of Genre," 65–96; Hellholm, "The Problem," 13–64; Musvosvi, "The Issue of Genre," 43–60; Barr, "Beyond Genre," 71–90; Kuykendall, "The Literary Genre"; Aune, "Understanding," 233–245.

151. Harrington, *Revelation*, 6–7. For a summary of Revelation in its early Christian context, see Koester, *History and Literature*, 253–262.

152. See Marshall, *Parables of War*.

153. Schlatter, *Das Alte Testament*. See Jenkins, *The Old Testament*; Rissi, *Time and History*, 18.

> "Apocalypse" is a genre of revelatory literature with a narrative framework, in which a revelation is mediated by an otherworldly being to a human recipient, disclosing a transcendent reality which is both temporal, insofar as it envisages eschatological salvation and spatial, insofar as it involves another, supernatural world.[154]

This definition stems from an awareness of other apocalypses circulating in John's time that shared these characteristics. Hellholm critiqued Collins' definition for its lack of a statement on the "function" of an apocalypse which he describes as: "intended for a group in crisis with the purpose of exhortation and/or consolation by means of divine authority."[155] Hellholm's important addition settles the matter of genre for our purposes.

## Conclusion

The preceding discussions covering a range of issues about the book of Revelation's composition, literary features, and intertextual characteristics indicate that doing justice to Revelation requires continued attention to the book's complex textual and audio-visual layers. The exegetical task requires keeping Revelation in close proximity to Israel's Scriptures and sacred traditions by carefully identifying *allusions* and *echoes* of these sources.

Two primary hermeneutical principles emerge from this Introduction: (1) understanding Revelation requires knowledge of the Judaic Scriptures' linguistic and theological landscape; (2) traveling through the hallowed grounds of the OT with Revelation as a map requires "Christological lenses."

In the next chapter, we will explore the DA in its Pentateuchal environs, which will help us visualize its language, imagery, actors, and theological themes. This vital exegetical effort will inform our study of the DA's reception in the NT and, more specifically, in Revelation.

154. Collins, "The Morphology," 1–20; Collins, *The Apocalyptic Imagination*, 2.

155. Hellholm, "The Problem," 23, 27. Hellholm considers "authorization" as "*the* characteristic function" of the Apocalypse of John because the source and authority of his vision are God" (Hellholm, "The Problem," 45). See also Vorster, "Genre," 103–23.

# 1

# THE DAY OF ATONEMENT IN THE OLD TESTAMENT

The introduction reviewed issues concerning Revelation's composition, literary features, and the way John engaged in a Christological reading of the OT. The present chapter focuses on the DA's rituals described in the Pentateuch—principally Leviticus 16. This detailed undertaking should inform the reader about the role the DA's rituals and actors played within the Hebrew cultus and beyond.

## The Theology of Levitical Rituals

Leviticus 16 has enjoyed a rich tradition of Christian commentary, beginning with church father Origen (*Homiliae in Leviticum*, 3rd century CE). Janowski calls the DA "the high point and culmination of the priestly purification and sin rituals" because it "provides the answer to the question of how Israel will overcome their sins and impurities to live in the proximity of a holy God."[1] It was, however, the Jewish scholar Jacob Milgrom who perhaps best grasped the Levitical system's significance and who influenced a new generation of scholars. This chapter draws primarily on Milgrom's reflections on the DA, along with the contribution of others.

In Rabbinic literature, the book of Leviticus is called תורת כהנים ("instructions for the priests") and *wayyiqrā* in the Hebrew Bible ("and he called," Lev 1:1).[2] The English title Leviticus comes from the LXX where it appears

1. Janowski, "Das Geschenk," 13, 14.

2. See m. Meg. 3:5; m. Menah. 4:3. For a discussion on the authorship of Leviticus, see Milgrom, *Leviticus 1–16*, 13–34; Archer Jr., "The Chronology," 359–374; Archer Jr., *A Survey*; Segal, *The Pentateuch*, 47.

as Λευιτικον, although the book does not deal with "Levites." Leviticus held enduring relevance in Jewish life; seventeen fragmentary scrolls of the book (including the *Targum* of Leviticus and two Greek copies) were found in the Judean desert, including atop the Masada fortification.[3]

Jewish scholar Y. Kaufmann observes how Leviticus "betrays its antiquity."[4] Arguing in favor of a pre-exilic date for Leviticus (Priestly), Milgrom adduces several lines of philological evidence: (1) the semantics of twenty-two Hebrew terms from P which fall into disuse after the post-exilic era; (2) "not a single Priestly term has been shown to be of post-exilic coinage"[5]; (3) no archaizing of P's language; and (4) terms such as *qōḏeš* and *miqdaš haqqōḏeš* (Lev 16:33) for the Most Holy Place (e.g., *qōḏeš haqqoḏāšim,* Exod 26:33, 34).[6]

"Theology," writes Milgrom, "is what Leviticus is all about. It pervades every chapter and almost every verse. It is not expressed in pronouncements, but embedded in rituals."[7] The book's great *Leitmotif* is the controversy between *holiness* vs. *impurity* because "the identification of impurity with death must mean that holiness stands for life," posits Milgrom.[8] Holiness in the Hebrew cultus was inextricably connected to creation: while creation separated light, darkness, heaven, and earth, God's purpose in the Levitical system is to separate "clean and unclean . . . holy and profane."[9] As Unger writes: "In Genesis we see man ruined; in Exodus, man redeemed; in Leviticus, man cleansed, worshiping and serving."[10] With meticulous attention to detail, Leviticus describes "rituals of restoration and reintegration" to fulfill God's promise to make Israel a holy nation of priests (Exod 19:5–6).[11] Leviticus is therefore central to Israel's "*raison d'être,*" concludes Hartley.[12]

Levine observes that Leviticus likely describes the rituals after they became part of Jewish life, a feature that Bibb calls "narrativized ritual" because

3. See Kugler and Baek, *Leviticus at Qumran,* 323.

4. Kaufmann, *The Religion,* 206.

5. Milgrom, *Leviticus 1–16,* 8. See Gane, *Cult and Character,* 34–36.

6. See Milgrom, *Leviticus 1–16,* 1063. Young, "The Impact," 36, writes that the notion of Leviticus 16 being "pre-exilic rather than the invention of P is now incontestable."

7. Milgrom, *Leviticus 1–16,* 42.

8. Milgrom, *Leviticus 1–16,* 46–7. See Jürgens, *Heiligkeit,* 425.

9. Janowski, "Das Geschenk," 22.

10. Unger, *Hodder Bible,* 85. Harrison, *Leviticus,* 9, calls Leviticus "a work of towering spirituality, which through the various sacrificial rituals points the reader unerringly to the atoning death of Jesus, our great high priest."

11. Hayes, "Atonement," 5–15. See also Kiuchi, *Leviticus,* 33.

12. Hartley, *Leviticus,* xxx.

"the narrative itself bears ritual significance within and beyond its story-telling."[13] This feature is evident in how the book intersperses ritual prescriptions with stories, such as the death of Nadab and Abihu (Lev 10). Milgrom also points out "striking" similarities between the Babylonian New Year's festival and Israel's Yom Kippur: (1) a purgation of the temple by the high priest; (2) impurity eliminated by animal sacrifices; (3) participants rendered impure; and (4) the king and high priest undergo a process of confession and penitence.[14] However, there are significant differences, the most important being that in Israel, this occurred only once a year and was a significant festival, different from the frequent purgations prescribed in the Babylonian rites. Further, the Levitical system of rituals differs from ANE "apotropaic" (emergency) rituals because of Israel's monotheism; responsibility for one's actions remains with the individual who alone can "drive God out of the sanctuary by polluting it with their moral and ritual sins," explains Milgrom.[15]

If theology in Leviticus appears in the form of rituals, what are they? Gane defines a ritual as a meaningful physical yet "symbolic activity" that carries out a "transformation process involving interaction with a reality ordinarily inaccessible to the material domain."[16] In turn, a "sacrifice" is "a religious ritual in which something of value is ritually transferred to the sacred realm for utilization by a deity."[17] This connection is created using something tangible, an animal, so that rituals, although *symbolic*, are not *abstract* in the sense of lacking connection with reality. Thus, Gane explains, "in a ritual a nonmaterial entity (e.g., sin) can be treated as if it belongs to the material domain, so that it can be subject to physical interaction and manipulation."[18] Further, a ritual must have constant meaning because "the full significance of an individual ritual or ritual activity can only appear within the context of the ritual system to which it belongs."[19] In this way, "nonphysical pollution,

13. Levine, "The Descriptive," 307–318; Bibb, *Ritual Words*, 35.

14. Milgrom, *Leviticus 1–16*, 1068.

15. Milgrom, *Leviticus 1–16*, 45, 43.

16. Gane, *Cult and Character*, 7, 15, 18. See Gane, "Schedules," 231–244; Marx, *Les Systèmes*, 13–20.

17. Gane, *Cult and Character*, 16.

18. Gane, *Cult and Character*, 8.

19. Gane, *Cult and Character*, 9, states that meaning comes from "clues" in the ritual. Davies calls this the "conceptual element," which gives the rite its meaning. See also Davies, "An Interpretation," 92–96; Klingbeil, *Bridging the Gap*, 14–18. See Janowski, "Das Geschenk," 4: "Rites possess a great performative intensity and must be correctly—even *rightly*—performed in order to be effective."

consisting of ritual impurities and moral faults, is purged from the sanctuary of supramundane Yahweh on behalf of the Israelites," leading to transformation.[20]

## *God Abides in the Sanctuary*

The sanctuary's ultimate function was not the sacrifice of animals but to preserve God's presence with Israel: "And have them make me a sanctuary, so that I may dwell among them" (Exod 25:8). God had confirmed to Solomon, "I have chosen and consecrated this house so that my name may be there forever; my eyes and my heart will be there for all time" (2 Chr 7:16). He promised that "if my people who are called by my name humble themselves, pray, seek my face, and turn from their wicked ways, then I will hear from heaven, and will forgive their sin and heal their land" (2 Chr 7:14).

While present with the people, God's presence was veiled in the recondite compartment of the tabernacle, the Most Holy Place, so they would be shielded from his power and glory and not die (Lev 10:2; 16:2; Exod 33:18–23). God's presence hovered on top of the mercy seat of the ark of the covenant and communicated with Israel through Moses and Aaron (Exod 25:22).

Obedience and repentance from transgressions followed by their atonement through sacrificial blood, as well as intercessory prayer kept the sanctuary holy and ensured God's continued presence with Israel. It was only within this cultic framework that the sanctuary could continue to function covenantally as God's abode.[21]

## *Defiling the Sanctuary Jeopardizes the Covenant*

Whereas the sanctuary housed God's presence, its rituals comprised its housekeeping: "Thus you shall keep the people of Israel separate from their uncleanness, so that they do not die in their uncleanness by defiling my tabernacle that is in their midst" (Lev 15:31). For loyal Israelites, the system of rituals became "a way of meaningfully interacting with God, to bring about a transformation or change of state."[22] While the driving force behind the

20. Gane, *Cult and Character*, 9, 12.

21. Milgrom, *Leviticus 1–16*, 50, 51. Elsewhere Milgrom argues: "Israel as a whole, priests included, enhances or diminishes its holiness in proportion to its observance of all of God's commandments." See also Milgrom, "The Changing Concept," 67; Wilson, *Systems, Concepts*, 16, 26.

22. Hundley, *Keeping*, 20.

people's compliance with the ritual system was their belief that the needed transformation would be achieved through obedience, the efficacy of any given ritual rested solely on God's grace and sovereignty. Thus, the rituals were not merely about "cult," but ultimately about "character."[23]

Contamination of the sanctuary occurred "aerially," argued Milgrom: "A sin committed anywhere [in the camp] will generate impurity that, becoming airborne, penetrates the sanctuary" and encroaches on the divine realm (see Lev 15:31; 20:3; Num 19:13, 20).[24] The severity and spatial extent of the defilement were in "proportion of the magnitude" of the sin/impurity, explains Milgrom; different types of violations by the Israelites affect different areas of the sanctuary as follows:

(1) an involuntary, communal violation, i.e., by the whole people or inadvertent impurity or physical impurity pollutes the outer altar, which is purged by the application of *ḥaṭṭāʾṯ* blood on its horns (Lev 4:25–35, 30; 9:9);

(2) an involuntary, individual violation or impurity on the part of the high priest or the community pollutes the inner-sanctuary, which the high priest cleanses through the application of *ḥaṭṭāʾṯ* blood to the altar of incense, and before the *pārōket*, the veil of the Most Holy Place (Lev 4:5–7, 13–21);

(3) intentional, "brazen and unrepented offenses" pollute the outer altar, but due to their severity, penetrate the Most Holy place where God resides.[25]

Moreover, the following subcategories according to expiability and reach within the sanctuary can be seen in Leviticus 5 and Numbers 15:[26]

| | | |
|---|---|---|
| Unintentional-non-defiant<br>(*Expiable-inadvertent*)<br>Outer altar | Intentional-non-defiant<br>(*Expiable-advertent*)<br>Holy Place→Holy of Holies | Intentional-defiant<br>(*Inexpiable-advertent*)<br>Holy of Holies |

23. Gane, *Cult and Character*, 9, 162; see Janowski, "Das Geschenk," 4.

24. Milgrom, *Leviticus: A Book of Ritual*, 31; Milgrom, *Leviticus 1–16*, 255–257. See Gane, *Cult and Character*, 160; Wright, "The Spectrum," 155, suggests "gradations of severity" of impurities based on whether they require a sacrifice and where they occur in the camp.

25. See Milgrom, *Leviticus 1–16*, 257.

26. For an extended discussion, see Gane, *Cult and Character*, 198–213.

The result of brazen, unatoned transgressions was clear: God could abandon the sanctuary and annul the covenant.[27] Warnings accompanied God's covenantal promises; if the people turned aside from "my statutes and my commandments," he would abandon the covenant, uproot them as a nation, and "this house, which I have consecrated for my name, I will cast out of my sight" (2 Chr 7:19; see Lam 2:7; Ezekiel 8–11; m. Shevuʿot 1.4).[28] Inadvertent sin and impurity defiled the sanctuary; willful sin and lingering impurities jeopardized the entire covenant. This brief overview highlights the role played by individual Israelites in keeping the sanctuary undefiled and the severe implications of an individual's actions for collective well-being.

### *Cleansing the Sanctuary: The Meaning of Kipper*

Central to the *ḥaṭṭāʾṯ* system of offerings in Leviticus were rites involving כִּפֶּר (*kipper*).[29] Scholarly treatment of *kipper* is extensive, but in sum, this verb, usually occurring in the *piʿel*—most likely stemming from the Akkadian *kuppuru*, "to wipe off"—is synonymous with מָחָה (*māḥā*) "to wipe off" (e.g., Jer 18:23), and סוּר (*sur*) "to remove" (e.g., Isa 27:9).[30] In cultic settings, *kipper* is often coupled with טִהַר (*tihar*) "purify" and חָטָא (*ḥaṭā*) "decontaminate" (e.g., Lev 14:52).[31] According to Milgrom, "in ritual texts the meaning 'rub off, wipe' predominates," and in all *ḥaṭṭāʾṯ* contexts, *kipper* bears this meaning exclusively. Sacrificial blood applied on the sanctuary "rubs off" its impurities."[32]

The question then arises about what was cleansed by the blood during *kipper*-rites. Here, scholarly views hinge on the meaning of the prepositional phrase כִּפֶּר עַל (*kipper ʿal*) when used alongside the preposition מִן (*min*). While Milgrom believes that *ḥaṭṭāʾṯ* blood absorbs impurity, Schwartz thinks its application eradicates impurity instantly, while sins are transferred to the high priest and then to the "goat for Azazel" on the DA.[33] Levine takes *kipper ʿal* as "to perform rites of expiation in proximity to—a person, object,

27. See Wright, "Day of Atonement," *AYBD* 2:73; Bergsma, *The Jubilee*, 32; Milgrom, "Israel's Sanctuary," 390–99.

28. Levine, *The JPS Torah*, 99. See Rooke, "The Day of Atonement," 354; for an extensive treatment on this subject, see Hundley, *Keeping*, 39–52.

29. See Watts, *Ritual and Rhetoric*, 136.

30. See Milgrom, *Leviticus 1–16*, 1079–1080 for a discussion on the correct translation of כִּפֶּר. See also Greenberg, *A New Look*, 12; *TDOT* s.v. כִּפֶּר.

31. Watts, *Ritual and Rhetoric*, 131.

32. Milgrom, *Leviticus 1–16*, 1080.

33. Schwartz, "The Bearing of Sin," 17–18.

etc.," involving direct contact.[34] Milgrom also contrasts impurities brought upon the sanctuary corporately from the iniquity of individual Israelites. As such, *kipper*-rites never have a person as a direct object, but rather cleanse the sanctuary of the impurity on the transgressor's behalf, as in Leviticus 14:19: "the priest shall offer the sin offering, to make atonement for the one to be cleansed from his impurity."[35] Milgrom thinks this is so because *ʿal* ("for, on account of, because of") is used synonymously with the preposition *min* with the meaning "for, because of, from," as in Leviticus 4:26: "Thus the priest shall make atonement on his behalf for his sin"; and in v. 35: "... the priest shall make atonement on your behalf." Since the blood is never applied on the offending party, its purging effect, when applied to the sanctuary, is done on behalf ("in proximity") of the offerer and only indirectly benefits him or her.[36] (However, it should be pointed out that Milgrom does not consistently take *min* as such, for in specific passages, he allows the privative rendering "from" where the context requires.) Foundational to Milgrom's view is the notion that "holiness never sanctifies impurity. Only the reverse occurs—impurity defiles holiness," and restoration only occurs when the impurity is removed.[37]

Conversely, Gane takes the prepositional phrase *kipper ʿal* alongside *min* as mostly privative: impurity is removed "from" the sinner so that "an offerer who has כפר performed on his/her behalf 'from' a physical ritual impurity becomes pure 'from' that impurity."[38] Purification by *kipper*-rites purges both sinner *and* sanctuary, but on different occasions: throughout the year, people are polluted and need to be purged by the *kipper*-rites, but on the DA, *kipper*-rites purge the sanctuary as the people's sins and impurities are removed from it.[39] The problem with Gane's reading is that it requires that *ḥaṭṭāʾṯ* blood change its function from purifier to pollutant: the impurity is removed "from" the sinner and transferred to the blood of the sacrifice, which then contaminates the altar when it is daubed on it; but on the DA this same blood acts as a purifier of the entire sanctuary. Milgrom calls this "chameleonic ability" of *ḥaṭṭāʾṯ* blood an "unsupported hypothesis," leaving us with

34. Levine, *In the Presence*, 65, 81.

35. See Milgrom, "Day of Atonement," 83.

36. Milgrom, "The Preposition," 162.

37. Milgrom, *Leviticus 1–16*, 255. See Schenker, "Das Zeichen," 199–205.

38. Gane, *Cult and Character*, 116, 155. See Milgrom, *Leviticus 1–16*, 1079–1080, for a discussion on the translation of כִּפֶּר. See also Lang, *TDOT* s.v. כִּפֶּר. See Janowski, "Das Geschenk," 26; Zohar, "Repentance," 609–618.

39. Gane, *Cult and Character*, 15, 18, 142.

Milgrom's view as the most cogent: *kipper* is necessary "because of" the sinner's impurity/sin, which allows God to forgive.[40]

Scholars have also noticed that *kipper* and *kōper* ("ransom") are closely related in some contexts. Levine offers a double-take on *kipper:* "(1) *kippēr* I, the primary *Piʿēl,* and (2) *kippēr* II, a secondary denominative, from the noun *kôper* 'ransom, expiation gift.'"[41] Drawing on two examples (Exod 30:12–16 and Num 35:31–33), Milgrom comes to a similar conclusion: "there exists a strong possibility that all texts that assign to *kipper* the function of averting God's wrath have *kôper* in mind: guilty life spared by substituting for it the innocent parties or their ransom."[42] This does not mean necessarily that *kipper* and *kōper* are homographs; elsewhere, Milgrom observes that non-cultic *kipper,* which carries the notion of *kōper* "must be sharply distinguished from that of the sanctuary" because the goal of *kipper* performed there is to secure the continued presence of God in the sanctuary, not one of averting his wrath.[43] In agreement, Schwartz explains that "cultic כפר, even in its metaphorical sense, does not include the notion of propitiation but only that of expiation."[44] Further, it should be pointed out that the notion of "ransom" is limited to non-cultic contexts where sin is present, as there are cases for which only purification can be meant by a *kipper*-rite, such as the case of a woman's post-partum impurity (Lev 12:8).

More recently, Sklar has argued that *kipper* means "purification," as well as "ransom" because "sin not only endangers, it also defiles, while impurity not only defiles, it also endangers."[45] The offender's life is endangered, requiring a ransom. Sklar summarizes the meaning of *kipper* as "a legally or ethically legitimate payment that delivers a guilty party from a just punishment that is the right of the offended party to execute or to have executed."[46] Taking this reading a step further than Milgrom, Sklar narrows the

40. Milgrom, "The Preposition," 163.

41. Levine, *In the Presence,* 67.

42. Milgrom, *Leviticus 1–16,* 1082. See Sklar, "Sin and Impurity," 20–21 for an explanation of the discrepancy between the printed version of Milgrom's commentary and this corrected version.

43. Milgrom, "Day of Atonement," 80.

44. Schwartz, "Prohibitions," 53; Rhyder, *Centralizing Cult,* 219–220.

45. Sklar, "Sin and Impurity," 24; see Sklar, *Sin, Impurity, Sacrifice, Atonement,* 183–187.

46. Sklar, "Sin and Impurity," 19. Sklar further observes: "The acceptance of this payment is entirely dependent upon the choice of the offended party, it is a lesser punishment than was originally expected, and its acceptance serves both to rescue the life of the guilty and to appease the offended party, thus restoring peace to the relationship." See *TDOT* 7:301: "for the recipient, it is represents [sic] compensation, reparation, indemnification; from the perspective of the offender, it represents a ransom (see Ex. 21:30: *pidyōn napsō,* "redemption of his life") for his own life, which is forfeit, a gift to propitiate the enraged injured party."

relationship between *kipper* and *kōper* into two distinct functions: *kipper*-rite and *kipper*-action, which achieve two types of *kōper*: *kōper*-purgation and *kōper*-payment. A *kipper*-rite involves the application of blood to a part of the sanctuary such as the altar and achieves *kōper*-purgation on it on behalf of the people or the offending party, as evidenced in Leviticus 17:11: "For the life of the flesh is in the blood; and I have given it to you to ransom your lives" (see Lev 16:19; Exod 30:15–16).[47] Moreover, *kipper* and *sālaḥ* often occur together in cultic settings, illuminating the relationship between the sinner and God, as in Leviticus 4:20b: "The priest shall make atonement [*kipper*] for them, and they shall be forgiven [*vᵉnislaḥ*]" (4:20, 31, 35; 5:10, 13, 16, 18, 26; see Temple Scroll [11QT] 26:9–10.) The reason for this interplay between ransom, atonement, and forgiveness, Sklar explains, is because "סלח can refer to the acceptance of a mitigated penalty in place of the penalty deserved, resulting in restored relationship between the sinner and the Lord."[48]

The preceding discussion provides an essential overview of how impurity and sin impacted the relationship between God and Israel and how the tabernacle was cleansed. These concepts have important implications for the NT's view of sin and its remedy, which we will review in chapter 3. With this overview behind us, we turn to specific aspects of the rituals encompassing the Levitical DA.

## The Origins of the Day of Atonement in Israel

The DA's official festal name does not appear in Leviticus 16 but is given in Leviticus 23:27 as "the day of atonements (*yōm hakippūrīm*), and as *hēmera exilasmou* and *tē hēmera tou ilasmou* in the LXX (Lev 25:9). The centrality of Leviticus 16 for Israel has been the object of extensive scholarly interest, and several theories for the DA's origin have been proposed. As W. Janowski observed, Leviticus 16 presents "compositional and conceptual" elements

47. Sklar, "Sin and Impurity," 29–31. In cases involving murder, whether intentional or unintentional, a more complex process is at play, as revealed in Numbers 35:30–34: "If anyone kills another, the murderer shall be put to death … Moreover, you shall accept no ransom for the life of a murderer … You shall not pollute the land in which you live; for blood pollutes the land …" (see also Prov 6:35). The implication is that when blood is spilled in murder, a blood *kōper*-payment is required: the blood (life) of the murderer achieves *kōper*-payment for life lost. However, because violence and bloodshed have defiled the land, the blood of the murderer now acts as a detergent, effecting *kōper*-purgation on the land.

48. Sklar, "Sin and Impurity," 21.

which stand at the center of the book of Leviticus.[49] Milgrom contends that the institution of the DA, along with the entire book of Leviticus, is "pre-exilic," even if, as Martin Noth observed, Leviticus 16 reveals "an elaborate process of growth."[50] As such, Leviticus 16 presents "the climax and crown of Israel's theology of sanctification," concludes Mays.[51] It was Radner, perhaps, who best captured the day's ethos:

> Here is where the summary character of the Day of Atonement finds its illumination: the approach of a family's mourning and diminution, the tabernacle's form, the articulating veil, the separated day each year, the priestly exclusions, the cosmic clothing, the victim beasts, the two goats, the divergent landscapes, the turmoil of angels, the world's unrest—all is laid out as a display by which the great chasm that is creation's grace is overcome somehow by God himself.[52]

Leviticus 16 is part of the unified *ḥaṭṭāʾṯ* system of rituals involving the manipulation of sacrificial blood in the Hebrew cultus: (1) The DA is introduced by pointing back to Leviticus 10; (2) God appears on the cloud over the ark; (3) Leviticus 16:16 assumes activities that occur elsewhere in the chapter (vv. 14–15), and are explained elsewhere in the Pentateuch (e.g., Exod 30:10); (4) Leviticus 16:16 assumes knowledge of evils mentioned in other chapters (4–5, 11–15); (5) Leviticus 16:24 assumes regulations present in Leviticus 1; (6) Leviticus 16:27 depends on 4:12 for the location of the burning of the *ḥaṭṭāʾṯ*. There is also allusive activity of the DA in Exodus 30:10; Lev 20:3, 23:27–30, 25:9 (the beginning of the year of jubilee coincides with the DA); Num 19:3, 20, 29:7–11.[53] In addition, the DA encompassed aspects of corporate sin, penal substitution, and remembrance as ancient as Israel itself; it presented existential issues for the nation, the high priest, his household, the priests, and the sanctuary as God's dwelling place.[54]

Other ancient aspects of the DA are: (1) the overtones of antiquity that suffused the rite; (2) Ugaritic and Hittite counterparts of the "goat for Azazel"

49. See Janowski, "Das Geschenk," 6; Wellhausen, *Die Composition*, 136–39, 147–49.

50. Noth, *Leviticus*, 117.

51. Mays, *The Book of Leviticus*, 5; see Hieke, *Levitikus 16–27*, 557–611.

52. Radner, *Leviticus*, 168.

53. See *Cult and Character*, 29–30.

54. Rendtorff, "Leviticus 16," 255; Rendtorff, *Theologie*, 118. See also Hartley, *Leviticus*, 218; Feinberg, "The Scapegoat," 320–333; Carmichael, "The Origin," 180.

rite; (3) the loss of the meaning of the term "Azazel," betraying its antiquity; and (4) the central role of the *kāppōrēṯ*, which disappeared after the exile.[55]

### *The Day of Atonement in the Israelite Calendar*

The DA took place once a year, "in the seventh month [Tishri], on the tenth day of the month" and marked the commencement of the new year, as well as the year of jubilee (Lev 16:29; 25:8–11).[56] The prescriptions for the people to "deny themselves" lasted twenty-four hours, although the rituals did not take twenty-four hours to perform (Lev 16:31; 23:32).

Rabbinic tradition suggests that the day Moses came down from Sinai with the second set of stones—after the episode of the golden calf—was the tenth day of Tishri, the same day Yom Kippur was to be celebrated. Because of Israel's sin of idolatry, Jewish communal practice of the DA entailed confession of personal sin to God and confession of faults to one another. The thirteen attributes of God found in Exodus 34:6–7 became a central liturgical piece of the DA in the form of *Selichot*, "prayers for forgiveness."[57]

## The Rituals of Yom Kippur

As Gane artfully put it, the DA "portrays the character of Yahweh, not by theological assertions, narrative, or even poetry, but by instructions for cultic deeds to be performed in his presence."[58] Such cultic deeds constitute the *ḥaṭṭāʾṯ* system of sacrifices of Leviticus 16, which are set up primarily by Leviticus 4, and secondarily, by the tabernacle's profanation by Nadab and Abihu (Lev 10).[59]

Although the *ḥaṭṭāʾṯ* purgations in Leviticus 4 functioned as a "prerequisite" for forgiveness as laid out in Leviticus 4:21: "The priest shall make atonement for them, and they shall be forgiven," the notion of forgiveness was not original to Leviticus 16 but is a later addition as found in the Temple

55. Radner, *Leviticus*, 168.

56. See Bergsma, *The Jubilee*, 190; Safren, "Jubilee," 107–113.

57. See Schoenberg, "A Good Argument," 190–192; Sanders, *Judaism*, 80, 117, 142–43.

58. Gane, *Cult and Character*, xix.

59. See Bibb, *Ritual Words*, 133. See also Hartley *Leviticus*, 233; Rooke, "The Day of Atonement," 345; Laughlin, "The 'Strange Fire,'" 559–65; Gradwohl, "Das 'fremde Feuer,'" 288–96; Kiuchi, *The Purification Offering*, 77–85.

Scroll.[60] It is also clear to the author of the Temple Scroll that the sacrifices were secondary to the people's attitude on the day.[61] As described in the Pentateuch, the DA entailed rituals of public atonement for the totality of individual transgressions accumulated on the sanctuary throughout the year, resulting in corporate impurity and covenantal jeopardy.[62]

The DA's rituals are established in Leviticus 16 with a reprise in 23:26–32 and Numbers 29:7–11. The sheer number of references to blood in Leviticus 16 highlights its importance on the DA: blood was daubed on the utensils and sprinkled in the sanctuary a total of forty-nine times, indicating the thoroughness of its purgative effects. The number "seven," according to Kapelrud, "was deliberately chosen" because it is "loaded with strength and danger ... intensity, quality, not directly quantity ... fulfillment, completion, finishing."[63] The applications of blood for purification on the DA are an expansion and culmination of the *ḥaṭṭāʾṯ* regulations, i.e., "purification offerings," given in Leviticus 4 and stated in Leviticus 16:16: "Thus he shall *kipper* the sanctuary, because of the impurities of the people of Israel, and because of their transgressions, all their sins; and so he shall do for the tent of meeting, which remains with them in the midst of their impurities."[64] The implications are clear: no one can approach God without atonement. The tabernacle needed to be purged of the human element periodically so that the divine could deign to remain in their midst (see Exod 25:8).[65]

The term *kipper* occurs sixteen times in Leviticus 16: *kipper*-rites are performed on the sanctuary altars, the veil of the Most Holy Place, and the "mercy seat," purging "impurities" and "all their sins" from the sanctuary (Lev 16:30–33). Two kinds of *kipper*-rites are prescribed for the DA: (1) *ḥaṭṭāʾṯ* sacrifices, involving the application of blood in the tabernacle for atonement for the high priest and the people (Lev 16:3–19); and (2) the dispatch of the "goat for Azazel" to the desert bearing the sins which had been transferred

60. See *Cult and Character*, 49–52. The commentary of Leviticus 16, 23 and Numbers 29:7–11 in the Temple Scroll (11QT)—a work on biblical interpretation for Second Temple Jews with slight variations from the biblical text—carries the notion of forgiveness: "... and he shall atone with it for all the people of the assembly and they shall be forgiven [ונסלח]" (11QT[a] 25:10). See the analysis of the section of the Temple Scroll, which deals with the DA in Volgger, "The Day of Atonement," 251–260. See also Ginsburskaya, "Leviticus," 265–277; Wise, *A Critical Study*, 219.

61. Körting, "Theology of Atonement," 232–247.

62. The notion of a sacrifice that purifies, cleanses, and sanctifies is present in Exodus 29:36, Lev 8:15, Ezek 43:20, 22, 23; 45:18.

63. Kapelrud, "The Number Seven," 499; see Warning, *Literary Artistry*, 27–29.

64. Hartley, *Leviticus*, 224, 228.

65. See Stevenson, *Power and Place*, 220.

to it by the high priest (Lev 16:20–22). The main distinction between these two types of *kipper*-purgation lies in the fact that the "goat for Azazel" was not sacrificed, and its blood was not used to purge the sanctuary; purgation was achieved by its dismissal.

The *kipper*-purgation rites performed in the inner rooms, utensils, and the tabernacle's court on the DA were performed in three phases, which more or less mirror each other and occurred in pairs.[66] All three sections were purified twice: once with the blood of the bull for the high priest and his household, followed by the same sequence with the blood of the "goat for the Lord" offered on behalf of the people (Lev 16:11–19). Purification was achieved by going from the holiest to the "less" holy sections: starting with the Most Holy Place, the high priest moves outwards, purifying first the "atonement plate" (*kāppōreṯ*) in the Most Holy Place, followed by the altar of incense in the Holy Place, and then the outer altar. Lastly, "all of the iniquities of the people of Israel, and all their transgressions, all their sin" (Lev 16:21) were transferred to the head of the "goat for Azazel" by the high priest through confession, and the goat was sent away from the community to a "barren region" (Lev 16:22).[67]

Because the cloud of incense prevented the high priest from seeing inside the Most Holy Place, furniture was sprinkled therein: once on the east side of the "atonement plate," and seven times in front of it (Lev 16:14b–16; 4:6, 7).[68] The Holy Place's purgation was done "likewise" by daubing blood on the four horns of the altar of incense and sprinkling it on the altar of incense seven times, as well as seven times in front of the veil (Lev 16:18–19; Exod 30:10). In the court, the high priest performed a similar purgation on the outer altar by daubing blood on its four horns and sprinkling on it seven times. The common element in all three purgations is the sprinkling of blood seven times. Through these actions, the high priest removed all the impurities from the sanctuary, and by proxy, from Israel when he transferred them to the "goat for Azazel."[69] Some elements of the DA's rituals are shared with those prescribed in Leviticus 4 for purification from the unintentional sins of the high priest, the congregation, the ruler, and regular members of the community, except that these regular purgations never involved the Most Holy Place.

66. *AYBD* 2:72.
67. Milgrom, *Leviticus 1–16*, 1043.
68. See Gane, *Cult and Character*, 71.
69. For a divergent view, see Kalimi, "The Day of Atonement," 72.

Leviticus 16 describes a sequence of rituals to be performed only by the high priest on the DA; no one else should be inside the tabernacle during the rituals. The order of the rituals was of utmost importance, as the Rabbis explained: "if he did one part of the rite before its fellow, he has done nothing whatsoever" because "each of them constitutes an act of atonement unto itself" (m. Yoma 5:7). At the same time, it seems clear that Leviticus 16 does not contain all that was performed on the DA, especially considering Second Temple practice. Lastly, Leviticus 16 stands as preparation for the "holiness code" of chapters 17–26, extending holiness from the sanctuary building to holiness, which is "coextensive with the land."[70]

This initial overview reveals the unity of chapter 16 with the rest of Leviticus because of the system of *ḥaṭṭāʾṯ* offerings. Without recurring purgations culminating in the DA, God could abruptly withdraw from their midst, abandon the sanctuary, and the people would be doomed.

### *Blowing the Šôp̄ar*

The DA's activities start with the loud sound of a שׁוֹפָר (*šôp̄ar*, Lev 25:9), an instrument made of a ram's horn. The sound of the *šôp̄ar* echoed the early history of Israel and was central to Jewish history: on the third day after they had gathered around Mount Sinai, they experienced "the voice of the *šôp̄ar* sounding very loud" (Exod 19:16, 19; 20:18). The people trembled, and as the days progressed, the sound of the *šôp̄ar* "grew louder."

The *šôp̄ar* was also used in times of war, and, possibly because of its connection with the DA, it was used in calls to reconsecration and worship.[71] The sound of the *šôp̄ar* had a profound spiritual meaning to Israel, and it should be played during such an important day as the DA, both as a reminder of Israel's recent delivery from Egypt, as well as a call to penitence and holiness.[72]

### *Israel's Role*

The corporate character of the DA rises to sharp relief as the entire nation was called to take part in the rituals. The activities required of the people ensured that the DA achieved its purification goals: (1) they should bring two male goats for the "purification offering" and one ram for the "burnt of-

70. Hartley, *Leviticus*, 217.

71. See Josh 6:4; Judg 3:7; 7:20; 2 Chr 15:14; Ps 47:6; 98:6; 150:3; Zech 9:14; Joel 2:1, 15.

72. Prashker, *The Day of Atonement*, 3, writes that, to the Jews, the *šôp̄ar* testified to "the setting free of slaves, the restoration of land to its ancestral owners."

fering"; (2) practice "self-denial"; and (3) do no work, a stipulation that applied even to foreigners.

The prescription for self-denial on the DA is given twice in Lev 16:29, 31 and repeated in 23:27, running "from evening to evening" (23:32). Self-affliction stands in contrast with the perpetual commandment to serve the Lord "joyfully and with gladness" (Deut 28:46–47). Along with the prohibition against working, self-denial highlights the intersection between intangible, symbolic meaning and tangible, corporate action inherent to the DA.[73] The day was so fraught with tension and peril that at the successful completion of the rituals, maidens danced and young men engaged in courtship.[74] Such celebrations would be out of sync with the spirit of "afflicting oneself" earlier in the day, but later in the day, they symbolized covenant renewal.

With time, the notion of denial or self-affliction on the DA coalesced into the practice of fasting, and Yom Kippur became known as "the Fast" (e.g., Acts 27:9).[75] Implicit in this practice is the notion that, in addition to abstaining from work and food, the people had to engage in soul-searching and solemn reflection on what this day meant for them individually and as a nation (see Isa 1:13; Amos 5:21).[76] Such a rite of penitence is exemplified in Ps 35:13, which, although not dealing with the DA per se, offers a glimpse of what afflicting oneself might entail: "I wore sackcloth; I afflicted myself with fasting. I prayed with head bowed on my bosom." As Wenham writes: "The law insists that if they are to be effective, the whole nation, Israelites and foreigners alike, must demonstrate true penitence" (e.g., Luke 1:8–13).[77]

The prohibition "and you shall do no work" is given once in Lev 16:29 and implied in the formula "it is a sabbath of complete rest" (*šabbat šabbatōn*, v. 31; see Lev 23:28–32). The prescriptions for the DA in Leviticus 23 focus on three elements: (1) personal affliction (penitence); (2) prohibitions against working; and (3) complete rest. While the prohibition against working was also central to other feasts, on the DA, the rest was the same as that of the weekly Sabbath, as both days are called a "day of complete rest" (Lev 23:3, 32; 25:4; Exod 31:15; 35:2). However, while the commandment to rest on the Sabbath is based on creation (Gen 2:1–13; Exod 20:11), the

73. See Wenham, *Leviticus*, 236; Kiuchi, *Leviticus*, 32; m. Yoma 8:1: "On the Day of Atonement it is forbidden to eat, drink, bathe, put on any sort of oil, put on a sandal, or engage in sexual relations. But a king and a bride may wash their faces."

74. See y. Taanit 4:8; 26b; 31a. Cf. Safren, "Jubilee," 112–113.

75. See Schiffman, "The Case," 181–188.

76. See Dan 10:12, Ezra 8:21; Ps 69:10; Milgrom, *Leviticus 1–16*, 51.

77. Wenham, *Leviticus*, 236.

reason for the prohibition against working on the DA was that "it is a day of atonement, to make atonement on your behalf before the Lord your God" (Lev 23:28).[78] By prescribing a sabbatical rest, writes Calaway, "the Day of Atonement becomes the ritual event that coordinates the Sabbath and the sanctuary, holy time and holy space, at their greatest intensity."[79] This relationship is all the more vivid in the great year of jubilee, "the fiftieth year," since it also commenced on the DA (Lev 25:9).

Similar to the commandment to refrain from work on the weekly Sabbath, the prohibition against working takes on life-and-death consequences on the DA: "And anyone who does any work during that entire day, such a one I will destroy from the midst of the people" (Lev 23:30). The severity of the penalty was concomitant with the DA's import, as individual Israelites were invited to rest solely on God's gracious gift of atonement.[80]

The repetition of the DA's stipulations in Leviticus 23:26–32 and Numbers 29:7–11 emphasizes different elements of the day's activities: while Leviticus 23 does not mention the *ḥaṭṭāʾṯ* offerings but focuses on the need to do "no work" and practice "self-denial" (v. 28–32), Numbers 29:7–11 mentions the prohibition to work only once but focuses on the animal and grain offerings.

## *The High Priest's Role*

The mediatory role of the high priest on the DA was not to be taken lightly. As a warning against carelessness by the priests, Leviticus 16 begins with a reminder of the death of Nadab and Abihu for bringing "strange fire" before God.[81] The chapter contains two explicit warnings about the risk of death when performing the rites on the DA, in addition to the veiled warnings embedded in the detailed instructions.[82]

The role of the Israelite priest was to "teach Jacob your ordinances, and Israel your law; they place incense before you, and whole burnt offerings on your altar" (Deut 33:10; 24:8). The high priest had "the cultic counterpart of

78. This rest "of atonement" is taken up by the author of Hebrews who frames a future "rest" (σαββατισμὸς, Heb 4:9) with the work of Jesus as a high priest.

79. Calaway, *The Sabbath and the Sanctuary*, 163.

80. See Weyde, *Feasts*, 99.

81. See Milgrom, *Leviticus 1–16*, 1011.

82. Milgrom, "Day of Atonement," 72, is correct to point out that the mention of Nadab and Abihu simply serve as a precaution in regards to the sanctity of the sanctuary, while Rooke suggests that the DA was instituted because of "the need to cleanse the sanctuary from the pollution caused by the corpses of Nadab and Abihu" ("The Day of Atonement," 345).

the prophet," observes Rooke.[83] Although all the other priests had been authorized to officiate daily at the outer altar, the high priest had specific roles: only he ministered at the incense altar daily and on the DA (see Exod 30:7–8). The high priest bore responsibility for the people; he carried the names of the tribes on his shoulder, executed "judgment" through the Urim and Thumim stones located inside his breastplate, and mediated the will of God.[84] The high priest was also responsible for medical diagnosis (Lev 13:1–2).

On the DA, regular priests faded into the background, and the high priest rose to prominence. Great care was taken to preserve his eligibility to perform the rites, as described in m. Yoma 1:1: "Seven days before the Day of Atonement, we sequester the high priest from his house to the chamber of the officials, and we prepare for him another priest in his place, [for] perhaps there will occur in him a disqualification." For example, if the high priest had a nocturnal emission, he had to perform ablutions and go home for the day (see Deut 23:10–11). Throughout this preparatory week, the heightened purification ritual of the red cow whose ashes were sprinkled for purification was also performed on behalf of the high priest (Num 19; see m. Parah 3:1; Heb 9:13).

The successful completion of the rituals by the high priest on the DA functioned "as a yearly ritual confirmation of his high priesthood" as he "moved from a state of impurity to purity," and from provisional to certain priesthood, concludes Rooke.[85] After dispatching the "goat for Azazel" and with his high priesthood confirmed, he donned his full regalia (Lev 16:24).

### *God's Role*

As the sole initiator of the means of atonement through sacrificial blood, God's role in the Hebrew cultus was not that of an angry deity to be appeased or propitiated but one of providing a way out of sin and impurity, akin to his role in providing the sacrifice in place of Isaac (Gen 22). As provider and recipient of the sacrifices of the DA, God initiated the instructions of the day by the Levitical formula, "and the Lord spoke" (v. 1); the sacrificial animals for the DA were presented "before the Lord" (v. 7); the male goat was "for the Lord" (v. 8).

83. Rooke, "The Day of Atonement, 56.
84. Spencer, "Aaron (Person)," 5. E.g., Exod 28:29, 30; Num 27:21; 1 Sam 10:20–24; 14:36–42, 27:6.
85. Rooke, "The Day of Atonement," 345, 357. See Babota, *The Institution*, 134–139.

God's role in the sanctuary cultus is explained in his own words in Leviticus 17:11: "For the life of the flesh is in the blood; and I have given it to you for making atonement for your lives on the altar; for, as life, it is the blood that makes atonement."[86] As pointed out by Schwartz, the unique construction "it was I who gave it" (*wa'ani nᵉtattiw*) must be understood alongside the equally emphatic *lāḵem ʿal-hammizbēaḥ lᵉḵappēr ʿal-napšōṯêḵem*, which renders the entire construction as: "It is not you who are placing the blood on the altar for me, for my benefit, but rather the opposite: it is I who have placed it there for you—for your benefit."[87] The one receiving atonement was not God, explains von Rad, but Israel: "Jahweh is rather the one who acts, in averting the calamitous curse which burdens the community."[88] Moreover, as Sklar perceptively observed: "Sacrifice was indeed something the Israelites gave to the Lord but it was first and foremost something he granted to them, in his grace as a means of atoning for sin and achieving the forgiveness they so desperately desired."[89]

Ultimately, the DA showed the lengths God was willing to go to overcome the separation brought on by sin. It was God's gracious acceptance of the atoning rituals that effected purification, thus ratifying his covenant with Israel and confirming his permanence in the sanctuary. The DA was the culmination of God's gift of salvation for Israel.

### *Ritual Ablutions*

High-priestly ablutions were a critical part of the DA. The specific instructions on what the high priest should wear accompanied the order to "bathe his body in water, and then put them on." Two ablutions were prescribed for the high priest: (1) before the rituals commenced; and (2) after the "goat for Azazel" ritual, but before the burning of the sacrifices at the outer altar (Lev 16:4, 24). Milgrom observes that the purpose of the ablution after the entrance into the adytum was to remove "the super-holiness that he contracted" by officiating inside the Most Holy Place, which should not be allowed to "leak" into the Holy Place or the outer altar, much less into the camp.[90] Differing levels of holiness were also compartmentalized within the

86. See Gilders, "Blood as Purificant," 83.

87. See Schwartz, "Prohibitions," 51.

88. von Rad, *Old Testament Theology*, 270.

89. Sklar, *Leviticus*, 54.

90. Milgrom, *Leviticus 1–16*, 1049; Milgrom, "Day of Atonement," 73; Hartley, *Leviticus*, 242; Rooke, "The Day of Atonement," 355.

sanctuary to protect the people. As seen in the story of Nadab and Abihu, holiness was fatal to the unclean.[91]

Two additional ritual ablutions were required on the DA. The regular priest who led the "goat for Azazel" to the desert with its toxic load of sin was required to undergo purification with water lest he re-contaminate the community. Similarly, the regular priest who burned the carcasses of the animals in a "clean place outside the camp" had to bathe after the rite before reentering the camp (see Lev 4:11–12; Num 19:8).[92] While the high-priestly washings prevented the leakage of holiness into the unholy, the ablutions of regular priests prevented contamination of holiness with the impurity of dead sacrificial animals and for leaving the camp.

The importance of safeguarding covenantal purity on the part of the entire congregation was set out in several of the yearly Levitical stipulations but assumed heightened significance on the DA, highlighting the sense of collective responsibility that was attached to the day.

## *The High Priest's Clothing*

Before the high priest started the day's activities, he bathed and put on his ritual garment. His "holy vestments" (*bigḏê-qōḏeš*, Lev 16:4) are all made of linen (*baḏ*): "the holy linen tunic" (*kᵉṯōneṯ-baḏ qōḏeš*) the "linen undergarments" (*miḵnsê-ḇaḏ*), "the linen sash" (*ʾaḇnēṭ baḏ*), and "the linen turban" (*miṣnep̱eṯ baḏ*).[93] Once the high priest entered the sanctuary, he became inured to the impurities accumulated there throughout the year.

Several hypotheses have been advanced to explain the high priest's clothing for the DA. According to Swartz, the Second Temple period saw the development of a mystic understanding of the origins of the high-priestly clothing as the same clothing as God gave Adam.[94] Both Philo and Josephus believed the high-priestly dress represented the cosmos. Jewish commentator Rashi considered these garments the same as those of the regular priests, but there were important differences. For one, a regular priest's turban was always called *migbāʿōṯ* while the high priest's turban was always called the *miṣnep̱eṯ* (Exod 29:9; 39:28; Lev 16:4; Exod 39:28). The evidence, therefore,

91. Milgrom, "Day of Atonement," 162–163.

92. Pseudo-Jonathan explains that the animals "will be carried out *with poles by young men who will be priests, and they will carry them* outside the camp" (Lev 16:27).

93. בַּד is also used in descriptions of heavenly beings in Ezek 9:2–3, 11; 10:2; Dan 10:6; 12:3; Mal 2:7.

94. See *Bereshit Rabbah* 20:12; Swartz, "The Semiotics," 207–232.

points to a simpler high-priestly dress, not necessarily that of an ordinary priest. The goal of this change of attire may have been to strip the high priest of all honor in the presence of God (y. Yoma 7:3).[95] Deprived of his full regalia and his communication with God severed, he officiated solely on the atoning blood's efficacy, which in turn depended wholly on God's grace.

After offering the "goat for Azazel," the high priest changed back into his regular clothes and offered a burnt offering, which brought the day to a close (Lev 16:23–24). Wright suggests that the change of clothes had practical purposes, i.e., "to remove the soiled clothes and put on the clean, regular high-priestly clothing."[96] It is more likely, however, that the notion of a "transfer of holiness" is in view here, as pointed out by Milgrom and Rooke: "changing clothes signifies the transition between the sphere of the exceedingly holy and the sphere of the moderately holy."[97]

## *The Sacrificial Animals*

Leviticus 16 prescribes a "young bull for a purgation offering" (*lᵉḥaṭṭāʾṯ*), two rams "for the burnt offering" (*lᵉ ʿôlā*), one for the high priest and one for the people (vv. 3, 5), and "two male goats for a purgation offering" (v. 5).[98] The young bull and the ram were brought by the high priest and offered on behalf of himself and his household (vv. 3, 6, 24); the two goats brought by the people were offered by the high priest on their behalf (vv. 3, 5, 15, 24). The ram for the high priest and the ram for the people were offered as burnt offerings after the "goat for Azazel" rite was completed, and the high priest had donned his customary attire (v. 24).

Although not specified in Leviticus 16, it must be assumed that the animals selected for the sacrifices on the DA were "without blemish," following the standard set by the Passover lamb (Exod 12:5; Lev 4:3, 22, 28; Num 29:8).

## *Casting Lots for the Two Goats*

The two goats brought by the congregation were set "before the Lord" (Lev 16:5). Aaron then cast lots to decide which was "for the Lord" or "for

95. See Wenham, *Leviticus*, 230; Hartley, *Leviticus*, 236.

96. See Milgrom, *Leviticus 1–16*, 1017.

97. Rooke, "The Day of Atonement," 354.

98. According to the Temple Scroll (11QT 25:10–27:10), there were three rams: one for the burnt-offering and two for the sin-offering. See Maier, *The Temple Scroll*, 84. See the helpful discussion about both he-goats being called "לְחַטָּאת" in Gane, *Cult and Character*, 246–261.

Azazel," so that the decision ultimately belonged to God (Lev 16:7–10). As Milgrom points out, "if the high priest chose the animals, it would appear that he and the people he represented were offering an animal to Azazel." This selection process most likely took place before the sequence of the rituals started in v. 11 since it appears to repeat the prescriptions made in v. 6.[99] Although Leviticus is silent on the matter, the m. Yoma 4:2 indicates that the two goats had to be identical and lay in wait at the tent entrance. Distinct strips of cloth were affixed to each goat: one around the throat of the goat to be slaughtered, and a crimson strip of wool tied to the head of the "goat for Azazel" (see m. Yoma 4:1–2; Isa 1:18).[100]

Scholars have seen in the designation "one lot for the LORD and the other lot for Azazel" (Lev 16:8) the origins of an evil entity that stood in opposition to "the Lord." Milgrom reads the *lamed* in *layhwh* and *la ʿazā ʾzēl* as a *lamed auctoris,* that is, "belonging to," meaning that the live goat belonged to "Azazel," "a demon who has been eviscerated of his demonic powers by the Priestly legislators."[101] This conclusion has the support of non-canonical Jewish literature of the late first and early second century CE, where Azazel is presented as a fallen angel (see 3 Enoch 4:6; *Pirqe R. El.* 16; d. Ibn Ezra, Ramban). See the Excursus at the end of this chapter for an overview of the origins of the "goat for Azazel" rite as well as Azazel's identity.

### *The First Purification of the Most Holy Place: The Sacrifice for the High Priest and His Household*

The high priest had to offer a bull "for himself" in order to effect atonement for "himself and for his house" (Lev 16:6, 11) in order that he may intercede for the entire people. The rationale behind this sacrifice is that the high priest was not "sinless"; he bore responsibility for the entire congregation; his sins could "bring guilt on the people" (Lev 4:3).

The blood of the goat "for the Lord" was brought "inside the veil," i.e., inside the Most Holy Place, and sprinkled on the "atonement slate." It was subsequently brought out into the Holy Place and sprinkled in front of the veil of the Most Holy Place seven times (v. 14). This purification offering

99. See Milgrom, *Leviticus: A Book of Ritual,* 168; Gane, *Cult and Character,* 249. The casting of the lots for the goats in Lev 16:7–10 seems to explain what occurred sometime within the ritual and does not necessarily represent a precise sequence. The casting of the lots at this point of the ritual seems unnatural and appears to be an interpolation, as it must have occurred prior to the slaughtering of the bull. See Gane *Cult and Character,* 23; Noth, *Leviticus,* 114–115; m. Yoma 3:9.

100. See Stemberger, "Yom Kippur," 126.

101. Milgrom, *Leviticus 1–16,* 1021. See also Cazelles, "La question," 248.

by the high priest was followed by the sacrifice of the goat, thus purging the sanctuary (vv. 15–20; see Lev 4:3–12). The sacrifices for the high priest and his family and the sacrifice for the people followed the same pattern; the blood of the bull for the high priest and his family and the blood of the "goat for the Lord" offered on behalf of the people was sprinkled on the "atonement slate," and before the veil of the Most Holy Place.[102]

Inside the Most Holy Place was the כַּפֹּרֶת (*kāppōreṯ*), usually translated as "mercy seat" (see 1 Chr 28:11, "house of the *kāppōreṯ*").[103] Milgrom prefers leaving *kāppōreṯ* "untranslatable," while Hartley translates it as "Atonement slate" because it "both reveals and conceals his presence," and had a distinct cultic function as a boundary between God and the tablets of the covenant.[104] This reading is attractive, although not a decisive one since the function of the *kāppōreṯ* is not clarified in the Pentateuch. Kiuchi argues that "[i]n the light of LXX (*hilastērion*), it probably means 'propitiatory cover.'"[105] In support of this is the LXX text of Exodus 25:17, where at its first appearance *kāppōreṯ* is rendered as *hilastērion epithema,* in which *epithema* means "lid," although this is the only time where the gloss *epithema* is used (see 4QtgLev, "cover"). M. Görg suggests that *kāppōreṯ* is a loanword from the Egyptian *kappuri(e) t,* "footstool."[106] This view is also attractive since the ark of the covenant is frequently referred to as God's footstool (Ps 132:7; 1 Chr 28:2).[107] All preceding views are in agreement with the view that the *kāppōreṯ* which held the "golden cherubim" was the abode of the "Lord of hosts, who is enthroned on the cherubim" (1 Sam 4:4; see also Ps 99:1). As such, the *kāppōreṯ* constituted the DA's focal point and was where the day's purifications commenced.

## *The Offer of Incense*

Between the bull's slaughtering and the presentation of its blood on behalf of the high priest and his household inside the Most Holy Place, Leviticus 16 inserts the incense ritual. Although not explicitly stated, the incense ritual must have taken place before the high priest went into the Most Holy Place a second time with the blood of the "goat for the Lord" to make atonement for the people (Lev 16:15–19). Based on this, it appears that Aaron

102. *TDOT* 12:95–97.
103. *TWOT*, s. v. "כַּפֹּרֶת"; see Jastrow, כַּפֹּרֶת, *A Dictionary*, 658.
104. Milgrom, *Leviticus: A Book of Ritual*, 167; Hartley, *Leviticus*, 234.
105. Kiuchi, *Leviticus*, 290.
106. Görg, "Eine neue Deutung," 115–118.
107. See Milgrom, *Leviticus 1–16*, 1014; Brown, "Kipper," 191–194.

gathered the bull's blood from the altar of burnt offering, proceeded to gather coals from the altar of incense, placed the coals in the censer, put a large amount of "crushed sweet incense" on top of the coals, and entered the Most Holy Place.[108] This sequence would be difficult to perform without some assistance, which could have occurred in the outer court—since no one should be within the tent when the high priest was inside (v. 17). A large amount of incense produced a cloud of smoke around him and was meant to "cover the mercy seat that is upon the covenant" (v. 13; see Exod 30:34–38).

The offer of incense inside the tabernacle was representative of intercessory prayer, and the large amount used on the DA was emblematic of the day's import, highlighting the need for fasting, penitence, and intercession during the day's proceedings.[109] If the high priest entered the Most Holy Place without this intercessory shield of incense and became exposed to the Lord's presence residing over the *kāppōrēṯ*, he would die (v. 13; see Num 16:46–47).

### *The First Purification of the Holy Place: The Altar of Incense*

After offering the bull for himself and his family inside the Most Holy Place, Aaron must purge the Holy Place. A sequential cleansing moving from the innermost shrine to the exterior altar and the "goat for Azazel" rite is described in Lev 16:20: "When he has finished atoning for the Holy Place and the tent of meeting and the altar, he shall present the live goat." Based on Leviticus 4, Milgrom avers that "the purging of the shrine took place with the blood of the bull and goat separately, just as in the adytum."[110] There are questions as to which section of the tabernacle the phrase "tent of the meeting" refers (Lev 16:18–19). Both Wenham and Milgrom agree that "the tent of the meeting" in Leviticus 16:20 refers specifically to the Holy Place.[111] This conclusion is based on Exodus 30:10, where the offer "on its horns" once a year refers to the DA.[112]

The altar of incense inside the Holy Place was purged twice, with the blood of the bull and the blood of the goat "for the Lord" (Lev 16:18). This

108. See Noth, *Leviticus*, 122 for a discussion on the apparent discrepancy in the timeline.

109. See Luke 1:8–13 where prayers accompany an offer of incense inside the temple. Also Ps 141:2: "Let my prayer be counted as incense before thee, and the lifting up of my hands as an evening sacrifice." See Keil and Delitzsch, *Biblical Commentary*, 399; Milgrom, *Leviticus 1–16*, 238; Houtman, "On the Function," 458–65; Bechmann, "Duft," 49–98; Ritchie, "The Nose Knows," 59–73; Haran, "The Uses of Incense," 113–29; Heger, *The Development*, 458–65; Nielsen, *Incense*.

110. Milgrom, *Leviticus 1–16*, 1040.

111. Wenham, *Leviticus*, 232; Milgrom, *Leviticus 1–16*, 1034–5.

112. Milgrom, *Leviticus: A Book of Ritual*, 171.

altar of incense located inside the Holy Place must be distinguished from the "altar of burnt offering that is at the entrance of the tent of the meeting" (Exod 40:29; Lev 4:7, italics supplied), because the coupling of "altar" + "before the Lord" (*mizbēaḥ* + *lip̱nē-yhwh*) refers unequivocally to the altar of incense—unless a gloss is added to "altar" to indicate another altar.[113] How the "atonement" for the incense altar was accomplished is not explained fully in Leviticus 16:18, but it most likely followed the purification prescribed for the sins of the high priest and congregation in Leviticus 4:7, 18: "The priest shall put some of the blood on the horns of the altar of fragrant incense that is in the tent of meeting before the LORD . . ." There was a minor difference, however; in the regular *ḥaṭṭāʾṯ* rites performed on the incense altar, the blood of the bull was sprinkled in the direction of the veil seven times and daubed once on each of the four horns of the incense altar (according to the principle of *pars pro toto*), while on the DA the blood of the bull and the goat was daubed once on its four horns and sprinkled on it seven times (Lev 16:18–19). It appears then that on the DA, the double application of blood had distinct meanings, both for "purification" and "consecration" of the altar (Exod 29:36–37; tampering with its horns desecrated it, Amos 3:14).[114]

In sum, the application of blood on the altar of incense purged and reconsecrated it so that intercession could be made on it. The successful completion of this ritual depended on the people's repentance and "affliction" through confession. Displaying a defiant attitude could lead to swift judgment—as befell king Uzziah (2 Chr 26:16–21). Unrepented sin contaminated the altar of incense, and intercession made there was invalid because such ritual perpetuated impurity before the Lord. The guilty were cut off (Lev 23:29; Num 15:30–31).

### *The First Purification of the Outer Altar*

The purification of the altar of burnt offering is only implied in Leviticus 16:20: "When he has finished atoning for the holy place and the tent of meeting and the altar, he shall present the live goat." The movement from

113. See Exod 27:21; 28:35; 30:8; 34:34; 40:23, 25. See 2 Chr 1:6: "Solomon went up there to the bronze altar before the LORD [*lip̱nē-yhwh*]," which refers to the exterior altar where burnt offerings were made. Solomon's altar is "the altar of bronze" (*mizbēaḥ hannᵉḥōšeṯ*), clearly not the altar of incense, which was made out of acacia wood and on which no sacrifices were offered (Exod 30:7).

114. Milgrom believes the horns of the altar signify "the horns of a powerful animal (e.g., a bull or a ram) and are symbols of strength and force." (Milgrom, *Leviticus 1–16*, 236). E.g., 1 Sam 2:1, 10; 2 Sam 22:3; Jer 48:25; Zech 2:4; Ps 75:5–6, 11; 89:18, 25.

inner shrine → outer shrine → outer altar

is clear in the sequence; after Aaron had applied the bull's and the goat's blood on the *kāppōrēṯ* inside the Most Holy Place, "so he shall do for the tent of meeting" (v. 16), i.e., the Holy Place. After cleansing the Holy Place, he went out and purified the altar of burnt offering in the tabernacle's court (v. 18). Logically, then, the third and final element of the sequence must be the outer altar, which underwent purification by a seven-fold sprinkling (v. 19).

### *The Second Purification of the Most Holy Place: The Sacrifice for the People*

After the high priest offered the bull for himself and applied its blood inside the Most Holy Place, the Holy Place, and the outer altar, he slaughtered the "goat for the Lord" and brought its blood "inside the veil," i.e., inside the Most Holy Place. Once inside, he sprinkled the blood "as he did with the blood of the bull," i.e., seven times on top of the *kāppōrēṯ*, and in front of the veil. This offering purged the Most Holy Place (vv. 15–16), now on behalf of the people.

### *The Second Purification of the Holy Place*

Again, the second purification of the Holy Place with the goat's blood is only implied in the text and likely follows the seven-fold pattern detailed in the purification of the altar of incense (Lev 4:6, 7, 18). Like before, purification was achieved by daubing the blood of the "goat for the Lord" on the incense altar's four horns and sprinkling it before the veil seven times (Lev 16:15, 20).

### *The Second Purification of the Outer Altar*

The second purification of the outer altar of burnt offering is implied in v. 20, which describes a double process of purification with the bull's blood for the high priest and with the blood of the "goat for the Lord" sacrificed on behalf of all people.

### *The Rite of the "Goat for Azazel"*

No doubt, the most distinctive ritual of the DA was the dismissal of the "goat for Azazel" into the desert. After all the blood purifications of the Most

Holy Place, the Holy Place, and the outer altar were completed, the "goat for Azazel," or the "live goat," was presented "before the Lord."[115]

The ritual of the "goat for Azazel" encompassed several steps: (1) the high priest laid both hands on the head of the goat (v. 21);[116] (2) he confessed "over it all the iniquities of the people of Israel, all their transgressions, all their sins" (v. 21); (3) the goat was led away to a "barren region" (v. 22) by "the hand of a designated man" and sent "for Azazel" (v. 21); (4) once the goat was sufficiently removed from the community, it was set free.[117] Although the "goat for Azazel" was also a *ḥaṭṭāʾṯ* (v. 5), the purgative effect of the ritual differs from the goat of the Lord; its blood was not spilled, and its atoning function was not effected by blood but by transfer of sin, impurity, and their guilt from the sanctuary to the goat to be taken back to Azazel (v. 21–22). This ritual enacted visibly what the application of sacrificial blood achieved invisibly: the removal of sins from the camp.[118] Several aspects of this rite are explored below.

### *Confession of Sin over the "Goat for Azazel"*

After the "goat for Azazel" was presented "before the Lord," the high priest transferred Israel's sins and impurities on the goat's head by confession.[119] This act was part of a "cultic confession motif" involving "confessing one's sin, making some form of reparation, and offering an atoning sacrifice to expunge the sin."[120] As suggested by Young, for the Rabbis, confession

115. Aartun, "Studien," 84–86, argues that the "goat for the Lord" and the "goat for Azazel" function as one sacrifice. See Gane, *Cult and Character*, 255. For a summary of the views on the meaning of "for Azazel," see Hartley, *Leviticus*, 236–238; Rooker, *Leviticus*, 216–217; Tawil, "Azazel," 43–59; Rudman, "A Note," 396–401; Fauth, "Auf den Spuren," 514–534; Cheyne, "The Date and Origin," 153–156; Driver, "Three Technical Terms," 97–105; Loretz, *Leberschau*, 50–57; Pinker, "A Goat to go to Azazel," 1–25; Deiana, "Azazel in Lv. 16," 16–33; Sacchi, *Jewish Apocalyptic*, 211–231; Görg, "Beobachtungen," 10–16; Guinot, "L'Exégèse," 16–33; Helm, "Azazel," 217–26; Hodge, "A Historical"; Mojola, "The Chagga," 57–83.

116. For a discussion on the placing of both hands on the goat's head, see Péter, "L'Imposition," 48–55; see also Gane, *Cult and Character*, 244–246.

117. Westbrook, "Who Led," 417–422, argues that the person designated to lead Azazel was a criminal, similarly to ancient Hittite rituals. However, this view is countered by the fact that the person leading the goat to Azazel had to bathe to return to the camp (Lev 16:26). Rabbinic tradition reveals that another priest was designated as the "designated man" (Lev 16:21).

118. The dismissal of the "goat for Azazel" with its noxious load is akin to emptying the kitchen trash bin onto a garbage bin outside. When, the garbage bin is full, it is taken to the curb and to be hauled away. The DA was "trash day," and the "goat for Azazel" was the garbage truck, hauling away Israel's sins, impurities, and their guilt.

119. See Falk, "Scriptural Inspiration," 127–157; Num 27:18–23; Deut 34:9.

120. See Bautch, "The Formulary," 34–45; Pietersma, "Greek Jeremiah," 403–413.

of sin is "the feature of the DA which epitomized all they believed concerning expiation; that is, the forgiveness of all Israel's sins through repentant confession."[121] Although Aaron's confession was addressed to God, it also functions as an "accusation against Azazel," posits Gane, because he had instigated Israel's sin.[122] Having just left the Most Holy Place, he was infused with "the power required for the battle against Azazel," Levine suggests.[123]

An analysis of the preceding blood purification rituals indicates that the "goat for Azazel" ritual presents a discontinuity from the purifications of the inner shrines and the outer altar. Considering Milgrom's interpretation of sacrificial blood as a "detergent" that removed sins and impurities from the sanctuary, it would seem more logical if blood containing the sins removed from the sancta were to be applied onto the "goat for Azazel."[124] However, not only did this ritual *not* involve blood, its *ḥaṭṭā'ṯ* effects were achieved by confession on the goat's head and by enacting actual separation from sin by its dismissal from the camp.[125] One explanation is that "goat for Azazel" was not killed because the people's sins defiled it, "thus disqualifying it as a sacrifice."[126] Schwartz suggests that *ḥaṭṭā'ṯ* blood eradicated *impurities*, while *sins* were transferred onto the high priest, which he then transferred to the goat by confession, but this distinction seems strained.[127] It is more likely that Gane is on target when he contends that, although both goats are *ḥaṭṭā'ṯ*, the live goat's ritual necessitated remediation of sin by a different ritual action because of the presence of "guilt" or "culpability" (*ʿāôn*, Lev 16:21).[128] In other words, although the effects of sin and impurity on the tabernacle had been annulled through blood on the DA, the culpability for such rebellion still had not been addressed, which is then resolved by confession. This transfer of Israel's sin, impurities, and guilt onto the live goat was achieved by the high priest's mediatorial authority given to him by the Lord.

A similar transfer of culpability is seen in the condemnation of the blasphemer in Leviticus 24:14, as well as in the personal responsibility of sinners for their faults (Ezek 9:10; 11:21; 16:43; 22:31). Hartley conflates the "living bird" ritual (Lev 14:7) and that of the "live goat" as a way to provide "visual

121. Young, "The Impact," 371; see Wright, "The Gesture," 436.
122. Gane, *Cult and Character*, 264.
123. Levine, *In the Presence*, 82.
124. See Milgrom, "The Preposition," 160–161; Milgrom, "The Day of Atonement," 72.
125. Eberhart, *The Sacrifice*, 90.
126. Hartley, *Leviticus*, 238.
127. Schwartz, "The Bearing of Sin," 17–18.
128. Gane, *Cult and Character*, 258, 262–3.

representation to the assembly of the reality that on this day their sins had been completely wiped out and their power was terminated forever."[129]

Milgrom—based on his categorization of sins to be expiated on the DA—posits that confessing one's sins was a method to "convert deliberate sins into inadvertencies, thereby qualifying them for sacrificial expiation"; hence the confession "must be matched by the remorse of the people"; the people's purification was achieved by "repentance," and the *ḥaṭṭāʾṯ* blood purged the sanctuary.[130] It must be observed, however, that this conversion of "deliberate sins into inadvertencies" did not cover brazen, defiant sins and their actors. While their transgressions were purged from the sanctuary by sacrificial blood on the DA—since the covenant would not be jeopardized by their individual choices—defiant sinners were cut off, and "their guilt remains on them" (Num 15:30–31; 18:22).

### *The Meaning of laʿazāʾzēl*

The expression לַעֲזָאזֵל (*laʿazāʾzēl*) remains one of the most elusive appellations in the OT.[131] It appears four times in the OT, in Leviticus 16 (vv. 8, 10 [2x] and 26). There is marked disagreement on its etymology and meaning, and at least five interpretations have been proposed:[132] (1) the place to which it was dispatched; (2) removal; (3) on behalf of Azazel; (4) "the wrath of God"; and (5) a supernatural, demonic entity.[133] This study takes the last view as the most probable: *ʿazāʾzēl* as the symbol of a demonic figure that received the culpability of Israel's sin on the DA. Although the name *ʿazāʾzēl* remains cryptic in Leviticus—even in light of the worship of "goat-demons" (Lev 17:7)—there was a marked shift in Azazel's identity from a mysterious sin-bearer in the Pentateuch, to a demonic sin-originator in late Jewish thought, as indicated in the pseudepigraphal corpus. As observed by Gruenwald, "the central ritual in the Jewish calendar—the Day of Atonement—engages in a ritual that takes for granted the realness of the demonic."[134]

This view finds support in Rabbinic literature; e.g., b. Yoma 67b: "Only one of the Rabbis had a different view; he said that Azazel was a fallen angel and not the name of a place: The School of Ishmael taught: 'Azazel [it was so

129. Hartley, *Leviticus*, 238.
130. Milgrom, *Cult*, 119; Milgrom, *EncJud*, s.v. "Day of Atonement."
131. See Blair, *De-Demonising*; Grabbe, "The Scapegoat," 152–167.
132. Landersdorfer, *Studien*, 216–217.
133. See Hanson, "Rebellion," 195–233; Stuckenbruck, *The Myth*.
134. Gruenwald, *Rituals*, 220. See also Maccoby, *Ritual*, 90–91.

called] because it obtains atonement for the affair of Uza and Azaʾel,'" the latter being one of the spellings in 1 Enoch. Building on this tradition, medieval Rabbi Ramban explained: "the Holy One, blessed be He, commands us that on the Day of Atonement we should let loose a goat in the wilderness, to that 'prince' which rules over wastelands … [for] destruction and waste emanate from his power … Also in his portion are the devils called 'destroyers' in the language of our Rabbis, and in the language of our Scripture 'satyrs' [demons]."[135] A similar interpretation is found in the Sipra (Torat Kohanim) when commenting on the "calf of the herd" in Leviticus 9:2: "You must give [it] into the mouth of Satan. Send a gift ahead, before you enter the Temple, lest he hates you upon your entering the Temple."[136]

The earliest extra-canonical source depicting Azazel as a demon is the pseudepigraphal book of 1 Enoch, followed by the pseudepigraphal work Apocalypse of Abraham, in which Azazel is called a "dragon" (23:7).[137] In Christian thought, the view of Azazel as a demon dates back to church father Origen and enjoys the support of several modern scholars.[138] Nestle, for example, argues that "[i]f one reads Lev. chap. 16, with an open mind, the impression is that Azazel must be related to Yahweh in something of the same way as Ahriman to Ormuz, or Satan."[139] Keil and Delitzsch write: "The lots, one lot for Jehovah and one for Azazel, require unconditionally that *Azazel* should be regarded as a personal being, in opposition to Jehovah," i.e., "the devil himself."[140] That is "the most reasonable" view, concurs Wright.[141]

Three main arguments can be put forth in support of this view: (1) if one goat is "for the Lord," and the other to "for/to Azazel," *ʿazāʾzēl* more likely represented an entity that stood in opposition to the Lord, as did הַשָּׂטָן (*haśśāṭān*);[142] (2) elsewhere in the OT, the wilderness is seen as the abode of demons, and Leviticus 17:7 forbids sacrifices to goat-demons;[143] and (3)

135. Shevel, *Ramban's Commentary*, li, 89; see Pinker, "A Goat to Azazel," 6.

136. See Gruenwald, *Rituals*, 219.

137. See Hall, "The Christian Interpolation," 107–112.

138. *Contra Celsum* 6:43; Keil and Delitzsch, *Biblical Commentary*, 398; Nestle, "Azazel," 282–283; See Gane, *Cult and Character*, 247; Gane, *Leviticus and Numbers*, 288–290.

139. Nestle, "Azazel," 283.

140. Keil and Delitzsch, *Biblical Commentary*, 398. See also Segal, "The Religion of Israel," 250.

141. Wright, "Azazel," 536. See Feinberg, "Scapegoat," 330: "[i]t cannot be shown that the name Azazel occurs in the OT as the name of Satan or any evil spirit for that matter."

142. See Num 22:22; 1 Sam 29:4; 1 Chr. 21:1; 2:1; Zech 3:1, 2. See Hartley, *Leviticus*, 238: "Azazel is some type of being rather than a place."

143. See Isa 13:21–22; 34:11–15; Baruch 4:35; Tob 8:3; in the NT, Matt 12:34; 25:31–46; Luke 11:24; Rev 18:2.

the development of a demonic persona around the name *ʿazāʾzēl* in Jewish pseudepigraphal literature.[144] The passages below reveal the pervasive belief that Israel was surrounded by desert demons, whose influence and worship presented a constant source of covenantal jeopardy to Israelites.

(1) Leviticus 17:7 warns against offering sacrifices outside of the confines of the tabernacle, "so that they may no longer offer their sacrifices for goat-demons [שְׂעִרִם, *śeʿîrîm*], to whom they prostitute themselves."

(2) 2 Chronicles 11:15 describes Jeroboam's wickedness: "... and [he] had appointed his own priests for the high places, and for the goat-demons [*śeʿîrîm*]."

(3) In an oracle against Babylon in Isaiah 13:21 predicts that in its ruins, "ostriches will live, and goat-demons [*śeʿîrîm*] will dance."

(4) The oracle against Edom in Isaiah 34:14 predicts that "wildcats shall meet with hyenas, goat-demons [*śaʿîr*] all call to each other; there too Lilith [a female demon-goddess] shall repose, and find a place to rest." It is important to note that the coupling of *śaʿîr* and *lîlît* here led the LXX translators to render both words as δαιμόνια, "demons."[145]

(5) The *śeʿîrîm* mentioned in the context of the reforms of King Josiah: "he broke down the high places of the gates that were at the entrance of the gate of Joshua the governor of the city" (2 Kgs 23:8). According to the punctuation proposed by Hoffmann—via Lev 17:7 and 2 Chr 11:15—the nonsensical construction "the gates that were at the entrance of the gate" should be replaced with "the high places of the *śeʿîrîm*," which matches the idolatry motif in the passage.[146]

Echoes of the association between the desert and the demonic also reverberate in the NT when the synoptic Gospels connect *erēmon* with *diabolos*; Jesus is led "into the desert" (*eis tēn erēmon*) to be tempted by the devil (Matt 4:1; Mar 1:12–13 [*hypo tou Satana*]; Luke 4:1–2). Jesus also expressed this view: "When the unclean spirit has gone out of a person, it wanders through waterless regions looking for a resting place, but it finds none" (Matt 12:43).

144. E.g., 1 Enoch 8:1; 9:6; 10:4–8: 13:1; 54:5–6: 55:4; 69:2 Apoc. Ab. 13:6–14; 14:4–6; 20:5–7; 22:5; 23:11; 29:6–7; 31:5. See Orlov, "The Eschatological Yom Kippur," 3–35. Janowski and Wilhelm, "Der Bock," 109–169 who argue that *ʿazāʾzēl* is a "metathesized form" of "zz," "strong" and thus render the *lamed* in *laʿazāʾzēl* as the noun "god." See also Görg, "Beobachtungen," 10–16; Görg, "Asasel," 181–182; Grabbe, "The Scapegoat," 195–233.

145. *TWOT* 479.

146. Hoffmann, "Kleinigkeiten," 175. See Snaith, "The meaning of שׂערים," 115–118; Emerton, "The High Places," 455–67; Monroe, "A 'Holiness' Substratum," 45–49.

The preceding evidence on the demonic origins of the name Azazel begs the question: Why would the Levitical law-giver forgo the more common term for goat-demons (*śᵉʿîrîm*) in favor of *laʿazāʾzēl*? A couple of explanations could be advanced. First, the author likely wished to avoid a direct association of a sanctuary rite with pagan deities such as the mythological *śᵉʿîrîm*. As Milgrom explains: "Azazel is the name of a demon who has been eviscerated of his demonic powers by the Priestly legislators... They [demons] can represent the powers of the physical world ... but they are not deified ... and their worship is prohibited."[147] Second, the Levitical author likely wished to avoid confusing the purgation rite with an "offering" to the *śᵉʿîrîm*—precisely what Leviticus 17:7 forbids—while still ascribing executing judgment on a being in opposition to God (e.g., Exod 20:4–5; 22:9; Deut 4:19; 5:7–8; 17:3; Job 5:1). In this case, sending a toxic goat to Azazel offered a limited, highly controlled parallel with contemporary Canaanite goat-demon mythology while at the same time preserving the integrity of the Israelite purification rite within the confines of their monotheistic covenant. The author might have wanted to avoid dedicating more attention than necessary to Azazel and relegated this demon to a lower status, keeping the Lord at the center of the DA. This entity did not receive atonement through blood but only the toxic load of all of Israel's sins, impurities, and guilt.[148] The goat was not a substitute for loyal Israel, and a vicarious sacrifice was not implied in this ritual since the "goat for the Lord" had already assumed this function. Azazel received punishment and judgment and suffered "the fate of all angels and spirits in Scripture," observes Milgrom.[149]

The popular expression, "there is no such thing as a free lunch," is fitting here: sins removed from the tabernacle did not simply disappear into thin air; someone had to bear their guilt and pay their penalty; in this case, they were banished to their source, Azazel.[150] The goat did not carry a "peace offering" offered as to a god but a noxious load of abominations that had been accumulating in the tabernacle throughout the year, encroaching on the divine and jeopardizing the covenant.[151] Sins, impurities, as well as their culpability, which had been transferred to the goat and returned to Azazel, accrued yearly on his tab to be dealt with on the eschatological DA: Judgment Day.

147. Milgrom, *Leviticus 1–16*, 1021, 1072; Milgrom, *Leviticus: A Book of Ritual*, 168–169; Hartley, *Leviticus*, 238; Duhm, *Die bösen Geister*, 32.

148. See Hertz, *Leviticus*, 156; Milgrom, *Leviticus 1–16*, 1021; Zatelli, "The Origin," 263.

149. Milgrom, *Leviticus: A Book of Ritual*, 169; Milgrom, *Leviticus 1–16*, 1020. Nibley, *Temple*, 75.

150. See Hartley, *Leviticus*, 238; Ahituv, "Azazel," 1002; Caldwell, "The Doctrine," 29–33.

151. See Hanson, "Rebellion," 222.

Defiant Israelites who had become accomplices of Azazel's effrontery against YHWH suffered the same fate as he and his goat: they were banished, bearing their own sin and guilt, which often meant "death" (Num 15:30; 18:22).[152] Azazel is none other than Satan's alter ego.

We rest our case against Azazel for now and return to the day's rituals.

## *The Burnt Offerings*

After the "goat for Azazel" was led into the desert by an attending priest, Aaron returned to the tabernacle, removed his linen garments, bathed himself "in a holy place" (v. 24, presumably inside the tabernacle's compound), and put on "his garments," i.e., his regular, ornate attire (see m. Yoma 7:3: "golden garments.") Milgrom explains that "the high priest, exceptionally, is never contaminated by officiating at purgation rites," rather, the ablutions and change of clothing imply a "compartmentalization" of the holiness he encountered in the Most Holy Place in order to protect the people.[153] In addition, a return to the regular attire constituted a confirmation of his high priesthood. The day's proceedings had been successful, and the tabernacle had been re-dedicated as God's dwelling place.[154] Aaron must then "come out and offer his burnt offering and the burnt offering of the people, making atonement for himself and for the people" (v. 24). As far as the high priest's functions go, the DA's rituals are finally over.

The m. Yoma 6:2–6 describes additional activities performed during the "goat for Azazel" rite not present in the biblical text. According to the Rabbis, the "goat for Azazel" was led to a cliff, tied, and pushed off to die. While this occurred, the high priest waited for confirmation that the "goat for Azazel" had reached the desert before proceeding with the day's rituals.[155]

After Aaron offered the two rams as a burnt offering, an attending priest disposed of the bull and goat carcasses sacrificed earlier. These dead animals do not defile the sanctuary until they leave the camp on the DA. "The implication," posits Milgrom, "is that the holiness of the sanctuary is powerful enough to suppress the impurity-laden *ḥaṭṭāʾṯ* carcass until it leaves the sanctuary precincts."[156] Their carcasses were disposed of outside the camp, and the skin, flesh, and dung were consumed in fire (v. 27; see Num 19:8).

152. See Gane, *Cult and Character*, 264.
153. Milgrom, *Leviticus 1–16*, 1052, 1047.
154. Milgrom, *Leviticus: A Book of Ritual*, 172.
155. Milgrom, *Leviticus 1–16*, 1046.
156. Milgrom, *Leviticus 1–16*, 1064.

After this was done, the attending priest washed himself to decontaminate and reentered the community.

### *Atoning Unintentional vs. Intentional Sins*

The question now arises as to which transgressions were expiable by the *kipper*-rites on the DA. Wright contends that "intentional sins and presumably other unrectified sins and impurities pollute the adytum and the *kāppōrēṯ* and implicitly the ark" and were removed from the Holy of Holies on the DA.[157] Confession of sins, however, was only required for "brazen, presumptuous sins," so that the confession by the high priest on the head of the "goat for Azazel" is indicative of the scope of the DA's cleansing: it included even defiant sins (Lev 5:5, 20–26).[158] Thus, the removal of "all sins" from the sanctuary did not entail forgiveness/atonement for individual sinners but acted instead as a purgative offering for the sanctuary and the nation as a whole.

Therefore, the nature of the sin and the sinner's attitude and intention determine whether it is expiable or inexpiable, especially if "repentance is demonstrated through voluntary confession and restitution."[159] Throughout the year, only "unintentional" and "intentional-non-defiant" sins were expiable by *kipper*-rites. Conversely, "high-handed," intentional-defiant sinners, even when "confession" was forced out of them, as did Achan, faced dim prospects: they must be "cut-off" bearing their own guilt (Num 15:30–31; 18:22; Josh 7). The harsh punishment reserved for high-handed sinners precludes the possibility of remedy through repentance and penitence.[160] While their sin was purged from the sanctuary by the power rituals of the DA, these sinners suffered the same fate as the "goat for Azazel"—banishment and sometimes, death—which purged "the evil from Israel" (Deut 17:12). As Gane concludes, "sacrificial כפר through outer-altar or outer-sanctum purification offerings, a prerequisite to forgiveness, is not available to the offenders in such cases [i.e., high-handed sins]." Acceptance into the community is only guaranteed "for those of loyal character."[161]

157. Wright, "Day of Atonement," *AYBD* 2:73; see Boda, *A Severe Mercy*, 68.

158. Milgrom, *Leviticus 1–16*, 1042.

159. Gane, *Cult and Character*, 211.

160. Crüsemann, *The Torah*, 318, sees "no example by which serious infractions of the fundamental cultic order—especially for cases for which 'cutting off' is prescribed—can by confession and repentance be included among the offenses covered by the . . . Day of Atonement."

161. Gane, *Cult and Character*, 161–162.

## The Day of Atonement Covenant Lawsuit

The appendix in Leviticus 16:29–34 contains the covenantal formula: the yearly celebration of the DA was a "statute forever" (v. 29). At its center is the promise that by keeping the DA once a year, Israel "shall be clean before the LORD" (v. 30). This "cleansing" was the fundamental principle of the Levitical system.

While the tabernacle was purged from sin on the DA, and loyal Israelites enjoyed the benefits of the atonement, defiant sinners did not enjoy its effects but must be cut off bearing their guilt (Num 15:30–31; 18:22). This cutting-off often meant the death of the transgressor at the hands of the congregation and stood for the punishment that could befall the nation should they choose to become defiant (Josh 7). The covenantal formula found in Leviticus 26:14–46 carries a warning against disobedience: "If you continue hostile to me, and will not obey me, I will continue to plague you sevenfold for your sins" (v. 21). In Deuteronomy 28:15–68, this warning takes the form of curses following a covenantal breach.

## Conclusion

The themes embedded in the rituals of the DA encapsulate the ethos of the entire Levitical system of sacrifices which required holiness to preserve the divine presence with Israel. The main themes of the DA are:

(1) Israel's existential need to preserve the covenant with God;
(2) God's demand that his people be clean and holy through the removal of sin and impurity from "their midst" (Lev 16:30);
(3) God's grace in providing atonement for sin and impurity;
(4) Purification through the manipulation of sacrificial blood;
(5) Transfer of sins to the live goat by the high priest's confession;
(6) Retribution for sin ascribed to demonic Azazel;
(7) Defiant sinners and non-participants on the DA are banished;
(8) Restoration of the covenantal relationship with God.

As we'll see in the following chapters, the theology of the rituals of the DA constituted a continuous source of reflection within Judaism and reverberated in the life of Jews joining early Christianity.

## Excursus: The Origins of the Israelite Elimination Ritual in Its Ancient Near East Context

In several ways, the ritual of the "goat for Azazel" stands in parallel with contemporary Canaanite elimination rites. On the occasion of the discovery in 1937 of an ivory plaque of Megiddo (13th century BCE) depicting a sphinx fighting a caprine deity, Eissfeldt concluded that the discovery puts both images, the ritual of the "goat for Azazel" and the plaque in the same "homely" environment of Canaan.[1] Janowski notes how the "goat for Azazel" rite "belongs to the oldest core of the ritual tradition of Leviticus 16," and Martin Noth thinks that this "very ancient rite" was emblematic of Israel's *Sitz im Leben* in the deserts of Sinai.[2] Wright argues that the ritual of the "goat for Azazel" shares its roots with elimination rites in South Anatolia-North Syria and Mesopotamia.[3] In these rites, animals such as cattle, sheep, goats, donkeys, or mice were utilized. Moreover, Janowski and Wilhelm think that it is clear that the rite has its roots in Ugaritic and Greek rites of elimination and propose three possible basic types (Grundtypen) for the "goat for Azazel" rite: (1) nomadic ritual types; (2) Egyptian ritual types; and (3) the south-Anatolian-northern-Syrian ritual types.[4] Ahituv points out the similarities between the Babylonian New Year purgation festival of *akîtu* and the ritual of the "goat for Azazel."[5] A similar rite is found in a Hittite ritual that prescribes that a ram be driven away from a land afflicted with a plague to transfer the plague to an enemy.[6]

Moreover, the use of goats for purgation rituals in ANE cultures is well attested. Ancient Akkadian myths describe the guardian of the netherworld, Mamitu, as having the head of a goat, and at least one such custom involves the expulsion of a goat for purification.[7] Sumerian tablets excavated at Ebla in 1975 brought to light textual evidence of rites not dissimilar to the Israelite expulsion of the "goat for Azazel." One such text reads: "[And] we purge the mausoleum. Before the entry of Kura and Barama a goat, a silver bracelet

1. Eissfeldt, "Zur Deutung," 1–4.
2. See Janowski, "Azazel"; Noth, *Leviticus*, 124.
3. Wright, *The Disposal*, 31–74.
4. Janowski and Wilhelm, "Der Bock," 161.
5. Ahituv, "Azazel," 1001. See Milgrom, *Leviticus 1–16*, 1067–1070; Bergsma, *The Jubilee*, 31.
6. See Goetze, "Hitite Rituals," 347; Frazer, *The Golden Bough*, 354–412; Ferguson, "'I Never Did an Evil Thing,'" 55–60.
7. See Speiser, "A Vision," 109.

[hanging from the] goat's neck, towards the steppe of Alini we let her go."[8] In another example, the term used for the purgation of the cell of the god Nabu on the fifth day of the feast is *kuppuru*, a term that shares its roots with the Hebrew *kipper*. The use of blood for purgation is also present in the Hittite *Ulippi* ritual.[9]

## *The Greek Pharmakos Rites and the Ritual of the "Goat for Azazel"*

In 1903, Harrison published her findings on the elimination rites that accompanied the festivities of the ancient Greek harvest festival of Thargelia (from *thargelios*, the first loaf of bread of the harvest), a feast to Apollo that took place in Ionia and Athens. Part of the celebrations consisted of a purgation rite involving the expulsion of a *pharmakos*, a term that seems to have acquired the connotation of "refuse" and is used in connection with *katharma* ("cleansing") in ancient Greek sources.[10] On the sixth day of the month of Thargelion, the rite involved choosing two *pharmakoi*, i.e., undesirable, ugly, destitute, or "useless" characters chosen to cleanse the city of impurity.[11] These people were treated lavishly for a time and fed at public expense, and were subsequently led out of the city, taking with them the city's impurity.[12] Ancient sources indicate "it was the custom at Athens to lead in procession two *pharmakoi* with a view to purification (*katharmos*) ... to avert pestilential diseases," and protect crops.[13] A similar ritual is described by the poet Hipponax (ca. 6th century BCE), which required the expulsion of a *pharmakos* carrying twigs of a fig tree.[14]

DeMaris proposed five shared characteristics of ancient "scapegoat" rites: (1) a threat to the community; (2) a community member is designated to undergo a transformation; (3) a ritual action concentrates and directs divine

8. See Zatelli, "The Origin," 254–263; Bremmer, "Scapegoat Rituals," 271–93; DeMaris, "Jesus Jettisoned," 91–111.

9. Zatelli, "The Origin," 260.

10. See Harrison, *Prolegomena*, 97; Harrison "The Pharmakos," 298–99. Roberts, "The Pharmakos," 218–24, believes that *pharmakos* originated from the Turkic *vourmak*, which means "beat." He concludes that the later meaning of *pharmakos* as "magician" stems from the meaning of expelling evils based on the *pharmakos* rite. See also Steiner, "Diverting Demons," 71–100; Stern, "Scapegoat Narratives," 304–11.

11. See *Scholia on Aristophanes, Knights* 1136c; Parker, *On Greek Religion*, 216–7.

12. See Parker, *On Greek Religion*, 217; Bremmer, "Scapegoat Rituals," 273–277; McLean, *The Cursed Christ*, 65–104.

13. Photius *Bibl.* 534a quoted in McLean, *The Cursed Christ*, 89. For an extended discussion of the sources, see Hughes, *Human Sacrifice*, 140.

14. Bremmer, "Scapegoat Rituals," 300–301.

power; (4) expulsion of the designee from the community in the direction of the enemy; and (5) vicarious action by the designated person diverts disaster away from his community.[15] These shared traits led Burkert to conclude that the Hittite, Greek, and Roman rituals all "go back indeed to a ritual, described in the Old Testament, of Yom Kippur, the Day of Atonement."[16] Echoes of ancient *pharmakos* purgation rites appear in m. Yoma 6:3–5 when the Rabbis discuss the rite of the "goat for Azazel":

> They delivered it to him that should lead it away ... And they made a causeway for it because of the Babylonians who used to pull its hair, crying to it, "Bear [our sins] and be gone! Bear [our sins] and be gone!" Certain of the eminent folk of Jerusalem used to go with him to the first booth. There were ten booths from Jerusalem to the ravine, [at a distance of] ninety ris (which measure seven and a half to the mile). At every booth, they used to say to him, "Here is food, here is water," and they went with him from that booth to the next booth, but not from the last booth; for none used to go with him to the ravine; but they stood at a distance and beheld what he did.[17]

Nevertheless, not all scholars are convinced by the parallels between the ancient rites involving evil spirits and the "goat for Azazel" rite. Douglas calls the Greek rites a "Hellenized distortion" and thinks that the "right place to start" looking for a parallel is the book of Genesis, "where the theme of conspicuously uneven destinies occurs prominently." Douglas refers to the stories of Isaac/Ishmael and Jacob/Esau and Joseph (via the Book of Jubilees) and thinks these present a better source for the "goat for Azazel" rite because "atonement points to the central theological theme of the Pentateuch, a chosen people and the contrast with the people who have not been chosen."[18]

15. DeMaris, "Jesus Jettisoned," 103. See Dawson, *Studies in Violence*, 47.

16. Burkert, *Structure and History*, 65; See McLean, "On the Revision of Scapegoat Terminology," 168–73, considers the historical background for the *pharmakos* rite and proposes "scapeman" as a preferred term instead of "scapegoat."

17. See the commentary on Leviticus 16:10, 21–22 in the *Targum of Pseudo-Jonathan:* "The goat on which the lot for Azazel fell shall be set alive before the Lord to make atonement for the sinfulness of the people of the house of Israel (and) to be sent to die in a rough and stony place [...] which is in the desert of Soq, that is Beth Haduri [...] And he [Aaron] shall let (it) [the scapegoat] go, in charge of a man who has been designated previously, to go to the desert *of Soq, that is Beth Haduri.* (22) The goat shall carry on himself all their sins to a desolate *place* [...] and *the man* shall let the goat go into the desert *of Soq, and the goat shall go up on the mountains of Beth Haduri, and a blast of wind from before the Lord will thrust him down and he will die*" (Maher, *Targum*, 168–169).

18. Douglas, "The Go-Away Goat," 135.

## More on the Meaning of *La ʿăzā ʾzēl*

Levine's study of Akkadian *uttukû lemmuti* ("evil spirits" or "incantations") texts show that the belief in demons as denizens of the "netherworld" was widespread in ancient Mesopotamia.[19] Schur calls Azazel "König aller Wüstendämonen ... der schrecklichen Azazel," while Loretz warns that Leviticus 16 does not quickly allow rendering Azazel as "desert demon"[20] because, unlike God, it lacks a precise location.[21] In support of Azazel's demonic identity, Fauth draws on the following: (1) Late Antiquity Aramaic incantation bowls containing the letters הזע; (2) Greek texts of the Logos of Selene which contain αζα and αζαζ(α); (3) a medicinal amulet which reads αζαζ αραθ βαχυ.22 Building on ancient Akkadian and Ugaritic purification rites, Tawil lists parallels to the "goat for Azazel" rite and incantations as follows:

(1) Demons, the entities from the "netherworld," are the source of evil, destruction and desolation, iniquities and sins, diseases, and sicknesses;
(2) Demons inhabit the realm of the absence of life and vitality;
(3) Demons are described as "fierce" (Akkadian *ezzu*);
(4) The netherworld has easy access to the upper world;
(5) The netherworld is known as the "steppeland";
(6) Demons must not be allowed to remain in the land of the living but must be sent back to their place of origin;
(7) Disease and evil can be transferred to a substitute (i.e., a goat);
(8) Healing comes when the demons are sent away;
(9) The expulsion of the demons stops the evil.[23]

Significantly, Tawil points out how these ancient incantation rites have a clear parallel with the punishment of Azazel described in 1 Enoch 10:4:

19. See Levine, "Kippurim," 88–95. See Gurney, *Babylonian*, 86, for one such *uttukû lemmuti* incantation: "Let your pure and exalted mouth say, from the body of the sufferer go away. O all evil, arise and depart to the place of Ereskigal, take away the skin of the scapegoat from the body of the sufferer, into the carrefour, into the wide street [i.e. underworld] throw [it], so that all evil return to the netherworld."

20. See Schur, *Versöhnungstag*, 46.

21. See Loretz, "Asasel in Ugarit," 52: "a power lower than Yahweh and as he, without a specific location."

22. Fauth, "Auf den Spuren," 517. See Segal and Hunter, *Aramaic and Mandaic*; Hunter, "Who Are Demons," 95–115. Hunter quotes demonic entities such as devils, demons, spirits, amulets-spirits, idol-spirits, goddesses, and *liliths*. To these, we could add the *'aluqah* of Prov 30:15, which according to Shearman and Curtis is a vampire-demon, an interpretation based on the Targum rendering Ps 12:8. See Shearman and Curtis, "Divine-Human Conflicts," 234.

23. Tawil, "Azazel," 48–52. See Hanson, "Rebellion," 205.

"Bind Azaz'el hand and foot (and) throw him into the darkness!"[24] Tawil notes how "the demonic fallen angel Azazel ... a demonic creature, who ... personifies all evil, destruction and desolation, wars and bloodshed, wounds and plagues, diseases and sicknesses... is being disposed of in a similar way that demons and other hostile powers are treated in Akkadian incantation texts."[25] As will be explored in a later section, the pronouncement "to him ascribe all sin" is strikingly similar to the transfer of sins to the "goat for Azazel" by the high priest.

Tawil draws several comparisons between the description of the banishment of Azazel in 1 Enoch and the god Môt, "the god of death and Hades," in *uttukû lemmuti* texts: (1) the use of darkness as a description of the netherworld; (2) the imagery of binding up the demon; (3) the casting away of the demon to the netherworld; (4) the imprisonment of the demon in the netherworld; and (5) the dispatch of the demon and the substitutionary elements to the steppe land to dig/open a hole therein.[26] Tawil also draws on the Akkadian word *gasasu*, "raging demons" which bears a semantic relationship with *ʿazāʾzēl*, leading him to conclude that *ʿazāʾzēl* can only mean "fierce god," and is "an epithet of Môt which may also signify the location of his domain, the netherworld itself."[27] In support, Tawil cites the following philological evidence: (1) in Job 1:7; 2:2, the roaming of ʿ echoes the Akkadian *alaku-šâtu*, i.e., "verbs used to describe the movement of demons in the steppeland"[28]; (2) Ugaritic texts use the expression *kbd ars* for the "bottom of the netherworld," which is semantically equivalent to "belly of Sheol" (Jonah 2:3); (3) the Ugaritic *gr*//*gbʿ* parallels the Akkadian *šadû-huršanu* referring to the Mesopotamian "cosmic mountain of the netherworld"; and (4) the Hebrew "barren region" is equivalent to the Akkadian *seru* "the steppe land."

Some of the examples given by Tawil are less convincing than the evidence from Akkadian terms describing the demons of the underworld as *ezzu, šamru, nadru, gassu, gaspu, dannu*, which mean, respectively, "fierce, furious, raging, ferocious, overbearing, savage."[29] Despite some weaknesses, it is possible to agree with most of the philological arguments articulated by Tawil since the ANE parallels likely constitute the best source of the Jewish tradition surrounding Azazel as the demonic figure responsible for Israel's

24. *OTP* 17–18.
25. Tawil, "Azazel," 52, 59.
26. Tawil, "Azazel," 53, 56.
27. Tawil, "Azazel," 59.
28. Tawil, "Azazel," 49.
29. See Bauer, "Die Gottheiten," 95.

sins, iniquities, and guilt. The description of Azazel as a demon by the author of 1 Enoch may betray its antiquity, something the Levitical law-giver did not fully explore in his laconic account of the DA.[30]

## Alternative Views on the Meaning of *la*ʿ*azā*ʾ*zēl*

The views on the meaning of Azazel briefly explored below represent the diversity of understanding of the name, from ancient sources to current scholarship.

### *Azazel as the Goat's Function*

In this view, לַעֲזָאזֵל (*la*ʿ*azā*ʾ*zēl*) describes the goat's function, i.e., "to go away." This view capitalizes on the LXX translation of Azazel as *apopompaios* in Leviticus 16:8, 10. Further support is found in Leviticus 16:26 in the LXX, which renders the Hebrew ʾ*eṯ-haśśā*ʿ*îr la*ʿ*azā*ʾ*zēl* as "the goat to be sent away for remission" (*ton chimaron ton diestalmenon eis aphesin*). The Vulgate followed this rendering by the expression "*caper emissarius*," "the goat that is sent." In turn, this translation influenced Tyndale's rendering of the term as "scapegoat."

This position has the support of medieval Rabbi David Kimhi (1160–1235), who explained that Azazel was a combination of עז "goat" and אזל "to go."[31] However, this view ignores the syntactic function of the preposition ל in the expression, which is best explained as a *lamed auctoris* or "sign of proprietorship." This reading precluded seeing the goat itself as Azazel.[32] Indeed, Leviticus 16:10 would be incomprehensible if Azazel meant the goat itself when it says that the goat was to be sent "to Azazel in the wilderness."

30. See Blair, *De-Demonising*, 61: "The significance of *Azazel* is not who he is but what he symbolizes. In many ways his role is the opposite of Yahweh's. Like Yahweh, he is a deity, though it is made clear that he does not possess the same power. Yahweh receives sacrifice, *Azazel's* goat is not a sacrifice; Yahweh dwells in the very center, the Holy of Holies, *Azazel's* place is on the outside, the desert; Yahweh's dwelling place is pure, the desert is where all impurities can be found; worshipping Yahweh brings life to his people, following other gods brings death to them. Yahweh establishes order, *Azazel* is the bringer of chaos."

31. See *TWOT* s.v. "אָזַל"; See Hartley, *Leviticus*, 237.

32. Milgrom, *Leviticus 1–16*, 1020; see Cazelles, "La question," 93–101.

## *Azazel as the Place Where the Goat is Dispatched*

The view that sees Azazel as a "place" connects the name to the "barren region" (v. 22). However, it seems evident that *ʾel-ʾereṣ gᵉzērâhere* is synonymous with *miḏbār*, "wilderness" in Leviticus 16:10, and not Azazel.[33]

This view also capitalizes on themes found in Second Temple traditions, such as that found in Babylonian Talmud, which defines Azazel as "the hardest of mountains" and "a rocky precipice" (b. Yoma, 63b; 67b; see m. Yoma 6:6). This reading is transferred directly into the text of Leviticus 16:10 in Pseudo-Jonathan (original additions in italics): "The goat on which the lot for Azazel fell shall be set alive before the Lord to make atonement *for the sinfulness of the people of the house of Israel* [and] to be sent *to die in a stony and rocky place which is* in the desert *of Soq, that is Beth Haduri.*" Along the same lines, Targum Pseudo-Jonathan renders Leviticus 16:22 as: "The goat shall carry on himself all their sins to a desolate *place;* and *the man* shall let the goat go into the desert *of Soq and the goat shall go up on the mountains of Beth Haduri, and a blast of wind from before the Lord will thrust him down and he will die.*"[34]

Jewish commentator Rashbam (ca. 1080–1174) diverges from m. Yoma by saying that the "goat for Azazel" is led to "deserts" (plural מדברות, i.e., pasture for undomesticated animals) to graze. He compares the dismissal of Azazel with the rite of the cleansing of the leper in Leviticus 14:7, in which a bird is set free, and contends that "desert," does not necessarily mean a desolate place.[35] However, the position of m. Yoma that the goat was killed may be supported by the observation that *ʾel-ʾereṣ gᵉzērâhere* comes from the root גזר, "to cut off" and is synonymous with "desert" in Leviticus 16:22, so that the intent of the author of Leviticus may well be separation for destruction.[36] Moreover, it is unlikely that the nomadic nature of Israel would allow one specific place to be called Azazel.[37]

33. See Hartley, *Leviticus*, 238; Hoenig, "The New Pesher," 249.

34. The Rabbinic view is not without problems, for it may be an anachronism, an attempt to read the Second Temple practice of pushing the "goat for Azazel" off a cliff back into the pre-exilic text of Leviticus. See Ahituv, "Azazel," *EncJud* 3:1002.

35. Lockshin, *Rashbam's Commentary*, 91–92.

36. Milgrom, *Leviticus 1–16*, 1010, renders *miḏbār* as an "inaccessible region."

37. Feinberg, "The Scapegoat," 325. See Milgrom, *Leviticus 1–16*, 1020; Driver, "Three Technical Terms," 97. In non-Jewish literature, Sa'adya, an Arabic commentator on the Pentateuch, writing against Hiwwi al-Balchi, argued that Azazel comes from the Arabic *azazu(n)*, "rough ground," *azazilu* (broken plural), "precipice," a position that Driver follows. This view capitalizes on ʿzʿz as "rough ground," but it would require considering both the א and final ל as inconsequential.

## *Azazel as "Removal"*

This view sees Azazel as a *terminus technicus* meaning "removal."[38] This meaning is given by some lexicons based on the LXX rendering of Azazel as *apopompaios* (Lev 16:8, 10) and *diestalmenos* (16:26), i.e., "to send away."[39] Möller, for example, argues that the idea of removal points to the entity performing the removal: "Azalzel, or azazel, therefore, means one who removes by a series of acts ..."[40] Möller's position is not compelling; he contends that Azazel comes from the Aramaic word אזל (via the Arabic "*azala*"); however, אזל does not appear in the OT with the meaning of a ritualistic removal, but simply means "to go, to depart."[41] Further, only by biased inference could one construe the meaning "removal by a series of acts" from the idea of departing.

More recently, Rudman argued in favor of this view because he thinks the author of Leviticus does not subscribe to the notion of a demonic deity. Rudman's view appeals to the "desert" motif found in Leviticus 16 and builds on the duality between chaos and creation expressed through various symbols such as sea monsters, darkness, night, and death, as seen in ANE mythology and the Hebrew Scriptures.[42] Israel symbolized creation and the desert was the "home of chaos."[43] As such, "[n]ot only is the goat with its burden of sin removed from the camp of Israel (and creation's microcosm thereby purified of chaos), it is removed from creation proper."[44] While the Most Holy Place was "a microcosm of creation," the desert where the "goat for Azazel" is sent is the "home of chaos"; by sending sin back to chaos via the goat, the rite delivers Israel from sin, pointing to the eschatological cleansing of the entire creation.[45]

Rudman's view is akin to Hartley's that the wilderness is the source of Israel's sins, and the "goat for Azazel" simply returns them to its rightful place, "breaking the power that they had of binding and oppressing the people."[46]

38. See Feinberg, "The Scapegoat," 324. Hartley, *Leviticus*, 236.

39. Feinberg, "The Scapegoat," 320–31. See Brown, Driver, and Briggs, *Enhanced Brown-Driver-Briggs*; also "עֲזָאזֵל" in Thomas, *New American Standard Hebrew-Aramaic*.

40. Möller, "Azazel," 344.

41. See Deut 32:36; 1 Sam 9:7; 20:19; Job 14:11; Prov 20:14; Dan 2:17, 24; 6:19, 20; Ezra 4:23; 5:8; 15. See BDB, s.v. "Azazel."

42. See Gen 1, 2, 6–8; Ps 5:22; 46:3–4; 74:12–17; 89:10–15; 104:6–7; Job 38:8–10.

43. Rudman, "A Note," 399.

44. Rudman, "A Note," 400.

45. Rudman, "A Note," 396–401.

46. Hartley, "A Note on the Azazel-Goat Ritual," 241. See the discussion on Azazel as the symbol of a demon in Hamburger, *Fallen Angels*, 17–21, 46–9, 154–6. Also, Swanson, *Dictionary*, s.v. "תַּכְלִת"; Gerstenberger, *Leviticus*, 221; Gruenwald, *Rituals*, 222.

## *Azazel as "On Behalf of Azazel"*

This view is espoused by Wyatt, who states that "the expelled goat may not be 'to Azazel' (or 'for Azazel' in the same sense), but rather 'on behalf of' or 'in lieu of Azazel,' as a substitute for him."[47] Wyatt suggests that the god implied here, Attar, was rendered insignificant in the tabernacle service. In this case, the goat "for the Lord" was sacrificed as a substitute for God, while Azazel was a substitute for Attar. However, the "goat for the Lord" was not sacrificed "on behalf" of the Lord but, ultimately, on behalf of the people to purge their transgressions, and it follows that the "goat for Azazel" was likewise purged on behalf of the community.

## *Azazel as the "Wrath of God"*

This view was championed by Görg, who suggested that Azazel came to nomadic Israel via Seth, the Egyptian god of confusion. Thus, Azazel is "the expelled or removed culprit" because "the guilty one belongs there whence his guilt ultimately comes."[48] The meaning of Azazel as "for [the elimination of] divine anger" has also been suggested by Janowski via Hurrian elimination rites and the Akkadian *ezezu*, "to be angry."[49] Likewise, De Roo renders *laʿazāʾzēl* as a metathesized form of *ʿzzʾl*, i.e., "the powerful wrath of God."[50]

This view can also be countered. First, there would be no reason to distinguish the goats if both were somehow intended to be ultimately "for the Lord," or for "his wrath." Second, since the "goat for Azazel" was not originally meant to be sacrificed or killed (although it did meet that end in Second Temple times), this ritual could hardly be construed as one of "appeasement" of God's wrath. Moreover, the notion of appeasing God's wrath is entirely missing in the tabernacle cultus, including on the DA. In light of Leviticus 17:11, it was God who provided the means for cleansing and reconciliation through sacrificial blood: "For the life of the flesh is in the blood; it was I who gave it to you for making atonement for your lives on the altar; for, as life, it is the blood that makes atonement."[51] An angry God waiting to be appeased

47. Wyatt, "Atonement Theology," 429.
48. Görg, "Beobachtungen," 13.
49. Janowski and Wilhelm, "Der Bock," 162; Janowski and Wilhelm, "Azazel" in *DDD*, 128–131.
50. De Roo, "Was the Goat for Azazel," 233–242.
51. Gilders, "Blood as Purificant," 83.

would hardly take such a benevolent stance. There is no evidence that the rite of the "goat for Azazel" functioned outside of this atonement framework.

The preceding views do not adequately consider philological aspects of the name Azazel, especially how it was reworked in a larger swath of Second Temple Jewish apocalyptic literature as a fallen angel operating on earth in opposition to God.

## Conclusion

The evidence culled in this Excursus indicates that ancient Canaanite myths of demonic entities inhabiting the desert and responsible for chaos, plagues, and misfortunes remain the ideal source of the Israelite elimination rite of the "goat for Azazel." Although its identity is veiled in Leviticus, Jews came to view Azazel as a demon inhabiting the desert who received the toxic load of sin, impurities, and guilt that had been purged from the tabernacle and, by extension, from the congregation of Israel on the DA.

As will be argued later in this study, the view of Azazel as a demonic entity counters the view that it participated in "atonement" per se and is, therefore, a figure of Christ. Azazel's demonic identity is fully developed in Jewish literature and arrives as such in the book of Revelation.

# 2

# THE DAY OF ATONEMENT IN SECOND TEMPLE LITERATURE

THE IMPORTANCE OF YOM KIPPUR in Israel is evident partly in the fact that the Mishnah reserves an entire tractate, the Yoma, for commentary on the day's rituals.[1] Rabbinic literature—doubtless influenced by Second Temple practice—details aspects of the DA which fill the gaps left by the laconic Levitical account.[2] Nevertheless, readers should avoid concluding that the Mishnah and the Talmud contain precise depictions of what occurred in the Second Temple because no temple or functioning priesthood existed at the time of their final literary form (ca. 200 BCE).[3]

Both the y. and the m. Yoma tractates indicate that the high priest offered the *tāmîd* ("daily, continuous") sacrifices on the DA since this was a "perpetual ordinance."[4] The Rabbis comment that on the DA, the high priest had to offer "the incense of the morning, to trim the lamps, and to offer the head and limbs, baked cakes, and wine. The morning incense ritual occurred between the tossing of the blood and the offering up of the limbs" (m. Yoma 3:4–5). No doubt offering the *tāmîd* alongside the rituals of the DA added to the high priest's substantial workload.

About the clothing of the high priest, the Rabbis reveal: "At dawn he would put on a garment of Pelusium linen worth twelve *manehs*, and at dusk, he wore Indian linen worth eight hundred *zuz*" (m. Yoma 3:7). As the high priest enters the Most Holy Place, he says a short prayer "lest he put Israel in

1. All quotes from the Mishnah are from Neusner, *The Mishnah*.
2. See Stemberger, "Yom Kippur," 121–137; Cohn, *The Memory*, 41–48.
3. See Ben Ezra, *The Impact*, 23.
4. E.g., Exod 27:21; 30:7; Num 8:3; y. Yoma, 3:4–5; 2d; 3:5, a; m. Yoma 1:2; 3:4, 5; Exod 29:38–42; 30:7.

terror" (m. Yoma 5:1) while the people wait expectantly for the completion of the day's activities. The high priest's efficacious performance of the day's rituals spread joy in the camp, as evidenced by the "marriage" games in the afternoon of the DA.

## The Day of Atonement in the Book of Jubilees

The Book of Jubilees (Jub.), a Jewish pseudepigraphon from the second century BCE, was well-known in the early church and was considered canonical by the Ethiopian Orthodox Church. The work is a *midrash* on Genesis 1–Exodus 24 and conflates biblical material with Jewish traditions. As the author acknowledges, "God had made known to Moses more than what one reads in Genesis-Exodus."[5] Originally written in Hebrew, the only complete manuscript of Jub. is in Classical Ethiopic, with fragments in Hebrew, Syriac, and Greek.[6] Charles called it "the most advanced pre-Christian representative of the *midrashic* tendency" in Jewish intertestamental literature.[7]

Jub. contains at least two *allusions* to the DA. The first is Jub. 5:17–18, which utilizes a covenant lawsuit formula calling Israel to repentance in anticipation of Judgment Day: "It has been written and ordained that he will have mercy on all who turn from all their errors once each year."[8] The second one appears in 34:18–19, a *midrash* on the story of Joseph's betrayal by his brothers. According to the author, the day Jacob heard the news was the "tenth of the seventh month," the day of the DA, becoming the basis for the establishment of the ritual:

> 18 For this reason it has been ordained regarding the Israelites that they should be distressed on the tenth of the seventh month—on the day when (the news) which made (him) lament Joseph reached his father Jacob—in order to make atonement for themselves on it with a kid—on the tenth of the seventh month, once a year—for their sins. For they had saddened their father's [feelings of] affection for his son Joseph. 19 This day has been ordained so that they may be saddened on it for their sins, all their transgressions, and all their errors; so that they may purify themselves on this day once a year.[9]

5. VanderKam, "Moses Trumping Moses," 28.
6. VanderKam, *The Book of Jubilees*, ix.
7. *POT* 2:1.
8. VanderKam, *Jubilees* 1–21, 271.
9. VanderKam, *Jubilees* 22–50, 1003.

The passage adds a personal dimension to the DA, for the story of Joseph's betrayal, his exile in Egypt, Jacob's harrowing experience, and the Israelites' victory over Egypt constitute Israel's "family" story. Should Israel fail to repent, the thread of betrayal that connects them to that ancient sin is reattached, and they must dread judgment. Thus, Jub. connects the gravity of the sins of Jacob's sons with his mourning for Joseph's death; personal affliction is contextualized in Jacob's experience. In order to highlight the connection with the DA, the passage echoes the blood of the "goat for the Lord," which atoned for sin by being spilled and sprinkled on the mercy seat (Lev 16:15–16).

Two additional observations support the connection between the story of Joseph and the DA. First, the term "slaughter" (*šāḥaṭ*) which was mostly reserved for the slaughter of sacrificial animals in the Pentateuch, including the "goat for the Lord" in Leviticus 16, appears in the killing of the goat by Joseph's brothers: "and slaughtered a goat" (*wayyišḥaṭû śeʿir*, Gen 37:31). Second, the term for "dipping" in blood also appears in cultic settings (see Lev 4:6; 9:9; 14:6, 51). In addition, the story echoes the rite of the "goat for Azazel" in two ways: (1) Joseph's brothers transfer their guilt to the goat and remove it from their midst by sending its blood to Jacob; (2) in reverse fashion, the separation of Joseph from his brothers represents the fundamental notion of the separation of the righteous (Joseph) from the wicked (his brothers) which underpins the separation of the "goat for Azazel" from the camp. The association between the transfer of the brothers' sin and the rite of the "goat for Azazel" in Jub. is evident in how a sacrificed goat removes their impurity, while Leviticus reserves this function for the "goat for Azazel." Perhaps a better explanation for this use in Jub. may be that, by killing the goat and sending Joseph's coat with its blood to their father, they thought to remove their guilt.[10]

An overlooked *echo* of the "goat for Azazel" ritual is the notion of sending away evil in the form of "binding" in Jub. 10:11–12: "And we acted in accord with all of his words. All of the evil ones, who were cruel, we bound in the place of judgment, but a tenth of them we let remain so that they might be subject to Satan upon the earth."[11] The context of this passage is a complaint by Noah's sons about the influence of evil on their children (Jub. 10:2). Noah prays that his sons may be protected from their influence, asking God

10. See Dorman, "Commit Injustice," 55–56; Carmichael, "The Origin," 177.
11. VanderKam, *Jubilees* 1–21, 394.

to "imprison them and hold them fast in the place of condemnation." The passage connects evil with the ancient, antediluvian Watchers, the "fathers" of these evil spirits (Jub. 10:5) and seems to be based on the same tradition underlying the book of Enoch in which the Watchers, guided by the fallen angel Azazel, led the world into transgression. Although Azazel is not directly mentioned in Jub., it is possible to link the "binding" to a place of judgment to the condemnation of Azazel in 1 Enoch, which parallels the banishment of the "goat for Azazel" to the "wilderness/barren land" (Lev 16:22).

Absent in Jubilees are the temple, the high priest, goats, and uncleanness. According to Dorman, by omitting these elements and other aspects of the ritual, the author turns the DA into "a very personalized day of remembering and confessing sins ... an opportunity to escape judgment" through personal "repentance and mourning."[12]

## The Day of Atonement in the Apocalypse of Abraham

The Apocalypse of Abraham (Apoc. Ab.) is a Jewish pseudepigraphic work composed most likely in the first century CE, having survived only in an old Slavonic translation.[13] Like Jubilees, the book is considered a *midrash* on the calling of Abram interspersed with references to Azazel.[14] The context of the appearance of Azazel in the Apoc. Ab. is as follows: as Abraham struggles to understand why his father Terah has given himself to idolatry and false gods, God appears to Abraham and tells him to offer sacrifices with the help of the angel Yahoel (Apoc. Ab. 9:3–5). After Abraham has divided the animals and waits, an unclean bird flies over the carcass and starts berating Abraham for coming to a holy place to sacrifice. Yahoel then reveals to Abraham that this unclean bird is Azazel and casts a curse on him. Significantly, in Apoc. Ab., Yahoel officiates over Yom Kippur ordinances:[15]

(1) The context of sacrificed animals heightens the significance of the presence of Azazel in the passage, pointing to a DA background.

(2) The passage is based on the idea of two lots, which parallels the lots for the two goats on the DA. This overarching theme of the "two lots" is also

12. Dorman, "Commit Injustice," 52.
13. For a translation of the Apoc. Ab. with Hebrew retroversions, see Kulik, *Retroverting*.
14. Rubinkiewicz, "Apocalypse of Abraham," 685.
15. Orlov, *Yahoel and Metatron*, 113.

attested elsewhere in the Dead Sea Scrolls: "For they are the lot of darkness but the lot of God is for [everlast]ing light (1QM 12:5–6)."[16]

(3) The transfer of Abraham's corruption to Azazel conveys the idea of atonement: "For behold, the garment which in heaven was formerly yours has been set aside for him [Abraham], and the corruption which was on him has gone over to you (13:14)."[17]

(4) Yahoel bids Azazel, "Depart this man!" (Abraham), which parallels the sending away of Azazel into the "wilderness." The expression "inaccessible parts of the earth" may reflect the expression *eis gēn abaton* in Leviticus 16:22 (LXX).[18]

(5) The "dwelling place of your impurity" alludes to the purgative effect that the dismissal of the "goat for Azazel" attains for the community.

(6) Shaming Azazel parallels the later practice of abusing the "goat for Azazel" as it left the camp, a practice attested in rabbinic literature (e.g., m. Yoma 6:3–5).

Andrei Orlov argues that the DA is the most fitting background for this passage due to Azazel's role and the two lots.[19] Elsewhere, Orlov argues that the Hebrew term for "lots" (*gôrāl*) found in Leviticus 16:8–10, could underlie the Slavonic word for "lot" in the Apoc. Ab.[20] Further, the introduction of Azazel as a fallen angel and "arch-demon who rules over all evil agents" in Apoc. Ab. connects the book directly with the DA and is indicative of a well-developed Jewish apocalyptic tradition.[21] This explicit use of DA imagery in Apoc. Ab. is similar to the reconstructed text of 11QMelchizedek.[22]

In addition, Orlov et al. point out how Yahoel's attire mimics that of the OT high priest: the linen around Yahoel's head recalls the Aaronic high-priestly headdress (Exod 28:39); his purple robe is reminiscent of the purple color used in the OT high-priestly dress; his golden staff may have priestly connotations as it mirrors Aaron's budding rod; the rainbow-colored

16. Martínez and Tigchelaar, *The Dead Sea Scrolls*, 135.

17. See Grabbe, "The Scapegoat," 157; Helm, "Azazel," 223: "the transference of Abraham's corruption to Azazel may be a veiled reference to the scapegoat rite."

18. See Ben Ezra, *The Impact*, 94.

19. Orlov, "The Eschatological Yom Kippur," 7.

20. Orlov, "The Likeness of Heaven," 237; see also Orlov, *Heavenly Priesthood*, 73–92; Orlov, *Dark Mirrors*, 27–46; Orlov, *Divine Scapegoats*.

21. Orlov, *The Atoning Dyad*, 87–89; Orlov, "The Pteromorphic Angelology," 830–42; Grabbe, "The Scapegoat," 157.

22. Ben Ezra, *The Impact*, 94; see Rubinkiewicz, "Abraham, Apocalypse of," 42, 43; Rubinkiewicz, *L'Apocalypse d'Abraham*, 98–255.

turban seems to recall the effect of the turban and the golden plate worn on the high priest's forehead. Orlov concludes that Yahoel is not merely an angel but "a priestly figure initiating an apprentice into celestial sacerdotal praxis."[23]

Lastly, Apoc. Ab. portrays Abraham as a sacrifice since "the patriarch's movement upward as an eschatological sacrifice is juxtaposed to Azazel's movement downward as an eschatological scapegoat paralleling the antagonistic movement of the two goats of Leviticus 16," observes Moscicke.[24] Based on the above, it appears that the whole of Apoc. Ab. is built on a purgation rite such as the DA: the sins of idolatry by Terah and Nahor jeopardize the covenant and *echo* the impurity brought into the Most Holy Place by the sins of all Israelites, while Abraham's ascent to heaven reaffirms the covenant.[25]

In addition to the works reviewed above, other pseudepigraphal works allude to the DA. For example, a *quid pro quo* relationship between the earthly and heavenly sanctuaries can be seen in the Testament of Levi 312; the high-priestly entrance to the Most Holy Place symbolizes ascents into the heavenly Holy of Holies, and the offering of intercessory prayer there.[26] In 11QMelchizedek II, 6–8, Melchizedek, the leader of the heavenly forces, atones for all the sins of the sons of light on the DA at the end of the tenth jubilee. The text, as reconstructed by Parry and Tov, reads:

> And this [wil]l [happen] in the first week of the jubilee (that occurs) after [the] ni[ne] jubilees. And the D[ay of Atone]ment i[s] the e[nd of] the tenth [ju]bilee, in which atonement shall be made for all the sons of [light and for] the men [of] the lot of Mel[chi]zedek[ ] over [th]em [ ] accor[ding to] a[ll] their [doing]s.[27]

Three additional references to the DA are found in the Book of Giants (4Q203), which expand aspects of the punishment meted out on the "goat for Azazel" by making him suffer for the sins of all the fallen angels. The text as reconstructed by Martinez and Tigchelaar reads:

23. Orlov, "The Eschatological Yom Kippur," 81. See Orlov, *Yahoel and Metatron*, 111–115.
24. Moscicke, *The New Day of Atonement*, 80.
25. Orlov, "The Eschatological Yom Kippur," 110.
26. Ben Ezra, *The Impact*, 79, 82, 91.
27. Parry and Tov, *Exegetical Texts*, 25.

> and [yo]ur power [...] Th[en] 'Ohyah [said] to Hahy[ah, his brother ...] Then he punished, and not us, [bu]t Aza[ze]l and made [him ... the sons of] Watchers, the Giants; and n[o]ne of [their] be[loved] will be forgiven [...] ... he has imprisoned us and has captured yo[u] ...[28]

A similar concept is found in the Ages of Creation (4Q180–181). Martinez and Tigchelaar render the text thus:

> [And] interpretation concerning 'Azaz'el [עזזאל] and the angels wh[o came to the daughters of man] [and s]ired themselves giants. And concerning 'Azaz'el [עזזאל] [is written ...] [to love] injustice and to let him inherit evil for all [his] ag[e ... ] [ ... ] (of the) judgments and the judgment of the council of [...].[29]

In 1QpHab, a *pesher* on the book of Habakkuk, when commenting on Hab 2:15 ("Alas for you who make your neighbors drink, pouring out your wrath until they are drunk, in order to gaze on their nakedness!"), the author explains: "This refers to the Wicked Priest, who pursued the Teacher of Righteousness to destroy him in the heat of his anger at his place of exile. At the time set aside for the repose of the Day of Atonement he [the Wicked Priest] appeared to them to destroy them and to bring them to ruin on the fast-day, the Sabbath intended for their repose" (col. XI, 4–8).[30]

## Azazel in 1 Enoch

Azazel is quite prominent in the book of 1 Enoch as the leader of the fallen angels and demonic adversary (8:1; 9:6; 10:4–8; 13:1–2; 54:4–6; 55:4; 69:2). Unfortunately, some sections of 1 Enoch (such as chapter 54) did not survive in their Greek version to allow an analysis of the text in light of the LXX and the Greek NT. Due to the importance of these *allusions* to Azazel in 1 Enoch to our study, their extensive intertextual connections with Leviticus 16 and Revelation will be explored at length in chapter 4.

28. *The Dead Sea Scrolls*, 1:411.
29. *The Dead Sea Scrolls*, 1:370–373.
30. Parry and Tov, *Exegetical Texts*, 91.

## The Day of Atonement in Philo

In *De Specialibus Legibus* 1.186–188, Philo describes the DA as "the fast."[31] Several elements stand out in this passage. First, the high priest is conspicuously absent. Second, Philo states that even the non-religious among the Jews participate in "the Fast" because of its solemnity and describes the DA as a "national feast" (*heortē*), and a day for "purification and escape from sin" (*katharseōs kai psyguēs hamartēmatōn*). Philo then compares the DA to the preceding feast of trumpets because the same number of sacrifices was used. In his description of the animals sacrificed, Philo alludes to Numbers 29:7–11 by using the exact words for bull and ram as the LXX, *moschon* and *krion*, while using *arnas* for the seven lambs (instead of LXX's *amnous*). The process of choosing the goats by casting lots is akin to that described in m. Yoma, with the difference that in Yoma, the "goat for Azazel" was killed. Philo states that the goat carries "curses and offenses" (*atribē kai abaton*) into the desert. Philo forgoes any mention of the name Azazel and ends the passage by explaining that the offender's penitence turns to tangible transformation on the DA when the offender "changes for the better." Such purification was accomplished by God, to whom repentance (*metanoia*) is equal to not sinning at all.

There are also *allusions* to Leviticus 16 elsewhere in Philo. In *De Plantatione* 61, Philo mentions the "goat for Azazel" ritual: "on that day the people are enjoined to take by lot two goats, one for the Lord, and one to be the scapegoat [*tō apopompaiō*]." Philo revisits the "goat for Azazel" rite again in *De Posteritate Caini* 20: "He shall place it living before the Lord, that he may offer prayers over it, and send it out into the wilderness."[32] He also mentions the high priest's entrance into the Holy of Holies in two separate texts: once in *Quis Rerum Divinarum Heres Sit* 16, and twice in *De Somnis* 28, 34. In *Legum Alegoriae* II.56, Philo discusses the garment worn by the high priest on the DA, stating that he did not use his regular clothing to enter into the Holy of Holies. Other passages by Philo (e.g., *De Specialibus Legibus* 2:193–203) dealing with the high priest and the DA are largely allegorical and offer little, if any, insight into the practice of the DA in his context. Ultimately, when Philo makes literal references to the DA, he reflects the practice of the Diaspora.[33]

31. See Yonge, *The Works of Philo*, 551. For a discussion on Philo's *allusions* to the Day of Atonement, see Ben Ezra, *The Impact*, 107–114; Scullion, "A Traditio-Historical Study," 152–187; Deiana, "Il giorno del *Kippur*," 891–905.

32. Yonge, *The Works of Philo*, 138.

33. See Ben Ezra, *The Impact*, *114.*

## The Day of Atonement in Josephus

Despite the importance of the DA for Judaism, it is surprising that Jewish historian Josephus does not deal with the DA at any significant length. For example, in *Wars* 5.236, Josephus explains that the high priest did not wear his full attire when he went into the Most Holy Place. In *Ant.* 3.159–187, Josephus deals mainly with high-priestly clothing, while no mention is made of the DA. A more extended description of the DA is found in *Ant.* 3.240–243:

> (240) On the tenth day of the same lunar month, they fast till the evening; and this day they sacrifice a bull, and two rams, and seven lambs, and a kid [of goats] as sin offering. (241) But besides these they offer two kids, of which one is sent alive into the wilderness beyond the frontiers, being intended to avert and serve as an expiation for the sins of the whole people; while the other they conduct to the suburbs to a spot that is perfectly pure, and there burn it, skin and all, without any cleansing whatsoever. (242) Along with it is burnt a bullock, which is not offered by the community but is provided at his own expense by the high-priest. So soon as this bullock has been slain, he brings into the sanctuary some of its blood, as also of the blood of the kid, and with his finger sprinkles it toward the ceiling seven times, (243) and likewise on the floor, and as many times over the sanctuary itself and around the golden altar; the rest he carries into the outer court and sprinkles about the larger altar. Furthermore, they lay upon the altar the extremities, the kidneys, and the fat with the lobe of the liver. The high-priest also provides on his own account a ram for a burnt offering to God.[34]

In this passage, Josephus conflates Numbers 29:7–11 and Leviticus 16, with a few differences: he omits the priestly ablutions, the high-priestly attire, the offering of incense, and the name Azazel, simply speaking of that rite as *ho men zōn eis tēn hyperorion erēmian pempetai apotropiasmos*, which H. Thackeray translated as "of which one is sent alive into the wilderness beyond the frontiers, being intended to avert." Josephus also adds that the live goat served as *paraitēsis*, "intercession" for the whole people, likely a reference to the high-priestly confession of sin over the head of the goat (LXX = *exagoreusei*, "confess," Lev 16:21). In *Ant.* 17.165–166, Josephus mentions "the fast of the Jews" (*hēn Ioudaioi nēsteian*) in a passage describing high priest Matthias's disqualification to perform on that DA, which confirms the practice found in m. Yoma 1:7.[35]

34. *LOEB* IV:433.

35. See Begg, "Yom Kippur," 110; Ben Ezra, *The Impact*, 22; Milgrom, *Leviticus 1–16*, 1116.

## Conclusion

This brief chapter offered a brief overview of how the DA continued to reverberate in Jewish life, as indicated by how the authors of deuterocanonical literature built on the biblical DA, even as their reflections both enhance and depart from the biblical text. Azazel is portrayed as a demonic entity in several of these books, a symbolism that betrays an ancient undercurrent of meaning in Leviticus. More importantly, some of the references to the DA outside of the biblical canon clarify how Jewish understanding of this day evolved as it became inseparable from the experience of Jews in all times and places and provided significant theological motifs for Jewish authors and their readers. As we will see in the next chapter, the DA remained a powerful source of imagery for early Christian writers, including John the Revelator.

3

# THE DAY OF ATONEMENT IN THE NEW TESTAMENT

THIS CHAPTER EXPLORES HOW the Levitical DA was received and reworked in early Christianity in light of "the Christ event." We begin with a brief overview of the reception of the Jewish feasts in early Christianity, followed by an analysis of *allusions* and *echoes* of the DA in specific passages of the NT. This chapter constitutes a prelude to the intertextual approach applied to the book of Revelation in the next chapter.

## THE JEWISH FEASTS IN NASCENT CHRISTIANITY

The NT writers operated within a religious matrix of sacred texts and traditions pregnant with prophetic, typological, and eschatological meaning. The arrival of Jesus Christ as the *messiah* had been foreseen in ancient oracles emanating from the Hebrews Scriptures, enacted in the rituals of Jewish life, and hoped fervently in their hearts. Philip's invitation to Nathanael to "come and see" (John 1:46) is emblematic of the evangelists' confidence in the veracity of their witness: they had seen it with their own eyes Jesus die for their sins and resurrect on the third day "according to the Scriptures" (1 Cor 15:3–4). The OT is "was the swaddling cloths and the manger in which Christ lies," Luther wrote in the preface of his Bible translation.

Early Christians understood the sanctuary rituals and Jewish feasts as *prefigurations* of Jesus' life, death, resurrection, and exaltation. Applying a "figural christological reading," they reread their sacred texts and religious traditions in light of Jesus' life, death, resurrection, and exaltation, identifying intertextual signals emanating from the Hebrew Scriptures and reading

Jesus Christ back into them.[1] In a type of "retrospective signification," they ran a continuous, crimson thread through Scripture, weaving Jesus into the OT. As Hays eloquently stated, the NT authors expected their readers to experience a "conversion of the imagination" to find Christ's footprints all over their past.[2] This is palpable in the many *quotations, allusions,* and *echoes* of the OT found in the Gospels, Paul's frequent appeal to the Hebrew Scriptures to explain Jesus, the author of Hebrews' exposition of the tabernacle in light of Jesus' death and ascension, and Revelation's vast network of OT *allusions* and *echoes.*

There is even evidence that the early Christians, coming from this Judaic milieu, may have continued to observe some Jewish feasts.[3] This should not be surprising since. For example, Acts 2:1 has Jewish Christians gathered on Pentecost. In his letter to the Corinthian believers, Paul evokes the Passover lamb: "Christ, our Passover lamb has been sacrificed," and urges them to "celebrate the feast" (1 Cor 5:7, 8), likely an invitation to actual participation in Passover.[4] For Paul, Jesus had also been *prefigured* in the feast of First Fruits when he rose from the dead as the "first fruits of those who sleep" (1 Cor 15:20–23). Paul uses Pentecost and the DA as time referents: he times his stay in Ephesus "until Pentecost" in 1 Cor 16:8 (see Acts 20:16), and advises against continuing on their ocean voyage because "the Fast," i.e., the DA, had already passed, putting their weeks-long journey too close to winter (Acts 27:9).[5] Likewise, Peter compares the blood of Christ with that of a sacrificial lamb "without defect or blemish" (1 Pet 1:19; Exod 12:5), also an *allusion* to the Passover lamb, but also to the lambs of the daily *tāmîd* rituals in the tabernacle.

And yet, despite their typological significance in the NT, it is essential to note that *allusions* to the Jewish feasts may not have been commands that Christians should embrace Jewish practices. Paul criticized the Galatians' "Jewish time-keeping scheme" of "observing special days, and months, and seasons, and years" (Gal 4:10) as a means to gain salvation.[6] As he explained to the Corinthians, the OT constituted "types" (*typos*) that prefigured Christ

1. See Hays, *Reading Backwards,* 94; Hays, *Echoes of Scripture in the Gospels,* 2.

2. Hays, *Conversion of the Imagination,* 5–6.

3. Dunn, *Romans 9–16,* 806.

4. See Paxy, *Death,* 127–131, 137; Thiselton, *The First Epistle to the Corinthians,* 406.

5. Crossan, *The Cross That Spoke,* proposes that all passion narratives are built on the DA rituals via the Gospel of Peter. For criticism of this view, see Henderson, *The Gospel of Peter,* 26–42; Green, "The Gospel of Peter," 293–301; Fuller, Review of *The Cross That Spoke,* 71–73.

6. Martin, "Pagan and Judeo-Christian," 105. See the comprehensive analysis of the lists found in Gal 4:10 and Col 2:16 in Lightfoot, *Saint Paul's Epistles,* 193–4. See also Ben Ezra, "Christians Observing," 59–61.

(1 Cor 10:11). Colossian believers had been emancipated from having to perform under the old system because those were merely a "shadow" (*skia*) of what was accomplished in Christ (Col 2:16–17; 1 Thess 4:13–18). As in Colossae, Roman Christians should not become burdened with Jewish categories of "matters of food," but gentile Christians, whom he called "strong," could hold views that differed from those held by "weak" Christians (Rom 14:1–15:13).[7]

Even as Christianity's ties to Judaism waned towards the end of the first century, its relationship to Judaism was not monolithic. Irenaeus, for example, reveals that Christian martyr Polycarp (born ca. 80 CE) had kept Passover from childhood, while other church fathers were critical of Jewish Christians who observed the seventh-day Sabbath and Passover on the fourteenth of Nisan.[8] Ben Ezra suggests that Yom Kippur was observed in some Christian communities in Syria-Palestine well into the fourth century, while Passover and Pentecost held considerable appeal in other communities.[9] At the same time, there is little indication that the Christians who did observe them did so as the Jews or that the church followed a set calendar. It is more likely that the Jewish feasts held evangelistic significance for early Christians eager to preserve covenantal continuity with the OT in light of Jesus Christ's messianic claims.[10]

## The Day of Atonement in the New Testament

As previously suggested, the Hebrew Scriptures afforded explanatory power for the life, death, resurrection, and ascension of Jesus Christ in the eyes of the NT writers. In light of the atonement accomplished by Jesus, the author of the Epistle to the Hebrews declared the old covenant with Israel "obsolete" and "old" (Heb 8:13).[11] Standing in sharp relief in the typological

7. Meeks, *In Search*, 156. See also Young, "Romans 14:5–6," 51–70; Sampley, "The Weak," 40–52; Porter, *The Letter to the Romans*, 258.

8. *Adversus Haereses* iii. 3.4; Buchanan, "Worship," 297. For a discussion of Quartodecimanism, i.e., Passover on the 14th of Nisan, see Matson, "The Historical Plausibility," 302–306.

9. Ben Ezra, *The Impact*, 214, 221. See Fitzmyer, "The Ascension of Christ," 430; Burtchaell, *From Synagogue to Church*, 274; Tiwald, "Christ as Hilasterion," 198.

10. Davies, "Reflections," 132.

11. Davis, "Acts 2," 42, writes: "Whatever purpose God meant for failed Israel at Sinai, he means to fulfill through his church and Christ." Replacement theory has dominated Christian theology since patristic times, but rebuttals abound. Carroll, *Constantine's Sword*, 58, raised concerns about supersessionism because "replacement implied the elimination of the replaced." See also Wright, *Paul*; Vlach, *Has the Church Replaced*

landscape of the OT, the Hebrew cultus provided Christians clarity about the meaning of its rituals within a covenantal continuum, which now centered on the person of Jesus Christ. As observed by Oscar Cullmann, Jesus as a high priest underlies "the Christological statements" in the NT.[12]

As early Christianity emerged from Judaism, it continued to operate under the influence of Second Temple religious practices, as evidenced by how NT writers, writing many decades after the events, often drew on temple imagery. In this context, Leviticus provided relevant parallels to the atoning work of Christ, suggests Kiuchi.[13] As the yearly culmination of its rituals, the DA held a dominant influence in Judaism at the rise of Christianity and played a central role in developing the Christian understanding of Jesus' atoning sacrifice. "Good Friday," concludes Hartley, "became the Christians' Day of Atonement ... a day of self-denial, penance, expiation, and reconciliation."[14] Thus, we can agree with Rylaarsdam that: "The New Testament passion narratives, the Letter to the Hebrews and the writings of Paul are all in various ways under its [DA] impact."[15] The DA had meaningful applications for the readers of the Epistle to the Hebrews, both in its overarching typological framework and because of the DA's eschatological overtones as a microcosm of God's final purification of the created order.[16] The author builds on the DA to portray Jesus as a *sacrifice* and as *a high priest* who achieved victory for the believer by entering into the heavenly Most Holy Place with his own blood (Heb 6:19–20; 9:12, 24).[17]

Moving sequentially through the NT canon, the following sections explore how its writers, applying a "Christological exegesis" of the OT, read Jesus Christ back into the Levitical Day of Atonement.

12. Cullmann, *The Christology*, 107.

13. Kiuchi, *Leviticus*, 47; see also Eberhart, "To Atone," 231.

14. Young, "The Impact," 6; Hartley, *Leviticus*, 220.

15. Rylaarsdam, "Day of Atonement," 313.

16. Young, "The Impact," 9; Tiwald, "Hilasterion," 197; Ben Ezra, *The Impact*, 89. See also Aune, "Understanding," 242.

17. Moffit, "Blood, Life," 219 observes: "Thus, if there is any focal point of Yom Kippur, it was on the sprinkling of the blood in the holy of holies. That is to say, it was the moment when the life of the animal was taken into God's presence." Barker perhaps overstating her case, suggests that "the picture of Jesus as the great high priest in all his roles and aspects appears throughout the New Testament and is the key to understanding all early Christian teaching about hi." (*Revelation*, 4).

## The Day of Atonement in the Gospels

In the Gospels, "the Christ event" stands as the fulfillment of ancient OT Messianic prophecies, as well as the typological culmination of the Jewish system of blood rituals, sacrifices, offerings, and feasts. While *allusions* to OT Messianic prophecies occur primarily in the Gospel of Matthew, John uses four festivals to highlight some aspect of Jesus ministry: the Sabbath, the Feast of Passover, the Feast of Tabernacles, and the Feast of Dedication (e.g., John 2:13–25; 10:22–42; 13:19).[18] As seen below, a few *allusions* and *echoes* to the DA can be detected in the Gospels.

### *"My Blood Poured Out for Many" (Mark 14:24)*

The Gospel of Mark relates several sayings by Jesus on his last meal with the disciples, one of which has clear sacrificial connotations: "This is my blood of the covenant, which is poured out for many" (Mark 14:24). The Greek expression *haima ekchein* ("to pour out blood") appears nine times in Leviticus in the instructions for pouring blood at the base of the altar contexts of sacrificial blood.[19] Significantly, in an *allusion* to Isaiah 53:12, the parallel passage in Matt 26:28 contains the gloss "for the forgiveness of sins" (*eis aphesin hamartiōn*). Because blood was not poured around the altar on the DA, the exact phrase does not occur in Leviticus 16. At the same time, as such, the expression in the Gospels does not point to a single sacrifice per se, but the notion of blood spilled "for many" (*hyper pollōn*), along with Matthew's gloss, points to an atoning sacrifice for the sins of the entire community, which may *echo* the DA.[20]

### *The Release of Barabbas (Matt 27:15–23)*

Church fathers associated the passion narratives in the Gospels with the two goats of Leviticus 16, claiming that Jesus fulfilled both the typology of the "goat for the Lord," as well as that of the "goat for Azazel." Early Christian interest in the "scapegoat" typology of Leviticus 16 is due to four factors, as

18. Isa 7:14 in 1:22–23; Mic 5:2 in 2:4–7; Hos 11:1 in 2:15; Jer 31:15 in 2:17–18; Jesus' birth in Nazareth in 2:23; Isa 40:3 in 3:3; Isa 9:1–2 in 4:12–17; Isa 53:4 in 8:16–17; Isa 42:1–4 in 12:15–21; Isa 6:9–10 in 13:13–15; Ps 78:2 in 13:34–35; Isa 29:13 in 15:7–9; Zech 9:9 in 21:1–5; Ps 118:22–23 in 21:33–43; Zech 13:7 in 26:31; Zech 11:13 in 27:3–10; Ps 22:18 in 27:35. See Yee, *Jewish Feasts*, 30.

19. Lev 4:7, 18, 25, 30, 34; 8:15; 9:9; 17:4, 13; Exod 29:12.

20. See Collins, "Finding Meaning," 177; Collins, "Mark's Interpretation," 545–554.

articulated by Stökl: (1) the Christianization of the Jewish Scriptures; (2) an interest in the Jewish Yom Kippur; (3) the Greek *pharmakos* ritual; and (4) a reaction to the polytheistic interpretation caused by Julian's pagan revival.[21] Such "Christological goat typologies" as described in a recent monograph by Moscicke can be seen in the Epistle of Barnabas, Justin Martyr, Tertullian, Hippolytus, Origen, Jerome, Cyril of Alexandria, as well as the earliest commentary on the Gospel of Mark.[22]

The Gospel of Matthew reveals dependence on DA imagery, particularly in the passion narratives. The first is the release of Barabbas in Matt 27:15–23, which appears to allude to the "goat for Azazel"'s release. Scholars are virtually unanimous that the *privilegium paschalis*, i.e., the liberation of a criminal by a Roman authority before a Jewish feast, has not yet been historically attested, and a theological explanation for such episode has been sought. As early as the nineteenth century, scholars have argued that the Gospels' accounts of the release of Barabbas are based on the ritual of the "goat for Azazel," for a couple of reasons: (1) the use of a system of "lots" to decide the fate of each prisoner, as was used for both goats on the DA; (2) the release of one to be killed and the other, more objectionable candidate—to be released; and (3) a symbolic, inverted transfer of the guilt from the murderous Barabbas to the Jewish leaders, reminiscent of the transfer of guilt to the "goat for Azazel."[23] Building on these parallels, Maclean sees a parallel with the goats of the DA in that "one is killed, the other is released."[24] Maclean argues that the mob could be appealing to Roman urges to eliminate unwanted characters when they ask Pilate to "eliminate" Jesus from their midst while taking Barabbas' fate (blood) into their own hands. For this, she sees the Greek text as ambiguous: by saying, "His blood be on us and on our children!" the mob could be referring to Barabbas and not Jesus. Similarly, Ben Ezra suggests that the DA served as a "catalyst" in the narrative: "they choose the wrong goat, Jesus Barabbas, who is released in their midst (and consequently pollutes them), and hence as sacrificial goat, the wrong goat, Jesus of Nazareth, whose blood, spilled at the wrong place, also pollutes them."[25]

More recently, Moscicke has expanded the DA scapegoat typology found in the release of Barabbas to include four new concepts of his own (4–7 be-

21. Stökl, "The Christian Exegesis," 212.
22. Moscicke, *The New Day of Atonement*, 8; 99–137; see Hamilton, *The Death*, 221.
23. See Wratislaw, "The Scapegoat-Barrabas," 400–403.
24. Maclean, "Barabbas," 317.
25. Ben Ezra, *The Impact*, 171; Ben Ezra, "Fasting with Jews," 183.

low), which he summarizes as follows: (1) the similarity of the two goats; (2) the opposing designations of the two goats; (3) the priestly lottery between the two goats; (4) the dismissal of the scapegoat to Azazel; (5) the transference of iniquity by ritual hand-action and confession; (6) banishment and inhabitation in a wilderness; and (7) the inheritance of iniquity and a curse.[26]

Further, in support of a possible Roman elimination rite akin to the Greek *pharmakos* tradition, Koester observes that Matthew uses the term for Jesus' "scarlet robe" (*clamyda kokkinēn*, Matt 27:28), which differs from Mark's "purple cloak" (*porphyra*, Mar 15:17; see John 19:2, 5). Matthew's terminology is like that of Barnabas 7:8 (*to erion to kokkinon*), which the author uses to compare Jesus' humiliation to the dismissal of the "goat for Azazel." However, this rather loose reference based solely on the word *kokkinon*, if an *allusion* to the *pharmakos* rite, may have simply served as a rhetorical device to enhance the attitude and role of Jesus' killers (the Romans) in light of their own elimination rites, instead of attempting to liken Jesus' sacrifice to that of the "goat for Azazel" in the eyes of Jewish Christians.[27] Considering the well-established tradition that Azazel was a desert demon, it is highly improbable that Matthew would have connected Jesus to this ritual specifically. Be that as it may, there are enough correspondences in the episode of the release of Barabbas to establish at least some correspondence with the "goat for Azazel" ritual.

## *Jesus' Humiliation (Mark 15:16–20; Matt 27:27–31)*

Moscicke suggests that Matt 27:27–31 reflects a Matthean typology "that depicts Jesus as the 'goat for Azazel.'"[28] Indeed, in his landmark work, *The Death of the Messiah*, Brown explored the "verisimilitude" between the mocking of Jesus and four Graeco-Roman backgrounds for the episode: (1) historical incidents; (2) games of mockery; (3) theatrical mimes; and (4) carnival festivals.[29] Thus, it is not implausible that Matthew did intend to portray Jesus' procession to Calvary as the march of the "goat for Azazel" via ancient Greek elimination rites in which a *pharmakos* was abused on the way out of the city after being clothed in fancy clothes.[30] Collins agrees when

26. Moscicke, *The New Day of Atonement*, 135.

27. See Koester, *Ancient Christian Gospels*, 225–226; Collins, "Finding Meaning," 195.

28. Moscicke, *The New Day of Atonement*, 169; 202–218.

29. Brown, *The Death of the Messiah*, 874–877.

30. See Parker, *On Greek Religion*, 217; Bremmer, "Scapegoat Rituals," 273–277; B. H. McLean, *The Cursed Christ*, 65–104.

she suggests that the mocking of Jesus by the soldiers "seems to be a literary reconfiguration of the ritual in which the *pharmakós* takes on himself all the impurity, disease, and sin of the community."[31] If this was indeed the synoptists' intention, then, similarly to the release of Barabbas, the mocking of Jesus in the *Via Dolorosa* could be a portrayal of Jesus as a *pharmakos* in Graeco-Roman eyes and not necessarily a Judeo-Christian interpretation of the event. Again, this potential correspondence with the goat of Azazel rite need not weaken the far stronger connection between the pouring of Jesus' atoning blood with that of the "goat for the Lord" as an early Christian baseline understanding of his death.

## *The Veil of the Temple (Mark 15:38; Matt 27:50–54; Luke 23:45)*

The rending of "the veil of the temple" (*katapetasma tou naou*)—the *velum scissum*—reflects Mark's temple motif. It is the only element found in the parallel passages in Matthew and Luke describing a series of phenomena that took place simultaneously with Jesus' death: the darkening of the sun, the earthquake, and the resurrection of saints.[32] In all Gospel accounts, the rending of the veil of the temple "from top to bottom" implies a divine act, especially considering the Rabbinic tradition in the Mishnah, according to which the veil of the Most Holy Place was four inches thick.[33] Nevertheless, despite the dramatic nature of this event, none of the synoptists attempts to explain its meaning, perhaps because, as Gurtner suggested, "there is no precedent in Judaism for what the tearing of the veil symbolizes."[34] This deficiency, however, has not prevented scholars from offering explanations.[35] Nolland sees it as a "signal of the coming doom of the temple," a position also held by Hagner.[36] Thus, God's rending of the veil, indicating a cessation of the temple's ceremonial function, eclipses the parallel rending of Caiaphas's robe in Matt 25:65 as an act of outrage for "transgressions" inflicted on his office. Gurtner has capitalized on several motifs that run through Jesus' baptism and his death and sees cosmic relevance in the rending of the veil of the temple; according to him, it is "stock apocalyptic imagery" that creates a

31. Collins, "Finding Meaning," 195.

32. See Chronis, "The Torn Veil," 107; Gray, *The Temple*.

33. See Hagner, *Matthew 14–28*, 849; see m. Sheqal. 8:5.

34. Gurtner, "The Rending," 292–306; see Gurtner, *The Torn Veil*; Gurtner, "The Veil," 97–114. See also Plummer, "Something Awry," 301–16.

35. For an overview of the views, see Gurtner, "The Rending," 4–14.

36. Nolland, *The Gospel of Matthew*, 1212; Hagner, *Matthew 14–28*, 849.

thematic thread connecting the affirmation of Jesus' divinity at the "rending of the heavens" at his baptism and the similar confession made by the centurion at the cross (Mark 1:10; 15:39).[37]

The connection between the veil of the temple and the death of Christ may be indicative of a shared tradition underlying the Gospels and the Epistle to the Hebrews that associated the shedding of Jesus' blood on the cross with the blood rituals of the sanctuary.[38] The implication is that the veil in question is that of the Most Holy Place since this was the only veil connected to blood rituals and the only one that had cultic meaning. At least two observations support this conclusion. First, the veil of the Most Holy Place is a central element of the blood rituals on the DA: rituals occurred either "outside of the veil" or "within the veil." Each purification of the Most Holy Place and the Holy Place involved seven blood sprinklings before this veil (Lev 4: 6, 7, 18; 16:14, 15). Moreover, although the LXX does use the word *katapetasma* for the two curtains of the tabernacle building, the Hebrew terminology used in Exodus to describe the curtains of the sanctuary is distinct: (1) the coverings that surrounded the sanctuary are called *yᵉrî ʿōṯ* (Exod 26:1); (2) the curtain at the door of the tabernacle leading into the Holy Place is also called *yᵉrî ʿâ* (Exod 26:9) but also *māsāḵ* (Exod 26:36); (3) the curtain at the entrance of the court of the tabernacle is also called *māsāḵ* (Exod 27:16); (4) the curtains/hangings around the entire outer court which housed the tabernacle are called *qᵉlā ʿîm* (Exod 38:15); and (5) the veil separating the Holy Place from the Most Holy Place has a unique name not shared by any of the other sanctuary curtains, *pārōḵeṯ*.[39] This term appears in Leviticus 16:2, 12, 15 in the phrase "within the veil" (*mibbēṯ lappārōḵeṯ*) to specify that blood is to be sprinkled inside the Most Holy Place, and once in Exodus 26:33 to determine where the utensils of the Most Holy Place should be placed, i.e., "within the veil." The expression *mibbēṯ lappārōḵeṯ* is always translated as *esōteron tou katapetasmatos* in the LXX and is used in the Epistle to the Hebrews to speak of Jesus' going "within the veil" (*esōteron tou katapetasmatos*, Heb 6:19–20; 10:19–20). This evidence indicates that *katapetasma* in the Synoptics refers to the veil *par excellence* of the temple, the veil of the Most Holy Place.

37. Gurtner, "The Rending," 297. See Motyer, "The Rending," 155–157; Ulansey, "The Heavenly Veil," 123–25, argued that the torn veil was the outer *katapetasma*, based on Josephus's description that "it typified the universe" (*Wars* 5.5.4.211–212). See also Jackson, "The Death," 22.

38. Lindeskog, "Der Prozeß," 325–36; Lindeskog, "The Veil," 132–37.

39. See Gurtner, "The 'House of the Veil,'" 187–200.

This conclusion is not made on lexical evidence alone but also on functional grounds: as the main curtain of the temple, the veil of the Most Holy Place was the only veil possessing cultic significance.[40] Whereas the other coverings of the sanctuary veiled the sanctuary partially and had no cultic function other than covering the sanctuary, the veil of the Most Holy Place veiled God's presence in the tabernacle, except once a year on the DA. As Moscicke rightly concludes, "Matthew's *velum scissum* seems more specifically to evoke the high priest's entrance through the *katapetasma* into the Holy of Holies with the blood of the immolated goat on the Day of Atonement."[41] By opening the view into the Most Holy Place at the moment of Jesus' death, the synoptists connect it with the rituals performed "within the veil" on the DA, thus rendering the inner sanctum commonplace, open to the view of mere mortals.[42] Thus, the open access to the Most Holy Place in connection with the blood rites of the DA is the most likely source of the imagery of the *velum scissum* in the Synoptics.

### *Jesus as a High Priest in the Gospel of John*

As seen above, four Jewish festivals appear in the Gospel of John: the Sabbath, the Feast of Passover, the Feast of Tabernacles, and the Feast of Dedication (e.g., John 2:13–25; 10:22–42; 13:19).[43]

Heil presents evidence for the portrayal of Jesus as a high priest in the following Johannine passages: (1) the plot by the high priest Caiaphas to kill Jesus (John 11:45–53); (2) Jesus' arrest and trial before the high priest Caiaphas (John 18:1–27); (3) Jesus' seamless tunic (John 19:23–24) as a high-priestly robe.[44] Heil constructs his argument on the first two points by drawing contrasts between Caiaphas and Jesus. While plotting to kill Jesus, Caiaphas's arrogance in calling the Sanhedrin "ignorant" is contrasted with Jesus' humility in bestowing knowledge on his disciples (John 10:14–15; 11:49–50). High priest Caiaphas is under the influence of God himself (see "not of his own," 11:51) as he prophesies that Jesus would die for the whole nation (John 11:50). Heil also highlights the possible link between the expression "once a year" (*hapax tou eniautou*) in Leviticus 16:34 and Caiaphas designation as the high priest "that year" (*eniautou ekeinou*, John 11:51). The

40. See Nolland, *The Gospel of Matthew*, 1212; see Schneider, "καταπέτασμα," 629–630.
41. Moscicke, *The New Day of Atonement*, 199.
42. Witherup "The Death of Jesus," 580, sees the event as a "salvation-historical indicator."
43. See Lunn, "Jesus, the Ark," 736.
44. Heil, "Jesus as Unique High Priest," 729–745.

irony for Caiaphas in this possible *echo* of the DA Leviticus 16 is that it fell on him to perform the ultimate DA sacrifice by having Jesus killed as an atonement sacrifice for the nation.

Further, by contrasting Jesus' seamless tunic with the Caiaphas's torn robe, the Synoptics confer a superior high priesthood on Jesus. Heil also suggests a connection between Christ's seamless tunic "woven in one piece from the top" (*ek tōn anōthen hyphantos di' holou*, John 19:23; see Ps 22:18) with passages in the LXX describing the clothing of the high priest: it was "skillfully worked" (*ergon hyphanto poikiltou*, Exod 28:6) and the tunic and the ephod were woven "whole" (*ergon hyphantos holon*, Exod 28:31; 36:29). This *allusion* to high-priestly dress in the context of Christ's atoning sacrifice may strengthen its connection with the rending of the veil of the temple "from top to bottom" and its related DA themes.

## The Day of Atonement in Acts and the Epistles

The only chronological reference to the passage of the DA in the NT is found in Acts 27:9: "Since much time had been lost and sailing was now dangerous, because even the Fast [*tēn nesteian*] had already gone by ... "[45] The context pertains to Paul's travel to Rome to appear before Caesar, and the passage of the DA sometime before the events described (either in late September or early October according to the Jewish calendrical rules) indicates that conditions of travel by sea were quickly deteriorating. The use of "the Fast" as a temporal marker here may signify the lateness of the DA that year (when adding an intercalary month of Adar II before Passover), most likely in October, which would put the journey in the no-travel period of November through February.[46] James Dunn thinks the implication of this reference to the DA may be more serious, namely, that "Paul and his companions continued to observe this distinctive Jewish holy day."[47]

A possible *echo* of the DA may be found in the description of the ascension of Jesus in Acts 1:9: "When he had said this, as they were watching, he was lifted up, and a cloud [*nephelē*] took him out of their sight." Assuming a

45. See Ben Ezra, *The Impact*, 215.

46. See Polhill, *Acts*, 518.

47. Dunn, *The Acts*, 338; see Ben Ezra, "Whose Fast Is It," 259–282.

shared tradition between John, Acts, and the Epistle to the Hebrews that saw Jesus as heavenly high priest, the presence of the cloud at his ascension may present verbal and thematic links with the DA. The cloud that hid God above the mercy seat and the cloud of incense hiding the high priest on the DA may provide a source of the cloud imagery that hides Jesus at his ascension as he enters the presence of God. Moreover, there may be a thematic link between "entering" covered by a "cloud" into the Most Holy Place and Jesus' entrance into heaven with "a cloud."[48] As the Aaronic high priest "entered" into the presence of God residing in the Most Holy Place, Jesus "entered heaven itself," "within the veil" (Heb 6:19–20). As the high priest goes into the presence of the Lord on the DA, Jesus ascended into heaven itself to stand in the presence of the Father as a high priest to intercede for his people (Heb 7:25; 9:24; Rom 8:34; Eph 1:20–21).

### *The Day of Atonement in the Letters of Paul*

In the writings of Paul, we find the most extensive treatment of Christ's death as an atonement for sin in the NT.[49] Paul employs DA imagery when he compares Christ to the "mercy seat" in Romans 3:25: "through the redemption that is in Christ Jesus, whom God put forward as a sacrifice of atonement [*hilastērion*] by his blood, effective through faith."[50] The term *hilastērion* is used in the LXX to translate all twenty-one occurrences of the Hebrew *kāppōreṯ*—from the same root as *kipper* and *yom hakippurim*—most commonly known as the "mercy seat," the top of the ark of the covenant in the Most Holy Place (see "atonement cover" in the NIV; see Heb 9:5). According to Ladd, by using *hilastērion* "Paul makes a direct allusion to the sin offering that was presented by the High Priest on the great Day of Atonement," an *allusion* that Young calls "*prima facie* the most likely background for

48. Sleeman, *Geography*, 78, suggests this indicates "a clear demarcation between earth and heaven," writes Matthew Sleeman. See also Schreiner, *The Ascension*.

49. See Buchanan, "The Day of Atonement," 236: "The place to begin research on Paul's doctrine of redemption is . . . the Jewish understanding of sin, the land, legal and financial metaphors, and the function of the Day of Atonement." Calvin saw echoes of the Azazel purification rite in 1 Cor 4:13, where Paul has Greek purification rites involving *katharma* in mind when he uses the term *peri katharmata*. See *John Calvin's Bible Commentaries*, 107: "*katharma* denotes a man who, by public execrations is devoted, with the view to the cleansing of a city."

50. The question of whether this is an *allusion* to Leviticus 16 has been discussed by Schreiber, who compares Christ's death to a "votive offering" on our behalf. See Schreiber, "Das Weihegeschenk Gottes," 88–110; also Young, "Did St. Paul," 23–32; Bailey, "Jesus as the Mercy Seat," 155; Williams-Tinajero, *The Reshaped Mind*, 75–88.

Paul's usage in Romans 3:25."[51] This clear connection led Mason to affirm he had "no doubt at all that the dominant thought [in Romans 3] was that of the mercy-seat, that had once stood in the innermost sanctuary of the Jerusalem Temple, and of the solemn ritual of the Day of Atonement."[52]

However, the near-consensus view of the Hebrew *kāppōreṯ* as the source for the reference to *hilastērion* in Romans is not without detractors. Deissmann initially argued that *hilastērion* was not a noun but an adjective to explain *epithema* as in Exodus 25:16 [17]: "Then you shall make a mercy seat of pure gold" (*hilastērion epithema chrysiou katharou*). Deissmann later allowed the substantive meaning, while still denying the direct material connection between *hilastērion* and *kāppōreṯ* stating: "The links—*kāppōreṯ*, ἱλαστήριον, *Gnadenstuhl*—cannot be connected by the sign of equality, not even indeed, by a straight line, but at best, by a curve."[53] Morris reads *hilastērion* simply as "means of propitiation." Still, his contention stems from a tendency to downplay the occurrence of *hilastērion* in cultic settings in the LXX, as well as a misreading of the function of the OT sanctuary, which according to him, was "averting of punishment due to sin and the inclining of the Deity to be favourable." When Morris cannot deny its connection with the sanctuary, he acknowledges it by misunderstanding how cultic expiation occurred, i.e., as a "general reference to the removal of the wrath of God."[54] However, the notion of appeasing the wrath of God is absent in the sanctuary rituals; the sacrifices expiate the offenses from the offender and the sanctuary; God deigns to abide in it by gracious acceptance of its continuous purifications.

Since the temple that stood at the time of Jesus did not have a *hilastērion*—the ark had been lost at the time of the Babylonian invasion in the 6th century BCE—the cultic object is probably not what Paul is calling our attention to but to what occurred on it: "expiation." Leviticus 16 describes two sprinklings of blood on the *kāppōreṯ/hilastērion* on the DA which achieved expiation for sin: (1) the blood of the bull for Aaron; (2) the blood of the goat "for the Lord" offered for the people. Under this prism, Paul's use of *hilastērion* may indicate that he understood Jesus' death on the cross as a fulfillment of the DA in which the *hilastērion* assumed a central atoning role.[55] Thus, as

51. Ladd, *A Theology*, 466; see Young, "Hilaskesthai," 170; Beale, *A New Testament Biblical Theology*, 486–492; Thiselton, *The Hermeneutics*, 343; Mollaun, *St. Paul's Concept of* ʽΙΛΑΣΤΗΡΙΟΝ, 83.

52. Manson, "ΙΛΑΣΤΗΡΙΟΝ," 1–10.

53. Deissmann, *Bible Studies*, 135.

54. Morris, "The Meaning," 34, 43.

55. See Wiencke, *Paulus*, 52.

suggested by Tiwald, "an allusion to Leviticus 16:13–15 fits perfectly into the trajectory of argumentation in Romans 3 and into the whole theology of Paul: Christ's atoning and vicarious suffering is framed by cultic imagery from Yom Kippur."[56]

In sum, Paul's use of *hilastērion* in Romans strengthens the view that he understood Christ's death as the fulfillment of all Hebrew festivals and rituals culminating once a year on the DA. It is even possible that Paul's criticism of the feast "days" in Gal 4:10 may include the celebration of the DA, now made innocuous by the death of Christ, which fulfilled its typology. Thus, there is little reason to wrangle with Baigent's claim that the use of *hilastērion* in Romans 3:25 "hardly proves that Paul thought of Jesus as a priest,"[57] for while high-priestly imagery may be absent in Paul's writings, imagery of the DA is evident.

### *Did the "Goat for Azazel" Prefigure Christ?*

According to Stökl, the authors of the NT avoided connecting Jesus to scapegoat typology because it was connected to a demon (e.g., the demonization of goats in Matt 25:31–46).[58] Maclean furthers this notion by pointing out that "for a number of early Christian writers the scapegoat's association with demons clearly precluded any application to Christ."[59] However, the palpable shift in the understanding of Azazel that we see early on in Christianity is because Christian authors could not resist the "collective repertoire of motifs" contained in the "goat for Azazel" ritual, Ben Ezra suggests.[60] That is why the author of the Epistle of Barnabas, Justin Martyr, and Tertullian could argue that both goats in Leviticus 16 were types of the last Jewish Messiah.[61]

Considering the compelling evidence culled from the Pentateuch to the effect that the cipher Azazel pointed to a demonic entity who received the punishment for Israel's sin, the attempt to ascribe scapegoat typology to Christ lacks solid ground. At least one author who defends this idea quotes Isaiah 53:6, "and the Lord has laid on him the iniquity of us all," as a possible connection between Christ and Azazel.[62] However, this is not necessarily

56. Young, "Hilaskesthai," 170; see Tiwald, "Hilasterion," 194.
57. See Baigent, "Jesus as Priest," 38; Montefiore, *The Epistle to the Hebrews*, 5.
58. Stökl, "The Christian Exegesis," 226.
59. Maclean, "Barabbas," 317. See Miller, "The Social Logic," 382–383.
60. Stökl, "The Christian Exegesis," 228.
61. *Adversus Marcionem* 1.191.
62. Boyce, *Leviticus and Numbers*, 57.

a technical expression for the "goat for Azazel" ritual. By implication, the people's iniquity was vicariously placed on the goat "for the Lord" as well.[63]

John 1:29 has often been quoted in support of the view that Christ is symbolized by the goat that "takes away" the sin, i.e., the "goat for Azazel." But the language only seems similar for, in its effects, only the death of the first goat accomplished atoning purification. Although this has been the dominant view in evangelical scholarship, it has been increasingly challenged due to its philological and theological inconsistencies. Based on a close analysis of the "goat for Azazel" in its ritualistic context in Leviticus, Gane has argued that the "goat for Azazel" receives the responsibility for the sins of Israel and takes it to its symbolic source, Satan.[64] The implications of Gane's conclusion are readily apparent: the ritual makes sense because the disposal of "all sin" from Israel ultimately points to the final removal of "all sin" from the universe by casting it on the antitypical "goat for Azazel," i.e., the devil ("that old serpent," Rev 20:2).

Lastly, Schwartz suggests that Paul's use of the verb *exapostellō* in Gal 4:4: "But when the fullness of time had come, God sent [*exapesteilen*] his Son, born of a woman, born under the law"; and in 4:6: "God has sent [*exapesteilen*] the Spirit of his Son into our hearts, crying, "Abba! Father!" is based partly on the "goat for Azazel" imagery inherent in the *quid pro quo* relationship "sending away X redeems Y" (see Gal 3:13). Schwartz concludes that "Christ's action was that of a scapegoat."[65] Indeed, the two instances in the OT where the LXX uses *exapostellō* to translate שלח (*piʿel*) are the sending of the "live bird" (Lev 14) and the "goat for Azazel." But Schwartz overstates his case by arguing that the sending of Jesus from heaven to earth parallels the "sending away" of the "goat for Azazel"; for one, Jesus' departure from heaven can hardly be construed as a "purgation" rite. Paul's use of *exapostellō* in lieu of the more common *apostellō* may, quite simply, hinge on the range of motion inherent in the prefix *ex* ("out of") likely indicating Jesus' exit from an exalted position to assume one "under the law," rather than intending an exact match with the "sending away" of the "goat for Azazel" as a purgation rite.

63. Wenham is off target when he concludes that: "As it was led out to die in the wilderness bearing the sins of the people, so Christ was crucified outside Jerusalem for the sins of his people" (Wenham, *Leviticus*, 238). Caird, *New Testament Theology*, 153, suggests this may have been Isaiah's intention: "The sin-bearing goat was unclean and could not therefore be offered to God. But these two images had already coalesced in the prophetic vision of the Servant of the Lord, of whom it was said that the Lord laid upon him the guilt of us all, but also that he made himself a sacrifice for sin."

64. Gane, *Cult and Character*, 259.

65. Schwartz, "Two Pauline Allusions," 261.

## *The Day of Atonement in the Epistle to the Hebrews*

The most direct treatment of the DA rituals in light of the "Christ event" in the NT is undoubtedly found in the Epistle to the Hebrews.[66] "Christ as a high priest," posits Hagner, is the "central and unique theological emphasis in Hebrews."[67] Landgraf goes further, stating that the progression of the epistle follows "the significant architectural elements of the Day of Atonement" provides "a concrete, physical progression to many seemingly disjointed parts within Hebrews."[68] The Epistle to the Hebrews, according to Montefiore, contains "an elaborate explanation of Jesus' death and ascension in terms of the most important of all sacrifices described in the Old Testament, that of the Day of Atonement."[69] This understanding has been held since Origen, who argued that the whole letter of Hebrews dealt with Leviticus 16 (see *Homilies on Leviticus*, 9:2). The author's exposition on the sanctuary ritual points to the sacrifice of Christ and his priesthood as "better sacrifices" (Heb 9:23), and this is mainly based (although not exclusively) on the typology of the DA. Thus, the DA assumes "major, if not fundamental importance for the interpretation of Hebrews," concludes Gelardini.[70]

In the Epistle to the Hebrews, the Qumran tradition that conflates the Davidic figure of the Messiah with that of the high priest is visible, especially in the figure of this eschatological Davidic high priest.[71] The author's argument is often framed by apocalyptic terminology; e.g., "but in these last days he has spoken to us by a Son" who has appeared "at the end of the age" (Heb 1:2, 5; 9:26; 6:4–5; see 1 Cor 10:11).[72] The author draws a series of contrasts between the sanctuary rituals in general, the DA in particular, and the death of Christ. For example, in chapter 9, the author explains that while the earthly high priest entered "again and again/year after year" (v. 25) to officiate in the Most Holy Place, Christ entered "once for all" (v. 12) into "the inner shrine

66. See Young, "The Gospel According to Hebrews 9," 198–210; Philip, *Leviticus in Hebrews;* Ounsworth, *Joshua Typology*, 131–165; Mbamalu, "Jesus the Interceding High Priest." For a structuring of Hebrews based on the DA, see Landgraf, "The Structure of Hebrews," 19–27; Backhaus, Der Hebräerbrief, 61; Ladd, *A Theology of the New Testament*, 625.

67. Hagner, *Encountering*, 180. See Horbury, "The Aaronic Priesthood," 45; Stegemann and Steggeman, "Does the Cultic Language," 13.

68. Landgraf, "The Structure of Hebrews," 20, 26.

69. Montefiore, *Epistle to the Hebrews*, 37. See Johnsson, "Defilement," 229.

70. Gelardini, "The Inauguration," 227. See also McKnight and Church, *Hebrews-James*, 115; Langenhoven et al., "The Day of Atonement," 85, 86, argue that Christ's role as a high priest "in the context of the Jewish festival, the Day of Atonement" becomes a "hermeneutical key to the Christology of Hebrews."

71. See Mason, *You Are a Priest Forever*, 197–198; McRay, "Atonement," 1–9.

72. Isaac, "Priesthood," 55;

behind the curtain" as "a forerunner on our behalf" (6:19–20), "not with the blood of goats and calves, but with his own blood, obtaining eternal redemption" (v. 12; see 13:12; 10:19). His blood is that of "sprinkling" (12:24), and the expression "within the veil" is an *allusion* to the sprinklings occurring on the DA. (See 1 Pet 1:2: exiled Christians are called to be "obedient to Jesus Christ and to be sprinkled with his blood.")[73] The author urges his readers to approach each other "with ... hearts sprinkled clean from an evil conscience and ... bodies washed with pure water" (10:22; see 9:13–14).[74]

Significantly, the verb *hilaskomai* appears in the conclusion of the pericope of Heb 2:5–17: "to make a sacrifice of atonement for the sins of the people." To this end, his blood was presented "within the veil" (*esōteron tou katapetasmatos*), i.e., into the Most Holy Place of the heavenly sanctuary, in "heaven itself," in the very presence of God (6:19–20; 9:12, 24).[75] This rite of passage of sorts is parallel to the Israelite high priest's going "within the veil" once a year on the DA to offer blood inside the Most Holy Place. As explored previously, the Greek expression *esōteron tou katapetasmatos* comes from the LXX where it always translates the Hebrew *mibbēṯ lappārōḵeṯ* (Exod 26:33; Lev 16:2, 12, 15), which in the OT always refers to the veil of the Most Holy Place and the blood rituals involving it.[76]

In Hebrews 9, the author continues to draw on DA typology when he contrasts the limitations of the earthly tabernacle rituals with the superiority of Jesus' once-and-for-all sacrificial death. He begins by explaining that the activities of the "first tent," i.e., the earthly Holy Place (*prōten skēnēn*, v. 2, 6), served as a "parable of the present time" (v. 9) because it symbolized the limitations of access to God through rituals that occurred outside of the inner veil and out of the presence of God.[77] The way "into the sanctuary" (9:8–9), that is, the heavenly, was not yet disclosed because the same "gifts and sacrifices" could not perfect the worshiper (10:4). Jesus, however (v. 11), by his sacrifice and subsequent entry into the heavenly Most Holy Place ("heaven itself," v. 24), is in marked contrast to the earthly high priest: he

73. See Moore, "'Not to offer himself again and again.'"

74. Moffit, *Blood*, 221; Eberhart, "Characteristics," 58.

75. Schenck, "Hebrews," 179: "The literal event that the earliest believers related to an atoning sacrifice was the death of Jesus on a cross (see Rom 3:25). However, the earliest Christians also believed that the resurrected Jesus had gone to God's right hand, implying in their cosmology an ascension through the various layers of sky to the highest heaven."

76. Gane, "Re-Opening," 8. See also Gurtner, "Καταπέτασμα," 105–111; Gane, "LXX Syntax," 345.

77. See Stanley, "Hebrews 9:6–10," 385–399.

"entered once for all into the holy places [*ta hagia*]" (v. 12); his entry "once for all" is contrasted with the entrance by the high priest "once a year" (v. 7), into the "second tent," the Most Holy Place on the DA. For the contrast to make sense, Christ's entry must also be into the "second tent," i.e., the Mostly Holy Place, as is already implied in Hebrews 6:19–20: "We have this hope, a sure and steadfast anchor of the soul, a hope that enters the inner shrine behind the curtain [*esōteron tou katapetasmatos*], where Jesus, a forerunner on our behalf, has entered, having become a high priest forever according to the order of Melchizedek."

Christ's entrance "within the veil" with blood is conclusively linked with the DA; that it lay in the past is evident by the use of the aorist *eisēlthen*, "entered" in Hebrews 6:20. Whereas the high priest entered "once a year" into God's presence, Jesus, at his ascension, entered "once and for all" into the Father's presence. As the Aaronic "entrance" into the Most Holy Place provided security for the community, Jesus' entrance into "heaven itself" covered by a cloud provides the anchor for the believer. Moreover, this entrance into the "veil" clarifies the use of *ta hagia* instead of *Hagia Hagiōn* in Hebrews 9:12: *ta hagia* points to a typological passage through the entire sanctuary, beginning with the Holy Place and culminating with the application of his blood in the heavenly Most Holy Place. Thus, the argument advanced by some that the author of the Epistle to the Hebrews envisions an "inauguration" ceremony of the heavenly sanctuary must be rejected (see next section). While blood never went into the tabernacle to inaugurate it, the new covenant (*diathēkē*) or "will"—which required the death of the testator (9:16–17)—was inaugurated by Christ's blood offered inside the heavenly sanctuary in the manner of DA blood.[78]

The DA also provides the context for the *allusion* to the ritual of the ashes of the red cow in Hebrews 9:13, which involved "cedarwood, hyssop, and crimson material" (see Num 19; see Heb 9:19: *meta hydatos kai eriou kokkinou kai hyssōpou*; and Ps 51:7). According to Milgrom, the ritual of the red cow offers a "cogent parallel" with the handling of blood on the DA: its blood was daubed on the horns of the outer altar and sprinkled in front of the tabernacle seven times.[79] More importantly, however, is the fact that this advanced purification ritual using an unblemished adult animal became a fitting purgation rite for the high priest in preparation for the DA during the

78. See Matera, "The Theology," 197.

79. Milgrom, *The Commentary to Numbers*, 440.

Second Temple period, when the ashes of the red cow were sprinkled on him for seven days (m. Parah 3:1; b. Yoma 1).[80]

As the author closes his defense of the superiority of the blood of Jesus in chapter 9, we see terminology from the DA again: "he has appeared once for all [*hapax*] at the end of the age to remove sin by the sacrifice of himself (9:26b). For the author, Jesus' self-sacrifice accomplishes the removal of sin, consummating the typology of removing all "impurities of the people of Israel and, because of their transgressions, all their sins" (Lev 16:16; 30) on the DA. As Bruce, *The Epistle to the Hebrews*, 214, put it: "When on the cross he offered up his life to God as a sacrifice for his people's sin, he accomplished in reality what Aaron and his successors performed in type by the two-fold act of slaying the victim and presenting its blood in the holy of holies."[81] Believers now "have confidence to enter the sanctuary by the blood of Jesus, by the new and living way that he opened for us through the curtain [*dia tou katapetasmatos*] (that is, through his flesh)" (Heb 10:19–20). Despite the *crux interpretum* present in this verse, the parallel rending of the veil of the Most Holy Place in connection with Jesus' death in the Synoptics lends support to this reading of the veil as "his flesh," because it was "through his flesh" that we have secured access to God's presence.[82] "What was once limited to the

80. m. Parah 3:1: "They sprinkled the priest that was to burn the cow on each of the seven days, but the priest that was set apart for the Day of Atonement they sprinkled only on the third and seventh days." See Horbury, "The Aaronic Priesthood," 52: "The association of the two rites in Hebrews 9.13 thus probably reflects not unconcern over details of the cult, and not (only) the exigencies of argument, but first-century understanding of the Day of Atonement." See Michel, *Der Brief*, 168, 313.

81. Bruce, *The Epistle to the Hebrews*, 214.

82. Although the NRSV takes *dia tou katapetasmatos = tout' estin* [*dia*] *tēs sarkos autou*, the second *dia* is omitted, raising the following problem: Is "of his flesh" (*tēs sarkos autou*) connected to "veil," "way," or "inaugurated" and, if naturally taken as an appositive to the more immediate "veil," can *dia* be taken locally in the case of *katapetasma* but instrumentally in the case of *sarx*? An elegant, albeit seemingly neglected solution, was proposed long ago by Gardiner when he took *dia* both locally and instrumentally, "so that the real thought of the author is precisely that which is impossible to allow to the exact grammatical force of his expression" (Gardiner, "On Heb. 10:20," 142). Ellingworth takes a similar position, arguing that "it is probably better to suppose a change from one well-attested meaning of *dia* to another, rather than to give a meaning to *sarx* which is either unlikely in itself, or foreign to Hebrews, or both" (*The Epistle to the Hebrews*, 521). Building on Gardiner, Young takes *tout' estin tēs sarkos autou* appositionally to *katapetasma* by appealing to the fact that *sarx* is instrumentally related to *haima* as a means of access in v. 19, which strengthens the parallel connection between *katapetasma* and *sarx* in v. 20b (see Young, "TOUT' ΕΣΤΙΝ," 104). Lane takes a similar position, stating that "[t]he internal logic of the sentence presupposes a shift in thought from *dia* taken locally with *tou katapetasmatos*, "the curtain," to *dia* (unexpressed) taken instrumentally with *tēs sarkos autou*, "his flesh" (Lane, *Hebrews 9–13*, 275). See also Jeremias, "Hebräer 10:20," 131; Hofius, "Inkarnation," 132–43; Johnsson, "Defilement," 353–355; Koester, *Hebrews*, 443; Young, "TOUT' ΕΣΤΙΝ," 104.

high priest and once restricted to one day in the year is now open to all and forever," posits Young.[83]

Another *echo* of the DA can be heard in Hebrews 10:26: "For if we willfully persist in sin after having received the knowledge of the truth, there no longer remains a sacrifice for sins," which echoes Lev 23:29–30: those who did not participate in the spirit of the DA and were recalcitrant sinners must be "cut-off"; not even the all-encompassing sacrifices offered on the DA covered them. In the new covenant, it is no longer the sanctuary that needs to be "cleansed" (9:28; 10:2, 12, 17), but the Christian's conscience, accompanied by a life of self-denial, rest in God's grace, and faithfulness to God.

Lastly, the sabbatical rest mandated for the DA provides the background for the "sabbatical" rest found in Hebrews 4, especially as the people of God look forward to the permanent "Sabbath" (*sabbatismos*, Heb 4:9) guaranteed through Christ's atoning blood.[84] As in the OT, God's holiness could be experienced through his presence *spatially* in the sanctuary, as well as *temporally* through the experience of holy time on the Sabbath, the Christian's ultimate rest in God's presence in the heavenly sanctuary—achieved by Christ's entrance "into heaven itself"—will coalesce both spatial and temporal aspects of God's all-encompassing holiness.[85]

## *"Within the Veil": Day of Atonement or Inauguration?*

Whereas the view that the Epistle to the Hebrews portrays Christ's entrance into heaven as fulfilling the typology of the Mosaic DA is virtually consensual in academia, some have argued that the tabernacle inauguration is in view instead while downplaying the importance of the DA in Hebrews. In his commentary, Ellingworth avers that the imagery in Hebrews 9:21 "presupposes a comparison between two covenant inauguration ceremonies."[86] Nelson has argued that the OT provides two "templates," which the author of Hebrews uses to describe the sacrifice of Jesus: "the Day of Atonement as described in Leviticus 16 and the ceremony of covenant confirmed by sacrificial blood in Exodus 24:3–8."[87] However, while present in Hebrews 9, references to the inauguration of the Mosaic tabernacle remain peripheral in the author's discussions.

83. Young, "TOUT' ΕΣΤΙΝ," 104.
84. See Radner, *Leviticus*, 168.
85. Calaway, *The Sabbath and the Sanctuary*, 163.
86. See Calaway, *The Sabbath and the Sanctuary*, 21.
87. Nelson, "'He Offered Himself,'" 252.

On this point, a more important question should be, what kind of sacrifice did Jesus offer and when? Whereas, as Kibbe posits, "Christ's death [as] the inaugural act of the new covenant" is beyond dispute, controversies about *when* the atonement was accomplished linger in Christian theology.[88] The debate first arose in the 16th century when Socinus (1537–1604) published his book *De Jesu Christo Servatore* (1578), in which he argued that Christ's atoning work was not accomplished on the cross but at his ascension when he initiated his heavenly priesthood. Christ's death, Socinus concluded, was not "propitiatory" but rather only "preparatory" for his more important work inside the heavenly sanctuary. Christ's atoning work on behalf of believers can only take place as he continually offers his blood before the Father in heaven, he argued.

The Socinian view of atonement experienced a revival of sorts in 19th-century America in the aftermath of the revivalist movement called Millerism (1831–1844). Millerites applied a historicist interpretation to the cleansing of the sanctuary in Daniel 8:14 as referring to the cleansing of the earth by fire at an eschatological DA, which they interpreted as Jesus' Second Coming at the end of 2,300 literal years. The *terminus a quo* of this period was Artaxerxes's decree to occupy Jerusalem in 457 BCE, and its end reached Yom Kippur, October 22, 1844. When Jesus failed to return, the Millerites sought to revise the prophetic views that led to their Great Disappointment. Building on the sanctuary ritual which underpinned their interpretation of the book of Daniel, they pivoted the fulfillment of the book's prophecies from a fiery DA cleansing on Judgment Day to Christ's passage from the Holy Place to the Most Holy Place of the heavenly sanctuary to commence an eschatological DA in 1844.

The historicist debate about the time of the commencement of the final atonement in heaven later bifurcated into disagreements not only about *where* the atonement occurred—either on the cross or in heaven—but also *when*: at Christ's death, at his ascension, or at a future point in time. Notwithstanding the intractable problems with the historicist interpretation of Daniel, the view has encroached upon several historicist understandings of NT theology. The Epistle to the Hebrews has logically taken center stage as historicist interpreters have sought to establish on which OT background the author depended when explaining Jesus' entrance into heaven.

88. Kibbe, "'Is It Finished,'" 34.

In the early 20th century, historicist theologian Albion Ballenger argued that Jesus had gone "within the veil" of the heavenly Most Holy Place at his ascension to initiate his mediatorial role. This view was followed closely by Andross, who argued that "Christ, after making His offering on Calvary, passed within the veil of the heavenly sanctuary and anointed the ark of the testament, and with His own blood performed the service of consecration."[89] He then returned to officiate inside the heavenly holy place until 1844. The debate was revived in the late 1970s in the work of prominent historicist scholar Desmond Ford who took Ballenger's position that Christ entered into the Most Holy Place of the heavenly sanctuary to intercede on behalf of believers, according to the Epistle to the Hebrews.[90]

Perhaps the most complete discussion on the two main historicist currents—inauguration vs. DA in Hebrews 9–10—involved inauguration proponent Davidson and DA proponent Young published in the *Andrews University Seminary Studies*.[91] The conversation between the two scholars was prompted by Gane's seminal article in the same issue, in which he demonstrated that the expression "within the veil" (*esōteron tou katapetasmatos*) in Hebrews 6:19–20 comes from the LXX translation of the Hebrew expression *mibbēṯ lappārōḵet*, which always refers to the veil of the Most Holy Place.[92]

Young thought that Gane's article "argued convincingly that the LXX background to Heb 6:19–20 supports the interpretation that Christ entered 'the inner part of the heavenly sanctuary at the time of Jesus' ascension."[93] Young builds on Gane's piece by refuting an article by Rice that argued that the expression *esōteron tou katapetasmatos* in Hebrews 6:19–20 did not refer exclusively to the veil of the Most Holy Place but could refer to the *katapetasma* of the Holy Place.[94] He concludes that "[t]here is only one passage in the OT that speaks of the high priest going within the veil—that is the Day of Atonement chapter, Leviticus 16," because the expression "'the innermost place from the veil' cannot be dissociated from the contextual terms 'high priest' and 'entered.'"[95] Further, Young argued that Heb 6:19–20 must be read synoptically with 10:19–20 and concludes that "[t[he parallel nature of the passages leaves little doubt that the veil in both texts is the same—that is

89. Andross, *A More Excellent Service*, 52.

90. See Ford, *Daniel 8:14*.

91. Young, "Where Jesus Has Gone," 165–173; Davidson, "Christ's Entry," 176–190; Young, "The Day of Dedication," 61–68; Davidson, "Inauguration,'" 69–88.

92. Gane, "Re-Opening." See Gurtner, "Καταπέτασμα," 105–111; Gurtner, "LXX Syntax," 345.

93. Young, "Where Jesus Has Gone," 165.

94. Rice, "Hebrews 6:19," 229–234.

95. Young, "Where Jesus Has Gone," 171.

the inner veil,"[96] and that "any first-century Jew who read Hebrews' language of an annual entrance of the high priest by means of blood through the veil into the sanctuary, would think of the Day of Atonement. This was the only occasion when *all these acts occurred at one time*" (italics original).[97]

In turn, Davidson accepted Gane's conclusions but pivoted, stating instead that the expression "within the veil" is "a moot point in comparison to the larger issue: What Old Testament event provides the background for this passage?"[98] Davidson's premise is that the entrance in Hebrews 6 is devoid of "distinctive terminology or motif ... that points decisively to one event and not the other."[99] He then argued that the decisive argument comes from Heb 10:19–20, a passage which, in his view, explains 6:19–20: "Therefore, my friends, since we have confidence to enter the sanctuary [*ta hagia*] by the blood of Jesus by the new and living way that he opened for us [*enekainisen*] through the curtain." In his view, both *enkainizō*, "inaugurate" and *ta hagia*, "sanctuary," require readers "to consider the OT background of the entire sanctuary and its inauguration" and that "[t]he latter passage elaborates on the nature of Christ's entering, showing that the event in both passages is that of inauguration."[100] Based on his interpretation of *ta hagia* as referring to the sanctuary as a whole, Davidson argued that the expression proves that Jesus' entrance is parallel with the entrance to inaugurate the sanctuary.

Davidson's position is open to considerable criticism. First, Davidson is correct when he follows current NT scholarship that the use of *enkainizō* in Hebrews 9:18 and 10:20 points to inauguration motifs, but the term is not exclusively used to refer to the sanctuary in the LXX.[101] Further, the entrance "within the veil" in Hebrews 6:19–20 comes earlier in the book and should control the meaning for the later "entrances," as pointed out by Young. Third, while Davidson accepts that the entrances in Hebrews 6:19–20; 9:12 and 10:19–20 are parallel and that the veil must be the same in all, he sees a "sanctuary inauguration motif" as dominant to the detriment of other themes. But this conclusion is arbitrary since he accepts DA imagery in Hebrews 9:7, 25 but rejects it in 9:11–12, despite the thematic synchrony between the two passages. Fourth, while Davidson attempts to apply a philological analysis of some LXX terms and their context in Hebrews, he shows

96. Young, "Where Jesus Has Gone," 172.
97. Young, "Where Jesus Has Gone," 172.
98. Davidson, "Christ's Entry," 179.
99. Davidson, "Christ's Entry," 179.
100. Davidson, "Christ's Entry," 181, 182.
101. See Ellingworth, *The Epistle to the Hebrews*, 466.

bias by downplaying the importance of the OT expression "within the veil," which never occurs in any of the inauguration passages but primarily refers to entrances with blood into the Most Holy Place on the DA (four times in Lev 16). While Davidson calls on Young to extend his methodology "to other key LXX terminology used by the author of Hebrews, including *enkainizō, tragos, moschos,* and *ta hagia*" in Hebrews," Davidson is guilty of the same inconsistency when he cherry-picks a preferred meaning for the expression "within the veil."

The main argument against an inauguration background for the entrances "within the veil" in Hebrews is the fact that the use of blood to dedicate the entire tabernacle is not attested in the OT. Although the author of Hebrews suggests as much in Hebrews 9:21, none of the sanctuary dedication passages in the OT indicate that either the blood or any part of sacrificed animals was brought into the tent of the meeting to dedicate it. It is more likely that the author conflated several Pentateuchal passages that deal with the dedication of the tabernacle and all its vessels with "blood," although not all cultic utensils were thus dedicated. Blood in the tabernacle rituals was consistently reserved for purgation/purification offerings, while the dedication of the tabernacle and its utensils was accomplished by the "holy anointing oil" made of myrrh, sweet-smelling cinnamon, aromatic cane, cassia, and olive oil.[102] During the establishment of the Aaronic priesthood, the blood of a bull calf was presented as a "purification offering" (*ḥaṭṭāʾṯ*) and "atonement" for Aaron and his sons; this had functional implications so they could act as mediators in the tabernacle. A bull was sacrificed on each of the seven consecutive days as a sin offering for the priests and for the altar, which is similar to the DA ritual for the high priest (Lev 8:14–15, 22–24, 33–35; 16:14). On the eighth day, another "bull calf" was sacrificed as *ḥaṭṭāʾṯ* for Aaron as his sons (Lev 9:2, 8–9). In addition, two rams were both "burnt offering" and "ordination offering" (Exod 29:15–18; Lev 8:21, 8). While both blood and oil were daubed on Aaron and his sons to accomplish a dual function of purgation-dedication, the interior compartments of the tabernacle were not dedicated by blood for an evident reason: the tabernacle had not yet assumed its mediatory function, and God had not yet descended into it. Therefore, no purgation of its interior by blood was necessary or even valid. Only the altar of burnt sacrifices was dedicated with blood during the dedication, and only after fire from God had consumed the sacrifices did the tabernacle assume its

102. See Exod 26:22–38; 29:23–24; 30:26–28; 37:29; 40:9; Lev 8:10, 12, 23–24.

cultic function and could, finally, receive sacrificial *ḥaṭṭāʾṯ* blood in its inner rooms (Lev 8:11, 15; 9:24).

Moreover, the expression "all the vessels used in worship" (*panta ta skeuē leitourgias*) in Hebrews 9:21 appears as *panta ta skeuē leitourgika* two times in the LXX text of Numbers 4:12, 26, and refers unequivocally to the tabernacle equipment (see also Lev 8:11; Num 7:1). Conversely, *skeuos* is used to refer to people elsewhere in the NT: (1) Paul is called a "chosen vessel" (*skeuos eklogēs*, Acts 9:15; (2) Paul refers to the human body metaphorically as "clay vessels" (*ostrakina skeuē*, 2 Cor 4:7); (3) the wicked are called "vessels of wrath" (*skeuē horgēs*, Rom 9:22); (4) women are called "weaker vessels" (*asthenesterō skeuei*, 1 Pet 3:7); and (5) the Thessalonians are urged to "control their vessels [bodies]" (*heautou skeuos ktasthai*, 1 Thess 4:4). This figurative use of *skeuos* in the NT may point to the same meaning in Hebrews, indicating that the author may have conflated the dedication of the tabernacle with oil with the dedication of the priests with oil and blood. Be that as it may, the critical conclusion is that while the blood of dedicatory sacrifices did not go into the Most Holy Place during any of the dedication ceremonies in the OT, it did on the DA, and that provides the best OT background for Christ's entrances into the sanctuary in Hebrews.

The association of blood with the dedication of the entire tabernacle may be part of a list of technical imprecisions found in Hebrews about the sanctuary and its rituals:

(1) In Hebrews 9:4, the author appears to place the "altar of incense" inside the Most Holy Place instead of the Holy Place (see Exod 30:6);

(2) The inclusion of the "golden urn holding the manna, and Aaron's rod that budded" (9:6) inside the ark of the covenant alongside the tablets of the ten commandments is not attested in the Pentateuch (1 Kgs 8:9; 2 Chr 5:10).

(3) The use of "water, scarlet and hyssop" is not found in the dedication of the tabernacle but in the prescriptions for the purification of a leprous person and the ceremony of the red cow (Lev 14:6; Num 19:6). The ashes of a red cow were sprinkled on the high priest in preparation for the DA.[103]

(4) During the dedication ceremony, Moses read from the book of the law (Exod 24:4), while the author of Hebrews states that he sprinkled both the book and the people (Heb 9:19).[104]

103. See m. Parah 3:1: "They sprinkled the priest that was to burn the cow on each of the seven days, but the priest that was set apart for the Day of Atonement they sprinkled only on the third and seventh days."

104. See Johnson, *Hebrews*, 241–245; Spence-Jones, *Hebrews*, 235: "the force of the argument does not depend on these added details."

Young negotiates these difficulties by suggesting that the author of Hebrews "is by no means averse to manipulating the type to fit the antitype," and cites as a possible source b. Yoma 4a, where the oil of dedication stood for the blood.[105] Young further points out that the entrances into the Most Holy Place during the inauguration did not involve a high priest, while Jesus is thus treated in Hebrews.[106] Arguing convincingly for a DA background, Young proposed the following synoptic view of the pertinent passages in Hebrews which indicate a recurring DA theme:[107]

| **Aaronic** | | | **Christ** |
|---|---|---|---|
| **Day of Atonement** Heb 9:7 | **Day of Atonement** Heb 9:25 | **Day of Atonement** Heb 13:11 | **Day of ???** Heb 9:11–12 |
| High priest | High priest | High priest | High priest |
| Goes into | Enters | Brought into | Entered |
| The second [tent] | Holy place | Sanctuary | Holy Place |
| Once a year | Year after year | ———— | Once and for all |
| Not without … blood | With blood | Blood | With his own blood |

In sum, the view of the sanctuary inauguration as background for Christ's entrance "within the veil" and "into heaven itself" in Hebrews contains significant blind spots, as reviewed below:

(1) Hebrews 9 presents Jesus in a high-priestly, mediatorial role, whereas during the tabernacle inauguration, the high priest took a secondary, non-mediatorial role.

(2) Most of the sacrifices offered at the inauguration were not "expiatory," but dedicatory/celebratory.

105. Young, "The Gospel," 205. See also Johnsson, "Defilement," 338–51.

106. Young, "The Day of Dedication," 62.

107. Young, "The Day of Dedication," 64; see Young, "Where Jesus Has Gone," 173; Cortez, "From the Holy," 527–547; Cortez, "Atonement," 175–188.

(3) The inner tabernacle was dedicated with oil. Sacrificial blood did not enter the tabernacle, let alone the Most Holy Place, during the OT inauguration ceremonies but was only applied externally and on the priests.

(4) The sanctuary could not accept the application of blood, let alone inside the Most Holy Place during the inauguration rituals, because it had not yet assumed a mediatory role, which was only confirmed by the manifestation of God's glory at the end of the ceremony (see Exod 40:34–38).

(5) The author of Hebrews can hardly be referring to the inauguration of an actual sanctuary in heaven with two compartments without contradicting his earlier claim that the division of the earthly sanctuary into two "tents" reflected the limitations of the "present time" (Heb 9:6). In Christ, the barrier has been torn down, and free access to God's presence has been opened once and for all to the believer.

We can reasonably conclude that, whereas it is evident that the author of the Epistle to the Hebrews draws on some inauguration imagery, he focuses on the expiatory DA blood of Jesus, offered "heaven itself" in intercession for the believer by alluding to DA language and imagery.

## The Expression *Peri Hamartias* in the New Testament

As discussed in the previous section, the NT authors understood Jesus' death, resurrection, and exaltation as having been *prefigured* in the sanctuary and Jewish Feast typology, especially the DA.

One of the most important indicators of this dependence on the Hebrew cultus and Leviticus 16 is found in the use of the expression "for sin" (*peri hamartias*). In the LXX, *peri hamartias* (and the variants *to peri hamartias tēs hamartias, to peri tōn hamartiōn, hyper hamartias,* and *hyper hamartiōn*) appears fifty-four times—translating various Hebrew expressions such as *ḥaṭṭāʾṯ, lᵉḥaṭṭāʾṯ* and *haḥaṭṭāʾṯ* in which *ḥaṭṭāʾṯ* is used as a substantive = "sin/purgation offering."[108] This unique Greek expression and its variants occur sixty-six times in the LXX, nine of which in the prescriptions of the DA (Lev 16:3, 5, 9, 11 [2x], 15, 16 (pl. *peri pasōn tōn hamartiōn*); 25 (pl. *peri tōn hamartiōn*); 27 [2x]; Num 29:11).

In the NT, we first encounter *peri hamartias* in John 8:46: "Which of you convicts me of sin [*tis ex hymon elenchei me peri hamartias*]?" followed by two

108. The exception is Isaiah 53:10 where *peri hamartias* translates אָשָׁם.

similar uses in John 16:8–9. The common feature in these two passages is that all three occurrences have *peri hamartias* alongside the verb *elencho*, "to convince, to expose," which requires one to take *peri hamartias* not as the substantival phrase "sin offering" as in the OT, but rather take *peri* literally as "about/over/of." It would strain the Greek to take *elencho* differently from its ordinary meaning and read *peri hamartias* as an *allusion* to "sin offering" as in the LXX. Most Bible versions translate the passage in John literally as "convince of sin," and this is where we shall leave it.

It is, however, in the letters of Paul and the Epistle to the Hebrews where we find *peri hamartias* used in a sense that is closer to how it is used in the LXX. In a discussion of law and sin in Romans 8:3, Paul states: "For God has done what the law, weakened by the flesh, could not do: by sending his own Son in the likeness of sinful flesh, and to deal with sin [*kai peri hamartias*], he condemned sin in the flesh." Other Bible translations translate *peri hamartias* as: "on account of sin" (NKJV), "to be a sin offering" (NIV), "for sin" (ESV, YLT), "as an offering for sin" (NASB), "as a sacrifice for sin" (NEB, NJB) to name a few. Why the discrepancy? The use of *peri hamartias* in Romans 8:3 has elicited a vigorous debate, with an almost equal number of scholars supporting the substantival "sin offering" translation as there are detractors.[109] Early on, Norton took *kai peri hamartias* with *katekrinen* ("to pronounce a sentence," "to condemn") instead of with *pempsas* ("to send") because "περὶ with the genitive to mean 'on the charge of' or 'on the grounds of' in a judicial setting is common in the New Testament."[110] But even if we were to take *peri hamartias* with *katekrinen*, is there a significant objection to conflating judicial imagery with sacrificial imagery in Paul's polemic against wicked living? In various instances, Paul uses *krinō* and *katakrinō* alongside notions of "sin," "spiritual death," and "repentance," concepts that are not strictly "judicial" (see Rom 1:18–32; 2:1; 14:23; 1 Cor 11:32). Forensic justification for Paul occurs through Jesus' sacrificial, substitutionary death. In 2 Thess 1:5–12, God's righteous judgment (*kriseōs*) on the wicked will not happen until "that day" when they will be "cut off." Moreover, as Wright convincingly demonstrated, *peri hamartias* has "inescapably sacrificial associations."[111] Wright argues that the context of Romans 8:3 reflects a thematic linkage with the usage of

109. See Wright, *The Climax*, 220; Schreiner, *Romans*.

110. Norton, "The Meaning," 516.

111. Wright, "The Meaning," 454. See also Wright, *The Climax*, 221; Dunn, *Romans 1–8*, 422; Dunn, "Paul's Epistle to the Romans," 2853.

*lᵉḥaṭṭāʾṯ/peri hamartias* in Leviticus: a verb of sacrificing, the sacrifice, followed by *peri hamartias* which presents a "strong argument" for the "sin offering" translation. Paul is dealing here with "unwilling" sin or "sin through ignorance" as a result of "weakness of the flesh."[112]

Paul's Christology illuminates his theology of atonement, for the presence of sacrificial language in Romans 8:3 points to the finality of Jesus' death to "condemn sin in the flesh": Christ is a superior sacrifice that stands in stark contrast to the repeated sacrifices required by the Torah because of the "weakness of the flesh" (Rom 4:13–15; 7:7). This weakness caused the law to have the reverse effect on sin: it caused sin to increase (Rom 5:20), an incurable condition that was taken care of by the decisive offering of Jesus as "sin offering" (*peri hamartias*).[113] Note also how the presence of *hamartia* in the thematically parallel 2 Cor 5:21 has led scholars to take it as "sin/purgation offering" as in Romans 8:3.

The preceding analysis begs the question of which "sin offering" Paul has in mind when he uses *peri hamartias*: Does Paul compare Jesus to the "sin/purgation offerings" required as emergency sacrifices for sins occurring daily throughout the year? Or could he have the DA in mind, thus interpreting the cross as the author of Hebrews does, as the final DA sacrifice that solved the problem of sin "once and for all"? The attractiveness of a DA background to *peri hamartias* in Romans 8:3 is undoubtedly enhanced compared to the alternatives. In light of Paul's comparison of Jesus with the *hilasterion* of the Most Holy Place earlier in the epistle as well as his use of "once and for all" (*hapax*, Rom 3:25, 26), terms which are fraught with DA overtones, it seems that in Romans 8:3, Paul is not merely contrasting Jesus' sacrifice with the rituals performed regularly in the sanctuary as a whole but rather, it was Jesus' "once and for all" DA sacrifice that put an end to the ineffectual requirements of the old system. Although scholars have not generally seen the DA in Romans 8:3, it provides an attractive background to what Jesus accomplished on the cross.

Sacrificial language from the DA is also present in 1 John 2:2: "and he is the atoning sacrifice for our sins [*hilasmos estin peri tōn hamartiōn hēmōn*], and not for ours only but also for the sins of the whole world"; and in 4:10: "In this is love, not that we loved God but that he loved us and sent his Son

112. Wright, "The Meaning," 455.

113. See Mounce, *Romans*, 175; Dunn, *Romans 1–8*, 422: "Paul can merely allude to it [i.e., "sin offering"] since this way of thinking of Jesus' death was already well established in the Christian congregations." See also Osborne, *Romans Verse by Verse*; also Harris, *The Second Epistle*, 454.

to be the atoning sacrifice for our sins [*hilasmon peri tōn hamartiōn hēmōn*]." It should be noted that the plural *peri tōn hamartiōn* does occur in Leviticus 16:16 and twice as *apo pasōn tōn hamartiōn* (v. 30, 34). The difference between *peri* and *apo* is based on the interchangeable nature of the Hebrew prepositions *ʿal* "for, on account of, because of" and *min* "from, for," which Milgrom considers synonymous in cultic settings, thus making *peri tōn hamartiōn* and *apo pasōn tōn hamartiōn* synonymous. This concept, in turn, is echoed in John's expression "for the sins of the whole world" [*peri holou tou kosmou*], which echoes the purification of the "all sin" from Israel on the DA.[114]

It is, however, in the Epistle to the Hebrews where the cultic meaning of *peri hamartias* comes into sharper focus. Heb 10:6 has: "in burnt offerings and sin offerings [*peri hamartias*] you have taken no pleasure"; and Heb 10:8 reads: "You have neither desired nor taken pleasure in sacrifices [*thysias*] and offerings [*prosphoran*] and burnt offerings [*holokautōmata*] and sin offerings [*peri hamartias*]." These statements are made in the context of Jesus' surrender of his life as a sacrifice to fulfill "God's will" and to abolish "the first to establish the second" (10:8–10; 8:13). As in Hebrews 9:11, 24–25, Jesus' death in Hebrews 10 is again contrasted with the earthly sanctuary rituals offered "year after year" (vv. 1, 3), "day after day" (v. 11; 7:27), and "again and again" (v. 11). Jesus' DA sacrifice was offered "once and for all" (v. 10), "a single sin offering" (v. 12), "for all time" (v. 14; see 7:3) which saves "for all time" (see "to the uttermost," KJV) "those who come to God through Him" (7:25). In addition, the author of Hebrews uses the variant *hyper hamartiōn* synonymously with *peri hamartias* in two passages: Heb 10:12: "But when Christ had offered for all time a single sacrifice for sins [*hyper hamartiōn*], 'he sat down at the right hand of God'"; and in Hebrews 5:1: "For every high priest taken from among men is appointed for men in things pertaining to God, that he may offer both gifts and sacrifices for sins [*hyper hamartiōn*]."[115] Although *hyper hamartiōn* does not appear in the OT, *hyper hamartias* appears

114. See Milgrom, "The Preposition," 163.

115. See the distinct use of *hyper* ... *hamartiōn* in Heb 7:27: "who does not need daily, as those high priests, to offer up sacrifices, first for his own sins and then for the people's [*hyper tōn idiōn hamartiōn thysias anapherein epheita tōn tou laou hamartiōn*]." The last passage presents the exegete with a difficult choice: how to negotiate the use of "sin offerings" offered "daily" (*kath' hēmeran*) for the high priest and for the people. It seems expensive, exegetically speaking, to question his use of "sin offering" here, which is parallel with a similar argument in other passages. It may be more palatable to think that "daily" may be an imprecision. It seems clear that our author had the *tāmîd* offered daily in the sanctuary in mind (Exod 29:38, 42). Conversely, the closest OT parallel to this offering of *ḥaṭṭāʾṯ* sacrifices for high priest and people is the DA, since only on this day were such sacrifices offered (Lev 16:6–10). In this case *kath' hēmeran* could be an ancient "typo" or refer to the DA, but that stretches the Greek. Lane, *Hebrews 1–8*, 194, calls "daily" here "problematical."

nine times there, eight in the book of Ezekiel, all of which are synonymous with the substantival use of *peri hamartias* as "sin offering."[116] These references, in light of the use of the plural *peri hamartiōn* used elsewhere in the Epistle to the Hebrews, may indicate that the author is using *hyper hamartiōn* with the meaning of "sin offering." In this case, the word "sacrifices" (*thysias*) in both passages could explain what type of *hyper hamartiōn* sacrifices these are: "sin[s] offerings" (see Heb 10:26: *ouketi peri hamartiōn apoleipetai thysia*).

In Hebrews 10:18, *peri hamartias* is used in contrast with *aphesis*, "remission": "Now where there is remission [*aphesis*] of these, there is no longer an offering for sin [*peri hamartias*]" (NKJV). The entire exposition on Jesus' sacrifice as *peri hamartias/peri hamartiōn* in Hebrews 10 comes full circle by the preposition "therefore" (*oun*) used thirteen times, which ties everything together and moves the argument to its natural conclusion: where forgiveness (see "cleansing," 10:2) had been accomplished, there is no more need for *peri hamartias*. Also, "therefore" in Hebrews 10:19–20 stands in parallel with Jesus' entrance into the heavenly Most Holy Place described in Hebrews 6:19–20. Thus, the following reading of Heb 10:19–20 emerges:

> Therefore, brethren, having boldness [*echontes oun* = 6:19: "a sure and steadfast anchor"] to enter the Holiest [6:19: "within the veil"] by the [Day-of-Atonement] blood of Jesus [20] by a new and living way which He consecrated for us, through the veil [6:19: "within the veil"], that is, His flesh, and having a High Priest [*hierea megan*] over the house of God, [22] let us draw near with a true heart in full assurance of faith, having our hearts sprinkled from an evil conscience and our bodies washed with pure water (NKJV).

Lastly, the author of Hebrews utilizes the plural *peri hamartiōn* in two passages: Heb 5:3: "Because of this he is required as for the people, so also for himself, to offer sacrifices for sins [*peri hamartiōn*]," and Heb 10:26: "For if we sin willfully after we have received the knowledge of the truth, there no longer remains a sacrifice for sins [*ouketi peri hamartiōn apoleipetai thysia*], but a certain fearful expectation of judgment, and fiery indignation which will devour the adversaries." In Hebrews 10:26 (as in 5:1, 7:27, and 10:12), *thysia* functions as a gloss to *peri hamartiōn* rather than a distinct type of sacrifice (as does *prosphoras* in 10:18). Significantly the plural *peri tōn hamartiōn* is used in Leviticus 16:25: "The fat of the sin offering [*to peri tōn hamartiōn*] he shall burn on the altar." The "defiant sin" mentioned in

116. See Ezek 40:39; 43:22, 25; 44:29; 45:17, 22, 23; 46:20; 1 Esdras 7:8; *Odes* 12:10.

Hebrews 10:26—when read in parallel with 10:18—is reminiscent of the ineligibility of defiant sinners to be purified on the Israelite DA. Whereas those of loyal character are covered by Jesus' DA blood—in which case *peri hamartias* is no longer needed (10:18)—defiant sinners must be "cut off" and await judgment" because *peri hamartias* sacrifices are no longer available (10:26). Just as defiant Israelites were to be "cut off" (Lev 16:29–30) and barred from the benefits of the *ḥaṭṭāʾṯ* offerings on the DA, defiant sin on the part of Christians also annuls the applicability of Jesus's blood on their behalf.

In sum, in virtually all instances of *peri hamartias* (and cognate variants) in the letters of Paul, the Epistle to the Hebrews, and 1 John, Jesus' sacrifice is portrayed in the cultic language of the DA.

## Atonement in the New Testament: The Meaning of *Hilaskesthai*

As a corollary of the presence of *peri hamartias* in the NT is the use of the Greek word *hilaskesthai* in the NT, a term borrowed from the LXX where it and its cognate *exhilaskesthai* mostly—but not always—translate *kipper* as in, for example, *yôm hakkippurim* translated as *tē hēmera tou hilasmou* and *hēmera exilasmou* (Lev 25:9; 23:27; Num 5:8).

The basic meaning of *hilaskesthai* and *exhilaskesthai* in classical and koine Greek is "to propitiate, to placate, to appease."[117] The *NIDNTT* defines the idea behind *hilasmos* as "man's effort to dispose in his favor the awful and frequently calamitous power of the dead, the demons and the gods, and to strengthen his own actions by the assistance of supernatural forces."[118] In light of the use of this term in the context of the sanctuary service in the LXX, the question for our purposes here is whether the underlying Hebrew term *kipper* did convey the meaning of "appeasement" or "propitiation" of God in cultic settings. In the LXX, *hileōs einai* (or *hileōs genesthai*), "to be gracious" translates the Hebrew *sālaḥ* ("to forgive") a total of fifteen times. *Hilaskomai* appears twelve times—in the middle and passive voices with God as the subject effecting "forgiveness"—and *exilaskomai* appears 105 times, 83

117. See Homer, book 3, line 418–419: "αρπαλίμως μοι, τέκνα φίλα, κρηήνατ' ἐέλδωρ ὄφρ' ἤτοι πρώ τιστα θεῶν ἱλάσσομ' Ἀθήνην ("Quickly, my dear children, fulfill my desire, that first of all the gods I may propitiate Athena" (Murray, *The Odyssey*).

118. *NIDNTT* 3:149.

translating *kipper* in cultic settings in Exodus, Leviticus, and Numbers. It is in these cultic settings where the use of *exilaskomai* becomes problematic. There is little question that *exilaskomai* has the meaning of "propitiation" in the non-cultic settings of Zechariah 7:2; 8:22 and Mal 1:9, but in these three cases, it does not translate the Hebrew *kipper* but rather *ḥālāh* ("afflict oneself"; NRSV: "entreat the favor"). In the story of the purification performed by Phinehas in Numbers 25:13, *exilaskomai* translates *kipper*, but when the same event is mentioned in Ps 106[105]:30, *exilaskomai* translates *pālal* ("intervene, interpose"). In at least one case, the concept of purgation is conflated with *exhilaskesthai*, where the phrase "with the blood of the atoning sin offering" (*middam ḥaṭṭa'ṯ hakkippurim*) is translated as *tou haimatos tou katharismou tōn hamartiōn tou exilasmou* in the LXX (Exod 30:10).

The use of *exilaskomai* to translate *kipper* in Genesis 32:21 (MT) deserves consideration. The text reads: "For he said, 'I may appease him [*'aḵappᵉrâ p̄ānāyw*] with the present that goes ahead of me, and afterward I shall see his face [*'er'ê p̄ānāyw*]; perhaps he will accept me.'" The passage is similar to Prov 16:14: "As messengers of death *is* the king's wrath, but a wise man will appease it [*wᵉ'îš ḥāḵām yᵉḵappᵉrennâ*]." The literal meaning of the expression *'aḵappᵉrâ p̄ānāyw* in Genesis 32 is "to do *kipper* to the face of X"—but the wooden translation put forth by Schenker as "appease the face" is nonsensical.[119] Although the overall thrust of these passages is that of "averting the anger," this has generated problematic arguments in favor of reading *kipper* as "appease." Hill, for example, argued that "it may well be that it is precisely where the term is not a religious and conventionalised cult-word that we can discern its basic meaning," i.e., "propitiation."[120] Schwartz, however, laments the fact that scholars have too quickly fallen into the "pitfall" of reading *kipper* as "appease" in Genesis 32:21, and argues that the passage reflects a more primitive meaning of *kipper*, not primarily as "appease the wrath" but rather as "wiping" the face so that one could "see the face." Schwartz does so based on the etymology of both *kipper* ("rub off") and *ḥēmâ* ("wrath"), the latter stemming from "foam, froth," which Schwartz takes as something that needs to be wiped off from someone's face so the face can be seen.[121] It is also apparent by the four-times repetition of "face" (*p̄ānê*) in the passage that "Y doing something to the face of X will also lift Y's own face." In this case, the "sole meaning" intended in Genesis 32:21 is that *kipper* means "to wipe away." Fur-

119. Schenker, "*koper* et expiation," 32–46; see Schwartz, "Prohibitions," 53–54.
120. Hill, *Greek Words*, 31.
121. See Levine, *In the Presence*, 69, n. 39.

ther, he argues that *kipper* in cultic settings is used "metaphorically" and "does not include the notion of propitiation but only that of expiation."[122] Similarly, Milgrom warns that *kipper,* which required "ransom," "must be sharply distinguished from that of the sanctuary," because the goal of *kipper* in the tabernacle rituals was not for appeasing God's wrath but to avoid "causing the indwelling God to leave."[123]

The meaning of *hilaskesthai* in the NT has been a matter of extensive debate. The *TDNT* defines *hilaskomai* as "related to the same root as ἵλεως" such as "the verbs ἵλημι, 'to be gracious,' ἱλάσκομαι (ἱλάομαι, also ἱλέομαι, ἱλεόομαι) with the causative significance, 'to make gracious,' and in much the same sense, and particularly common in the LXX, ἐξιλάσκομαι."[124] In a seminal article in 1931, Dodd argued that the translation of *hilaskesthai* and *exilaskesthai* as "propitiation" when rendering *kipper* is "illegitimate" because it reflects a meaning "strange to non-biblical Greek."[125] Dodd built his conclusion on the fact that *kipper* is variously translated in the LXX by words such as *hagiazō* ("sanctify"), *katharizō* ("purify"), *athōoō* ("forgive"), and *analeiphō* ("rub off"), which do not carry the meaning of "propitiation." Based on these synonymous renderings, Dodd concludes that "we should therefore expect to find that they regard the ἱλάσκεσθαι class as conveying similar ideas."[126] Dodd's conclusions have been highly influential; in his commentary on Romans, Barrett followed Dodd when he concluded that "the common Greek meaning 'to propitiate' becomes practically impossible when, as sometimes happens, God is the subject of the verb. God cannot be said to propitiate man: he cleanses, forgives man and expiates (wipes out) his sin."[127]

Notwithstanding Dodd's forceful conclusions, Morris, Hill, Nicole, et al. attempted to undermine Dodd's thesis.[128] Critiquing Dodd's conclusion that concepts of purification and sanctification must decide the meaning of *hilaskesthai,* Hill argued, instead, that the few cases where *hilaskomai/exilaskesthai* mean "propitiation" in non-cultic contexts can regulate their meaning in cultic contexts because "what the verb meant in ordinary usage" can define "what made it specially fitted for us in connection with the cult."[129] Similarly,

122. Schwartz, "Prohibitions," 53.

123. Milgrom, "Day of Atonement," 80.

124. *TDNT* 3:314.

125. Dodd, "*Hilaskesthai,*" 360.

126. Dodd, *The Bible,* 84.

127. Barrett, *The Epistle to the Romans,* 72.

128. See Hill, *Greek Words,* 23–48; Morris, "The Use," 227–233; Morris, *The Apostolic Preaching,* 144–213; Nicole, "C. H. Dodd," 117–157.

129. Hill, *Greek Words,* 31.

Morris argued that "the averting of anger seems to represent a stubborn substratum of meaning from which all the usages can be naturally explained," even though his reading of Genesis 32:21 is questionable and his appeal to supporting evidence is often not self-evident (see Ps 25:11; 65:4).[130] Nicole, on the other hand, criticized Dodd's method, pointing out that his argument against "propitiation" considers only thirty-six percent of the cases.[131]

Reacting to Dodd's critics, Young—rather than seeing *exilaskomai* as synonymous with words such as *hagiazō* and *katharizō*, etc.—thinks that "the more cogent explanation is that the LXX translators considered *exilaskomai* unsuitable" in all contexts, especially when God is the subject and sin is the object of *kipper*.[132] Klaus Koch agreed when he pointed out that "*hilaskomai* and its derivative terms in the entire Old Testament never render *kipper* when God is the subject and the sin the object of the expiation."[133]

What becomes apparent is that the use of *hilaskomai* or *exilaskomai* in the LXX is inconsistent when rendering Hebrew words that may not all have the same meaning. Part of the problem, as pointed out by Joseph Do, is that "the discussion of expiation and propitiation for the noun ἱλασμός has been limited to the background of its LXX and NT Greek, not its Hebrew roots." Further, he argues, "the word-group ἱλάσκομαι or ἐξιλάσκομαι is used in the LXX in a manner very different from that of classical Greek."[134] Perhaps therein lies the source of disagreements on the matter. The problem for the advocates of the "propitiation" view is an over-dependence on the LXX for the meaning of a word used in the NT when the original Hebrew *Vorlage* of that word is readily available, as in the case of *kipper* and *hilaskesthai*. When *hilaskesthai* is used in the NT, it comes from a Hebrew cultus background that becomes vital to understanding the sacrificial atonement achieved by Jesus. As we have seen above, the Hebrew *kipper* in cultic settings never carries the meaning "propitiation" but only "expiation."

Although Dodd's position was open to criticism, and his assumptions may have been weakened by the fact that the idea of "appeasing" God does occasionally appear in the OT alongside the use of *hilaskomai*—although with high anthropopathic overtones—the notion of "appeasing" God is absent from the Hebrew cultus because it necessitates a concomitant "wrath" that needs to be appeased, a dynamic that is foreign to the rituals of the tab-

130. Morris, *The Apostolic Preaching*, 173.

131. Nicole, "C. H. Dodd," 129.

132. Young, "C. H. Dodd," 69.

133. Koch, "Die israelitische Sühneanschauung," 102.

134. Toan Do, "Jesus Death," 563–564.

ernacle.[135] The rituals were prescribed under the umbrella of God's gracious acceptance of loyal Israelites who entered into a covenant with him, not one of appeasement of an angry deity. While God is sometimes the direct object of *exilaskomai* in the LXX, he is never the direct object of the Hebrew *kipper*. Thus, Dodd remains correct that "the LXX does not regard the cultus as a means of pacifying the displeasure of the Deity, but as a means of delivering man from sin, and it looks in the last resort to God himself to perform that deliverance, thus evolving a meaning of ἱλάσκεσθαι strange to non-biblical Greek."[136] Von Rad explains the same principle thus: "the one who receives expiation is not Jahweh, but Israel: Jahweh is rather the one who acts, in averting the calamitous curse which burdens the community."[137] Similarly, Young warns that "the initiative of God in this action [of atonement] must be jealously preserved, and all intimations of the grotesque notion of God propitiating himself, or his justice, banished."[138] Here again, the syntax of Leviticus 17:11 comes into sharper focus: "It is not you who are placing the blood on the altar for me, for my benefit, but rather the opposite: it is I who have placed it there for you—for your benefit."[139] In the Hebrew cultus, God is the primary agent of atonement and forgiveness; his grace attracts the sinner, provides a way out, and accepts the sinner's acceptance of his divine solution. Such initiative reveals a preemptive, self-expiatory act that is independent of the offerer's actions, except for their attitude of contrition for sin and willing participation in the expiatory rites.

The preceding discussion has important implications for understanding *hilaskesthai* in the NT since it is from the cultic settings in the OT that the references to the atonement accomplished by Jesus emerge. We can now briefly examine the use of *hilaskesthai* in the NT. While *exilaskesthai* does not appear in the NT, there are six examples of the use of *hilaskesthai* and its cognates. The first comes from Luke 18:13: "'God, be merciful to me [*hilasthēti moi*], a sinner!'" which has the sinner as the object of God's mercy. Further, as discussed above, in Romans 3:25, Paul draws a parallel between Jesus and the sanctuary's *hilastērion*, the "atonement plate" found inside the Most

135. The Hebrew terms for wrath in the OT (*ʾap̱* and *qāṣap̱*), do not appear in the context of the sanctuary cultus, except for Lev 10:6: "Do not dishevel your hair, and do not tear your vestments, or you will die and wrath [*qāṣap̱*] will strike all the congregation," but the text does not deal with any ritual for the atonement of sins, instead with the disobedience of the priests and their disqualification from the service.

136. Dodd, "Hilaskesthai," 359.

137. Von Rad, *Old Testament Theology*, 270.

138. Young, "C. H. Dodd," 78.

139. See Schwartz, "Prohibitions," 51.

Holy Place: "whom God put forward as a sacrifice of atonement [*hilastērion*] (NRSV)." This comparison expands the meaning of Leviticus 17:11: God was the active agent in Jesus' DA-styled atonement.[140] Despite the peculiar construction in Hebrews 2:17, here again, the object of *hilaskesthai* is "sin," not God: "to make a sacrifice of atonement for the sins of the people [*to hilaskesthai tas hamartias*]." Two further examples of the use of *hilaskesthai* alongside the cultic expression *peri tōn hamartiōn* are 1 John 2:2: "and he is the atoning sacrifice [*hilasmos*] for our sins [*peri tōn hamartiōn hēmon*]," and 1 John 4:10: "... he loved us and sent his Son to be the atoning sacrifice [*hilasmon*] for our sins [*peri tōn hamartiōn hēmon*]."

In all of these NT examples—consistent with the use of *kipper/hilaskesthai* in cultic settings in the OT—the object of *hilasmos* is never God but rather the sinner and their sins, which leaves us with one possible conclusion: *hilasmos* and cognates in the NT must be read as "expiation," or "atonement," and never as "propitiation." Since the concept of "propitiation" was absent in the DA, it provides the most appropriate OT background for the meaning of *peri hamartias* in the NT in light of Jesus' atoning sacrifice.

## Conclusion

This chapter explored how the DA presented the NT authors with a mine of significant motifs, imagery, and a theological framework by which to proclaim Christ as a "sin/purgation offering." Jesus is portrayed in the NT both as a sacrifice—as evident in the use of "with his own blood" in Hebrews 9:12—and heavenly high priest, having entered "within the veil," the heavenly Most Holy Place, where he intercedes "always" for the faithful (Heb 7:25).[141] More importantly, it was God who provided the ultimate DA atoning offer in Jesus on the basis of his own gracious divine initiative for the sole benefit of the believer.

The NT authors' Christological exegesis of the DA forms a springboard for our intertextual study of Revelation, a task to which we now turn.

140. Ridderbos, *Paul*, 191, warns that "every representation as though an *Umstimmung* [retuning] were brought about in God by the propitiatory sacrifice of Christ and as though his wrath were only to be 'appeased' in the sacrifice of Christ, is completely contrary to the Pauline gospel."

141. Longenecker, "The Christology," 116, commenting on high-priestly Christology, points out that "[a]ll of the elements brought together in such a conception—messianic priesthood, the association of Melchizedek with the Messianic Age, redemptive sacrifice, and heavenly intercession" are present in the NT.

# 4

# THE DAY OF ATONEMENT IN THE BOOK OF REVELATION

In this chapter, our study finally arrives at the destination it set out to reach, as we explore how John drew on the themes, language, and imagery of the DA to present a unique high-priestly Christology. John's multifaceted visions of Christ as a high priest, atoning sacrifice, and universal ruler have overarching implications for Revelation's soteriology and eschatology.

## John's Allusive Method

As discussed previously, the early Christians lived and moved within a religious landscape suffused with the typological emanations of the OT and punctuated by the fulfillment of God's promises to Israel recorded there and enacted in the symbols of the sanctuary and its feasts. John operated within this same religious matrix of texts and traditions as Jesus and his disciples, and he used this vast network of intertextual signals to reveal Jesus to his readers. In keeping with the way the NT writers engaged the OT in their *kerygma* of Jesus Christ, John saw him *prefigured* in the Hebrew Scriptures. Utilizing his own flavor of "Christological exegesis" of Israel's Scriptures and sacred traditions, John read Jesus Christ back into them. Perhaps more than any other NT author, John expected his readers to experience a "conversion of the imagination" so they could find Jesus in the OT.[1] Here again, the analogy of a "map" used previously is helpful. As John traveled through the hallowed grounds of the Hebrew Scriptures with his "Christological map," he left clues of his voyage, setting up landmarks along the way to help us find

1. Hays, *Conversion of the Imagination*, 5–6.

Jesus Christ there. Reading and interpreting John's *apokalypsis* ("unveiling") of Jesus Christ today requires attention to these textual clues.

As discussed in the Introduction, John makes no quotations of the OT; allusive activity in Revelation takes the form of *allusions* and *echoes*. In general, *allusions* are established through direct and specific lexical correspondence with intertexts, while *echoes* are non-lexical, *thematic allusions* or "reverberations" of an idea or event familiar to both author and reader. In this chapter, *allusions* are listed as such (without qualifiers such as "clear" or "probable," etc.) because, when it comes to the influence of the DA on John's thought, the occasion was so unique and rare, and its rituals so distinct that any direct correspondence in Revelation to what happened on that day can be called an *allusion*, whether it contains verbal parallels, or by thematically alluding to its themes or rituals. For example, the presence of incense inside the Most Holy Place in Revelation 5 constitutes an *allusion* to the DA because this event only occurred then. Conversely, less clear thematic correspondences to the DA in Revelation are labeled "soft," "medium loud," or "loud" *echoes*, depending on their thematic and contextual coherence.

Significantly, John often makes one main *allusion*, which is accompanied by secondary *echoes*, forming a chamber of thematic resonance. An example of John's evocations of the OT is the vision of the slaughtered Lamb, where the dominating theme—atoning blood offered inside the Most Holy Place—forms an *allusion* to the DA that is enhanced by thematic *echoes* that bounce off the central *allusion* and off each other, forming what Hollander calls a "cave of resonant signification" (see pages 140–141).[2] Consequently, *allusions* often generate both *loud* and soft *echoes*, thus, an *echo* of a precursor text or idea is not any less important than an *allusion* to that intertext. The author uses these *allusions* to intentionally evoke and invoke intertexts, even if he may adapt them to his own rhetorical ends.

Even if Revelation is deemed to contain both *allusions* and *echoes* of the DA, the assessments found at the end of each section tend to err on the side of caution; the result is that *echoes* appear more frequently than *allusions*. Whereas this chapter moves sequentially through Revelation, this is not an exhaustive commentary on the subject of "atonement" in Revelation, and not all chapters are discussed.[3] This control is necessary because it would be beyond the scope of this study to pretend to exhaust all latent intertextu-

2. Hollander, *The Figure of Echo*, 64, 19. See Reis, *The Figure of Typological Echo*, forthcoming.
3. For a discussion of atonement in Revelation, see Johns, "Atonement," 124–46.

al relationships in Revelation. At the same time, I was also careful not to overestimate the importance of DA to the detriment of other intertexts in Revelation, lest I fall under condemnation for adding or taking away from the book. I prioritized exploring how the presence of DA imagery enhances the understanding of a given passage.

The current scholarly interest in the minutiae of intertextual theory would probably be intriguing to John. If we were to explain to him what we understand as *allusions* and *echoes* and ask him if he meant to allude or just echo a certain OT idea, he would likely answer: "Yes!" Considering the way he composed Revelation, he was more interested in how past revelatory events and voices testified to and prefigured Jesus Christ, not the vagaries of philology (he certainly wasn't concerned about consistently using correct Greek grammar either!). This does not diminish the value of studying Revelation as literature, it simply means that when doing so, we shouldn't miss the forest for the trees.

At this point, it should be evident to those interested in the intersection of biblical intertextuality and authorial intention that only the biblical author and perhaps the original readers hold the key to unveiling intertextual relationships latent in the text. Modern readers of Revelation can only hope for a glimpse, as "through a glass darkly," of John's mind and how his readers might have read (or heard) Revelation. Thus, the definitive list of *allusions* and *echoes* of the OT in Revelation will remain a matter of enduring debate. I can only reassure readers of *this book* as to my authorial intentions: that you learn to hear John's voice as it echoes in the text.

## The Day of Atonement in Revelation: An Overview

A vital part of John's theological mainframe were the sanctuary rituals and the Jewish feasts which he understood as *prefigurations* of Jesus' life, death, resurrection, and exaltation. Even Revelation's literary structure appears to be under the influence of the tabernacle service.[4] At the same time, the tabernacle rituals per se are not John's concern; he may speak of an "altar," "incense," a "slaughtered" lamb, and "souls under the altar," while bypassing the details of the rituals underlying this imagery.[5] Apparently, he had no qualms about adapting the rituals for his rhetorical ends. Like other NT au-

4. See Paulien, "The Role," 249.
5. See Johns, "Atonement and Sacrifice," 138.

thors, John draws on the typology of the Jewish feasts: Jesus is the Passover lamb, but also a type of the "goat for the Lord" whose blood was offered as a DA sacrifice in the heavenly Most Holy Place "as if slaughtered" (5:6).[6] He is also the heavenly high priest who invites us to become royal priests of a better temple, the priestly New Jerusalem; unlike the earthly high priest who offered ineffective yearly sacrifices, Jesus made a superior sacrifice on behalf of the church (Lev 16:6; Heb 6:19–20).[7] Jesus continues his heavenly intercession inside the figurative Most Holy Place in heaven, applying the benefits of his blood on behalf of the believer. As a result of Jesus' redemptive work, God will soon "tabernacle" with his people as He did with Israel of old (*skēnoō*, 7:15; 21:3).[8] Based on his prerogative as "the firstborn of the dead" as celebrated in the feast of the First Fruits (1:5; see 1 Cor 15:23), Christ will one day resurrect the dead saints in the "first resurrection" (20:5). The harvest theme present in the feast of First Fruits frames positively the harvest of the saved by the "Son of Man," but negatively the reaping of the wicked (14:4, 10, 16, 19). Pentecost—the fifty days of harvest and the covenant of the law embedded in the sound of the trumpet (1:10; Exod 19:16)—now symbolizes the new covenant of the Spirit with the church (1:10; 2:11, 17; 4:5; see Acts 2). The Spirit now guides, comforts, and rebukes the church (chapters 2–3). The eschatological DA announces good news for the blood-bought church but judgment on the wicked world. On the DA, the people were purified from their sin, a theme that reverberates throughout Revelation in the pure white robes of the saints symbolizing righteousness; sin is never part of their description in Revelation (chapters 7, 14). The judgment meted out on Azazel—an ancient, mysterious entity whose identity developed into a demonic figure in Jewish apocalyptic literature—is echoed in the punishment of the harlot, the beast, and the dragon (chapters 17–20).[9] The trumpet sound during the Feast of Trumpets reminds the people of their responsibilities within the covenant of which the DA was a culmination. It seems evident, therefore, that the book's original readers, likely familiar with the sanctuary cultus and the Jewish feasts, would easily identify the *allusions* and *echoes* of the DA found in Revelation.

6. See Odek, "The Heavenly Sanctuary," 217–227.

7. Barker, *Revelation*, 49: "The Christian hope of the return of the Lord was identical with the hope of the culmination of the tent Jubilee and the restoration of the creation for the time of the Messiah."

8. See Draper, "The Heavenly Feast"; Briggs, *Jewish Temple*, 54; Spatafora, *From the Temple of God.*

9. See 1 Enoch 13:1–2; 9–10; 14:2–16:2.

As the preceding overview indicates, as the culmination of all the rituals of the sanctuary service, the DA afforded John a treasure trove of imagery and theological motifs.[10] The result is a gallery of theological artistry that overpowered John's mind as he engaged in prophetic ministry on behalf of the seven churches of Asia Minor.

In the following pages, we will engage in "literary forensics," seeking to trace John's thumbprints as he pored over the Hebrew Scriptures and its traditions in search of images and ideas to unveil Christ. In our investigation, the correct interpretation of the data will require careful consideration of how John evokes and invokes sacred texts in his Christological exegesis of the OT.

## Revelation 1: Jesus as Heavenly High Priest

In Revelation 1:5, Jesus is introduced as "the faithful witness, the first-born of the dead, and the ruler of the kings of the earth." It is striking that in the first few verses of the book, we encounter sacrificial imagery: Jesus redeemed the church "by his blood" (*en tō haimati autou*).[11] The imagery of sacrificial blood and priesthood accompany the vision of the resurrected Jesus walking inside the sanctuary among the candlesticks (v. 12), which immediately establishes a sanctuary background to chapter 1, if not for the entire book.

### *Atoning Blood in Revelation 1*

Among the potential *echoes* of DA in Revelation are the references to "blood" in Revelation 1 in the context of Jesus' sacrificial death and his heavenly priesthood. As explored in chapter 2, the manipulation of atoning blood was foundational to the purification rites in the sanctuary service, and accordingly, blood was the central element of the DA. On that day, the cleansing of the tabernacle and its compartments was achieved by the application of sacrificial blood—which acted as a detergent removing impurity—followed by the dismissal of the "goat for Azazel" to the desert bearing the transgressions that were removed by the sacrificial blood (Lev 16:29, 34).

10. See Wolff, "Die Gemeinde," 189. Briggs, *Jewish Temple*, 54 writes: "Christ is a priest there [in Revelation], certainly a high priest in light of His person."

11. Compare with *en tō haimati Iesou* in Heb 10:19. See Schabow, *Gemacht*; Schüssler-Fiorenza, *Priester für Gott*.

Decock places the use of "blood" in Revelation in three categories: (1) the blood of Christ (as saving power); (2) the blood of the martyrs (as a cry for justice); and (3) and the blood of divine justice.[12] As previously discussed, just as the references to the blood of Jesus and his atoning sacrifice throughout the NT include *allusions* and *echoes* of the DA, the same occurs in Revelation. One potential line of evidence may be the fact that the central element of the DA ritual described in Leviticus 16, "blood" (*haima*), appears ten times there and five times in Revelation, specifically in connection with the blood of Jesus Christ (1:5; 5:9; 7:14; 12:11; 19:13). As in the Epistle to the Hebrews, Jesus is introduced in Revelation as the perpetual high priest, having attained a perfect renewal of the covenant by "his own blood" (see Heb 6:19–20; 9:12).[13] Jesus is at the same time high priest and atoning sacrifice. The other fourteen references to *haima* in Revelation appear in scenes of judgment arising from violence against the saints perpetrated by Babylon, during the harvest of the earth (6:10; 14:2; 16:3–4, 6 [2x]; 17:6 [2x]; 18:24; 19:2), and in cosmic/earthly cataclysms (Rev 6:12; 8:7–8; 11:6).

It is plausible that the references to "blood" in the book's prologue may simply point to an overarching sanctuary theme rather than specifically to a DA background. However, as will be seen below, the presence of atoning blood in conjunction with other thematic elements in the chapter (e.g., high-priestly robe, the candlesticks, the golden sash, trumpet imagery) amplifies this *echo* forming an audio-visual landscape where the DA becomes prominent.

### *"A Loud Voice as a Trumpet"*

Revelation 1 moves from the introductory remarks in vv. 1–9 to a vision of the resurrected Christ (vv. 10–20). While "in the spirit on the Lord's day" (1:9), John hears "a loud voice [or sound] as a trumpet" (v. 10). The first observation to be made here is the fact that the first actual interaction between Jesus and John in the book occurs at the sound of a trumpet, a daily occurrence in the Second Temple service and the annual festivals, including the DA.[14]

12. See Decock, "The Symbol of Blood," 157. Although categories 1 and 2 are helpful, category 3 may be questionable as he considers the blood on the robe of the rider of the white horse as the "blood of nations," which is not a decisive reading.

13. Discussions of the thematic parallels between the book of Hebrews and Revelation do not necessarily imply knowledge of Hebrews by readers of the seven churches. These parallels may, however, point to shared Christological traditions.

14. Caird, *Revelation*, 110–112. Beale, *Revelation*, 203, sees here an *allusion* to Exodus 19:16, 19,

In the Pentateuch, the blowing of ram's horns/trumpets announced the acts of God (see Exod 19:16; Num 10:10). Rabbinic literature mentions the use of trumpets on the first day of the Autumn month of Tishri as a prelude to the DA ten days later. The Feast of Trumpets and the DA were regarded as one single festival that "ushered in the time of judgment that led up to the Day of Atonement" and had eschatological overtones.[15] Paul's reference to the "archangel's call" and "the sound of God's trumpet" announcing Judgment Day in 1 Thess 4:16 is indicative of this tradition.

The phrase "a loud voice [or sound] as a trumpet" (*phōnēn megalēn hōs salpingos*) is significant because underlying it comes from the Hebrew *qôl šôp̱ar*, usually translated as *tēn phōnēn megalēn tēs salpingos* in the LXX (e.g., Exod 20:18). This phrase also appears in 2 Sam 15:10 and is translated in the LXX as *phōnēn tēs keratinēs* ("sound of the horn") where *keratinēs* translates *šôp̱ar* literally. The *šôp̱ar* was used in other cases of theophanic revelations, in calls to festal celebrations, and in battle.[16] The main difference between the frequent OT expression *qôl šôp̱ar* and the trumpet of Revelation 1 is the addition of the adjective "loud" (*megalē*). The source of this imagery comes from at least three passages of the OT. The first is the LXX text of Exod 19:16, which describes "the voice of the trumpet very loud" (*phonēn tēs salpingos ēchei mega*) at Sinai, which is synonymous with *phōnēn megalēn hōs salpingos* in Revelation 1. Strengthening this connection with the loud trumpet sound at Sinai is the fact that the giving of the law on Sinai is thematically parallel to Jesus' portrayal as "the ruler of the kings of the earth"; he pronounces the new covenant's code of ethics in the form of the messages to the seven churches (1:5, 11).[17] Thus, as the blowing of the trumpet is associated with the Sinaitic covenant and its annual renewal on the DA, Jesus' trumpet-like voice ushers in the new covenant established "by his [DA] blood."

Jesus' appearance shows that he speaks to John from the Holy Place after ministering inside the heavenly Most Holy Place. If the trumpet blast in Revelation 1 is associated with Sinai—a call that was daily reiterated by the trumpets at the sanctuary service—the call is now for the church to be a witness of the acts of God to the world. This call to be a witness is also repeated

*phonēn tēs salpingos ēchei mega; phonai tēs salpingos ēchei mega* as an attempt on the part of John to bestow prophetic authority on himself, as did Moses at Sinai. This conclusion is questionable as it shifts the passage's focus from the exalted Jesus to John.

15. Paulien, "The Role," 259, 261.

16. E.g., Ps 47:6; Isa 18:3; Joel 2:1; Zeph 1:16; Zech 9:14.

17. Beale, in "The Descent," 100–102, argues that the OT theophanies are often connected with the temple and that Sinai is also portrayed as a temple.

in 11:1–3, where the church is referred to as a "candlestick," shedding light in a dark world. The mention of "key of David" in 1:18 and 3:7 points to Isaiah 22:22: "I will place on his shoulder the key of the house of David ... he shall open, and no one shall shut; he shall shut, and no one shall open."[18] Allusions to these OT passages point to Jesus' exalted position as ruler/high priest over the church, presiding in his heavenly sanctuary. As the high priest of the new covenant, Jesus bestows the priesthood on the seven churches (1:6).

The second potential OT source for *phōnēn megalēn hōs salpingos* is Isaiah 27:13 where *b<sup>e</sup>šôp̱ār gāḏôl* ("a great trumpet"; LXX, *tē salpingi tē megalē*) heralds the eschatological redemption of Israel, but the context lacks thematic correspondence with Revelation 1.

A third source may be Leviticus 25:9: "Then you shall have the trumpet sounded loud [*šôp̱ar t<sup>e</sup>rûʿâ*] on the tenth day of the seventh month—on the day of atonement—you shall have the trumpet [*šôp̱ar*] sounded throughout all your land." The underlying Hebrew is "a blast of the *šôp̱ar*" a meaning lost in the LXX's *diangeleite salpingos phōnē*, lit. "proclaim with the trumpet." There are reasons to think Leviticus 25:9 could be the source for the trumpet imagery in Revelation 1: (1) the underlying imagery is the same, i.e., a loud blast of a trumpet/*šôp̱ar*; (2) Leviticus 25:9 provides the closest thematic source to Revelation 1, namely, a blast of the *šôp̱ar* at a time when the high priest comes into prominence on the DA; (3) the trumpet appears in the context of the application of sacrificial blood inside the sanctuary; and (4) the connection of the trumpet with "the day of the Lord" is a parallel to the call of the prophet Joel to prepare for "the day of the Lord:" "Blow the trumpet in Zion; sound the alarm on my holy mountain! Let all the inhabitants of the land tremble, for the day of the LORD is coming, it is near"; the people should be "sanctified" in preparation for this day (Joel 2:1,12–16). Significantly, the prescriptions for the DA are like Joel's preparations for the "day of the Lord" in that they call for self-affliction in the form of fasting, weeping, mourning, and the rending of hearts. Thus, by associating the sound of the *šôp̱ar* with the vision of the resurrected Christ, John builds on the association of the *šôp̱ar* with "the day of the Lord," thus echoing the eschatological overtones of the DA. The similarity of the themes of Revelation 1 and Joel 2 may even point to an understanding of the expression "the day of Lord" in Revelation 1:10 as an early Christian understanding of Christ's death in terms of an

18. The mention of a "key" may also be an *allusion* to 2 Enoch 42:1: "I saw the key-holders and guards of the gates of hell standing, like great serpents, and their faces like extinguished lamps, and their eyes of fire, their sharp teeth." See also Apocalypse of Zephaniah 6:11–15.

eschatological DA initiated at the cross and extending to the eschatological judgment upon the wicked world and the final eradication of sin.[19]

Since the Feast of Trumpets occurred in preparation for the DA as we have seen previously, this initial appearance of the trumpet sets the stage for the ensuing vision of the seals (6:1–7:8), the seven trumpets (8:6–11:19), and the seven bowls (16:1–21). In an eschatological sense, then, the trumpet from Revelation 1 is a harbinger of a cosmic DA calling the church to holiness through the blood of the Lamb and proclaiming judgment on his enemies.

In sum, the reference to the *šôp̱ar*, alongside high-priestly imagery in the chapter, constitutes a *loud echo* of the DA.

## *Jesus' High-Priestly Attire*

In addition to the *echoes* of the DA discussed above, the distinct high-priestly attire in Revelation 1 portrays Jesus ministering among the lampstands, which represent the seven churches (1:20), offering the intercession of his atoning blood on their behalf.[20]

In Revelation 1:13, Jesus appears "clothed with a long robe [*podērēs*] and with a golden sash across his chest." His presence inside the sanctuary, walking amidst the golden lampstands, dressed in a long, white *podērēs* with a golden sash around his waist, leaves little to the imagination: he is the heavenly high priest.[21] The high-priestly attire as found in the Hebrew

19. This reading of *kyriakē hēmera* was briefly entertained by Stott, "A Note," 70–75. See Strand, "Another Look," 174–181.

20. See Winkle, "Clothes," 366; Haran, *Temples*, 174; Himmelfarb, *Ascent*, 19; *Ant.* 15.403–409; 18.90–95; 20.6–16

21. Beginning with Irenaeus, commentators have agreed that Revelation 1:13 alludes to priestly attire, having Daniel 10:5 as the primary source followed by Ezek 9:2–3, 11. It should be noted that the LXX text of Daniel 10:5 does not follow the MT precisely; it renders *ûmoṯnāyw ḥagurim bᵉḵeṯem ʾûp̱āz* ("belt of gold of Uphaz") as *ek mesou autou phōs* ("light out of his middle"). If this is an *allusion* to Daniel, we can then be sure that John was using a Hebrew text at this point, not the LXX. See Hahm, "The Priestly Influence." Wolff, "Die Gemeinde," 189, writes: "The description of the Son of Man in v. 13 shows, while alluding to Dan. 10:5, the high-priestly features of the sash and the name of the garment: ποδήρης." So Caird, *Revelation*, 25; Beale, *Revelation*, 210; Mounce, *Revelation*, 58; Kistemaker, *Revelation*, 95; Osborne, *Revelation*, 89; Beale, *Revelation*, 210; Beale, *Daniel in Revelation*, 160; Aune, *Revelation 1–5*, 93–94; Koester, *Revelation*, 246; Barker, *Revelation*, 84–85; Rowland, "A Man Clothed," 99–110; Sweeney, "Ezekiel," 136. Aune disagrees, maintaining that "the most common Hebrew term for the robes of the high priests and priests in the OT is כְּתֹנֶת, usually translated as χιτών" and not *podērēs*, because it is "hardly understood as a technical term" and that there is "no clear indication on the part of the author to conceptualize the appearance of the exalted Christ in priestly terms." (*Revelation 1–5*, 93–94). Aune draws on the fact that *podērēs* in the LXX translates five Hebrew words related to the high-priestly attire: *ḥōšen* ("breastplate," Exod 28:15, 22), *mᵉʿil* ("cloak," Exod 28:4; 29:5), *ēp̱ôḏ* ("ephod," Exod 28:31); *ḇaḏ* ("linen," Ezek 9:2, 3,11), and

text (MT) of Exodus 28:4, 42: the linen undergarments (*miḵnsê-ḇāḏ*), a blue, wooly robe (*mᵉʿil*), a linen tunic (*kᵉṯōneṯ-baḏ*), the ephod (*ʾēp̄ōḏ*), the linen turban (*miṣnep̄eṯ baḏ*), a linen sash (*ʾaḇnēṭ baḏ*), a breast piece (*ḥōšen*), and the *ṣiṣ zahāḇ ṭahôr*, a diadem of pure gold tied around the turban containing the words: "Holy to the Lord" (Exod 28:36; 39:30).[22]

On the DA, the high priest was stripped of his daily, elaborate clothing and dressed like an ordinary priest. His "holy vestments" (*bigḏê-qōḏeš*, Lev 16:4) were all made of linen (*baḏ*): "the holy linen tunic" (*kᵉṯōneṯ-baḏ qōḏeš*; LXX, *chitōna linoun*), the "linen undergarments" (*miḵnsê-ḇaḏ*; LXX, *periskeles linoun*), "the linen sash" (*ʾaḇnēṭ baḏ*; LXX, *zōnê linē*), and "the linen turban" (*miṣnep̄eṯ baḏ*; LXX, *kidarin linēn*).[23] To these, we could add the *ṣiṣ nēzer-haqqōḏeš*, the golden diadem attached to the turban (Exod 28:38). After the "goat for Azazel" rite, he bathed and donned his full high-priestly attire (Lev 16:24).

The term *podērēs* used to describe Jesus' long robe (1:13) is an *hapax legomenon* in the NT and carries adjectival connotations; as the root of the Greek word implies, a *podērēs* reaches to the feet (*pous*).[24] Though both the high-priestly *mᵉʿil* and the *kᵉṯōneṯ* could be understood as *podērēs*, i.e., reaching to the feet, the *mᵉʿil* did not have sleeves (as did the *kᵉṯōneṯ*), and was "blue" with pomegranate adornments and bells at the hem and was always worn with the ephod (Exod 28:31–35).[25] In the LXX, *podērēs* is used exclusively in two contexts: (1) to refer to high-priestly attire (Exod 25:6; 28:4, 27; 29:5; 35:8; Zech 3:4); (2) to describe a heavenly being (Ezek 9:2, 3, 11).[26] Thus, *podērēs* has divine, high-priestly overtones, and this is why John re-

*maḥalāṣôṯ* ("fine robe" in Zech 3:4). Nevertheless, Aune seems to miss the forest for the trees since *podērēs* exclusively translates high-priestly and heavenly attire in the LXX. For example, the Hebrew term for the blue priestly robe, *mᵉʿil* (occurring twenty-seven times in the MT), is variously translated in the LXX outside cultic setting as *diploida* (2 Sam 2:19; 24:4, 11; 28:14; Job 29:14; Ps 19:29), *stolē byssinē* (1 Chr 15:27), *thōraka* (Isa 59:17), and *himation* (Ezra 9:5; Isa 61:10).

22. Josephus calls the *miḵnsê-ḇāḏ* as the "Machanase, which means something that is fast tied. It is a girdle, composed of fine twined linen, and is put about the privy parts, the feet to be inserted into them, in the nature of breeches; but above half of it is cut off, and it ends at the thighs and is there tied fast" (*Ant.* 3.152).

23. בַּד is also used in descriptions of heavenly beings in Ezek 9:2–3, 11; 10:2; Dan 10:6; 12:3; Mal 2:7.

24. See BDAG, s.v. "ποδήρης."

25. Josephus describes the *kᵉṯōneṯ* as sitting close to the body and having sleeves (*Ant.* 3.153) while the *mᵉʿil* did not have sleeves. See *HALOT* 2:612. See Gesenius and Tregelles, *Gesenius' Hebrew and Chaldee Lexicon*, s.v. "מְעִיל."

26. Outside the OT, *podērēs* appears in Wisdom of Solomon 18:24; Sirach 27:8; 45:8 and in the Epistle of Aristeas 96.

serves it for Jesus in Revelation, while all the other white (linen) robes in the book are either *himatia* or *stolas*; the robes promised to the churches of Sardis and Laodicea are *himatiois leukois* and *himatia leuka* (3:5, 18). The same *himatia* are worn by the twenty-four elders in Revelation 4:4 (*himatiois leukois*), while the robes of the souls under the altar and the great multitude are *stolas* (6:11; 7:9, 13–14; see 22:14).[27] All white robes in Revelation symbolize "righteousness" (19:8).[28] In addition, the avenging angels, who carry the seven plagues, also wear white linen robes with a "golden sash," and "a shining, white linen robe" (*linon katharon lampron*, 15:6) like Jesus.

The term *podērēs* does not occur in the Greek text of Leviticus 16; the "holy linen tunic" (*kᵉṯōneṯ-baḏ qōḏeš*) worn by the high priest on the DA is translated in the LXX as *chitōn linoun hēgiasmenon*.[29] This absence, however, is not fatal to seeing Jesus as a high priest in his DA attire in Revelation 1 because, as indicated by Trench, *podērēs* is "properly an adjective" more than a noun: it simply describes the length of the robe.[30] Since the undergarments of the high priest were the only pieces of his attire that did not reach to the feet but were tied to his thighs (Exod 28:42; see *Ant.* 3.152), it was the *k̲ᵉṯōneṯ-ḇāḏ*, the long linen robe worn regularly by Aaron under the *mᵉʿil* that was a *podērēs*, i.e., reaching to the feet. This is also found in the LXX text of Exod 29:5 where *k̲ᵉṯōneṯ-ḇāḏ* is rendered as *ton chitōn ton podērēs*.[31] Therefore, assuming *podērēs* denotes the long, white, linen, high-priestly, tunic, it is the *absence* of the other accessories that allows us to identify with precision which robe Jesus was wearing: "the holy linen tunic" prescribed for the DA.

Despite the preceding evidence, Winkle writes about Revelation 1:13: "Despite the appearance that ποδήρης here translates כתנת, one cannot conclude that it stands for any high-priestly dress item other than מעיל … the high priest's woolen, hyacinth-dyed, foot-length robe, thus com-

27. See the helpful discussion in Trench, *Synonyms*, 184–187.

28. It is also noteworthy that while Matthew describes the high priest as rending his *himation* (Matt 26:65), Mark uses *chitōn* (Mark 14:63).

29. Plutarch uses a similar expression in his description of the Jewish high-priestly attire "on feast days" as *chitōn podērē* likely referring to the Jewish Yom Kippur (see *Symposiacs* IV.6). Bernardakis, *Plutarchus Moralia*, 173.

30. Trench, *Synonyms*, 187.

31. E.g., Exod 28:40; 39:27; see Gen 37:3; 2 Sam 15:32; Isa 22:21 See Josephus, who translates *k̲ᵉṯōneṯ-ḇāḏ* in Leviticus 16:4 *podērēs chitōn*, a robe that "reaches down to the feet, and sits close to the body and has sleeves that are tied fast to the arms"; *Ant.* 3.153. See also Sirach 45:8 where מכנסים כתנת ומעיל in the Greek is *periskelē kai podērē kai epōmida*, where *podērē* stands for the כתנת and *epōmida* for the מעיל.

municating his high-priestly identity."[32] This conclusion can be challenged as follows:

(1) The high-priestly *mᵉʿil* was never worn as a single piece of clothing. As the root מעל, "to cover," implies, it is meant to be worn as an outer garment over the *k̠ᵉṯōneṯ*, "the linen tunic," which, in turn, was worn over the *mik̠nsê-ḇāḏ*, the "linen undergarments" (Exod 28:42).[33] At least one lexicon defines *mᵉʿil* as a "sleeveless, coat-like upper garment" (see 2 Sam 13:18).[34]

(2) As an accompanying accessory, the high-priestly *mᵉʿil* was always worn in conjunction with other high-priestly accessories, such as the *ēp̄ôḏ*. It is called the "robe of the ephod" (*mᵉʿil hāʾēp̄ôḏ*; e.g., Exod 28:31). The ephod supported the *ḥōšen*, "breast piece," which housed the Urim and the Thummim (Exod 28:30), and the shoulder pieces with two onyx stones (Exod 28:12).[35] The *mᵉʿil* had golden bells and pomegranates at the hem. As the crowning jewel of the high-priestly attire, Aaron wore the *ṣîṣ nēzer-haqqōḏeš*, a golden diadem tied around the turban containing the words: "Holy to the Lord" (Exod 28:36; 29:6; 39:24–30; Lev 8:9). There is no hint in Revelation 1 that the exalted Jesus is wearing the *mᵉʿil hāʾēp̄ôḏ* and its accessory pieces.[36]

(3) The high-priestly *mᵉʿil* was not made of linen but of "blue wool yarn."[37] In turn, the robes of all angelic beings in Revelation are made of white linen, a material that had sacral connotations.[38] Moreover, John uses "white" sixteen times in Revelation (e.g., *leukainō*, "to make white," 7:14) and provides the key to understanding its meaning: purity and righteousness (19:8).[39]

32. Winkle, "Clothes Make," 182.

33. *TWOT* s.v. "מְעַל."

34. Koehler and Baumgartner, *Lexicon*, s.v. "מְעִיל."

35. The Urim and the Thummim were a symbol of judgment: "thus Aaron shall bear the judgment of the Israelites on his heart before the Lord continually" (Exod 28:3). This piece is also missing in Leviticus 16:4. What is the significance of not wearing the Urim and the Thummim on the DA? Rooke suggests: "The obvious consequence is that he is rendered ritually deaf and dumb while inside the Tent of Meeting . . . he is deprived of everything that marks him out as a high priest, and is left vulnerable" (Rooke, "Day of Atonement," 352). This may be echoed in the messianic prophecy in Isaiah 63:2: "I have trodden the winepress alone; from the nations no one was with me."

36. Winkle admits this when he writes: "Consequently, it is significant to note that in translating the מְעִיל, the translators of the LXX typically used a word that was characterized by its relationship to another article of dress that the high priest wore" ("Clothes," 159).

37. Swanson, *Dictionary*, s.v. "תְּכֵלֶת"; see *TWOT* s.v. "תְּכֵלֶת." In *Ant.* 3.159 Josephus describes the robe as "reaching to his feet (in our language it is called Meeir) . . . tied round with a girdle, embroidered with the same colors and flowers as the former, with a mixture of gold interwoven."

38. See Exod 28:42; 39:28; Lev 6:10; 16:4, 23, 32.

39. E.g., Rev 1:14 (2x); 2:17; 3:4, 5, 18; 4:4; 6:2, 11; 7:9; 7:13; 14:14; 19:11, 14 (2x); 20:11. See Tavo, *Woman, Mother*, 167: "Clearly, the act of being clothed in white, whether by robe, garment or linen, connotes a life of purity and integrity."

Revelation 19:13 depicts "the armies of heaven, wearing fine linen, white and pure," riding white horses. We should rightly assume, then, that the rider of the horse—who has been historically interpreted as symbolizing the exalted Jesus—wears the same "fine linen, white and pure." The New Jerusalem itself is symbolically "clothed with fine linen, bright and pure for the fine linen [i.e., "white"] is the righteous deeds of the saints" (19:8). The promise to the righteous in Sardis also sheds light on the color of Jesus' *podērēs* in 1:13: "they will walk with me, dressed in white, for they are worthy" (3:4).[40] Likewise, the high priest's "holy linen tunic" worn on the DA was white (see Yoma 3:6).[41] After Aaron's work inside the tabernacle was completed, these "linen vestments" were replaced by his full high-priestly garments, called *b^egādim* since they were not all made of linen (Lev 16:24; m. Yoma 3:7). This change of attire implies that the service of the DA was accepted, and Aaron could now offer the *tāmîd* wearing his full high-priestly dress.

(4) Throughout Revelation, John shows a keen interest in the color of what he sees. We read of a golden sash, hair white as wool/snow, eyes as fire, feet as bronze, scarlet robes, red dragon, four colored horses, to name a few. In addition, the color of clothing has a spiritual connotation and reveals the character of those who wear it: in general, black, purple, and scarlet connote evil, while white connotes purity and righteousness and is reserved for heavenly beings and saints.[42] It is highly improbable that John would simply "miss" the color of Jesus' *podērēs* if it were the blue, heavily decorated, high-priestly *m^eʿil*.

(5) The long robes of the heavenly beings in Ezekiel 9:2, 3, 11; 10:2, 6, 7 and Daniel 10:5; 12:6, 7 are likewise made of linen. John is alluding to Ezekiel 9 and Daniel 7 in Revelation 1:13, which indicates that, along with all other heavenly beings in Revelation, Jesus is clothed in pure, white linen. It appears, then, that John understands the terms *podērēs* ("long robe") and *byssinos* ("linen robe") to be synonymous. In other words, a white *byssinos*, like the one given to the Lamb's bride (19:8), was also a *podērēs*. Ultimately, all those who follow the Lamb will be figuratively clothed as he.[43]

40. Note the presence of *axioi*, which is the same word used for the lamb in Revelation 5.

41. See Neufeld, "Under the Cover," 72: "golden" robe.

42. The harlot who rides the beast in Revelation 17 is "clothed in purple and scarlet" (*peribeblēmenē porphyroun kai kokkinon*, v. 4), a dress that is identical to Babylon's attire with the addition of *byssinon*: "... the great city, clothed in fine linen, in purple and scarlet" (*peribeblēmenē byssinon porphyroun kai kokkinon*, 18:16).

43. See Barker, *Revelation*, 84–85: "On balance, we should probably assume that the robe in Revelation 1.13 was the white linen worn by the high priest when he entered the holy of holies as no other vestments are mentioned. Had it been the long coloured robe worn elsewhere, he would have

Based on his conclusion that *podērēs* in Revelation refers to the high-priestly *m$^{e}$ʿil hāʾēp̱ôḏ*, Winkle further argues: "Since the foot-length garment of Jesus is hyacinth-colored, it cannot be referring to Yom Kippur or Day of Atonement imagery but rather imagery corresponding to the regalia worn by the high priest on every other day but one." [44] First, this is a circular argument based on his a priori, unsupported conclusion that Jesus was wearing the blue *m$^{e}$ʿil*. Secondly, this surprising conclusion is based on the argument of silence since John nowhere mentions the color of the robe. Further, while Winkle is correct that the term *podērēs* does not appear in Leviticus 16:4—the term there is *chitōna linoun*—*podērēs* translates *m$^{e}$ʿil* only twice in the LXX (see *hypodytēs*, nine times).[45] As such, *podērēs* is hardly a *terminus technicus* for *m$^{e}$ʿil*, as Winkle seems to imply. Fourth, while the term *m$^{e}$ʿil* does not refer exclusively to the high-priestly robe in the OT when it is thus used, it is introduced primarily as *m$^{e}$ʿil hāʾēp̱ôḏ*, "the robe of the ephod" because they were worn together as one piece.[46] In sum, our different conclusions stem from our presuppositional lenses; while Winkle argues that the absence of high-priestly imagery in Revelation 1 presupposes its *presence*, I argue that its *absence* indicates the high-priestly imagery comes from a different sanctuary context: Yom Kippur.

As an addendum, there are parallels between the heavenly, high-priestly Yahoel, who officiates during Yom Kippur in the Apocalypse of Abraham, and the exalted, high-priestly Christ in Revelation 1. For example, Yahoel has "the likeness of a man" (Apoc. Ab. 10:4), while Jesus is called the "Son of man" in 1:13. Yahoel's hair is "like snow" (Apoc. Ab. 11:4), while Jesus' hair is "white as snow" (1:14). Yahoel's body is likened to precious stones (Apoc. Ab. 11:2), while Jesus' feet are like "burnished bronze, refined in a furnace (1:15). In sum, both books seem to draw on similar traditions and high-priestly representations of heavenly beings (see Dan 10:5; Ezek 9:2–3, 10).

In conclusion, it is implausible that John would omit high-priestly accessories and their color had Jesus been wearing the blue "robe of the ephod." John's readers likely took the absence of the regular high-priestly attire in

been wearing over it the embroidered tunic, the ephod, and the breastplate set with twelve gem stones. These are not mentioned." See Vogel, *Cultic Motif*, 49: "In chaps. 10 and 12, Daniel meets 'a certain man clothed in linen,' pointing to a high-priestly figure officiating on the Day of Atonement, who engages him in lengthy dialogues that make up the main content of these chapters."

44. Winkle, "You Are What You Wear," 343; Winkle, "Clothes," 304.

45. E.g., Exod 28:4, 31; 33; 34; 36:29–33.

46. E.g., Exod 28:31, 34; 29:5; 39:22, 23, 24, 25, 26; Lev 8:7; 1 Sam 2:19; 15:27; 18:4; 24:4, 11; 28:14; 2 Sam 13:18; 1 Chr 15:27; Ezra 9:3, 5; Job 1:20; 2:12; 29:14; Ezek 26:16.

1:13 to mean that Jesus' robe was the long, white, high-priestly "holy linen tunic" worn by the high priest on the DA while offering atoning blood inside the sanctuary. For this reason, Jesus' high-priestly dress in Revelation 1:13 constitutes an *allusion* to the high-priestly dress worn on the DA.

## *Podērēs in the Epistle of Barnabas*

Further support for the previous conclusion is found in the Christian traditions underlying the Epistle of Barnabas, where *podērēs* describes Christ's garment. In a passage comparing the sacrifice of Jesus with the ritual of the "goat for Azazel," the author states: "For they shall see Him in that day wearing the long scarlet robe [*podērē*] about His flesh, and shall say, Is not this He, Whom once we crucified [*katakentēsantes*, lit. "pierced"] and set at naught and spat upon; verily this was He, Who then said that He was the Son of God" (Barn. 7:9).[47] The use of *podērē* in Barnabas is relevant for a couple of reasons: (1) it connects *podērē* to the appearance of the exalted Christ as John does in Revelation 1:13; (2) it connects *podērē* to the lament of the nations who "pierced him" (*katakentēsantes*) as does John in Revelation 1:9, "even those who pierced him" (*exekentēsan*) which frames Christ's death in cultic terminology; and (3) the *allusion* to the goat Azazel connects Jesus' *podērē* to a DA background, despite its scarlet color.[48]

## *Jesus' Golden Sash*

The presence of a high-priestly "golden sash" provides further support for seeing Jesus as a high priest officiating on the DA. This sash was one of the pieces of clothing prescribed for the high priest on the DA: "He shall put on the holy linen tunic, and shall have the linen undergarments next to his body, fasten the linen sash [*ab̲nēṭ b̲ād̲*; LXX: *zōnē linē*], and wear the linen turban; these are the holy vestments" (Lev 16:4). Josephus describes how the sash was worn: "[I]t is girded to the breast a little above the elbows, by

47. See Lightfoot and Harmer, *The Apostolic Fathers*, 276; Ben Ezra, *The Impact*, 152–3.

48. In *Legum Alegoriae* II.56, Philo states that the high priest never went into the Most Holy Place wearing a *podērēs*: "On this account the high priest "will not come into the holy of holies clad in a garment reaching to the feet [*en tō poderei*] ... to make an offering of the blood of the soul, and to sacrifice the whole mind to God the Savior and Benefactor." Philo also uses *podērēs* in *De Vita Mosis* II.118 to describe the blue *mᵉʿil*, the blue tunic (Exod 28:31–35), which was not worn on the DA. It appears then that Philo and John both use *podērēs* adjectivally to describe garments that "reach down to the feet" while having different colors and functions. Furthermore, Philo is incorrect that the robe used on the DA did not reach the feet since the "holy linen tunic" worn on the DA did.

a girdle often going round, four fingers broad, but so loosely woven, that you would think it were the skin of a serpent" (*Ant.* 3.154). This description matches the position of the sash as seen in Rev 1:13: "girded on the chest with a golden sash." Lastly, Lev 8:7 indicates that the *k*ᵉ*ṯōneṯ* was tied around with the *aḇnēṭ* forming a set, and this is how John sees Jesus.

## *The Day of Atonement as Validation of Jesus' High Priesthood*

The significance of the preceding discussion of the exalted Jesus' high-priestly clothing on the DA lies in the fact that typologically, as the ultimate high priest, he no longer needs to return to the regular priesthood clothes and the daily rituals, a return that betrayed the inefficacy of the earthly sanctuary (Heb 10:5–18). Instead, having done his high-priestly work "once and for all" (Heb 9:12), Jesus appears in his high-priestly DA attire, interceding for the seven churches of Asia Minor. He is the high priest *par excellence,* not only because he wears high-priestly garments but also because he purchased humankind with his blood in death. His redeeming sacrifice granted him the authority to exhort the churches.

John's vision of the high-priestly Jesus Christ affirms the notion embedded in the OT rituals that the DA was a confirmation of the high-priestly office. As Rooke suggests, as "it is a rite of entrance . . . the Day of Atonement ceremonial in Leviticus 16 can be seen as the first official duty that Aaron undertakes after his consecration, which in turn could imply that the Day of Atonement is to be regarded as the validation of Aaron's high priesthood" (e.g., Zech 3:7).[49] Thus, as his first high-priestly act after his unveiling to John, Jesus exhorts and offers cleansing from sin to the churches of Asia in the form of white robes. His DA sacrifice on the cross has made him a "high priest forever" (Heb 6:20; 5:6; 7:3, 17, 21–25, 28).

| **Assessment: The Day of Atonement in Revelation 1** | |
|---|---|
| *Allusive Type*: Allusion; loud echoes. | *Thematic Coherence*: DA high-priestly clothing worn while offering atoning blood in the sanctuary; the sound of the trumpet. |

49. Rooke, "The Day of Atonement," 357.

## Revelation 2 & 3: The Day of Atonement as Precursor to the Letters to the Churches of Asia

As discussed in chapter 2, the DA stands at the gate of the section of Leviticus 17–26, which scholars have viewed as a covenant lawsuit, a legal code separate from the rest of Leviticus, known as *Heiligkeitsgesetz,* i.e., "the holiness code."[50] Brueggemann sees the OT as full of "metaphor and imagery of the courtroom trial," which, according to him, frame it "as a series of claims asserted for Yahweh, the God of Israel."[51] By appealing to OT covenantal themes, John seeks to assert his authority as the successor of OT prophets.

The regulations of the Levitical *Heiligkeitsgesetz* ("holiness law") pertained to the following aspects of Israel's life:

(1) Slaughtering of animals (Lev 17:1–9)
(2) Prohibitions of the consumption of blood (17:10–16)
(3) Sexual relations (18:1–29)
(4) Ritual and moral purity (19:1–37)
(5) Sanctions for impurity (20:1–27)
(6) Priestly holiness (21:1:24)
(7) Use of offerings (22:1–16)
(8) Kinds of acceptable offerings (22:16–33)
(9) Holy Feasts:
  Sabbath (23:1–3)
  Passover (23:4–5)
  Feast of Unleavened Bread (23:5–8)
  Feast of First Fruits (23:9–14)
  Feast of Weeks (23:15–22)
  Feast of Trumpets (23:23–25)
  Day of Atonement (23:26–32)
  Feast of Tabernacles (23:33–44)

50. The term was coined by Klostermann, *Der Pentateuch*, 385.

51. Brueggemann, *Theology of the Old Testament*, xvi. See also Davidson, "The Divine Covenant Lawsuit," 45–84. For a full discussion on the various explanations for what scholars call a separate legal code known as *Heiligkeitgesetz,* see Sun, "Holiness Code," 254–258. Sun summarizes arguments for the unity of this section with the rest of Leviticus thus: "The following formal considerations are not suggestive of an originally independent legal corpus: (1) the plurality of speech report formulae (17:1; 18:1; etc.); (2) the two compliance reports (21:24; 23:44); and (3) the repetition of material within the corpus (e.g., 19:3 = 19:30; 19:4, 30 = 26:1–2; 19:5–8 = 22:29–30 [see Lev 7:15–18]; 19:9–10 = 23:22; 19:27–28 = 21:5; 19:31 = 20:6; 19:34 = 24:22; 20:6–8 = 20:27; 25:18–19 = 26:4–5)."

(10) Care of the lampstand of the Holy Place (24:1–4)
(11) Bread for the tabernacle (24:5–9)
(12) Punishment for blasphemy (24:10–23)
(13) Sabbatical year (25:1–7)
(14) Year of jubilee (25:8–55)
(15) Rewards for obedience (25:1–13)
(16) Sanctions for violations (26:14–46)

The DA, the day of renewal of God's covenant with Israel, stood as the gatekeeper of this holiness code. The placement of these regulations immediately after the institution of the DA is not haphazard: as the covenant was renewed on the DA, Israel should strive to safeguard it. In turn, their continued effort to keep these regulations makes the yearly celebration of the DA viable. There is, therefore, a bi-directionality, or codependency, in the relationship of these holiness instructions and the DA, as Wenham writes: "God's call to Israel to be his holy people preceded the revelation of the law at Sinai, but only obedience could make holiness a living reality."[52]

According to Bandy, the "prophetic lawsuit" found in Deuteronomy 32 also plays a vital role in Revelation, influencing how John structured the book.[53] It is indeed intriguing that John places the instructions, praises, and reproaches of the seven churches of Asia immediately following the revelation of Jesus Christ as the heavenly high priest officiating inside the sanctuary in a DA setting. Jesus has successfully fulfilled the antitypical DA by his death on the cross, followed by his installment as heaven's high priest at the ascension. Now the seven churches of Asia Minor are invited to follow a set of "holiness" prescriptions just as ancient Israel. The themes shared by the instructions in the Levitical code and the admonitions present in the messages to the seven churches "presume the existence of a spiritual gap between the Lord and the people," explained Kiuchi.[54] After Jesus is presented as a high priest officiating on the DA, he exhorts the seven churches.

The messages to the seven churches reveal God's desire that his people, now symbolized by the church, should pursue holiness (Exod 19:6). Revelation 1:6 alludes to the Greek text of Exodus 19:6: Israel was called to be a "kingdom of priests and a holy nation" (LXX: *basileion hierateuma kai ethnos*

52. Wenham, *Leviticus*, 31; Caird, *Revelation*, 110.
53. See Bandy, *The Prophetic Lawsuit*.
54. Kiuchi, *Leviticus*, 28.

*hagion*; cf. 1 Pet 2:9: *basileion hierateuma ethnos hagion*) the church is also a "kingdom, priests" (*basileian hiereis*). This *allusion* is repeated in Revelation 5:10: "you have made them to be a kingdom and priests [*basileian kai hiereis*] to our God."[55] The church is now invited to safeguard its place in the new covenant that Christ has instituted with "his own blood" (opposed to the OT high priest's use of the ineffective blood of animals; see Heb 9:11–12). By his perfect sacrifice in the antitypical DA, Jesus has confirmed his status as heaven's high priest once for all; by his confirmation as a high priest on the merits of his perfect DA sacrifice, he can grant priesthood on the "saints from every tribe and language and people and nation" (5:9–10).

The church's royal high priesthood (or priestly kingdom) is established through Christ's blood, shed on the typological DA as explained in the Epistle to the Hebrews and echoed in Revelation 1.[56] As the successful completion of the DA reconsecrates and renews the tabernacle's "lease" for Israel, so it is Christ's successful ministration of the typological DA at the cross and his subsequent ascension into "heaven itself" (Heb 9:24) that makes the church's priesthood possible and meaningful. According to Paul, Christ's rulership comes from victory in death (see Col 2:15: "and having disarmed the powers and authorities, he made a public spectacle of them, triumphing over them by the cross"); his victorious death has raised him to the right hand of God where the church is also, as rulers-priests, "seated with Christ in heavenly realms" (Col 3:1; also Eph 1:20; 2:5; 1 Cor 15:20; 1 Pet 3:18, 22).[57]

John, however, takes this OT promise of priesthood further by conferring actual high priesthood status to the saints of Sardis: "they will walk with me, dressed in white, for they are worthy" (3:4).[58] This high-priestly privilege of ministering before God alongside Jesus echoes the full access to the heavenly Most Holy Place now granted to all Christians: "where Jesus, a forerunner on our behalf, has entered" (Heb 6:19–20). Such a promise is extended to all Christians; theirs is not a high priesthood of repeated blood sacrifices, but of privileged access to the presence of God granted because of Christ's DA sacrifice. They serve continuously before a holy God as the high

55. See Fiorenza, *Revelation*, 43.
56. See Beale, *Revelation*, 193.
57. Beale, *Revelation*, 194.
58. Note the presence of *axioi*, which also describes the Lamb in Revelation 5:4, 9, 12.

priests ministered inside the Most Holy Place on the DA. This high priesthood will one day culminate in the New Jerusalem, God's high-priestly city.[59]

### *Jesus' High-Priestly Intercession Portrayed*

As the cross stands as an eschatological DA sacrifice, Jesus lives perpetually before the Father to intercede through the continuous merits of his blood (Heb 7:25). He has purchased us and "washed us" by his blood, an action that remains effective for the seven churches long after the initial sacrifice on the cross had been completed, which mirrors the needed application of blood subsequently to the sacrifice proper in the sanctuary rituals. Nevertheless, it must be said that the typology should not be overextended to create an actual, parallel ritual in a literal, heavenly sanctuary, which, as has been argued by some, is an exact copy of and subservient to the earthly. The earthly realities were shadows of the heavenly; the author of the Epistle to the Hebrews saw in the cross and Jesus' subsequent ascension the fulfillment of the typology of the DA (Heb 9:12, 24). Jesus went into the heavenly Most Holy Place with better blood, his own. In Revelation, the DA frames the messages of purification and judgment, initially to the seven churches of Asia Minor and then to the world.

Not only is Jesus introduced as a high priest giving instructions to the seven churches, but John appears to stand in the place of Aaron, assuming a partial, earthly high-priestly role as he mediates the transmission of divine messages to the seven churches.[60] Moses and Aaron represented the unity between priesthood and prophecy; Jesus and John stand at the convergence of heavenly high priesthood and prophetic ministry (e.g., Deut 24:8; 33:10; 1 Sam 2:28). In Revelation, the same dynamics are at play: the church is first addressed in exhortations (Rev 1–3); in the second part of the book, the wicked world receives the judgment (Rev 4–22). Thus, the progression of the transmission of the holiness instructions found in Revelation seems to parallel that of the transmission of holiness instructions to Israel:

59. See Brownlee, "The Priestly Character," 224–225.

60. Hurtado, "Revelation 4–5," 110, points out how "the vision of the risen Christ in Revelation. 1 certainly determines the content and imagery employed in the following messages to the seven churches." See Barker, *Revelation*, 4: "The picture of Jesus as the great high priest in all his roles and aspects appears throughout the New Testament and is the key to understanding all early Christian teaching about him." See also Barker, *Temple Themes*.

| | | | | | |
|---|---|---|---|---|---|
| God → | Moses → | Aaron → | Chieftains → | Israel | → Heathen nations |
| God → | Jesus → | John → | Elders | → Churches | → Wicked world |

As only the high priest could mediate between God and the people on the DA, Christ appears as the only mediator between God and the church in Revelation, relaying messages to the seven churches through his mouthpiece, John. As Milgrom suggested, violations of the Israelite covenant set up "reverberations that upset the divine ecology," and the same is true of the church under the new covenant; Jesus knows "their deeds" within the covenant and offers them reproach and encouragement (2:2, 13, 19; 3:1).[61]

The notion of collective responsibility for sin that we find in Leviticus can be seen in the messages to the seven churches, where admonitions are directed to the church at large. The churches were guilty of jeopardizing the new covenant established by Jesus' DA sacrifice by tolerating competing, demonic priesthoods in their midst: Smyrna tolerated the "Synagogue of Satan" (2:9), some in Pergamum were followers of "Balaam" and the "Nicolaitans" (2:14–16); Thyatira welcomed the "deep secrets of Satan" in the false prophecies of Jezebel, which led to sexual immorality and idolatry (2:20; see Ezek 16:13–14; 23:1–4; Hos 1:2; 2:2–23; 4:12).

In sum, the covenantal admonitions found in Revelation 2–3 appear to echo the ancient covenantal lawsuit between God and Israel in Leviticus 17–24, of which the DA was the precursor. Like the OT prophets, John writes letters to the churches to establish his leadership among them and calls them to honor the covenant established by Jesus' DA sacrifice.

| **Assessment: The Day of Atonement in Revelation 2 & 3** | |
|---|---|
| *Allusive Type*: Soft echoes. | *Thematic Coherence*: Covenant lawsuit; holiness expected of the church. |

61. Milgrom, *Leviticus: A Book of Ritual*, 42.

## Revelation 4 & 5: The Throne Room and the Slaughtered Lamb

After the letters to the seven churches, "the first voice ... like a trumpet" (4:1) belonging to the exalted Jesus makes an invitation to John: "Come up here, and I will show you what must take place after this" (4:2). John finds himself immediately "in the spirit" in heaven where he sees a throne surrounded by a rainbow with someone who looks like "jasper and carnelian" seated on it (4:2–3) and, around the throne, twenty-four thrones and seated on the thrones "twenty-four elders, dressed in white robes" with golden crowns on their heads (4:4). Dramatic atmospheric phenomena in the form of "flashes of lightning, and rumblings and peals of thunder" fill the room where also are present the seven spirits of God symbolized by "seven lamps" (4:5–6). Around these thrones are four "living creatures" who defy description (4:7). They praise God without ceasing, singing, "Holy, holy, holy, the Lord God the Almighty, who was and is and is to come" (4:8). The twenty-four elders follow these chants with acclamations and cast their crowns before the throne (4:10–11).[62] The expressions of praise by the four creatures and the twenty-four elders is extended to all creation who sings, "Worthy is the Lamb that was slaughtered to receive power and wealth and wisdom and might and honor and glory and blessing!" (5:12). This acclamation is followed by an "Amen" by the four cherubim and worship by the twenty-four elders (5:13–14).

The description of the "four living creatures around the throne" (4:6) creatures alludes to Ezekiel 1 and Isaiah 6, which speak of winged *kᵉrûbim* around (*kyklō*) God's throne (see the use of *kyklō* in Isa 6:2). These *kᵉrûbim* are also represented by the two *kᵉrûbim* placed on top of the ark's mercy seat inside the Most Holy Place (e.g., Exod 25:18–22; see Heb 9:5) and engraved throughout Solomon's temple (1 Kgs 6:23, 27).[63] All communication from God emanated from these two *kᵉrûbim* and their presence in the throne room in Revelation mirrors the descriptions of the Most Holy Place in the OT. Their eyes could be interpreted as symbolizing God's all-seeing eyes from which Aaron had to be veiled by incense when inside the Most Holy Place.

62. The representative works on Revelation 4–5 are Johns, *The Lamb Christology*; Stefanović, "Background and Meaning"; Frilingos, *Spectacles of Empire*; Hoffmann, *The Destroyer*.

63. Josephus uses similar language to describe the *kᵉrûbim*: "Upon its cover were two images, which the Hebrews call Cherubim; they are flying creatures, but their form is not like to that of any of the creatures which men have seen, though Moses said he had seen such beings near the throne of God" (*Ant*. 3.137).

The scene is continued in Revelation 5 with the appearance of a sealed scroll in God's hand. A mighty angel asks with a "loud voice": "Who is worthy to open the scroll and break its seals?" (5:2). When no one is worthy, John weeps bitterly but is told by one of the twenty-four elders that the "Lion of the tribe of Judah, the Root of David," is worthy of taking the scroll and opening its seals (5:5). John then turns to the throne and to the Lamb standing "between the throne and the four living creatures and among the elders ... as if it had been slaughtered," who then takes the scroll (5:7). This event elicits praise from the four creatures, the twenty-four elders, and the angelic hosts (5:8–14).[64] Beale presents evidence for the influence of Daniel 7 and, to a lesser degree, Ezekiel 2–3 in Revelation 5. Thus, as in the OT backgrounds, the focus of these chapters is one of exaltation for Christ's dominion over the entire created order.

The scroll or book (*biblion*) in God's hand, which the Lamb takes possession of, has been interpreted in many ways. Since the opening of its seals introduces scenes of judgment, the book is best understood as God's "book of covenant" with humanity containing redemption for the faithful followers of the Lamb and judgment on the followers of the beast.[65] It is the Lamb's atoning death that makes him worthy to open the book and execute judgment.

### *The Slaughtered Lamb Offered Inside the Heavenly Most Holy Place*

As Beale rightly concludes, the slaughtered Lamb of Revelation 5 is steeped in atonement language and imagery, ultimately pointing to the rituals of the DA, "where the sacrificial animal is a representative penal substitute for Israel."[66] In the "form of a slaughtered Lamb," Tonstad contends, "Jesus brings the character of the divine government to light. This disclosure is designed to answer the questions raised in Revelation, and to save God's embattled reputation." The Lamb is "the definitive manifestation of God's character in history," because he gives his life as an atoning sacrifice.[67] As in the Levitical system, it was God who provided atonement for humanity by sending Jesus Christ "as a lamb to the slaughter" (Isa 53:7; Lev 17:11).

64. Beale, *Revelation*, 314–315.

65. See Beale, Revelation, 340–341: "The "book" in ch. 5 should be understood as a covenantal promise of an inheritance ... concerning paradise lost and regained."

66. Beale, *Revelation*, 660–661; Ben-Daniel, *The Apocalypse*, 31.

67. Tonstad, *Saving God's Reputation*, 3.

In Revelation 4–5, we hear one main *allusion* to the DA accompanied by secondary *echoes*, forming a chamber of thematic resonance. The main *allusion* serves as a unifying factor in the vision, bouncing off the secondary *echoes* while being enhanced by them. These secondary echoes radiate thematic "pings" to each other, creating an auditory loop in surround sound style. Like a contrapuntal Bach chorale, John composed a veritable "theological symphony," orchestrated to overwhelm the listener with the realization that it was the Lamb's atoning death that made him worthy to judge and to have dominion over creation. He is enthroned in heaven on the merits of his atoning blood. In this cosmic crescendo, while the voice of the mighty angel reverberates throughout the cosmos asking, "Who is worthy?" the four cherubim sing without ceasing (4:8): "Holy, holy, holy, is the Lord God Almighty, who was, and is, and is to come," while the high-priestly elders join in, singing "You are worthy, our Lord and God, to receive glory and honor and power, for you created all things …"

When John sees the Lamb, the elders sing a "new song" in praise of the Lamb, saying: "You are worthy to take the scroll and to open its seals, because you were slain, and with your blood you purchased for God persons from every tribe and language and people and nation. You have made them to be a kingdom and priests to serve our God, and they will reign on the earth." They are soon joined by all the angels who proclaim, "Worthy is the Lamb, who was slain, to receive power and wealth and wisdom and strength and honor and glory and praise!" As a grand finale, the entire universe joins in worship, saying: "To him who sits on the throne and to the Lamb be praise and honor and glory and power, for ever and ever!" After this universal acclaim, the four creatures around the throne exclaim, "Amen!" and their praise ceases, having accomplished their goal of eliciting universal praise for God and the Lamb.

Thus the imagery of atoning blood offered inside the heavenly throne room, its Most Holy Place, constitutes a dominating *allusion* pointing to the DA, while appearing alongside the imagery of a lamb, an *echo* of Passover and the daily sacrifices of lambs in the tabernacle; the four cherubim, which echo the cherubim over the mercy seat and Solomon temple; the high-priestly clothing of the elders and their offer of incense inside the Holy of Holies, another *allusion* of the DA; scenes of exultation, echoing the Levitical music ministry in the temple, as well as the heavenly worship that accompanied theophanies in the OT; a scroll or book of God's covenant, echoing the imagery of heavenly books in Daniel 7 and Ezekiel 2–3; and lastly, omens of judgment in the form of atmospheric disturbances, which take us back to the imagery of judgment attached to the Passover lamb. (See diagram below).

Not only does the Lamb's atoning death resonate internally within the chapter, but it also continues to reverberate throughout the entire book, constituting the book's foundational vision. Each opening of the book's seals by the Lamb triggers visions of rewards for the just and judgment on the wicked.

**Chamber of Thematic Resonance of Revelation 4 & 5**

*The Lamb's Atoning Death Makes Him Worthy to Judge and to Reign*

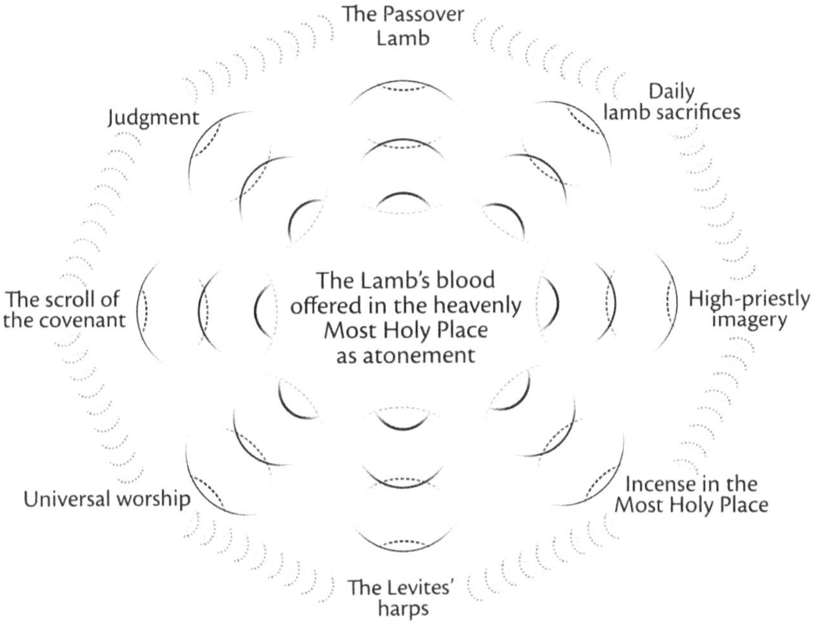


Theoretically, if space allowed, schematics such as the one above could be created for all passages containing *allusions* and *echoes* of the DA in Revelation. But this sample should illustrate for the reader the level of John's intertextual engagement throughout the book.[68]

## *The High-Priestly Elders*

One of the most striking features of Revelation 4–5 is the appearance of the enigmatic twenty-four elders who minister inside the heavenly throne

68. The vision's clear atonement and cultic imagery counter the suggestion that it has less atoning than political implications. Johns, for example, contends that "there is little in the Apocalypse of John to support this understanding of Jesus' death as Atonement" (Johns, *Lamb Christology*, 130; see also Johns, "Jesus in the Book of Revelation," 235). Blount agrees that "purchase by blood ... is more political than it is expiatory" (Blount, *Revelation*, 37). See also Kraybill, *Apocalypse*, 165.

room. Their identity has provided fodder for much theological speculation. Seated on "twenty-four thrones" and dressed in "white robes, with golden crowns on their heads" (4:4), they act in synchrony with the "four living creatures," and move in the throne room, at times bowing down before the throne in worship, throwing their crowns, offering incense, and interpreting the visions to John (4:5, 10, 14; 5:8). Commenting on the identity of the twenty-four elders, Beale suggests that they are "priests" who "represented the people of Israel in their appointed service in the temple."[69] Indeed, a closer look at the chapters' extensive sanctuary imagery indicates that the service of the Solomonic temple provides the most appropriate background for the symbology of the twenty-four elders: (1) the twenty-four orders of priests of the sanctuary (1 Chr 24:3–19); (2) the twenty-four Levitical gatekeepers (1 Chr 26:17–19); (3) the twenty-four orders of Levites charged with offering music and worship in the sanctuary (1 Chr 25:6–31).

The twenty-four elders' high-priestly role comes into sharp focus in Revelation 4–5: (1) they wear long white robes as did the high priests (along with the victor's crown, 4:4); (2) they perform a high-priestly, mediatorial function by offering incense inside the heavenly Most Holy Place (5:8); (3) they perform a liturgical function as each plays a Levite's harp in worship (5:14); and worship the slaughtered Lamb. In their mediatorial role, these elders are intimately related to the redeemed saints who, elsewhere in Revelation, are seen wearing "white robes" and playing "harps" (7:9, 13; 14:2; 15:2).

### *The Offer of Incense in the Heavenly Most Holy Place*

"Every incense offering," observed Farrer, "was a symbol of Atonement Day."[70] The imagery of offering incense by the twenty-four elders inside the heavenly Most Holy Place connects it directly to the offering of incense on the DA when a large amount of incense was used. This imagery is repeated later in the book in the scene involving a high-priestly angel who holds the golden censer, whose great quantity of incense also stands for the prayers of the saints, again connecting the imagery to the DA (8:3, 9:13). On this point, Milgrom suggests that "in Israel, the ascent of the smoke of incense became the visible manifestation of prayer."[71]

69. Beale, *Revelation*, 324; 660–661.
70. Farrer, *A Rebirth of Images*, 178.
71. Milgrom, *Leviticus 1–16*, 238.

Even though the *tāmîd* sacrifices involved burning incense at the incense altar daily, no incense was offered inside the Most Holy Place except on the DA. Thus, the offering of incense by the twenty-four elders inside the heavenly Most Holy Place—alongside the offer of the Lamb's atoning blood there—is an *allusion* to the offering of a double portion of incense inside the Most Holy Place on the DA, which signified an escalation of the importance of the prayers of the people and a heightened commitment that the DA sacrifices be pleasing to God (Lev 16:12–13).[72]

## *Day of Atonement or Sanctuary Inauguration?*

Notwithstanding the clear evidence discussed above, some see sanctuary dedication as the dominant theme in Revelation 5. Paulien, for example, gives the following reasons for this conclusion: (1) Revelation 3:21 associates the scene of Revelation 5 with the cross and the enthronement of Christ, events that are linked with the establishment of the heavenly sanctuary service by the author of the Epistle to the Hebrews; (2) lambs were offered during the tabernacle dedication (Exod 40:29; Lev 1:10), whereas on the DA male goats are the main sacrifices; (3) terminology associated with the inner room of the sanctuary (*naos* and *kibōtos*) is absent, and so is the language of judgment; and (4) the structure of Revelation associates the DA with a later portion of the book.[73] Nevertheless, the view of a sanctuary "inauguration" background for Revelation 4–5 can be countered on several fronts.

(1) The vision of Revelation 4 begins with an entrance into the heavenly throne room, which mirrors the entrance by the high priest into the earthly Most Holy Place on the DA. John's admittance into heaven is a spiritual entrance into the heavenly Most Holy Place where God's throne is situated and where Jesus was seated (Heb 8:1–2; 12:2; 9:24).

(2) As to the objection that "lambs were appropriate for sacrifice during the service of inauguration" and that the lambs sacrificed on the DA were "regular burnt offerings," the fact remains that none of the inauguration sacrifices—regardless of which animal is in view—had the function of purgation/remission of sins as does Revelation's slaughtered Lamb. The lamb sacrificed

72. This idea is reflected in Luke 1:10, where Zechariah offers incense in the temple: "And when the time for the burning of incense came, all the assembled worshipers were praying outside." The temple was, after all, not only a place for cultic intercession but a "house of prayer for all people" (Matt 21:13; see Isa 56:7). See Hayward, "Understandings," 388.

73. Paulien, "The Role," 251, 257.

for the people during the inauguration was a "burnt offering" (Lev 9:3) and not for "atonement" as Revelation 5:9 requires: "for you were slaughtered and by your blood you ransomed for God saints from every tribe and language and people and nation ..." In fact, virtually all the inauguration sacrifices were "peace offerings," the system of burnt/peace/thanksgiving offerings (*ʿōlōṯ/šᵉlāmim*), which included grain offerings and had the goal of invoking God's presence as a "pleasing odor."[74] These *tāmîd* offerings only involved the sacrifice of two lambs, one in the morning and one in the evening (Exod 29:48–46; Num 28:1–8), along with grain offerings (Num 28:5), while the burnt offerings on the DA required seven one-year-old male lambs (Num 29:7–11). During the inauguration, "one male goat" was sacrificed on the outer altar for the people as a "purification offering" (*ḥaṭṭā'ṯ*), but its blood was not brought inside the sanctuary, much less inside the Most Holy Place. In addition, the people offered a lamb for "burnt offering," and "an ox and a ram" as "peace offering" (Lev 9:3–4; see Num 7). Lastly, a lamb was prescribed as a "guilt offering" for Nazirites and lepers (Num 6:12; Lev 14).

(3) The slaughtered lamb of Revelation 5 died to expiate sin, not as a "burnt offering." The "purification offering" and "guilt offering" had the same meaning (Lev 7:7; see Num 18:9). The word for "guilt offering" (*'āšām*) in Lev 7:7 also appears in Isaiah 53:10, a messianic passage that connects the suffering servant and the death of a lamb: "When you make his life an offering for sin" (*'āšām*). Moreover, the same word for "slaughtering" the "goat for the Lord" in Lev 16:15 (*sphaxei*) is used for the "lamb as if slaughtered" (*arnion estēkos hōs esphagmenon*, v. 6) which, along with the offer of its blood inside the heavenly Most Holy Place connects it thematically to the DA.[75]

On balance, then, the sacrifice of a Lamb in Revelation 4–5 is best understood in relation to its function inside the heavenly Most Holy Place: to offer atonement. By utilizing the imagery of a slaughtered Lamb, John disre-

74. Exod 20:22–26; 29:35–37; Lev 7:11–18; 8:21, 28; Num 15:2; 2 Chr 7:1–11; 1 Kgs 8:64; 18:20–40. Leviticus 1:4 describes a rite where an offerer places his hand on a burnt offering in order "to make atonement." The placing of the hands on the sacrifice has the connotation of transfer of sin and purgation, a notion that is missing in the inauguration burnt offering sacrifices. See Levine, *In the Presence*, 6.

75. Gulley, "Revelation 4 and 5," 60–64, summarizes the objections to a DA background in Revelation 4–5 thus: (1) the chapters depict jubilation, not judgment; (2) language pertaining to the Most Holy Place is missing; (3) the scene describes the commencement of Christ's exaltation by receiving the scroll; (4) no authority is given to Christ in Revelation 4–5; (5) Christ's worthiness is connected to his death, which points to his exaltation after the cross; and (6) the sealed scroll has with the history of the world. Evidently, Gulley's objections are untenable, as a cursory reading of the passage demonstrates. For similar views, see Davis, "Heavenly Court"; Davidson, "Sanctuary Typology," 112–126; Paulien, "Seals and Trumpets," 183–198; Stefanović, "Background and Meaning."

gards ritual technicalities by creating a composite symbol drawing from several OT sacrificial contexts and culminating with the offering of *ḥaṭṭāʾṯ* blood before the mercy seat on the DA. Thus, the slaughtered Lamb constitutes a DA *ḥaṭṭāʾṯ* offering whose blood was figuratively applied inside the heavenly Most Holy Place, as occurred in the earthly sanctuary.[76]

In sum, the vision of the "slaughtered Lamb" inside the heavenly Most Holy Place is based on a conflation of imagery from several OT atonement themes such as the Passover lamb (Exod 12:21; 1 Cor 5:7; John 1:29, 36), the suffering lamb of Isaiah 53:7, and, most significantly, the offer of atoning blood inside the Most Holy Place on the DA (Lev 16:15).[77]

| **Assessment: The Day of Atonement in Revelation 4 & 5** | |
|---|---|
| *Allusive Type:* Allusions; loud and soft echoes. | *Thematic Coherence:* Sacrificial blood offered inside the heavenly Most Holy Place; incense offered inside the Most Holy Place; universal worship for the Lamb's atonement; imagery of judgment. |

## Revelation 6: The Souls Under the Altar of Incense

Revelation 6 introduces the opening of the scroll that the Lamb was worthy to receive and open (5:9). The subsequent vision of the "souls of those who had been slaughtered [*esphagmenon*] for the word of God and for the testimony they had given," now seen "under the altar" and dressed in white, follows the opening of the fifth seal (6:9; 8:3–4). This event leads to the opening of the sixth seal, which unleashes a seismic cataclysm and presages the final punishment on the wicked (6:12–17). The souls cry out to God, saying, "Sovereign Lord, holy and true, how long will it be before you judge and avenge our blood on the inhabitants of the earth?" (6:10; see Zech 1:12). The urgency of time and the impending judgment is evident in the cry, "How much longer?" Their cry for justice has eschatological implications since the resurgence of their role in history after being slain points to the imminence

76. Aune also reached this conclusion: "The metaphor of Jesus as a sacrificial lamb whose blood (i.e., death) has atoning significance is based on the confluence of two traditions: Jesus as the (Passover) lamb (1 Cor 5:7; John 1:29, 36) and the conception of the death of Jesus as atoning in a way similar to the חטאת, 'purification offering'" (*Revelation 1–5*, 373).

77. See Paxy, *Death*, 137; Aune, *Revelation 1–5*, 367–373.

of the judgment on their behalf. Their cry is emblematic of the prayers of the saints of all ages represented by the incense rising before God (5:8; 8:4).[78]

The imagery of the incense offering corresponds to other features of the tabernacle service, such as the offering of incense in the *tāmîd* rituals (Exod 30:7–8). However, because their supplication is made in the context of eschatological judgment, it may be beneficial to probe the relationship of these prayers to the eschatological connotations of the DA. Since the prayers of the souls under the altar are directed to God, this altar may be best understood as the same "golden altar before God" (*thysiastēriou tou chrysou tou enōpion tou theou*) that we see in 9:13 (also in 8:3).[79] This conclusion seems to be confirmed by the giving of the white priestly robes (*stolē leukē*) to the slaughtered souls, which signify fitness to serve before God (6:11). Although the term for "robe" here is different from *podērēs* and *himation*, their attire is identical to the high priest's attire on the DA and that of the exalted Jesus in Revelation 1—a long white, linen robe. In context, therefore, their receiving white robes is the preliminary answer to their prayer and could signify their fitness to be in the presence of God while they await the final judgment. Their righteousness symbolized by white robes is contrasted by the sentence meted out on unbelieving/unrepentant humanity during the opening of the sixth seal.

It seems evident that this altar cannot be the altar of burnt offering or have any connotation of "sacrifice" because the souls are "under the altar," not on it. Ultimately, the context is intercession and their slaughter, one of violence and martyrdom. Further, these souls are likely not the same souls seen reigning with Christ in 20:4, since the "testimony of Jesus" is not included in the description of the souls under the altar. Because their beheading coincides with the eschatological emergence of the beasts, these souls probably symbolize the eschatological Christian martyrs of which the original readers were a part.

The imagery of the climactic judgment passed on the "inhabitants of the earth" by the ominous rituals of the DA appears to be echoed in this vision (6:10). The two groups, believers and non-believers, present in the souls' outcry may also point to the separation of the two goats on the DA.[80] This

78. See Beale, *Revelation*, 390.

79. So Beale, *Revelation*, 391: "The better identification is with the golden altar of incense, which stood in the vicinity of the holy of holies (clearly referred to in 8:3–5 and 9:13 and in the developments of those references in 11:1; 14:18; and 16:7). The sacrificial blood of the Day of Atonement was poured on this altar, and incense was burned on it (Exod 30:1–10; Lev 4:7; Heb. 9:4)."

80. See Paulien, "The Role," 257; Hayman, "Book of Enoch," 43.

contrast may also be built on the cultic motif of separation of pure from impure and atoned from unrepentant, which was central to the tabernacle service, culminating in the corporate purification rituals of the DA.

| **Assessment: The Day of Atonement in Revelation 6** | |
|---|---|
| *Allusive Type*: Soft echoes. | *Thematic Coherence*: Intercession at the altar of incense; separation of loyal and disloyal groups; eschatological judgment. |

## Revelation 7 & 14: The Priestly 144,000

Revelation 7 describes the vision of the 144,000 and is parallel to the vision of the same group in Revelation 14. According to the interpreting elder, the "great multitude" is made up of those "who have come out of the great ordeal; they have washed their robes and made them white in the blood of the Lamb" (7:14), a description which is parallel to the 144,000 of 14:1–5:

> And with him were one hundred forty-four thousand who had his name and his Father's name written on their foreheads. [2] And I heard a voice from heaven like the sound of many waters and like the sound of loud thunder; the voice I heard was like the sound of harpists playing on their harps, [3] and they sing a new song before the throne and before the four living creatures and before the elders. No one could learn that song except the one hundred forty-four thousand who have been redeemed from the earth. [4] It is these who have not defiled themselves with women, for they are virgins; these follow the Lamb wherever he goes. They have been redeemed from humankind as first fruits for God and the Lamb, [5] and in their mouth, no lie was found; they are blameless.

The vision of chapter 7 is a continuation of the events initiated inside the heavenly throne room in Revelation 4. After John hears the number of the sealed, 144,000 (v. 4), a great multitude suddenly appears "standing before the throne and before the Lamb, robed in white, with palm branches in their hands" (v. 4). Moreover, the reappearance of one of the twenty-four elders as an *angelus interpres* in chapter 7 connects the vision to the themes of heavenly priesthood and DA in chapter 5. Despite the difference in terminology, it is undeniable that the great multitude's white robes (*stolas leukas*) associate them with the white robes (*himatiois leukois*) of the twenty-four elders who minister as priests in the heavenly throne room.

The 144,000 are the representatives of the "kingdom of priests" established by Christ "through his blood" (1:6). This priesthood established "by blood" echoes the dedication of the Aaronic priests who were set apart by having blood applied directly on them (Lev 8:23, 24); "they have washed their robes and made them white in the blood of the Lamb" (7:14). The imagery of washing one's robes is also reminiscent of the purifications performed on the DA by the high priest and by the priest who led the "goat for Azazel" away. While the high priest washed his body on the DA, Lev 16:26 prescribes the only washing of clothes of the ritual: "The one who sets the goat free for Azazel shall wash his clothes [LXX, *himatia*] and bathe his body in water, and afterward may come into the camp." The same *himatia* appear six times in Revelation, four related to the eligibility of the saints to stand before God, and two in the vision of the rider of the white horse.[81] Thus, the washing of priestly garments in the cultic context of the DA appears to be similar to the washing of the saints' clothes "in blood" as an act of eschatological purification. Moreover, the permission to "come into the camp" as well as the high priest's eligibility to enter the Most Holy Place on the DA are thematically related to the saints' eligibility to be present "before the throne of God" and "within his temple" (7:15). Like the one who led Azazel to the desert, the saints have actively participated in eradicating sin from creation; by washing their robes in the atoning blood of the Lamb, they have become eligible to enter into the eternal community of the faithful.[82] Thus, the theme of the eschatological elimination of sin from creation that pervaded the rituals of the DA is echoed in the eschatological cleansing of sin that makes it possible for the saints to stand in God's presence.

The vision of the sealed saints in heaven comes after the opening of the scroll's sixth seal, which unleashes cataclysms and judgment on the earth. In the Synoptics, similar phenomena accompany the Second Coming of Christ.[83] The question "and who is able to stand?" in 6:17 is answered by the vision of the great multitude standing before the throne. As discussed previously, the atoning/cleansing effect of sacrificial blood on the DA was actuated when it came in physical contact with the tabernacle sections it was

81. Rev 3:4; 5, 18; 4:4; 16:15; 19:13, 16.
82. See Aune, *Revelation 6–16*, 475.
83. Matt 24:29; Mark 13:24–27; Luke 21:25–28.

meant to cleanse. Like Midas and gold, atoning blood made holy whatever it touched. An Israelite whose clothes came in contact with sacrificial blood had to perform ablution in a holy place to remove the blood (Lev 6:27). In the figurative cleansing of the robes of the saved in atoning blood, a similar dynamic is in view: they have been sanctified by holy blood, but instead of washing away the holy blood from their clothes, they proceed to dip them deeper in that blood; they have no intention of letting go of holiness. Through spiritual contact with the holy, atoning blood of Christ, their clothes are forever infused with holiness, and they have become eternally his. Because the context deals with a final purification of the saints seen inside the heavenly Most Holy Place, the DA's blood—which contained elevated levels of holiness and achieved the "ultimate" purification of priesthood and people—seems to be the best background for this imagery. The saints' active engagement with atoning blood highlights Revelation's theology of atonement: "Jesus' triumph over sin and evil, as well as a strong exemplary focus" for the followers of the Lamb, posits Ian Paul.[84]

A second characteristic of the 144,000 is that they have "his name and his Father's name written on their foreheads" (14:1), which stands for the sealing in 7:3–8.[85] The imagery of a name or seal on the forehead echoes the golden plaque worn on Aaron's forehead continuously, including the DA (Exod 28:36; 39:30). This plaque had inscribed on it "Holy to the Lord," and performed a similar function as the name on the foreheads of the 144,000: it indicates ownership, as well "fitness," i.e., righteousness. Aaron offered atoning blood on behalf of the people before God with this plaque on his forehead. The plaque on the foreheads of the 144,000 bestows on them the same prerogatives as those of the OT high priest: they can serve God before the throne, inside the heavenly Most Holy Place.[86] This sign of ownership stands in contrast with the "mark and the name of the beast" seen on the foreheads of the wicked in 13:16–17.

By describing the priestly 144,000 as "virgins" (14:4a), John conflates them with Christ's bride, the priestly New Jerusalem (19:7, 21:2, 9; 22:17).[87] The dominating imagery of virginity in the passage is emblematic not only

84. Paul, *Revelation*, 46; Berger, *Die Apokalypse*, 511.

85. See Aune, *Revelation 6–16*, 804.

86. Blount considers the imagery of a "seal" as a "protected witness to the lordship of God and the Lamb" (*Revelation*, 266). See Beale, *Revelation*, 736.

87. See Klaassen, "The Ascetic Way," 394.

of bridal purity but also enhanced cultic purity by refusing to partake in the idolatrous fornication of the harlot.[88] Like the Israelites who stood sanctified at the end of the DA, the 144,000 are "blameless" (14:5; see Lev 16:30). Thus, the references to virginity and incorruptibility may allude to the heightened sense of self-denial and abnegation suffusing the DA.

Lastly, the saints are the *aparchē*, "first fruits" (14:4b) forms an *allusion* to the Spring festival of the First Fruits. This imagery prepares the ground for the vision of the earth's harvest (14:14–20).

### *Cultic Purity Instead of Forgiveness*

Significantly, the passages dealing with the purity of the saved and their ability to stand before God in Revelation do not mention "sin" or "forgiveness." As discussed previously, the rituals of the DA as laid out in Leviticus 16 did not encompass the notion of "forgiveness" of sins but only their purgation from the tabernacle and consequently from the people. Forgiveness was a later development in Jewish thought—as evidenced in the Dead Sea Scrolls.[89]

The word "forgiveness" in the NT translates two Greek words, *aphesis* and *apolyō*. BDAG define *aphesis* as "the act of freeing and liberating from something that confines, *release* from captivity" and "the act of freeing from an obligation, guilt, or punishment, *pardon, cancellation*."[90] Conversely, *apolyō* has a similar meaning, i.e., "to grant acquittal, set free, release, pardon," and even to "divorce" (Matt 5:31) and similar meanings throughout the NT.[91] Two exemplary passages utilizing *aphesis* and *apolyō* in the sense of "forgiveness" are Matt 26:28: "for this is my blood of the covenant, which is poured out for many for the forgiveness [*aphesis*] of sins"; and Luke 6:37: "Forgive [*apolyete*], and you will be forgiven." Neither *aphesis* nor *apolyō* appear in Revelation.

Commenting on the washing of the robes in 7:13, Beale states: "This generally reflects the OT metaphor of cleansing polluted garments, which connotes forgiveness of sins in Isaiah 1:18; 64:6; Zech. 3:3–5."[92] Howev-

88. See Beale, *Revelation*, 738. Bauckham, *The Climax*, 217–29, sees an "ironic holy war" in the passage. See also Stefanović, *Revelation*, 437.

89. See Ginsburskaya, "Leviticus," 268–9.

90. BDAG 155. E.g., Matt 26:28; Acts 2:38; 10:43; Col 1:14; Heb 9:22; 10:18.

91. BDAG 117.

92. Beale, *Revelation*, 436.

er, none of these OT passages deal directly with the notion of "forgiveness" of sin, but with "purification" from it: Isaiah 1:18–19 promises that though Judah's "sins are like scarlet" and "red like crimson," they will be "like snow" and "wool." The Isaianic passage appears to draw words from Leviticus 26 such as "obey" (*šāmaʿ*), "sword" (*ḥereḇ*), and "devour" (*ʾāḵal*) in the context of the Levitical formula of blessings and curses and the purgations attached to the tabernacle service. Notice also the use of *leukainō* in Isaiah 1:18 (LXX) and *eleukanan* in Revelation 7:14. The word "unclean" (*ṭāmēʾ*) in Isaiah 64:6 occurs twenty-seven times in Leviticus. We come closest to the notion of "forgiveness" in Zechariah 3:4: "See, I have taken your guilt [*ʿāôn*] away from you, and I will clothe you with festal apparel," but even here, removing guilt (or iniquity) is synonymous with making "clean," because the passage deals with restoring Joshua's eligibility to officiate in the temple: "Remove the filthy garments from him … Let them put a clean turban on his head." (v. 5).

In sum, the similar absence of the concept of "forgiveness" in favor of cultic purity in Revelation 7 and 14 echoes the rituals of the DA. As such, John's emphasis on eschatological cultic purity highlights the urgency of covenantal loyalty and the imminence of judgment in these passages.

### *Casting Lots Over Humankind: The Three Angels*

The binary separation of humankind as clean vs. unclean, followers of the Lamb vs. worshipers of Babylon, and the commandments and the faith of Jesus vs. the mark of the beast proclaimed by the three angels introduces the vision of the harvest in 14:14–20. Like Israel of old, humanity is given two choices: fear God and worship him or face the calamitous consequences of the alternative. This call appears to echo the great divide created on the DA of the entirely holy from the entirely unclean, as well as the casting of lots over the goat of the Lord and the "goat for Azazel."[93]

The "casting of lots" dynamic emanating from the DA rituals is enhanced by the bipartite harvest of the earth that separates the just from the wicked. The harvest metaphor in oracles of judgment is common in the OT and the Synoptics and applied to the reaping of the saved, as well as the reaping of the wicked.[94] Likewise, in Revelation 14, the harvest of the earth occurs

93. Paulien, "The Role," 257, writes: "Such a division along spiritual lines took place also in relation to the lots cast over the two male goats on Yom Kippur. On that day individuals chose between two types of atonement, the one offered by the service and the one represented by their own ultimate death."

94. See Isa 17:5; 18:4–5; 24:13; Jer 51:33; Hos 6:11; Joel 3:13; Mic 4:12–13; 4 Ezra 4:28–32; 2

in two phases: (1) the harvest of the "first fruits" by the "Son of man" that are purportedly gathered up with him (vv. 4, 14–16; Dan 7:13); and (2) the harvest of what was left from the first reaping (ripe "clusters of the vine"), i.e., the wicked by an avenging angel who throws them into the "wine press of the wrath of God" reserved for the followers of the beast (vv. 17–20).[95] Additional cultic imagery in the passage, such as "temple," "fire, "altar," alongside judgment imagery, enhance the passage's thematic coherence with the themes of the DA.

| **Assessment: The Day of Atonement in Revelation 7 & 14** | |
|---|---|
| *Allusive Type*: Loud echoes. | *Thematic Coherence:* Reappearance of the slaughtered Lamb; the heavenly Most Holy Place; white, priestly robes symbolizing cultic purity; character loyalty; the harvest of the earth. |

## Revelation 8: The Seventh Seal and the Angel with the Golden Censer

Revelation 8:1–5 describes the opening of the seventh and final seal of the scroll, which the slaughtered Lamb took from the hand of God in the throne room. The opening of the seal is followed by "half an hour of silence" (v. 1). Seven angels "who stand before God" are then given "seven trumpets" (v. 2). At this point in the vision, "another angel"—who is not one of the seven who have the trumpets—comes and stands by "the altar" (*epi tou thysiastēriou*) with a golden censer. He is given a "great quantity of incense" (*thymiamata polla*) offered "with the prayers of all the saints," which, in turn, echoes the incense offered by the twenty-four high-priestly elders in 5:8: "golden bowls full of incense, which are the prayers of the saints."

The scene is again introduced by the sound of trumpets, which had once accompanied the DA, and later assumed eschatological meaning in the prophets (Lev 23:24; 25:9; Isa 27:13; Joel 2:1).[96] Ford sees allusions to the

Syriac Apocalypse of Baruch 70:20; Matt 3:11–12; Matt 13:24–30, 36–43; John 4:35–38.

95. So Bauckham, *The Climax*, 283–296.

96. See Tonstad, *Revelation*, 289.

trumpets used in rituals and on special occasions such as the DA.[97] Similarly, Aune connects the trumpets to the Apocalypse of Zephaniah (1st century BCE–1st century CE), where trumpets introduce scenes of judgment.

A more critical term used in Revelation 8 related to the tabernacle service in general and prominently on the DA is "altar" (*thysiastērion*) which appears eight times in Revelation.[98] The phrase "the golden altar which is before the Lord" (*tou thysiastēriou tou chrysou tou enōpion tou theou*) in 8:3 (see 9:13) follows almost verbatim the rendition of Lev 16:12 in the LXX: *tou thysiastēriou tou apenanti Kyriou*, and slightly modified as *to thysiastērion tou to on apenanti Kyriou* in Lev 16:18.[99] In the MT, the expressions used in Lev 16:12, 18 are *hammizbēaḥ millipnē yhwh* and *hammizbēaḥ ʾăšer lipnē-yhwh* respectively, "the altar before the Lord" and "the altar that is before the Lord."[100] In the LXX, *thysiastērion tou chrysoun* refers to the golden altar of incense.[101] The "golden altar" (*mizbēaḥ hazzahāb*, Exod 39:38) is also called "the altar of incense" (*mizbēaḥ miqṭar*, Exod 30:1), rendered in the LXX as *thymiama, thysiastērion thymiamatos, thysiastērion tou thymiamatos*, and *thysiastērion tōn thymiamatōn*. Ministering at the "altar of incense" is exclusively reserved for the high priest because the altar is "most holy to the Lord" (Exod 30:7–9, 10).[102]

It is relevant that the Hebrew word *mizbēaḥ* is not used *exclusively* to refer to the "altar of incense" in the OT. The distinguishing feature of the altar of incense is that it is "before the Lord" (*lipnē yhwh*), a *terminus technicus* occurring 224 times in the OT and variously rendered as *enanti Kyriou, enanti*

97. Ford, *Revelation*, 136.

98. Rev 6:9; 8:3 [2x], 5; 9:13; 11:1; 14:18; 16:7.

99. A similar expression is used in the LXX text of Lev 17:6: "the altar of the Lord which is at the entrance of the tent of meeting," which could be construed as an exception to seeing the *thysiastērion apenanti Kyriou* as the altar of incense. But although the LXX text reads *thysiastērion kyklō apenanti Kyriou para tas thyras tēs skēnēs tou martyriou*, the MT reads *ʿal-mizbaḥ yhwh petaḥ ʾōhel môʿēd*. The expression *lipnē yhwh* "before the Lord" is missing from the MT text, which turns the LXX translation questionable at this point.

100. Milgrom, *Leviticus 1–16*, 1025, considers the *mizbēaḥ* in Lev 16:12 as the outer altar in part because "only the former had a perpetual fire" and also because he considers both altars as being "before the Lord" in Lev 1:5 and 4:6. However, Lev 1:5 does not describe an altar which is "before the Lord" but *rather ʿal-hammizbēaḥ sābîb ʾăšer- petaḥ ʾōhel môʿēd*, and Lev 4:6 does not mention a *mizbēaḥ* at all. Further, there is no mention that the fire needed to be from the perpetual fire from the outer altar, so Milgrom's conclusion is not inevitable. Kiuchi (*Leviticus*, 298) also considers this the altar of incense. In favor of reading this altar as the golden altar is the possibility that the coals were gathered from the *tāmîd* sacrifices, which also occurred on the DA (see Exod 30:7–8; m. Yoma 3:4; m. Tamid 5:1–6:3). The Yoma is unclear about where the coals were gathered from ("they brought the ladle and the fire pan out to him," 5:1).

101. See Exod 39:38; 40:5; 40:26 [LXX 40:24]; Num 4:11; 1 Kgs 7:48 [LXX 7:34]; 2 Chr 4:19.

102. Ford sees a reference to DA in the "four horns" of the altar. See Ford, *Revelation*, 145.

*tou Kyriou, apenanti Kyriou,* and *enōpion Kyriou.* The altar's designation as standing "before the Lord" places it in front of the veil that separated the Holy Place from the Most Holy Place. Aune argues that in Revelation, *thysiastērion* refers to the "altar of incense" only in 8:3, 5, and 9:13, while the other five occurrences "apparently refer to the altar of sacrifice of burnt offerings."[103] However, this is not a necessary conclusion. Since *thysiastērion* unequivocally refers to the altar of incense in at least three passages in Revelation, it is reasonable to assume that, in the absence of a clear indication of which altar is in question, all of the references to this *thysiastērion* likely refer to the same "golden altar," the "altar of incense" that was before the veil of the Most Holy Place.[104] If this is the case, then the role the altar of incense assumed on the DA may be a critical background in these passages. Just as the angel in 8:3 offers incense symbolizing the prayers of "all the saints," the high priest also interceded on behalf of all Israel by offering a large amount of incense and purifying the altar twice on the DA.

As seen previously, Revelation 8:5 is the book's only *verbal allusion* to Leviticus 16 (v. 12), as indicated in *NA*[28] and *UBS*[5]. This *allusion* is established by lexical correspondences between 8:3–5 and Leviticus 16:12–13 in the LXX: (1) both events deal with the "altar/golden altar" (*tou thysiastēriou/ thysiastērion tou chrysoun*); (2) both events involve the offering of a large amount of incense (*plēsei tas cheiras thymiamatos/thymiamata polla*); (3) the expression "smoke of incense" (*atmis tou thymiamatos*) in Leviticus 16:13 is synonymous with "smoke of incense" (*kapnos tōn thymiamatōn*) in Revelation 8:4; (4) both events occur "before the Lord" (*enanti Kyriou/enōpion tou Kyriou*). Language shared by both passages includes "altar" (*thysiastērion*), "incense" (*thymiamatos*), "fire" (*pyros*), "hand" (*cheiras*), and "before the Lord/ God/the throne" (*apenanti Kyriou/enanti Kyriou; enōpion tou theou/enōpion tou thronou*). The correspondences highlighted above can be visualized in the following table (with shared language underlined in Greek):

103. Aune, *Revelation 6–16*, 511.

104. Stefanović, "The Angel at the Altar," 79–94, argues that the angel stands "on" the altar of burnt offerings. He capitalizes on the expression *epi tou thysiastēriou*, which refers to someone standing on the altar of burnt offering. However, nothing in Rev 8:3 prevents seeing the angel as standing "on" the altar of incense, especially since the presence of incense in connection with an altar should point one to the offering of incense at the altar rather than the outer altar.

| Verbal Comparison of Leviticus 16 and Revelation 8 | |
|---|---|
| **Leviticus 16:12–13** | **Revelation 8:3–5** |
| [12]He shall take a censer full of coals of fire from the altar before the LORD, and two handfuls of crushed sweet incense, and he shall bring it inside the curtain | [3]Another angel with a golden censer came and stood at the altar; he was given a great quantity of incense to offer with the prayers of all the saints on the golden altar that is before the throne. |
| [13]and put the incense on the fire before the LORD, that the cloud of the incense may cover the mercy seat that is upon the covenant | [4]And the smoke of the incense, with the prayers of the saints, rose before God from the hand of the angel<br>[5]Then the angel took the censer and filled it with fire from the altar and threw it on the earth; and there were peals of thunder, rumblings, flashes of lightning, and an earthquake. |
| [12]καὶ λήμψεται τὸ πυρεῖον πλῆρες ἀνθράκων πυρὸς ἀπὸ τοῦ θυσιαστηρίου τοῦ ἀπέναντι Κυρίου, καὶ πλήσει τὰς χεῖρας θυμιάματος συνθέσεως λεπτῆς καὶ εἰσοίσει ἐσώτερον τοῦ καταπετάσματος | [3]καὶ ἄλλος ἄγγελος ἦλθεν καὶ ἐστάθη ἐπὶ τοῦ θυσιαστηρίου ἔχων λιβανωτὸν χρυσοῦν, καὶ ἐδόθη αὐτῷ θυμιάματα πολλά, ἵνα δώσει ταῖς προσευχαῖς τῶν ἁγίων πάντων ἐπὶ τὸ θυσιαστήριον τὸ χρυσοῦν τὸ ἐνώπιον τοῦ θρόνου |
| [13]καὶ ἐπιθήσει τὸ θυμίαμα ἐπὶ τὸ πῦρ ἔναντι Κυρίου· καὶ καλύψει ἡ ἀτμὶς τοῦ θυμιάματος τὸ ἱλαστήριον τὸ ἐπὶ τῶν μαρτυρίων | [4]καὶ ἀνέβη ὁ καπνὸς τῶν θυμιαμάτων ταῖς προσευχαῖς τῶν ἁγίων ἐκ χειρὸς τοῦ ἀγγέλου ἐνώπιον τοῦ θεοῦ.<br>[5]καὶ εἴληφεν ὁ ἄγγελος τὸν λιβανωτὸν καὶ ἐγέμισεν αὐτὸν ἐκ τοῦ πυρὸς τοῦ θυσιαστηρίου καὶ ἔβαλεν εἰς τὴν γῆν, καὶ ἐγένοντο βρονταὶ καὶ φωναὶ καὶ ἀστραπαὶ καὶ σεισμός |

The great quantity of incense given to the angel in 8:3 is an *allusion* to the two handfuls that the high priest places in the censer on the DA.[105] More-

105. A similar scene is described in the Life of Adam and Eve (Greek Apocalypse of Moses) 33:4–5: "I myself saw golden censers and three bowls, and behold, all the angels with frankincense

over, the throwing of a temple object described in 8:5: "Then the angel took the censer and filled it with fire from the altar and he threw it to the earth," echoes the practice of throwing the *magrepha* in the Herodian Temple. As the Rabbis explain in m. Tamid 5:6: "One [of the priests] took the *magrepha* and cast it between the porch and the altar; no one in Jerusalem could hear his neighbor's voice because of the sound of the *magrepha*." Some Jewish scholars have understood this *magrepha* as a shovel used by the high priest during the *tāmîd*.[106] As pointed out in part by Yasser, the important thematic resonances between the m. Tamid and Revelation include: (1) the context of the sanctuary service (earthly and heavenly); (2) the indirect reference to the use of coals in m. Tamid and "fire" in Revelation; (3) the throwing of a sanctuary utensil; (4) the effect of the throwing in the form of noise/disturbances. The fact that the *tāmîd*, along with the throwing of this enigmatic *magrepha*, was also offered on the DA strengthens this *allusion* to the incense, and John seems to have been familiar with this practice.

Aune suggests that "[t]here is every likelihood that this angel would be identified as Michael by readers acquainted with early Jewish angelology."[107] Indeed, like Michael, this angel ministers directly "before God" (8:4). Michael's preeminence in divine affairs is seen in other parts of the Scripture (e.g., Dan 10:13, 21; 12:1; Jude 9), as well as Jewish literature; in the b. Hagigah 12b, Michael is "the great prince," drawing from Daniel 10:13 (cf. Theodotion of Daniel 12:1: *ho archōn ho megas*).[108] Michael also ministers before the throne of God (b. Menahot 110a; b. Zebahim 62a) and is the "chief of the holy angels" in the Ascension of Isaiah 3:16, a description echoed in Revelation 12:7 (see also Ascension of Moses 10:2).[109]

and the censers and the bowls came to the altar and breathed on them, and the fumes of the incense hid the sky." The Testament of Levi 8:10 connects the offering of a large amount of incense with the notion of being fit to serve before the Lord: "The seventh placed on my head a diadem of priesthood, and filled my hands with incense, that I might serve as priest to the Lord God." Beale, *Revelation*, 456, hears an *echo* of Leviticus 16:12–1 in Revelation 8:5. However, the thematic and verbal correspondences are too extensive to be just an "echo" and should be considered an *allusion*.

106. See Yasser, "The Magrepha," 24–42. The noise of the *magrepha* is given an exaggerated quality in the m. Tamid 3:8 purportedly capable of being heard as far as Jericho, eighteen miles away.

107. Aune, *Revelation 6–16*, 515.

108. The popularity of the name Michael among Jews could indicate knowledge of this angelic tradition (see Num 13:13; Ezra 8:8; 1 Chr 5:13, 14; 6:25; 7:3; 27:18).

109. For similar views, see Collins, *King and Messiah*, 189; Barker, *Revelation*, 171, states assertively that the mighty angel "is the Lord himself." For a discussion on the representation of Christ as an angel in Revelation, see also Gundry, "Angelomorphic," 662–78; Gundry, "Angelomorphic," 377–394; Gieschen, "Angelomorphic."

Taking the angel with authority over the fire of the incense altar in 14:18 as background, the mighty angel in Revelation 8 too may symbolize a heavenly high priest—who in the OT was the only one allowed to officiate at the altar of incense—and is above all the other angels in authority and power. This angel ministering at the altar of incense has a "loud voice" (*phōnē megalē*; cf. "mighty voice" [*en ischyra phōnē*] in 18:2, and the *phōnē megalē* of the rider of the white horse in 19:17).[110] It is even possible that Revelation 14 describes the same event as Revelation 8 but from a different perspective. The angel appearing as a high priest with authority over the fire of the incense altar now bestows the authority on "another angel" to reap the earth with a sickle, as does the "Son of Man" (14:14; 17). The same *angelon ischyron* from 5:2 and 10:1 calls "my people" out of Babylon and declares judgment on Babylon (18:3, 21).[111] A similar "voice" calls the earth to "praise God," and a mighty angel with power over the sun calls all birds for the feast (19:5, 17). All these "mighty voices" echo Jesus Christ's *phōnē megalē hōs salpingos* (1:10, 12, 15).

Whereas the expression "loud voice" per se does not confer divinity, the presence of "authority" (*exousian*) and the high-priestly ministration before the Lord may clarify the identity of these divine beings. For example, the *angelon ischyron* who wonders about the worthiness of the Lamb in Revelation 5, reappears in 10:1 but now has similar features as the exalted Christ—his face is like the sun (*to prosōpon autou hōs ho hēlios*), a description that matches almost verbatim 1:16 (*hē opsis autou hōs ho hēlios*), and echoes Jesus' transfiguration when his face "shone like the sun" (*to prosōpon autou hōs ho hēlios*, Matt 17:2). Around the angel's head is a rainbow (*iris*) surrounding the heavenly throne in 4:3 (see Ezek 1:26–28).[112] He is full of glory (*doxa*), a term often used for God or Christ in Revelation.[113] The description of his body is an *allusion* to Daniel 7:13 where the Son of Man appears in a cloud (Rev 1:7; 14:14), which connects it to the descriptions of the coming of Christ elsewhere in the NT (Matt 24:30; 26:64; Mark 13:26; Luke 21:27; Acts 1:9). He has the authority to announce when the end will occur (10:6). A similar "loud voice" emanates from the temple in 16:1, commanding the seven

110. This Greek expression occurs twenty times in Revelation (see 1:10; 5:2, 12; 6:10; 7:2, 10; 8:13; 10:3; 11:12, 15; 12:10; 14:7, 9, 15, 18; 16:1, 17; 19:1, 17; 21:3). It occurs fifty times in the LXX and betrays the Hebrew גדול הקול.

111. See Aune *Revelation 1–5*, 347.

112. Beale, *Revelation*, 524, considers the article before *iris* to be an "article of previous reference," tying the rainbow of the angel with the rainbow around the throne.

113. E.g., 1:6; 5:12–13; 4:9, 11; 5:13; 7:12; 11:13; 14:7; 15:8; 16:9; 19:1; 21:11, 23.

angels with the seven bowls to do their work and proclaiming, "It is done" (16:17). This pronouncement unleashes the same disturbances connected to the throwing of the golden censer to earth in 8:5, which are virtually identical to the ones occurring during the unveiling of the ark of the covenant in the Most Holy Place in heaven (11:19), and the ones that occur during the vision of the throne room in 4:5. (The absence of the earthquake in 4:5 should be self-explanatory: the vision relates to events transpiring in heaven, not on earth.) Significantly, these phenomena occur in passages with DA *echoes.*

In sum, whereas Christological angelomorphism in Revelation may still be open to debate, what is consistent in these visions of celestial beings is the high-priestly imagery that connects them to the Hebrew cultus, specifically with motifs suffusing the DA. Since the incense altar came into prominence on the DA, the imagery of the mediation at the incense altar in the context of eschatological judgment makes the DA the most relevant source for the judgment scenes involving incense in Revelation. The rite of the incense reached the apex of its cultic significance on the DA on which the high priest brought the blood, together with a large amount of incense, inside the Most Holy Place to intercede for the people (Lev 16:12–13).

The preceding analysis demonstrates that Revelation 8:3–5 forms a clear *allusion* to Leviticus 16:12–13, 18, along with equally loud thematic *echoes.*

| **Assessment: The Day of Atonement in Revelation 8** | |
|---|---|
| *Allusive Type:* Allusions; loud echoes. | *Thematic Coherence:* Reappearance of the slaughtered Lamb; high-priestly mediation at the altar of incense; a large amount of incense used; the throwing of a sanctuary utensil; eschatological judgment based on character loyalty. |

## Revelation 9: The Golden Altar of Incense and Defiant Humanity

Revelation 9:13 introduces the judgment on unrepentant humanity unleashed by the sixth trumpet: "Then the sixth angel blew his trumpet, and I heard a voice from the [four] horns of the golden altar before God."[114] All preceding trumpets indicate a gradual increase of damage inflicted on nature and humanity; the sixth triggers large-scale devastation on the earth.

As pointed out above, the "golden altar of incense before God" in 9:13 is the same "golden altar of incense before the throne" in 8:3. While the scene in chapter 8 is associated with the opening of the scroll's seventh seal scroll, the scene in 9:13 concerns the blowing of the sixth trumpet. A "voice from the four horns"—probably God's—tells the angel who has the sixth trumpet, "Release the four angels who are bound at the great river Euphrates" (v. 14). They, in turn, unleash a cavalry of 200,000,000 dreadful soldiers who ride horses with lion-like heads that spew "fire and smoke and sulfur" from their mouths and have tails like serpents (v. 6, 17). This army and their hellish horses kill one-third of humanity, ostensibly those who could no longer repent (vv. 15–21).

Like the scene in chapter 8, the scene in 9:13–21 also occurs "before the throne," a circumlocution synonymous with "before the Lord" in 8:3–5, and indicates judgment that emanates from the horns of the golden altar of incense. Additional elements not mentioned in 8:3 are the "[four] horns of the golden altar which is before the Lord" and the "voice."

The horns of the incense altar take center stage in the sanctuary's purgation rites. Two rituals in Leviticus involve applying sacrificial blood to the horns of the incense altar: (1) the purification offering for the unintentional sins of the high priest and the people performed throughout the year (Lev 4:2, 6, 7, 18); and (2) the blood rituals performed on the DA. On the DA, this altar was purified twice: once with the blood of the bull, offered for the sins of the high priest and his household, and once with the blood of the "goat for the Lord," offered on behalf of the people (Lev 16:11, 15, 16).[115] Whereas the purification ritual on the four horns of the altar of incense in Leviticus 4 is

114. The word *tessarōn* is missing from some ancient manuscripts. See Rev 9:13 in *NA*[28].

115. The incense altar was purified from the sins of the high priest and his household with the blood of a bull. The sins of the "ruler" (Lev 4:22–26), as well as the sins of the "ordinary people (Lev 4:27–31) required that goats (male and female respectively) be offered, and their blood daubed on the four horns of the altar of the burnt offering.

intended to cover only "unintentional" sins committed throughout the year, on the DA, the tabernacle was cleansed, eliminating even brazen sins, even though their perpetrators were cut-off (Lev 16:16, 20; Num 15:30, 31).[116]

Nevertheless, because two rituals of purification of the four horns of the altar of incense are prescribed in Leviticus, it is necessary to probe how the imagery of incense may point to the DA rather than to the regular purification offerings. This question may be answered by examining the themes of final judgment accompanying the DA, which are present in Revelation 9. Standing as the judgment day for the people of Israel, the DA's successful ministration meant that God could continue to abide in their midst.[117] If at any point, the DA failed to bring about restoration because the nation had turned unrepentantly away from God, he would permanently abandon the sanctuary, and Israel would be rejected (2 Chr 7:19; Lam 2:7).[118] Repentance and obedience would lead to prosperity (Lev 26:3–13; 2 Chr 7:14), while "hostility" towards God in the form of unrepentant sin and idolatry would bring destruction (Lev 26:14–39). Hence the importance of purging the altar of incense because it was there where intercession was made. Intercession offered on the altar of incense was only binding based on the people's ability to display repentance and "affliction" on the DA because unrepented sin contaminates the altar of incense and encroaches on the divine. Those who do not repent through self-denial and affliction risk being cut off from the people. Although the tabernacle and its rooms were purified on the DA, including the four horns of the golden altar of incense, unrepentant sinners were condemned; purification and restoration were not available to them (Num 15:30–31).[119]

A significant element in 9:21 is the statement that wicked humanity continued "worshiping demons" (*proskynēsousin ta daimonia*) which may be an *echo* of the ritual of the "goat for Azazel" that involved not the worship of a demon per se but points to a demonic entity responsible for Israel's sins, including the idolatry of "goat-demons" of the ancient Canaanite pantheon

116. Milgrom, "Day of Atonement," 73.

117. Milgrom, "Day of Atonement," 73.

118. Caird, *New Testament Theology*, 406, is off target when he bemoans the shortcomings of the DA: "Even the Day of Atonement, which was intended to cover the national sin, only reinforced the sense of separation of the average Israelite from God. Only Passover maintained a vital connection with the life of the people, reminding them that God had redeemed them from slavery in Egypt."

119. Gane, *Cult and Character*, 161–2.

(Lev 17:7). This connection is strengthened by the fact that the LXX translates "goats" (*śeʿîrîm*) in Isaiah 13:21 as *daimonia*.

It seems that the vision of 9:13–21 depicting a final judgment pronounced from the four horns of the golden altar of incense on unrepentant humanity echoes ancient cultic themes associated with the DA. Twice the rest of humanity not affected by the three plagues of "fire, smoke, and sulfur (9:17) "did not repent of the works of their hands or give up worshiping demons and idols of gold and silver and bronze and stone and wood," or from "their murders or their sorceries or their fornication or their thefts." This group suffers under the seven plagues (15:1) poured out on those "who had the mark of the beast and who worshiped its image" (16:2). Similar language of recalcitrance is used to describe the victims of the outpouring of the fourth bowl: "they were scorched by the fierce heat, but they cursed the name of God, who had authority over these plagues, and they did not repent and give him glory" (16:9). Likewise, those who fall under the "darkness" from the fifth bowl "cursed the God of heaven because of their pains and sores, and they did not repent of their deeds" (16:11).

In sum, the judgment pronounced from the four horns of the altar of incense by the voice of God points to the termination of probation on unrepentant humanity, indicating that no further intercession is available to them. Likewise, the purification of the altar of incense enables intercession based on repentance offered on it, both on regular sacrifices and on the DA. Its restoration as the center of intercession and mediation represents covenantal renewal for repentant Israel, but condemnation to high-handed, unrepentant sinners (Lev 23:29; Num 15:30–31). Their lack of repentance leads to the judgments of the seventh trumpet and the seven bowls/plagues of Revelation 16 (e.g., 11:15–19). Here again, the motif of eschatological judgment connected with the cessation of intercession forms loud *echoes* of the DA.

| **Assessment: The Day of Atonement in Revelation 9** | |
|---|---|
| *Allusive Type*: Loud echoes. | *Thematic Coherence*: High-priestly mediation at the altar of incense; the four horns of the altar of incense; worship of demons (Azazel, goat-demons); defiant sinners "cut off"; eschatological judgment based on character loyalty. |

## Revelation 11: Measuring the Temple, the Altar and the Ark of the Covenant

Revelation 10:1–11:13 creates a hiatus between the blowing of the sixth and seventh trumpets.[120] Paulien sees in the second half of the Apocalypse introduced at this juncture a "repeated focus on the *most holy* or inner sanctum of the temple where the central activities of Yom Kippur took place."[121] Specifically, Paulien suggests that "the association of the inner shrine of the temple with judgment in 11:18, 19 can point to no other aspect of the Hebrew cultus than the Yom Kippur liturgy."[122]

Chapter 11 begins with the measuring of "the temple of God and the altar and those who worship there." This scene mirrors the vision in 21:15, depicting the angel measuring the New Jerusalem with a golden rod. The use of "measuring" in both passages echo Ezekiel 40–48 and denotes God's protection of his people in judgment, while the part not measured is trampled underfoot (v. 2).[123] All references to "temple" in Revelation refer to the heavenly temple; the "two witnesses" are the "two lampstands that stand before the Lord," and direct the reader to the Holy Place of the tabernacle where the golden lampstand was, and to the seven churches as the "seven lampstands" (1:20; see Exod 25:31–40).[124] The connection between the two witnesses and the seven churches is clear: the two witnesses are God's servants operating on earth on his behalf with authority to inflict judgment on those who attempt to silence them.

As briefly explored in the Introduction, Strand suggested that Leviticus 16 is the ideal background to the measuring seen in Revelation 11 because the DA "was a sort of final day of 'measuring' within the Israelite cultic year."[125] In support, Strand points out that the only two places in Scripture where the terms "sanctuary," "altar," and "people" occur in combination are Leviticus 16 and Revelation 11:1–2.[126] But Strand seems to have ignored Lev 4:13–21, which prescribes the sacrifice of a bull for the sin of the congregation, whose blood was daubed on the four horns of the altar of incense.

120. Beale, *Revelation*, 520.
121. Paulien, "The Role," 257.
122. Paulien, "The Role," 253, 256.
123. See Beale, *Revelation*, 559.
124. E.g., 3:12; 7:15; 11:19; 14:15, 17; 15:5–6, 8; 16:1, 17; 21:22.
125. Strand, "An Overlooked," 322.
126. Strand, "An Overlooked," 322. See Paulien, "The Role," 256.

As such, the measuring in Revelation 11 is more likely a soft *echo* of the DA since the people of Israel were spiritually "measured" throughout the year.[127]

The blowing of the seventh trumpet in 11:15 elicits loud praise, like the praise given by the four cherubim and the twenty-four elders when the slaughtered Lamb takes the scroll (5:9–14). However, while this trumpet evokes praise, it also foreshadows punishment for the wicked: "The nations raged, but your wrath has come, and the time for judging the dead, for rewarding your servants, the prophets and saints and all who fear your name, both small and great, and for destroying those who destroy the earth" (11:18).

More significant in Revelation 11 is the transition from Holy Place to Most Holy Place by the appearance of the "ark of the covenant within his temple." The expression "ark of the covenant" (*kibōtos tēs diathēkēs*) appears much more frequently in the LXX than the synonymous *kibōtou tou martyriou*.[128] The "ark of the covenant" was viewed only once a year by the high priest on the DA, or whenever the ark accompanied Israel in battle (2 Sam 6; see 1 Chr 13:1–14; 15:25–16:3). This sudden opening of the heavenly Most Holy Place triggers a series of judgments in the form of "flashes of lightning, rumblings, peals of thunder, an earthquake, and heavy hail" (11:19), which enhance the motif of measuring/judgment in the passage. Whereas the measuring in 11:1 is a positive sign for the people of God, the atmospheric disturbances that occur when the Most Holy Place opens announce punishment on the wicked. This vision of judgment is expanded by that of the dragon, the beast, and those who have "the mark, that is, the name of the beast or the number of its name" (13:17).

The implied removal of the heavenly "veil," thus revealing the ark of the covenant, echoes the rending of the "veil" of the temple at the moment of Jesus' death in the Synoptics. The significance of this unveiling in the context of judgment should be evident: it is the Lamb inside the heavenly Most Holy Place who effects judgment on the wicked. Whereas the appearance of the ark of the covenant symbolizes protection for the people of God who have been "measured" and found fit (11:1–2), it unleashes judgment on unrepentant humankind.[129]

127. See references to measuring in 2 Sam 8:2 and Matt 7:2.

128. E.g., *kibōtos tēs diathēkēs* in Num 10:33; Exod 39:15; 31:7; Jer 3:16; 14:44; Deut 10:8; 31:9, 25, 26; Josh 3:3, 6, 8, 11, 13, 14, 15, 17; 4:7, 9, 11, 14, 16, 18; 6:8,9, 11, 12, 13; 9:6 [MT 8:33]; Judg 20:27; 1 Sam 5:4; 6:3, 18; 7:1; 2 Sam 6:10; 15:24; 1 Kgs 2:26; 3:15; 6:17; 8:1; 1 Chr 15:25, 26, 27, 29; 16:4, 16, 37; 17:1; 22:19; 28:2, 18; 2 Chr 5:2, 7. E.g., *kibōtou tou martyriou* in Lev 16:2; Num 7:89; Exod 25:21.

129. See Beale, *Revelation*, 619.

Paulien sees 11:19 as a pivot point in the book, marking the beginning of "an increasing focus on judgment," especially in the increasing use of words of judgment such as *krinō* (16:5; 18:8; 18:20; 19:2; 20:12; 20:13), *krisis* (14:7; 16:7; 18:10; 19:2), and *krima* (17:1; 18:20; 20:4).[130] Considering the presence of judgment motifs in Revelation 11, it is not coincidental that the appearance of the ark of the covenant unleashes atmospheric phenomena in the form of "flashes of lightning, rumblings, peals of thunder, an earthquake, and heavy hail," which are nearly identical to those described in 4:5, 8:5 and 16:18, except for the earthquake which is absent in Revelation 4. The disturbances affect the earth, beginning with the blowing of the seven trumpets, which announce judgment on unrepentant humans not covered by the blood of the Lamb (7:14). The first earthquake occurs when the angel throws the golden censer to earth (8:5; see Ezek 10:2), reoccurs when the seventh angel blows the seventh trumpet (11:19), and intensifies when the seventh angel pours his bowl on the earth's atmosphere (16:18). The addition of "great hail" in 11:19 indicates a progression in the extent and intensity of the phenomena from the seventh trumpet to the seventh bowl: this hail affects the earth on a massive scale. There is also a progression in the severity of the earthquakes, from the seventh trumpet to the seventh bowl: Revelation's last earthquake is an unprecedented cataclysm, "so great and violent was the earthquake" (*tilikoutos seismos houtō megas*).

In sum, the connecting element of the *echoes* in the chapter is the heavenly throne room, the Most Holy Place, where the slaughtered Lamb offers his atoning blood.[131] Like the judgment inflicted on recalcitrant Israelites on the DA, earth's inhabitants are judged by their rejection of the Lamb's atoning sacrifice; they brought it upon themselves.

| **Assessment: The Day of Atonement in Revelation 11** | |
|---|---|
| *Allusive Type*: Soft echoes. | *Thematic Coherence*: The theme of "measuring" = "judging"; the ark seen inside the heavenly Most Holy Place. |

130. Paulien, "The Role," 252, 260.

131. Bauckham, "Judgment," 5, points out that, although the judgment issues from God's presence, "in none of these cases is it directly said that God commands or executes them."

## Revelation 15: The Opening of the Heavenly Most Holy Place

Revelation 15:5–8 depicts the opening of the "temple, which is the tabernacle in heaven," out of which come seven angels carrying the "seven last plagues" (v. 6) contained in the seven "bowls of God's wrath" that are poured out on wicked humanity in chapter 16. The "seven plagues" allude to the plagues threatened in the "covenantal lawsuit" between God and Israel of which the DA was the precursor: "If you continue hostile to me, and will not obey me, I will continue to plague you sevenfold [*plēgas hepta*] for your sins" (Lev 26:21).[132] As we have explored previously, this covenantal lawsuit forms the whole of the cultic life of Israel, which culminated each year with the DA.

Within this covenantal framework, it is significant that the angels with the seven plagues are "robed in pure bright linen, with golden sashes across their chests" (v. 6), a description that mirrors that of the exalted Christ who is clothed with "a long robe and with a golden sash across his chest" (1:13). As in the portrayal of the exalted Jesus in the opening visions, the avenging angels' clothing of linen and a golden sash mirrors the high-priestly attire on the DA. They appear as Christ's high-priestly representatives as they mete out judgment on the earth, flying in angelic formation.[133]

An *allusion* to Leviticus 16:13, 17 is found in Revelation 15:8: "and the temple was filled with smoke from the glory of God [*kapnou tēs doxēs tou theou*] and from his power, and no one could enter the temple until the seven plagues of the seven angels were ended." Paulien sees here an *allusion* to the inauguration of the tabernacle as described in Exodus 40:34–35: "Then the cloud covered the tent of meeting, and the glory of the Lord filled the tabernacle. Moses was not able to enter the tent of meeting because the cloud settled upon it, and the glory of the Lord filled the tabernacle."[134] Nevertheless, the evidence in support of inauguration as the background for this scene is questionable, while the DA rises to prominence as the better alternative, as follows:

132. The parallel passage in Deuteronomy 28:14–68 contains the curses for covenant failure and speaks of "the boils of Egypt" as punishment (v. 27; 60, 68; see Rev 16:2).

133. Cf. Beale, *Revelation*, 804; Barker, *Revelation*, 259.

134. Paulien, "The Role," 253. See also 1 Kgs 8:10–11; 2 Chr 5:13; Isa 6:1–4; Ezek 10:2–4; 11:23; 44:4. See Beale, *Revelation*, 806–807: "The description may be a collective echo of similar Old Testament descriptions of God's presence in the earthly temple."

(1) Leviticus 16:13 also describes the filling up of the tabernacle temple with smoke: "put the incense on the fire before the LORD, that the cloud of the incense [*atmis tou thymiamatos*] may cover the mercy seat that is upon the covenant." This "cloud of incense" was directly associated with God's presence within the Most Holy Place, as we see in Revelation 15:8.

(2) The "smoke" (*kapnos*) that fills the heavenly temple reappears here from 8:4: "And the smoke of the incense [*kapnos tōn thymiamatōn*], with the prayers of the saints, rose before God from the hand of the angel." In Revelation, *kapnos* appears both in cultic settings and in scenes of judgment and devastation.[135] In the LXX, *kapnos* always translates *ʿāšān*, "smoke," and does not appear in tabernacle/temple dedication theophanies; what fills the sanctuary there is either "cloud" (*nephelē*) or "the glory of God" (*k̲ᵉb̲ôd̲-yhwh*).[136] As such, *kapnos* is closer in meaning with *atmis*, "smoke" as in "the smoke of incense [*atmis tou thymiamatos*]" that covered the high priest on the DA.[137] In other words, the glory of God that fills the temple in 15:8 emanates from the smoke of incense, symbolizing completed intercession for the saved while foreshadowing judgment on the wicked. God's glory is not displayed in flashy theophanies alone but also in goodness, mercy, and justice (see Exod 33:19).

(3) A temporary prohibition to enter the tabernacle is not exclusive to the inauguration ceremonies but also occurred on the DA: "No one shall be in the tent of meeting from the time he enters to make atonement in the sanctuary until he comes out and has made atonement for himself and for his household and for all the assembly of Israel" (Lev 16:17).

(4) More importantly, the *allusion* to Leviticus 16:17 is strengthened because on the DA, as we see in Revelation 15:8, entering the sanctuary is barred "until" something else occurs: while no one can enter the heavenly temple *until* the seven plagues are poured out, on the DA, no one could enter the tabernacle *until* the high priest had come out. This *quid pro quo* dynamic is absent in the dedication ceremonies; Moses had already "finished the work" (Exod 40:33) of dedication when the tabernacle was filled with a cloud (see 2 Chr 7:2).

135. E.g., Rev 9:2, 3, 17, 18; 14:11; 18:9, 18; 19:3.

136. Exod 40:34–35; 2 Chr 7:2.

137. See *kapnos* in the non-cultic contexts of Isaiah 4:5 and 6:4. The vision of the heavenly Most Holy Place in which Isaiah sees the hem of God's robe filling the whole temple (Isa 6:4) carries the idea of "affliction" for uncleanness (v. 5) instead, and that of "purification" from "guilt" and "sin" by a coal from the incense altar (vv. 6–7). Louw Nida, *Greek-English Lexicon*, 8: "The closest equivalent of ἀτμίς is normally a term which refers to the steam rising from a boiling pot or cauldron."

(5) The revelation of God's glory inside the inaugurated sanctuary in the OT does not fit the context of judgment inherent to the pouring out of the "seven plagues"; the context of sanctuary/temple dedications was one of thanksgiving and praise, not judgment.

(6) Lastly, the filling up of the heavenly temple with God's glory in the context of the eschatological judgment is indicative of the cessation of intercession rather than its initiation, as in the sanctuary dedication.

In sum, although the vision in Revelation 15:8 appears to draw on OT temple theophanies, the judgment motif along with cultic imagery present in the passage indicate that the filling of the heavenly temple with smoke, the prohibition to enter the temple "until" judgment was complete, and the cessation of intercession form an *allusion* to the DA, accompanied by loud *echoes*.

| **Assessment: The Day of Atonement in Revelation 15** | |
|---|---|
| *Allusive Type*: Allusions; loud and soft echoes. | *Thematic Coherence*: The temple filled with incense; cessation of intercession; cultic purity; high-priestly clothing; cultic bowls; "high-priestly" angels; judgment on defiant humanity. |

## Revelation 17: The Harlot, the Beast, and the "Goat for Azazel"

The vision of the harlot riding the beast follows the outpouring of the seven bowls on the earth in conjunction with the seven plagues. The vision jolts John because he probably expected that the end of the seven last plagues would signal the restart of intercession in the heavenly temple in light of the appearance of the ark of the covenant and the smoke of incense filling the temple. However, instead of going back to the heavenly temple, he is taken to a desert (v. 3).

Revelation 17–20 marks a shift in the target of judgment, from unrepentant humanity to the harlot/Babylon, the beast, the dragon, and the false prophet. The symbol of the harlot riding the grotesque beast is explained in Revelation 18: it is Babylon, the great city that stands against God and his people. The beast has "seven heads and ten horns," "blasphemous names," and holds a cup "full of abominations and the impurities of her fornication" (17:4). The reference to "impurities" here is significant and carries cultic connotations. The Greek words for "unclean/uncleanness" (*akathartos, akatharsia*) appear 132 times in the book of Leviticus alone (LXX) and denote that which is cultically impure. Whereas all of the purification rituals and offerings in the book of Leviticus are intended to separate the holy and clean from the unclean (*ṭāmēʾ/akathartos*), the rituals of the DA accomplished the absolute removal of all *akatharta* from Israel (*kai katharisei auto kai hagiasei auto apo tōn akatharsiōn tōn huiōn Israel*, Lev 16:19). A cup full of impurities echoes the large number of impurities cleansed by the rituals of the DA.

The harlot's name written on her forehead is "Babylon the great, mother of whores and of earth's abominations" (v. 5), who has become drunk with "the blood of the saints and the blood of the witnesses to Jesus" (v. 6), which are the same "impurities" that she carries in her cup. The "wine of the wrath of her [Babylon's] fornication" (v. 3) seduces the kings and merchants of the earth to commit fornication with her; they, in turn, have become rich and powerful from the affair.

Revelation 18 starts with the vision of an "angel coming down from heaven, having great authority; and the earth was made bright with his splendor." This scene follows the Hebrew of Ezek 43:2 closely when describing the glory of God (*wᵉhāʾāreṣ hēʾirâ mikkᵉḇōḏô*) but differs slightly in the LXX (*kai hē gē exelampen hōs phengos apo tēs doxēs kyklothen*). Akin to the angelomorphic theophanies in Revelation 8–9, the designation of glory to an angel is unique and significant since glory is otherwise reserved for God in Revelation. This designation may indicate that the angel of chapter 17 is the same high-priestly angel who has great authority in chapter 18. The angel calls God's people to "come out of her" lest they participate "in her sins" (*tais hamartiais autēs*, 18:4), which are so great that they are "heaped high as heaven" (v. 5). Again, the emphasis is on the clean vs. unclean couplet dominating the Levitical system.

The visions of judgment found in Revelation 17, 18, and 20 also echo ancient Greek *pharmakos* elimination rites, which underlie the rite of the "goat for Azazel."[138] As seen previously, during the *pharmakos* rites, an undesirable

138. Beale, *Revelation*, 634, observes: "Nevertheless, it is not implausible to see that the Old Testament, especially Daniel, is a filter through which extrabiblical traditions and myths are subordinated to biblical thought and accordingly transformed and applied to the dragon and to other figures in the Apocalypse."

person was dressed in extravagant attire and fed before being sent out of the community symbolizing its desire to eliminate a plague or disease. Echoes of this practice could be present in 18:7, except that the harlot dressed herself up: "As she glorified herself and lived luxuriously, so give her a like measure of torment and grief." The significance of this vision in connection with the *pharmakos* rite of the "goat for Azazel" arises from the thematic relationship between "sins" (*hamartias*) and "desert" (*erēmos*) in the passage. In the LXX text of Leviticus 16:22, the "goat for Azazel" is led into the *erēmos* after receiving the toxic load of Israel's sins and guilt. First, there is the portrayal of an animal connected with "abomination" and wickedness in v. 3. Second, as with the "goat for Azazel," the harlot holds a counterfeit high-priestly bowl full of the "abominations and the impurities of her fornication" (v. 4).[139] As the "goat for Azazel" carried sin back to its point of origin, i.e., the desert—a symbol of chaos and the demonic in the OT—the harlot too is sent to the desert and pairs up with an abominable beast. As in the ancient Greek elimination rights, she is dressed in "purple and scarlet," but instead of going to a palace or city, she is instead sent away to the desert ("barren region" in Lev 16:22). All who once admired her will ultimately "hate the whore; they will make her desolate and naked; they will devour her flesh and burn her up with fire" (17:16–17; 18:7). This imagery echoes the abuse inflicted on the ancient Greek *pharmakos* as it was driven away from the city, a practice that is also reflected in later Jewish attitudes towards the "goat for Azazel."

We also notice that "desert" (*erēmos*), a central element in the dispatch of the "goat for Azazel," appears three times in the LXX text of Leviticus 16:10, 21–22, and three times in Revelation: twice as the place to which the pregnant woman flees (12:6, 14); and as the territory of the harlot who rides the scarlet beasts (17:3). In Leviticus 16, *erēmos* is also the place where Azazel operates. Since the woman's presence in an inhospitable place such as the desert requires the provision of special protections (e.g., "wings," "a place prepared"), John's use of *erēmos* in Revelation 12 may be in line with the Jewish understanding of the "desert" as the abode of evil, a notion which suffuses the Levitical cultus, and most notably as the abode of Azazel. In the case of the harlot/Babylon, Isaiah 21:1 foretold its fall would be brought by the winds of the desert of Negeb, "a terrible land."[140] Moreover, the NT associates the desert with the habitation of demons in a manner that betrays ancient Canaanite myths; in Matt 4:1, Jesus is led "into the desert," the puta-

139. Ford, *Revelation*, 288, sees a parallel with the DA in the harlot's golden cup.

140. See Fekkes, *Isaiah*, 204–5, 213–14.

tive habitation of the devil to be tempted by him; demons expelled from the possessed wander the desert (see Matt 12:43; Luke 11:24). Thus, the presence of *erēmos* here connects the operations of the harlot with the habitation of the demonic in the desert, the demonic oppression of the pregnant woman there, the disposal of sin in the desert, and themes of judgment, forming a *probable allusion* to the DA.[141]

Furthermore, the vision of Revelation 17 also presents significant contrasts with the cultic language of Revelation 19, a passage that carries thematic parallels with the DA. First, the harlot riding the beast appears to be a counterfeit of the rider of the white horse in chapter 19. In contrast to her purple clothing, the rider of the white horse is clothed in linen. The harlot's royal attire disguises her real character, that of a violent prostitute, "drunk with the blood of the saints and offers the drink of her wrath and fornications." On his robe and thigh, the white horse's rider has the inscription "King of kings and Lord of lords" (19:16), while on the harlot's forehead is written: "Babylon the great, mother of whores and of earth's abominations." This profane inscription is also a counterfeit of the golden plaque worn on the high priest's forehead with the ascription: "Holy to the LORD" (Exod 39:30). The harlot's cup is full of "sin," while the rider of the white horse atones for sin with his DA blood; the cup at once echoes and contrasts the high priest's cup of atoning blood, which effected purification on the DA.[142]

Overall, the scene of the harlot in Revelation 17 contains at least one *allusion* to the "goat for Azazel" ritual, accompanied by *loud echoes* of the DA.

| **Assessment: The Day of Atonement in Revelation 17** | |
|---|---|
| *Allusive Type*: Allusion; loud echoes. | *Thematic Coherence*: An unclean beast full of sin and abominations wandering in the desert; counterfeit of the high priest attire. |

141. See Lev 16:22; Isa 6:11; 13:21; 32:15; 34:14; 64:9; Jer 4:27; 9:11; Ezek 29:9; 35:4. Beale's argument on the "desert" is convoluted at this point; at the same time that he accepts that the passage contains "symbolic geography," he then argues that John was taken into the desert because "it is the place of spiritual security and detachment from the world's dangers" (*Revelation*, 852). However, since the center of the vision is the harlot and the beast, "desert" in this context is connected to the impure, beastly realities of the harlot.

142. Ford, *Revelation*, 288.

## Revelation 18: Babylon as an Eschatological *Pharmakos*

In Revelation 18:1–24, John expands the description of the destruction of the harlot who rides the beast by alluding to the fall of Babylon. The scene opens with a heavenly being boasting "great authority" and "a mighty voice," whose splendor fills the whole earth.[143] He pronounces divine judgments against Babylon, which has become "a dwelling place of demons, a haunt of every foul spirit, a haunt of every foul bird, a haunt of every foul and hateful beast" (v. 2). As with the harlot of Revelation 17, the threefold repetition of "foul" (*akathartos*) reflects cultically charged imagery echoing the toxic load of sin and guilt removed on the DA. Fallen Babylon is a desolate, barren place full of "abominations and the impurities of her fornication" (17:4).

With its heavy load of abominations, beastly Babylon forms an *allusion* to the "goat for Azazel" at the same time, it contrasts with the high-priestly bride of the Lamb, the New Jerusalem, which is clothed in "fine linen, bright and pure" (19:8). While Babylon is full of "sin," no "unclean thing" is allowed inside the New Jerusalem (21:27; see Isa 35:8). The warning, "Come out of her [Babylon], my people, so that you do not take part in her sins" (v. 4), echoes the recurring motif of the separation of the holy from the unclean that suffused the Hebrew cultus culminating in the DA. Similar cultic terminology is found in Isaiah 52:11: "Depart, depart, go out from there! Touch no unclean thing; go out from the midst of it, purify yourselves, you who carry the vessels of the Lord" (see Jer 50:8; 51:6, 45).[144]

Softer *echoes* of the DA suggested by Ford are the "fine linen" in 18:11; according to the Rabbis, the high priest wore expensive Indian linen on the DA (m. Yoma 3:7), and the colors blue and scarlet, which stand for the false, eschatological priesthood of Babylon.

| **Assessment: The Day of Atonement in Revelation 18** | |
|---|---|
| *Allusive Type*: Allusion; loud echoes. | *Thematic Coherence*: A beast full of abominations; removal of impurities and sin in the eschatological destruction of Babylon; a call to character loyalty in the call to "come out" of Babylon. |

143. See Hangyas, "The Use."
144. See Beale, *Revelation*, 898.

## Revelation 19: Jesus, the High-Priestly Warrior

After the judgment against Babylon, Revelation 19 introduces the marriage supper of the Lamb. The chapter begins with a long hymn of praise extolling the slaughtered Lamb's atoning victory (vv. 1–10). This cosmic worship overwhelms the created order and includes familiar imagery such as "the great multitude," "the Lamb," "the twenty-four elders," "the four living creatures," "the throne," and "fine linen," forming a thematically coherent allusive vector back to Revelation 7 and 14 and the vision of the celestial Most Holy Place (Rev 4–5). The four "hallelujahs" in the passage amplify the resounding victory conquered by the Lamb.

The bride of the Lamb is clothed in "fine linen, bright and pure, for the fine linen is the righteous deeds of the saints" (19:8). These are the "garments of salvation" and "the robe of righteousness" promised in Isaiah 61:10, echoing the clothing of the high-priestly angels of 15:6 who carry the seven high-priestly bowls containing the seven last plagues of judgment "robed in pure bright linen, with golden sashes across their chests." The "wife of the Lamb" is the New Jerusalem (see 21:2, 9), the high-priestly city that houses the very presence of God, whose cubic shape parallels that of the Most Holy Place. The purity of this city-bride reflects the purity that permeates all who live inside its walls because "nothing unclean will enter it" (21:27).

The second half of the chapter (v. 11–16) describes the vision of the rider on the white horse who is called "Faithful and True," "The Word of God," and "King of kings and Lord of lords. There is no doubt who this rider is: Jesus Christ. The diadems on his head with an inscription that only he knows, and his white robe made of linen sprinkled with blood echo high-priestly attire and cultic imagery. Conversely, the theme of a warrior high priest is an *allusion* to the age-old high-priestly warrior tradition of the second song of Moses in Deuteronomy: "For he will avenge the blood of his children, and take vengeance on his adversaries; he will repay those who hate him, and atone the land for his people [*wᵉḵipper ʾaḏmāṯô ʿammô*]"; "with him were myriads [LXX, *myriasin*] of holy ones; at his right, a host of his own" (Deut 32:43; 33:2). The "myriads of holy ones" are echoed in the *myriades myriadōn kai chiliades chiliadōn* in Revelation 5:11, representing the host of holy ones who surround God's throne (9:16). It is significant that *kipper*—the central action of collective atonement on the DA—appears in Deuteronomy 32:43 in a context of corporate atonement and judgment, which is then echoed in Revelation's vision of the rider of the white horse. This scene provides a compelling thematic background for the portrayal of Jesus as a conquering high priest whose white robe is stained with sacrificial blood.[145]

The blood-stained garment of the rider of the white horse (v. 13), a symbol of Christ (see John 1:1–14), alludes to Isaiah 63:1–3: "I have trodden the wine press alone, and from the peoples no one was with me; I trod them in my anger and trampled them in my wrath; their juice spattered on my garments, and stained all my robes." However, in light of cultic imagery connected to the passage, it appears that John departs from the original meaning in Isaiah, for while Isaiah talks about the blood of the "peoples," Christ's white robe in Revelation 19 is stained with his own sacrificial blood as the slaughtered Lamb, revealing Revelation's *Leitmotif* of conquering by shedding one's own blood in atoning, vicarious death (e.g., 1:5; 5:5–10; 12:11). Furthermore, the juxtaposition of clothing and blood connects this imagery with the washing of the robes of the 144,000 in the blood of the Lamb, which denotes atonement and righteousness (7:14), not judgment, as in Isaiah.

In addition, the word "dipped" (*bebammenon*) in v. 13 is a *varia lectio* as manuscripts have "sprinkled" written variously as ῥεραντισμένον, ἐρραντισμένον, ῥεραμμένον, περιρεραμμένον, περιρεραντισμένον, and ἐρραμμένον.[146] It appears unlikely that the idea of sprinkling would have originated from dipping or that *bebammenon* originated the several variant forms of "sprinkle" (*rantizō*) in the manuscripts.[147] Significantly, the reading "sprinkled" instead of "dipped" is strengthened by the fact that the MT of Isaiah 63:3 to which Revelation 19:13–15 alludes, uses the verb "sprinkle": "their juice sprinkled [*wᵉyēz niṣḥām*] on my garments, and stained all my robes." The verb *nāzâ* is used for the blood sprinklings inside the tabernacle. Thus, it appears that Revelation 19:13, 15, although drawing some imagery from Isaiah, expands the meaning of the blood-stained clothes in light of Jesus Christ's sacrificial death: he is the conquering high priest who sheds his blood in battle in order to secure victory and atonement for his army, but suddenly resurrects to join

145. See Caird, *Revelation*, 243: "The Rider bears on his garment the indelible traces of the death of his followers, just as he bears on his body the indelible marks of his own passion." See also Barker, *Revelation*, 308: "This is the high priest emerging after taking blood into the holy of holies. His robe has blood stains, not from the battle which has yet to begin, but from the atonement sacrifice."

146. See *NA*[28], 780. On the importance of Revelation's manuscripts for its interpretation, see Allen, *Manuscripts*.

147. Mounce states that the reading *bebammenon* "can account for the variants better than any of the six forms of *rainō*/*rantizō* listed in the *UBS* apparatus" (*Revelation*, 353). It is more likely that another scribal phenomenon may be at play here: the scribe may have confused β and ρ thus *reramenon* in time became *bebammenon*, a possibility that may explain the several variants of *reramenon*. See the Vulgate's rendering as *"vestem aspersam sanguine"* ("clothes sprinkled with blood").

them in celebration; his blood obtains redemption while announcing judgment on the nations.[148]

Lastly, John's re-reading of Isaiah 63 in light of Jesus' blood may be indicative of a common tradition running through the Epistle to the Hebrews in which the *katapetasmatos*—the veil of the sanctuary, where the blood was sprinkled on the DA—is compared to the body of Christ: "by the new and living way that he opened for us through the curtain (that is, through his flesh)" (Heb 10:20).

In sum, Christ, the high-priestly warrior, conquers by his blood, shed on the eschatological DA; it is his blood that stains his clothes and purifies the church (1:5–6; 7:14). As Caird perceptively reminded us: "Wherever the Old Testament speaks of the victory of the Messiah or the overthrow of the enemies of God, we are to remember that the gospel recognizes no other way of achieving these ends than the way of the Cross."[149]

| **Assessment: The Day of Atonement in Revelation 19** | |
|---|---|
| *Allusive Type*: Soft echoes. | *Thematic Coherence*: Sprinkling of blood; high-priestly clothing in a context of atonement and judgment. |

## Revelation 12 & 20: The Judgment of the Dragon

After the fall of Babylon, the focus on judgment returns in Revelation 20, in the final punishment meted out on the dragon, a judgment that started with the vision of the pregnant woman, Michael's defeat of the dragon in heaven, and the dragon's foiled attack against the woman in Revelation 12.

John sees yet another angel coming down from heaven, having a key to the bottomless pit and a great chain (20:1). The scene echoes the "angel," "key," "bottomless pit" from Revelation 9. Since the "star from heaven" mentioned in chapter 9 is given control over the bottomless pit, it symbolizes

148. See Johnsson, "Revelation," 758–59; Boring, *Revelation*, 196–97; Harrington, *Revelation*, 192–93. See Beale, *Revelation*, 957, who argues that the imagery of blood in Revelation 19:13 and 15 is drawn from Isaiah 63 and is the blood of "judgment." For example, Beale calls the objection that the rider's clothes are stained before the battle begins "too mechanical" (*Revelation*, 959). However, the same can be said about his reading of Isaiah 63 in Revelation 19, for John may not be so strictly bound to Isaiah's original intention, as Revelation repeatedly demonstrates.

149. Caird, *Revelation*, 243.

"Abaddon" ("destruction"), "the angel of the abyss."[150] The star's fall echoes the description of the dragon falling with a third of the "stars" of heaven (12:9).

In this nightmarish scenario, this "star from heaven" opens the bottomless pit and releases smoke (*kapnos*) and locusts on the earth; they are given the power to torture the inhabitants of the earth for five months (9:3–5). These demonic beings are led by "Abbadon," the commander of the *abyssos* (9:11). Based on the preceding, it appears that the "dragon" of Revelation 20 is also the same Abbadon, "that ancient serpent, who is the Devil and Satan" (v. 2). The mighty angel of Revelation 20—likely Michael, who defeats the dragon in chapter 12— takes hold of the dragon, binds him, and throws him into the bottomless pit for a thousand years (v. 2; 12:9: "the great dragon was thrown down"). This prison term will be over after the "thousand years," and Abaddon/the dragon will be released one last time (vv. 7–8).

The abode of demonic entities such as "the harlot," "Babylon," and the "beast" in Revelation is the "desert" and the "bottomless pit" (11:7; 17:4, 8). Thus, Revelation 20 represents a reversal of Revelation 9; while Abbadon is released from the bottomless pit to inflict chaos on the earth in chapter 9, in chapter 20, he is sent back into the pit "in order that he might not deceive the nations" (v. 3; 12:9); the one who once controlled the abyss is now imprisoned by it. This reversal reverberates themes of the DA, primarily as an *echo* of the dismissal of the "goat for Azazel," carrying Israel's sin and abominations back to their source. On the DA, the second purgative ritual is the dispatch of the "goat for Azazel" to the desert, bearing "all the iniquities of the people of Israel, and all their transgressions, all their sins" (Lev 16:20–21). As discussed previously, the view taken in this study is that Azazel represents the demonic entity that causes people to sin. The "goat for Azazel" not only received the actual sins and impurities of Israel, but it also bore their guilt; the goat's fate symbolized the fate of Azazel himself.[151]

As observed by Janowski, "[t]he Jewish and Christian history of interpretation of the figure of Azazel stands in no relationship to its laconic treatment in Leviticus 16."[152] As previously noted, this demonic desert entity mirrored the mythology of nations surrounding ancient Israel in the form of "goat demons" operating in the desert, to which the "goat for Azazel" was

150. For a discussion of divergent views, see Aune, *Revelation 6–16,* 525; Koester, *Revelation,* 455–456; Beale, *Revelation,* 491–492. The representation of demons as falling stars has parallels in the OT (Isa 14:12) and Jewish literature: 1 Enoch 18:11–16; 86:1–2; 88:1–3; 90:23–26. See also Luke 10:18, where Jesus describes seeing Satan falling from heaven.

151. So Gane, *Cult and Character,* 259.

152. See Janowski, "Azazel," 128–131.

also sent "back." This long tradition of interpretation omitted in Leviticus 16 comes into full view in Revelation 20.[153] Jenks goes further by suggesting that the "Azazel myth" in early Christian writings is part of a "combat myth" tradition that gave rise to the antichrist in early Christianity.[154] Due to the cryptic nature of references to Azazel in the OT, the best approach to understand the development of the figure of Azazel in Christianity, according to Ben Ezra, is "to go beyond the biblical text and take later traditions of the scapegoat ritual into consideration, as they are reflected in texts of the Second Temple and Rabbinic periods."[155]

The Jewish understanding of Azazel evolved from a mysterious, demonic desert entity in the Pentateuch to a full-fledged demon in Second Temple literature and Satan's alter ego.[156] Allusions to Azazel in Jewish literature are significant because they tend to confirm the suspicion that the ritual of the "goat for Azazel" had eschatological and Judgment Day overtones involving the source of evil, Satan (*śāṭān/haśśāṭān*, 1 Chr 21:1; Job 1:6; 2:2). As the "goat for Azazel" carried sin and impurities back into the desert—which symbolized chaos and was the habitation of demons—so Satan, represented by the dragon and the beasts of Revelation, is the cause of the chaos in creation because he has deceived humankind (20:8). Chaos and darkness, represented by evil acts, undermine the created order.[157] Adding insult to injury, the dragon and his minions persecute and kill the saints (12:12, 17).

The dismissal of the "goat for Azazel" carrying away the sins of Israel was built on the idea that the separation of holiness from sin leads to the restoration of creation or re-creation.[158] Likewise, the dragon's destruction opens the way to a new creation. As in the separation of the two goats on the DA, one for the Lord and one for Azazel, John separates those marked with the mark of the beast from those sealed with the blood of the Lamb.[159] Below we explore the development of this demonic figure of Azazel in the Book of Enoch.

153. Young, "The Impact," 358: "John's use of this motif is not taken directly from the OT but as the Aza'zel figure was understood in certain quarters of Jewish apocalyptic."

154. Jenks, *The Origins*, 285–288, 358.

155. Ben Ezra, "Yom Kippur," 353.

156. E.g., 1 Enoch 8:1; 9:6; 10:4–8; 13:1; 55:4; 69:2; Apoc. Ab. 13:6–14; 14:4–6; 20:5–7; 22:5; 23:11; 29:6–7; 31:5. See Orlov, "Eschatological Yom Kippur," 3–35; Orlov, *Dark Mirrors*, 27–46.

157. See Job 24:14; Prov 2:13; Isa 57:20; Jer 49:9; Rom 13:12–13; Jude 13.

158. Marshall, *Parables*, 179: "those who dwell on earth and those who dwell in heaven."

159. So Barker, *Revelation*, 343: "The judgment implied in 20.4 is the Day of the Lord, the Day of Atonement when Satan has been bound and the Lord has come with his saints to judge the living and to establish his kingdom."

## *Azazel in the Book of Enoch and Revelation*

Perhaps the most relevant background for the themes of judgment against fallen angels, as seen in Revelation 20, can be found in the Jewish traditions of pseudepigraphal book 1 Enoch (ca. 300 BCE–100 CE). At least one quotation of 1 Enoch in the NT indicates that it was accepted in some Christian circles as authoritative in the first century CE. Evidence of this tradition is the fact that the judgment on the fallen angels described in Jude 6–7 draws primarily on 1 Enoch:

> 6And the angels who did not keep their own position, but left their proper dwelling, he has kept in eternal chains in deepest darkness for the judgment of the great day. 7Likewise, Sodom and Gomorrah and the surrounding cities, which, in the same manner as they, indulged in sexual immorality and pursued unnatural lust, serve as an example by undergoing a punishment of eternal fire.

Likewise, Jude 14–15 quotes 1 Enoch 1:9:

> 14It was also about these that Enoch, in the seventh generation from Adam, prophesied, saying, "See, the Lord is coming with ten thousand of his holy ones, 15to execute judgment on all, and to convict everyone of all the deeds of ungodliness that they have committed in such an ungodly way, and of all the harsh things that ungodly sinners have spoken against him.
>
> 1 Enoch 1:9: "Behold, he will arrive with ten thousand times ten thousand of the holy ones to execute judgment upon all. He will destroy the wicked ones and censure all flesh on account of everything that they have done, that which the sinners and the wicked ones committed against him."[160]

In addition, the punishment of being cast into darkness, which symbolizes an eternal verdict of condemnation in the eschatological parable of Matt 22:1–14, appears to draw on imagery from 1 Enoch 10:4 as found in its Greek text in Codex Panopolitanus (Gizeh fragment):[161]

160. *OTP* 1:14–15. See *POT* 2:189: "And behold! He cometh with ten thousand of ‹His› holy ones to execute judgement upon all, and to destroy ‹all› the ungodly: And to convict all flesh of all the works ‹of their ungodliness› which they have ungodly committed, ‹And of all the hard things which› ungodly sinners ‹have spoken› against Him." See also Asale, *1 Enoch*.

161. Orlov suggests that several traditions underpinning Q in connection with the temptation of Jesus (Matt 4) reflect an influence of the Enochic descent traditions. See Orlov, *Dark Mirrors*, 107–112; Swete, *The Old Testament in Greek*, xvii; *OTP* 1:6.

Matt 22:13a: "Then the king said to the attendants, 'Bind him hand and foot, and throw him into the outer darkness..."
[τότε ὁ βασιλεὺς εἶπεν τοῖς διακόνοις· δήσαντες αὐτοῦ πόδας καὶ χεῖρας ἐκβάλετε αὐτὸν εἰς τὸ σκότος τὸ ἐξώτερον· ἐκεῖ ἔσται ὁ κλαυθμὸς καὶ ὁ βρυγμὸς τῶν ὀδόντων]

1 Enoch 10:4a: "And secondly the Lord said to Raphael: 'Bind Azaz'el hand and foot, and throw him into the darkness"
[Καὶ τῷ Ῥαφαὴλ εἶπεν Δῆσον τὸν Ἀζαὴλ ποσὶν καὶ χερσίν, καὶ βάλε αὐτὸν εἰς τὸ σκότος][162]

This *allusion* indicates that the motif of judgment found in Revelation 20 draws on Jewish traditions about the role of Azazel in the rituals of the DA.[163] As we have previously seen, the school of Rabbi Ishmael believed that Azazel was a fallen angel (b. Yoma 67b).[164] In 1 Enoch 9:5–6, Azazel (or Asael) is portrayed as a fallen angel operating in the antediluvian world as a teacher of "unrighteousness" who revealed "the eternal secrets which were (preserved) in heaven, which men were striving to learn."[165]

A comparative analysis of the judgment on Azazel described in 1 Enoch 10:4–6 shows that it is strikingly similar to the judgment on the dragon in Revelation 20:1–3, 10:

162. 1 Enoch 10:4 in Black, *Apocalypsis Henochi,* 24. See the Greek text in Syncellus: Καὶ τῷ Ῥαφαὴλ εἶπε Πορεύου, Ῥαφαήλ, καὶ δῆσον τὸν Ἀζαήλ· χερσὶ καὶ ποσὶ συμπόδισον αὐτόν, καὶ ἔμβαλε αὐτὸν εἰς τὸ σκότος. Scholars have also discerned similarities between Matt 19:28 and 25:31; see Theisohn, *Der auserwählte Richter,* 56–63; Knibb, Review of *Der auserwählte Richter,* 197–200; Knibb, *Essays,* 151–158.

163. For a discussion on the use of 1 Enoch imagery in Revelation and the NT, see Hannah, "The Throne of His Glory," 68–96; Vorster, "1 Enoch," 1–14; Macaskill, "Matthew and the Parables," 219–230; Walck, "The Parables of Enoch," 231–268.

164. See Ben Ezra, *The Impact,* 87: "the punishment of the demon resembles the treatment of the goat in aspects of geography, action, time and purpose." See Davies, "Sons of Cain," 48; Robins, "The Pleiades," 341–344.

165. On the fact that Asael and Azazel deal with the same entity, Dimant writes, "In my judgment such an identification (of Asa'el and Aza'zel) is already assumed in the adaption of the material in chap 10, where the punishments are commanded" (Dimant, "1 Enoch 6–11," 327); see also Knibb, *Essays,* 56–76.

| Verbal Comparison of Revelation 20 and 1 Enoch 10 | |
|---|---|
| **Revelation 20:1–3, 10** | **1 Enoch 10:4–6** |
| [1]Then I saw an angel coming down from heaven, holding in his hand the key to the bottomless pit and a great chain [καὶ ἅλυσιν μεγάλην]. [2]He seized the dragon, that ancient serpent, who is the Devil and Satan, and bound him [καὶ ἔδησεν αὐτὸν] for a thousand years, [3]and threw him [καὶ ἔβαλεν αὐτὸν] into the pit [ἄβυσσον], and locked and sealed it over him [ἔκλεισεν καὶ ἐσφράγισεν], so that he would deceive the nations no more, until the thousand years were ended. After that, he must be let out for a little while. | [4]And secondly the Lord said to Raphael: 'Bind [δῆσον] Azaz'el hand and foot and throw him [καὶ βάλε αὐτὸν] into the darkness." And he made a hole in the desert [τὴν ἔρημον], which was in Duda'el, and cast him there; [5]he threw on top of him rugged and sharp rocks. And he covered his face [καὶ ἐπικάλυψον αὐτῷ] in order that he may not see light; |
| [10]And the devil who had deceived them was thrown into the lake of fire and sulfur [εἰς τὴν λίμνην τοῦ πυρὸς] where the beast and the false prophet were, and they will be tormented day and night forever and ever. | [6]and in order that he may be sent into the fire on the great day of judgment [εἰς τὸν ἐμπυρισμὸν].[166] |

A similar fate awaits demon Semjâzâ and his companions v. 11–13):

> [11]And the Lord said unto Michael: 'Go, bind [*dēlōson*] Semjâzâ and his associates who have united themselves with women to have defiled themselves with them in all their uncleanness. [12]And when their sons have slain one another, and they have seen the destruction of their beloved ones, bind them fast for seventy generations in the valleys of the earth, till the day of their judgement and of their consummation, till the judgement that is for ever and ever is consummated. [13]In those days they shall be led off to the abyss of fire [*to chaos tou pyros*]: [and] to the torment and the prison in which they shall be confined forever.[167]

This imagery is expanded in the Similitudes of Enoch (1 Enoch 54:1–6), in which the visionary sees "the kings and the mighty" being cast into a

166. *OTP* 1:17. Cf. Thompson, "The End of Satan," 257–268.
167. *POT* 2:194.

deep valley burning with fire.[168] In this valley, iron chains of "immeasurable weight" are made, and these will be used in the execution of judgment on the kings and mighty (1 Enoch 53:3–4). Unfortunately, no Greek text of 1 Enoch 54:4–6 exists, so we read it in Charlesworth's translation:

> And I asked the angel of peace, who was going with me, saying, "For whom are these imprisonment chains being prepared?" And he said unto me, "These are being prepared for the armies of Azaz'el, in order that they may take them and cast them into the abyss of complete condemnation, and as the Lord of the Spirits has commanded it, they shall cover their jaws with rocky stones. Then Michael, Raphael, Gabriel, and Phanuel themselves shall seize them on that great day of judgment and cast them into the furnace (of fire) that is burning that day, so that the Lord of the Spirits may take vengeance on them on account of their oppressive deeds which (they performed) as messengers of Satan, leading astray those who dwell upon the earth.[169]

It is important to note that "Satan" in the passage above is probably not to be differentiated from Azazel because the plural "Satans" appears four times in Similitudes (40:7; 53:3; 54:6; 65:6–7), which indicates that all fallen angels are "Satans." This reading may be based on the use of the word in the OT to indicate a demonic adversary.[170] It is also possible to compare it with 2 Enoch, which also shows the development of Azazel's identity as Satan. In 2 Enoch, the demonic roles ascribed to Semihaza and Azazel as leaders of the fallen angels are now transferred to Satanael. This is an *allusion* to the Adamic story of Genesis 3, which is also echoed in Revelation 20:2, where the author connects the dragon to "that old serpent."

168. The date of composition of the Similitudes of Enoch or Book of Parables (1 Enoch 37–71) is a contested issue. Charles (*POT* 2:171) contends that "the date of the Similitudes could not have been earlier than 94 B.C. or later than 64 B.C." Collins, *The Apocalyptic Imagination*, 178, dates the Similitudes to "early of mid first century CE, prior to the Jewish revolt of 66–70 CE to which it makes no reference." This position follows VanderKam, "1 Enochic," 33–101. Milik, *The Books of Enoch*, 89–98 gives it a third-century date based partly on its absence in Qumran, but this theory has not been widely accepted. This study takes the majority position that the Similitudes is a Jewish work from the first century BCE to early 1 first century CE. For a discussion on this issue, see Charlesworth, "The Date and Provenience," 37–57; Bock, "Dating the Parables," 58–113; Knibb, "The Date of the Parables," 345–359; Suter, "Weighed in the Balance," 217–21; Greenfield and Stone, "The Enochic Pentateuch," 51–65; Erho, "Historical–Allusional Dating," 493–511; Erho, "The A-historical Nature," 23–54; Erho, "Internal Dating," 83–103; Hindley, "Towards a Date," 551–65; Nickelsburg, *Jewish Literature*.

169. *OTP* 1:38; *POT* 2:220–221.

170. 1 Sam 29:4; 2 Sam 19:23; Num 22:32; 1 Kgs 5:18; Job 1:6; 2:2; 1 Chr 21:1; Zech 3:1.

The cause for Azazel's judgment is given in 1 Enoch 13:1–2:

> As for Enoch he proceeded and said to Azaz'el, "There will not be peace unto you; a grave judgment has come upon you. They will put you in bonds, and you will not have (an opportunity for) rest and supplication because you have taught injustice and because you have shown to the people deeds of shame, injustice, and sin."[171]

Significantly, before the final judgment on Azazel and his angels described 1 Enoch 54:1–5, the author(s) inserts a war between the "kings" and the saints in 1 Enoch 54:6–8, repeated in 62:3–5.[172] This parenthetical description of a worldwide war with Azazel and his angels immediately before judgment day has important thematic and verbal correspondences with the war described in Revelation 20:7–9 in which Satan deceives "Gog and Magog, in order to gather them for battle" against "the camp of the saints and the beloved city." Similarly, in 1 Enoch 56, Azazel's angels "shake up the kings (so that) a spirit of unrest shall come upon them"; they rise "like lions" and "hungry hyenas" and "trample upon the land of my elect ones" (v. 5–6) and the "city of my righteous ones." The judgment passed on the wicked kings/kings of the earth is mentioned in several passages in Revelation.[173] The large number of "corpses" (v. 7) resulting from this war mirrors the number of the wicked who are as the "sands of the sea" in Revelation 20:8. In 1 Enoch 56:8, it is said that Sheol "shall open her mouth" and they will be "swallowed up into it and perish," a judgment echoed in the "burning furnace" in 54:6 and the "lake of fire" in Revelation 20:10, 14–15. The defeat of Satan and his armies in Revelation is probably dependent on 1 Enoch 55:4: "Kings, potentates, dwellers upon the earth: You would have to see my Elect One, how he sits in the throne of glory and judges Azaz'el, and all his company and his army, in the name of the Lord of Spirits."

Several similarities between the judgment of the fallen angel Azazel in 1 Enoch and that of the dragon in Revelation 20 are readily apparent:

(1) An angel of the Lord executes the judgment on both;

(2) Azazel is bound with "chains" (1 Enoch 54:3, 4, 56:1; 69:28; 103:8) while Satan is bound with a "great chain" (*halysin megalēn*, Rev 20:1);

171. *OTP* 1:19.

172. See Aune, "Palestinian Jewish Apocalyptic," 4–8. Charles, *The Book of Enoch*, xcv–ciii, lists Revelation 6:15 as one of several NT passages showing dependence on the Book of Enoch.

173. E.g., Rev 6:15; 16:12, 14; 17:2, 9, 12, 18, 18:3, 9; 19:18, 19.

(3) The binding of the dragon echoes the command for Raphael to "bind Azazel" (1 Enoch 10:4);

(4) The "darkness," "hole in the desert," "sharp rocks," and the cover of darkness in 1 Enoch 10:5 are echoed in the "bottomless pit," which is sealed over the dragon in Revelation 20:2. The "darkness" and the "abyss" in 1 Enoch 54 are synonymous with the *abyssos*, the "bottomless pit";

(5) The Lord's order to "let him [Azazel] abide there forever, and cover his face that he may not see light" is echoed in the dragon's long sentence of "a thousand years" (1 Enoch 10:5; 13:1) in the abyss (Rev 20:3);

(6) The corruption of "the whole earth ... by Azazel's teaching" (v. 8) is echoed in the dragon's deception of the nations;

(7) The reference to making "swords and knives, and shields, and breastplates" under the guidance of Azazel in order to make war on the saints and the "city of my righteous" (1 Enoch 8:1; 56:6) is echoed in the dragon's gathering of the nations "for battle" in Revelation 20:8;

(8) The "lake of fire" (Rev 20:10–15) alludes to the valley of burning fire into which the kings and the mighty are thrown (1 Enoch 54:1; 56:8);

(9) Azazel suffers the same fiery end: "on the day of the great judgment he shall be cast into the fire" (1 Enoch 10:6), the same as the dragon: "And the devil who had deceived them was thrown into the lake of fire and sulfur" (Rev 20:10).

As occurred with the return of impurities back to Azazel on the DA, the punishment on Azazel described in 1 Enoch inaugurates an era when "the whole earth will be worked in righteousness" (1 Enoch 10:17–22). This imagery shows dependence on the cleansing of the people on the DA (Lev 16:30), a new era of righteousness which is a forerunner of the "new heaven and the new earth" (21:1) following the final destruction of Satan. Moreover, and quite significantly, at the end of this judgment passage, cultic language is used in 1 Enoch to describe the absolute purification of creation: "And the earth shall be cleansed [*kataristhēsetai*] from all pollution [*pantos miasmatos*], and from all impurity [*pasēs akatharsias*], and from all plague, and from all suffering, and it shall not happen again that I shall send (these) upon the earth from generation to generation and forever" (1 Enoch 10:22).[174] Allusions to Leviticus 16 can be clearly detected in the references to "cleansing,"

174. The Greek text of the Gizeh fragment reads: καὶ καθαρισθήσεται πᾶσα ἡ γῆ ἀπὸ παντὸς μιάσματος καὶ ἀπὸ πάσης ἀκαθαρσίας καὶ ὀργῆς καὶ μάστιγος, καὶ οὐκέτι πέμψω ἐπ᾽ αὐτοὺς εἰς πάσας τὰς γενεὰς τοῦ αἰῶνος. Black, *Apocalypsis Henochi*, 26.

"all defilement," "all impurity," the latter commonly translated as "all sin."[175] This is the sin that had been ascribed to Azazel: "And the whole earth has been corrupted through the works that were taught by Azâzêl: to him ascribe all sin [*kai ep' autō grapson tas hamartias pasas*]" (1 Enoch 10:7). The imagery of placing "all sin" on Azazel is an *allusion* to Lev 16:21: "and confess over it all the iniquities of the people of Israel" (*exagoreusei ep' autou pasas tas anomias*)" (see 1 John 3:8).

In Revelation, "that ancient serpent, who is called the Devil and Satan," is called "the deceiver of the whole world" (12:9). In his judgment, he receives back the sins of the whole world, which is an *allusion* to the transfer of culpability for sins by confession on the "goat for Azazel." The dragon, the beast, and the harlot/Babylon form an unholy partnership that generates "abominations" on the earth, and they all suffer the same fiery end (18:4, 5; 20:10). As Ben Ezra suggests, "the restoration of the earth by removing sin ... and the destruction of the evil forces in a war incited by Gabriel ... allude to the cathartic rationale behind Yom Kippur."[176]

Cultic language is used again when a similar sentence is given to Azazel's companion Semjâzâ: "Go, bind Semjâzâ and his associates who have united themselves with women so as to have defiled themselves with them in all their uncleanness [*en tē akatharsia autōn*]" (1 Enoch 10:11). This imagery is in escalated contrast with the description of the 144,000 who have not "defiled themselves with women, for they are virgins" (14:4). The author's use of the DA's themes of purification from "uncleanness" as a harbinger for the eschatological cleansing of creation is quite clear.

As seen previously, the curses proffered by the heavenly high priest Yahoel on the fallen angel Azazel in the Apocalypse of Abraham are also evocative of several descriptions of Satan in the Gospels, the letters of Peter, and Revelation. In Apoc. Ab. 23:7–8, Azazel is compared to the serpent that tempted Adam and Eve in Eden, an ascription reserved for Satan in Revelation 20:2. While "Abraham's lot is in heaven," Azazel's fate is on the earth" (Apoc. Ab. 13:8). Azazel's banishment to the "untrodden (or inaccessible) parts of the earth" parallels the dragon's fate to dwell "on the earth" for a thousand years as an eschatological Azazel (Apoc. Ab. 14:6; Rev 20:3; see Isa 14:12–15). While Azazel is "the firebrand of the furnace of the earth," the devil is thrown into the "lake of fire" (Apoc. Ab. 13:5; 31:3–5; Rev 20:10).

175. See *OTP* 1:19; *POT* 2:195.

176. Ben Ezra, *The Impact*, 87.

Like Satan (John 8:44), Azazel is called a liar who inflicts "wrath and trials" on the elect (Apoc. Ab. 13:9; see Rev 12:12; 1 Pet 5:8). Moreover, heaven is a temple in the Apocalypse of Abraham, which echoes Jesus' entrance into the heavenly Most Holy place as an entrance into "heaven itself" (Heb 9:24) on the antitypical DA.[177]

Lastly, the sequence of "purification" of creation from Satan's "sins" by the atoning blood of the Lamb and the fiery judgment that purges creation mirror the sequence of the rituals on the DA in which the "goat for the Lord" was sacrificed first, followed by judgment on Azazel (1:5; 4–5; see Lev 16:11, 20). Satan, as both originator and final trustee of all sin, is judged at the end of time with the penalty for all transgressions, just as the live goat carried the community's transgressions away from the camp, never to return. On this point, it is significant that the locking up of the dragon in Revelation 20 comes after the depiction of the rider on a white horse, which has been almost universally understood as symbolizing the *parousia* when the returning Jesus and his angels inflict the final judgment on unrepentant humanity.[178]

If Revelation 19 echoes the purification by blood and judgment over enemies which permeated the DA, the rite of the "goat for Azazel" functioned as a type of the "eschatological defeat of demonic power" echoed in the binding and imprisonment of the dragon in chapter 20.[179] It may well be then that, like in mystery novels, the elusive identity of villain Azazel is revealed in the story's final chapters.

| **Assessment: The Day of Atonement in Revelation 12 & 20** | |
|---|---|
| *Allusive Type*: Allusions; loud echoes. | *Thematic Coherence*: Judgment on the dragon (Satan) based on the "judgment" on Azazel. |

177. See Himmelfarb, *Ascent*, 66.

178. E.g., Beale, *Revelation*, 949–950; Koester, *Revelation*, 753ff; Aune, *Revelation*, 1053; Caird, *Revelation*, 240–248.

179. See Helm, "Azazel," 225: "Thus ancient Jewish traditions appear to be in agreement with the interpretation which finds in the expulsion of the scapegoat a type or model of the eschatological defeat of demonic power."

## Revelation 21: The High-Priestly New Jerusalem

The judgment on Satan, the beast, the false prophet, and all who follow them into the "lake of fire" ushers in the "new heaven and a new earth" (20:15; 21:1; 1 Enoch 10:17–22). As in the final chapter of the story of Job, the accuser is gone.

The marriage supper of the Lamb promised in Revelation 19 is consummated by the descent of the "holy city, the New Jerusalem coming down out of heaven from God, prepared as a bride adorned for her husband" (21:2). God is present in the New Jerusalem as prophesied by Isaiah 52: "He will dwell with them as their God; they will be his peoples, and God himself will be with them" (21:3), in fulfillment of the promises of the covenant found in Lev 26:3, 11: "If you follow my statutes and keep my commandments and observe them faithfully … I will place my dwelling in your midst, and I shall not abhor you." This promise was especially true on the DA when the whole nation was purged from sin and granted a new beginning; Israel's covenant renewal was a foretaste of the restoration of the created order.[180]

Beale suggests that the New Jerusalem is described as a type of the Most Holy Place and the saints are its priests, "serving in the temple and privileged to see God's face in the new holy of holies, which now encompasses the entire temple-city."[181] These saints-priests have the Lamb's name written on their foreheads (22:4), an *allusion* to the "rosette" placed on the high priest's forehead, bearing the inscription "Holy to the Lord" (Exod 28:36; 39:30). Further, the act of measuring the New Jerusalem echoes the measuring of the temple in chapter 11: "The city lies foursquare, its length the same as its width; and he measured the city with his rod, fifteen hundred miles; its length and width and height are equal" (21:16). The New Jerusalem's cubic shape mirrors the Holy of Holies (1 Kgs 6:20; 2 Chr 3:8; Ezek 41:4).[182] As Koester observes, "The massive size of the cubic city exhibits holiness on a cosmic scale."[183]

Significantly, the chronological information in Ezek 40:1 connects the new temple oracle with the DA: "In the twenty-fifth year of our exile, at the beginning of the year, on the tenth day of the month … the hand of the Lord was upon me …" The only other passage in the OT where the year begins

180. See Ben Ezra, *The Impact*, 89.
181. Beale, *Revelation*, 1113–1114.
182. Beale, *Revelation*, 1075–1076.
183. Koester, *Revelation*, 816.

on the "tenth of the month" is Lev 25:9–10, which coincides with the DA. Further, the vision comes in "the twenty-fifth year," which can only be explained as the middle of a jubilee period. In Ezekiel's new temple, "My dwelling place shall be with them; and I will be their God, and they shall be my people" (Ezek 37:27). The importance of this *allusion* to Ezekiel's temple is clear: the establishment of the eschatological city-temple, the New Jerusalem, coincides with the jubilee inaugurated by the DA sacrifice of the Lamb offered inside the heavenly Most Holy Place. This theme is familiar in the prophets, for Isaiah 40–28, 61 connect the DA with the year of jubilee in passages dealing with the eschatological restoration of creation. Not surprisingly, these same themes are echoed in Revelation 21–22: (1) cultic purity (Isa 44:1–31; Rev 21:7, 27); (2) the renewed presence of God (Isa 43:1–9; Rev 21:3–4; 22:5); (3) restoration to ancestral land (Isa 47:13–48:35; see the "new earth" Rev 21:1); and (4) social equity (Isa 45:9–12; 46:18; 47:21–23).[184]

In this city-temple, writes Alexander, "[t]he entire New Jerusalem is an expanded Holy of Holies."[185] The implication of the *echoes* of the dimension of the Holy of Holies is that, although only the earthly high priest entered the Most Holy Place, and only once a year on the DA, the saints now enjoy the continuous presence of God inside the heavenly Most Holy Place, the New Jerusalem. As the high priest on the DA must go through a decontamination process to minister before the very presence of God, so did the inhabitants of the New Jerusalem: they have washed their robes "so that they will have the right to the tree of life and may enter the city by the gates" (22:14). As with God's presence in the earthly Holy of Holies, the holy city must be free of undesirables such as "anyone who practices abomination of falsehood" as well as "dogs, sorcerers and fornicators and murderers and idolaters and everyone who loves and practices falsehood" (21:17; 22:15).

John sees "no temple in the city, for its temple is the Lord God the Almighty and the Lamb" (21:22). The New Jerusalem does not have a temple because the city itself constitutes a cosmic Most Holy Place; the dwelling place of God and the Lamb replaces the need for a temple. The city fulfills

184. See Bergsma, *The Jubilee*, 188–190.

185. Alexander, *From Eden*, 20; see Smalley, *Revelation*, 552: "the cubic shape of Jerusalem is a clear reminder of the holy of holies, also a cube, which stood at the heart of the Temple in the old city of Jerusalem." See Koester, *Revelation*, 816: "[l]ike the holy of holies, the walls of the New Jerusalem are covered in gold."

on a cosmic scale God's promise to dwell with ancient Israel, a promise that was renewed every year on the DA.[186] By turning the New Jerusalem into a temple, John sees the fulfillment of Solomon's prescient words: "But will God indeed dwell on the earth? Even heaven and the highest heaven cannot contain you, much less this house that I have built!" (1 Kgs 8:27).

| **Assessment: The Day of Atonement in Revelation 21** | |
|---|---|
| *Allusive Type*: Medium loud echoes. | *Thematic Coherence*: The New Jerusalem as the heavenly Most Holy Place; universal cultic purity; God's presence with the saints. |

## Revelation 20 & 22: Day-of-Atonement Retribution for the Wicked

In Revelation, the retributive aspects of the DA are set in the context of the punishment of the dragon and its followers (20:12). All those who are not covered by the atoning blood of the Lamb have the mark and the name of the beast and fall under divine judgment. Furthermore, the concept of ritual purgation inherent in the rituals of the DA may be echoed in 22:11, 14: "Let the evildoer still do evil, and the filthy [*ryparos*] still be filthy, and the righteous still do right, and the holy still be holy ... Blessed are those who wash their robes, so that they will have the right to the tree of life and may enter the city by the gates." The warning resembles the warning given by Isaiah to Israel to "turn and be healed" (Isa 6:9–10; see Ezek 2:2–7; 3:27: "Let those who will hear, hear; and let those who refuse to hear, refuse"). The warning is given in the context of the "unsealing" of John's visions (v. 10) which implies that not all is fulfilled and that a probation period may still be in view for the church.

Beale and other scholars see here an *allusion* to Daniel 12:10: "Many shall be purified, cleansed, and refined, but the wicked shall continue to act wickedly. None of the wicked shall understand, but those who are wise shall understand." However, the passage in Daniel only provides a partial thematic

186. See Rowland, "The Temple," 478.

link with Revelation while lacking lexical correspondences.[187] Thus, a better OT source for the couplet "filthy-washed" must be sought. This source may be found in the word "filthy" (*ryparos*) in 22:11; while it is an *hapax legomenon* in the NT, it occurs in the LXX of Zechariah 3:3, 4 where the high-priest Joshua's "filthy clothes" are *himatia rypara*. In the vision, Joshua's "filthy clothes" are replaced with a *maḥalāṣôṯ* translated as *podērē* in the LXX, which, as noted earlier, is reserved for high-priestly attire in the LXX and in 1:13 refers to Jesus' DA robe. The use of *maḥalāṣôṯ* in Zechariah 3 probably indicates a white linen robe which, together with the high-priestly "turban," could symbolize the high priest's righteousness enabling him to officiate on behalf of the people on the DA. The context of Satan's accusations against Joshua certainly fits the imagery. Joshua's status as *ryparos* stands for cultic uncleanness or "guilt" (v. 4), while the *podērē* symbolizes his "righteousness" as a high priest and his worthiness to preside over Israel (vv. 4–7; see Job 29:14). This connection is apparent in that *ryparos* is a gloss of *ho adikōn*, lit. "the unrighteous" (22:11). This OT background indicates that John has cultic uncleanness in mind in 22:13 since it has this meaning in Zechariah 3. Cultic uncleanness is also suggested in John's contrast of *ryparos* with the cultically purified robes of the saints (22:14), as in the case of the high priest Joshua.

This cultic context further frames the passage in a DA background by the fact that the robes of the saints are washed with the blood of the Lamb offered inside the heavenly Most Holy Place, while unrepentant sinners are barred from the benefits of this blood. The goal of the DA is to allow reciprocity of holiness: a purified people may stand before God, and God can stay in their midst. While the cleansing of the sanctuary removes impurities from the sanctuary and the people, unrepentant sinners are condemned to bear their guilt (Num 15:30–31; see 18:22). According to Paul, such retribution/reckoning does not include the saints: theirs is a reckoning of reconciliation accomplished through Christ's DA sacrifice.[188] The purgation on the DA has no effect on them, their relationship with the community of God is severed, and they are cut off. In this, Revelation 22:11 echoes the implacable judgment achieved on the DA: there was no midway on the DA, Israelites were either clean or unclean.

187. Beale, *Revelation*, 1132; Koester, *Revelation*, 840; Aune, *Revelation 17–22*, 1117.

188. E.g., 2 Cor 5:19; Col 1:22; 2:13; Rom 5:8–10; see Heb 6:19–20; 9:12, 24. See Buchanan, "Paul's Doctrine," 244–245.

The retributive character of the DA is also apparent in Revelation 22:12: "See, I am coming soon; my reward is with me, to repay according to everyone's work." This punitive background can be seen in the fact that the institution of DA was framed by the sudden death of Nadab and Abihu when they attempted to enter the inviolate realm of the Most Holy Place drunken and with "strange fire" (Lev 16:1). God's heart and eyes were in the sanctuary (2 Chr 7:16); the blessings of his presence depended on Israel's compliance with his standards of holiness at the risk of sudden retribution in case of disobedience.

By descending from heaven on the new earth, the high-priestly New Jerusalem consummates the DA's holiness ideals: "nothing unclean will enter it, nor anyone who practices abomination or falsehood, but only those who are written in the Lamb's book of life" (21:27). The scale of such purity was only attained on the DA when the whole nation of Israel was purged of impurities and made "clean" to stand before the Lord; this, in turn, safeguarded God's presence in their midst (Lev 16:30; 26:11). The escalated holiness achieved on the DA was a foretaste of the holy society of priests envisioned by Isaiah and Ezekiel (Isa 35:8; 52:1; Ezek 44:9).

Revelation ends with an *allusion* to the name on the forehead of the high priest: "they will see his face, and his name will be on their foreheads" (22:4). The saved now walk as high priests with Christ, the high priest in the New Jerusalem, dressed with him in white linen (3:4). The same characteristics that separated the high priest from the ordinary priests and people now characterize the saved: they are Holy to the Lord.[189]

Revelation 22:15 lists those who are excluded from the New Jerusalem: "Outside are the dogs and sorcerers [*pharmakoi*] and fornicators and murderers and idolaters, and everyone who loves and practices falsehood." Whereas the standard lexicon definition of *pharmakoi* is "sorcerer," it is significant that John places them outside the city precisely as occurred in the elimination rites of the *pharmakoi* in ancient Greece.[190] Bredin contends that Jesus' death as a *pharmakos* is reworked by John as a critique of violence and revenge in society, a reading that is based on the Greek elimination rites that blamed an individual for society's woes.[191] Although this is an intriguing rendering of

189. Ford, *Revelation*, 367: "They bear the name of Yahweh and stand in His presence, a privilege denied to all save the high priest on the Day of Atonement."

190. See BDAG, s.v. "φάρμακος."

191. Bredin, "Hate," 105–113.

*pharmakoi* in the passage, its use elsewhere in Revelation as "sorcery" probably precludes a different meaning here (9:21; 18:23; 21:8). Nevertheless, the double meaning of *pharmakos* as both "sorcerer" and "scapegoat" would be hard to miss for first-century Greek readers of Revelation, especially considering that, according to Roberts, the connection of *pharmakos* with "sorcery" is a later semantic change from its original connotation of cleansing, purifying and healing attached to the ancient *pharmakos* elimination rite.[192] Thus, it remains plausible that John's intended meaning for *pharmakoi* in 22:15 is framed by an eschatological elimination rite that excludes from the New Jerusalem all those who followed the harlot, Babylon, and the dragon, the infamous "*pharmakoi megaloi.*" Those who associate themselves with them become undesirable *pharmakoi*. Under this reading, the reference to the *pharmakoi* in 22:15 constitutes an *echo* of the goat-for-Azazel rite.

After the final DA cleansing is performed on the created order at the appearance of the "new heaven and a new earth" (21:1), the saved will inhabit the high-priestly New Jerusalem, the heavenly Most Holy Place, where "no unclean thing will enter" (21:27). This descent completes the "axis around which all biblical theology turns," i.e., "Creation, the Renewal of Creation (Redemption), the New Creation," wrote Dumbrell.[193] Only those who have "washed their robes" (22:14) in the DA blood of Christ will live therein and worship and "reign for ever and ever," ministering as high priests before the "throne of God and of the Lamb" (22:3, 5).

| **Assessment: The Day of Atonement in Revelation 20 & 22** | |
|---|---|
| *Allusive Type*: Medium loud echoes. | *Thematic Coherence*: Character loyalty of the inhabitants of the New Jerusalem; eschatological elimination rite of "all sin" and defiant sinners; the *pharmakoi*. |

192. See Roberts, "Pharmakos," 221. Roberts adduces geographical evidence for the ancient meaning of "expulsion" for *pharmakos* by mentioning Islands in the Mediterranean Sea used for banishing undesirables called Pharmacussae (coast of Attica) and Pharmacusa (coast of Asia Minor). Perhaps John himself was a *pharmakos* banished to the Island of Patmos.

193. Dumbrell, *The End*, 196.

## Conclusion

As explored in this chapter, the intersection between the Levitical DA and Revelation occurs in the form of *allusions* and *echoes* of its language, imagery, and theological motifs, which John culled from Israel's sacred texts and traditions using a "Christological exegesis." John's figurative interpretation of the OT became an essential lens through which he understood Jesus Christ and his message for the seven churches of Asia; as he revisited Israel's sacred texts and traditions, he read Jesus back into them. He invites his readers to put on these presuppositional lenses in order to comprehend his book and be transformed by it through a "conversion of the imagination."

Showing a heightened awareness of the DA and its centrality in Israel, John drew on the day's language and imagery in order to unveil Christ. Thus, a pattern emerges in Revelation: as the Levitical system of purification offerings culminated in the DA, on which the nation was purged from sin and stood "clean before the Lord," so the dawn of the eschatological kingdom of God is framed by the separation of the holy from the impure (21:27; 22:11, 15). As the observance of the DA confirmed Israel's status as the people of God, so the church's covenantal relationship with God continues to be based on the separation of holiness from sin and impurity, achieved solely by the washing one's figurative spiritual clothes in the DA blood of the Lamb. As Milgrom perceptively observed, "Holiness never sanctifies impurity. Only the reverse occurs—impurity defiles holiness."[194] This becomes a dominating metaphor in Revelation, highlighting the eschatological separation of God's people from unrepentant humanity and the rewards awaiting each group: eternal life in the priestly New Jerusalem for the followers of the Lamb, and annihilation for the followers of the beast, the dragon, and the false prophet.

194. Milgrom, "Day of Atonement," 162–163.

# SUMMARY AND CONCLUSION

This volume examined several aspects of the Levitical DA, from its origins in ancient Israel to its journey through Jewish pseudepigraphal literature, the NT writings, culminating with its reception in Revelation. As pertained to the primary goal of this study of tracing the presence of language and imagery of the DA in Revelation, only passages holding investigative potential were addressed, thus avoiding an exhaustive, "commentary" approach. The following summary highlights the most salient findings of this study.

As the yearly culmination of the Hebrew tabernacle service, the DA was the central day of personal and collective rest, confession, fasting, praying, and covenant renewal for the nation. The day's ethos was so deeply ingrained in the life of Jews that its overtones continued to reverberate in the life of Israel and became a dominant theme in Judaism, whose heroes and villains continued to star in leading roles in Second Temple literature and the NT.

As demonstrated here, the intersection between the Levitical DA and Revelation was framed by themes of the separation of holiness from uncleanness and judgment that suffused the tabernacle service, culminating in the annual rituals of the DA. As a microcosm of God's plan of redemption through Jesus Christ, the DA stands as a type of the eschatological judgment day: sin was eradicated from the tabernacle/temple, the people of Israel stood clean and holy before the Lord, the culpability for sin was laid on the "goat for Azazel" and carried away from the camp. God accepted the purification rites and renewed his covenant with Israel. This important Levitical feast became one of the typological lenses through which John the Revelator saw God's actions in history as he zooms in on the first advent of Jesus Christ and out into his second.

In the Introduction, Revelation's intertextual relationship to the biblical canon, the challenge of establishing John's authorial intention, and how this impacts the book's interpretation were discussed. By reviewing the literature, the most appropriate exegetical method to establish thematic or philological relationships between Revelation and the OT was sought, and previous research on the intersection between Revelation and the DA was reviewed. Foremost in the hermeneutical strategy developed here is the premise that John expected his readers to read Jesus' life, death, resurrection, and exaltation back into the Hebrew Scriptures and their religious traditions.

Based on this premise of continuity between the OT and Revelation, our study explored methods used by scholars to identify intertextual markers in Revelation. Following current practice, this study proposes that intertextuality in Revelation occurs as *allusions* and *echoes* of the OT language and imagery, in addition to other Jewish sources (such as the book of Enoch). While *allusions* are instances of graduated lexical or thematic correspondence with precursor texts, ideas, or images, *echoes* are *thematic allusions* (or non-lexical correspondences) of themes, ideas, or images shared by the author and his readers.

In chapter 1, the DA stipulations found in the Pentateuch were explored, resulting in a clear picture of what the ancient Jewish DA entailed:

(1) Israel's existential need to preserve the covenant with God;

(2) God's demand that his people be clean and holy through the removal of sin and impurity from "their midst" (Lev 16:30);

(3) God's grace in providing atonement for sin and impurity;

(4) Purification through the manipulation of sacrificial blood;

(5) Transfer of sins to the live goat by the high priest's confession;

(6) Retribution for sin ascribed to demonic Azazel;

(7) Defiant sinners and non-participants on the DA are "cut off";

(8) Restoration of the covenantal relationship with God.

Chapter 2 examined how the DA continued to be reworked and reshaped in Jewish literature such as Rabbinic literature, pseudepigraphal writings such as 1 Enoch, the Apocalypse of Abraham, the Book of Jubilees, 11QMelchizedek, and the Book of Giants, as well as the writings of Philo and Josephus. This analysis explored the recurring *midrash* of the "goat for

Azazel" rite and how its eschatological overtones continued to reverberate throughout intertestamental Jewish literature, especially in the development of a typological understanding of that rite as prefiguring the eschatological judgment to be meted out on *haśśāṭān*, God's adversary and deceiver of humanity. By connecting Azazel with *haśśāṭān*, Jewish writers understood Azazel to be a demonic entity responsible for humanity's woes. Fittingly, then, the dismissal of the "goat for Azazel" became a symbol of the eschatological purification of the earth from transgression caused by *haśśāṭān*. John later picks up this motif when describing the judgment of the harlot, the beast, and the dragon.

Chapter 3 examined the presence of DA in the NT. That discussion provided a better understanding of how early Christian writers drew on the DA in their proclamation of "the event Christ." In the Epistle to the Hebrews, an overarching theme emerged: the sprinkling and daubing of atoning blood on the DA typified the shedding of Jesus' blood on the cross and his subsequent entrance into the heavenly Most Holy Place "with his blood." As in the tabernacle, this figurative heavenly ritual signifies the confirmation of Jesus' high-priestly ministry and his enthronement at the right hand of the Father (Heb 8:1–2).

Chapter 4 focused on the reception of the DA's language, imagery, and themes in the book of Revelation. As demonstrated, John's "Christological exegesis" of the OT suffuses the book with a high-priestly Christology. The seven churches of Asia are part of a "priesthood," and Jesus is the high priest mediating on their behalf, dressed in DA clothing (Rev 1). Jesus is a high priest who offers "his blood" as a redeeming sacrifice "from our sins" (1:5) in the mold of the ancient DA ritual. The DA blood of Jesus, the slaughtered Lamb—a composite of all sanctuary blood offerings—offered inside the heavenly Most Holy Place alongside the offer of incense there, cleanses the robes of the 144,000 who stand "clean before the Lord" as the Israelites of old on the DA (Rev 7, 14; Lev 16:30). Jesus, the Christian's high priest and defender, is the rider of the white horse dressed in white robes sprinkled with his own "atoning" blood (Rev 19). He is the high priest of the New Jerusalem—whose dimensions parallel those of the Most Holy Place—where the priestly saints serve and worship God forever (Rev 21).

The following is a summary of the passages in Revelation containing allusive interaction with the DA:

(1) Jesus' introduction as a high priest ministering inside the heavenly sanctuary, dressed in attire appropriate for the high priest on the DA (Rev 1);

(2) The call to holiness and removal of uncleanness given in the letters to the seven churches (Rev 2–3);

(3) The imagery of the blood of the slaughtered Lamb (Rev 5) offered inside God's throne room, the heavenly Most Holy Place. This is a recurring theme in the book and points to Jesus' blood as an atoning DA sacrifice;

(4) The theme of judgment connected to the DA appears in the form of atmospheric disturbances originating inside the heavenly Most Holy Place and repeated in subsequent scenes of judgment in the visions of the seven trumpets, seals, and bowls (Rev 8; 11; 16);

(5) The washing of the saints' robes in the blood of the Lamb (Rev 7; 14) echoes the DA motif of holiness and righteousness;

(6) The "seven plagues" poured on unrepentant humanity allude to the judgment of the "seven plagues" of the Levitical covenant lawsuit also associated with the DA (Rev 15; Lev 26:21);

(7) The motif of confession, penitence, and intercession embedded in the repeated use of incense imagery (Rev 8, 9);

(8) The judgment on the beast, the harlot/Babylon, and the dragon builds on the "goat for Azazel" rite via Jewish traditions (Rev 17–20);

(9) The cleansing effected by the DA blood of the Lamb leads to the subversion of the created order by the appearance of the "new heaven and a new earth" and the descent of the eternal, high-priestly New Jerusalem (Rev 21). As in the earthly sanctuary, God dwells in it.

In John's mind, the eschatological purification from sin leading to the saints' vindication in judgment may only be achieved by washing one's robe in the atoning blood of the Lamb Jesus Christ (7:14; 22:14). His blood frees his people from sin and makes them into a holy kingdom, a high priesthood (1:5–6; 3:4). All who confess their sin, repent and follow the Lamb may have his atoning blood offered figuratively inside the heavenly Most Holy Place on their behalf, while unrepentant, defiant humanity suffers the punishment contained in the seven-fold trumpets and plagues (5:8; 8–11; 16).

God's final act in this eschatological "cleansing" of his creation is accomplished by the destruction of the dragon and his minions (the beast, Babylon, the false prophet) in the lake of fire (20:10). This final cleansing is framed by the ritual of the "goat for Azazel," which Jews and early Christians understood to be a symbol of Satan, sin's originator and its final trustee on Judgment Day.

As the priestly New Jerusalem descends at the end of time, heaven and new earth reach a moment of singularity: the holy city overwhelms the earthly created order, completing the picture of a universe free from impurity and sin where "his servants will worship" God and the Lamb before the heavenly "mercy seat" forever (22:3). In the end, God wins.

---

Exegetical studies of the book of Revelation, such as the present tome, will continue to require careful analysis and reflection. While seeking to fill a lacuna in NT studies, this work does not claim to be exhaustive; future scholars will likely discern further *allusions* and *echoes* of the DA in Revelation.

As we end our journey through the fascinating sacred text that is Revelation, I renew my hope expressed in the Preface that by reading this book, you have gone through the "conversion of the imagination" that John expected of his readers, the same conversion I experienced writing it.

# BIBLIOGRAPHY


Aartun, Kjell. "Studien zum Gesetz über den grossen Versöhnungstag Lv 16 mit Varianten: ein ritualgeschichtlicher Beitrag." *ST* 34 (1980) 73–109.

Ahituv, Shmuel. "Azazel." *EncJud* 3:999–1002.

Alexander, T. Desmond. *From Eden to the New Jerusalem.* Grand Rapids: Kregel Academic, 2008.

Allen, Garrick V. *Manuscripts of the Book of Revelation: New Philology, Paratexts, Reception.* Oxford: Oxford University Press, 2020.

Anderson, Gary A. "Sacrifice and Sacrificial Offerings: Old Testament." *AYBD* 5:870–886.

Arasola, Kai. *The End of Historicism. Millerite Hermeneutic of Time Prophecies in the Old Testament.* Sigtuna: Datem, 1990.

Archer Jr., Gleason. "The Chronology of the Old Testament." In *The Expositor's Bible Commentary*, edited by Frank E. Gaebelein, 1:359–374. Grand Rapids: Zondervan, 1979.

———. *A Survey of the Old Testament: Introduction.* Chicago: Moody, 1964.

Arndt, William, Frederick W. Danker, and Walter Bauer. *A Greek-English Lexicon of the New Testament and Other Early Christian Literature.* Chicago: University of Chicago Press, 2000.

Asale, Bruk Ayele. *1 Enoch as Christian Scripture.* Eugene: Pickwick, 2020.

Attridge, Harold W. "Study of the New Testament in the Pluralistic Context of the Twenty-First Century." In *Foster Biblical Scholarship: Essays in Honor of Kent Harold Richards*, edited by Frank Ritchel Ames and Charles William Miller, 53–64. Atlanta: Society of Biblical Literature, 2010.

Auerbach, Erich. *Mimesis: The Representation of Reality in Western Literature.* Princeton: Princeton University Press, 2003.

Aune, David E. "The Apocalypse of John and Palestinian Jewish Apocalyptic." *Neo* 40 (2006) 1–33.

———. "The Apocalypse of John and the Problem of Genre." *Semeia* 36 (1986) 65–96.

———. "The Prophetic Circle of John of Patmos and the Exegesis of Revelation 22.16." *JSNT* 37 (1989) 103–115.

———. *Revelation 1–5.* WBC 52a. Dallas: Word Books, 1997.

———. *Revelation 6–16.* WBC 52b. Nashville: Thomas Nelson, 1998.

———. *Revelation 17–22.* Word Biblical Commentaries 52c. Nashville: Thomas Nelson, 1998.

———. "Understanding Jewish and Christian Apocalyptic." *WW* 25/3 (2005) 233–245.

Babota, Vasile. *The Institution of the Hasmonean High Priesthood*. Leiden: Brill, 2013.
Bakthin, Mikhail M. "Discourse in the Novel." In *The Novel: An Anthology of Criticism and Theory 1900–2000*, edited by Dorothy J. Hall, 481–510. Oxford: Blackwell, 2006.
Backhaus, Knut. Der Hebräerbrief: Übersetzung und Erklärung. Regensburg: Pustet, 2009.
Baigent, John W. "Jesus as Priest: An Examination of the Claim that the Concept of Jesus as Priest may be Found in The New Testament Outside the Epistle to the Hebrews." *VE* 12 (1981) 34–44.
Bailey, Daniel. "Jesus as the Mercy Seat: The Semantics and Theology of Paul's Use of Hilasterion in Romans 3:25." *TynBul* 51/1 (2000) 155–158.
Bandy, Alan S. "The Layers of the Apocalypse: An Integrative Approach to Revelation's Macrostructure." *JSNT* 31 (2009) 469–499.
———. *The Prophetic Lawsuit in the Book of Revelation*. NTM 29. Sheffield: Sheffield Phoenix, 2010.
Barker, Margaret. *Great High Priest: The Temple Roots of Christian Liturgy*. London: T&T Clark, 2003.
———. *The Revelation of Jesus Christ: Which God Gave to Him to Show to His Servants What Must Soon Take Place (Revelation 1.1)*. Edinburgh: T&T Clark, 2000.
Barr, David L. "The Apocalypse as a Symbolic Transformation of the World: A Literary Analysis." *Int* 38 (1984) 39–50.
———. "Beyond Genre: The Expectations of the Apocalypse." In *The Reality of the Apocalypse: Rhetoric and Politics in the Book of Revelation*, edited by David L. Barr, 71–90. Atlanta: Society of Biblical Literature, 2006.
———. "The Story John Told." In *Reading the Book of Revelation: A Resource for Students*, edited by David L. Barr, 11–24. Atlanta: Society of Biblical Literature, 2003.
———. "Waiting for the End that Never Comes: The Narrative Logic of John's Story." In *Studies in the Book of Revelation*, edited by Steve Moyise, 101–112. Edinburgh: T&T Clark, 2001.
Barrett, C. K. *The Epistle to the Romans*. London: Black, 1962.
Bauckham, Richard. *The Climax of Prophecy: Studies on the Book of Revelation*. Edinburgh: T&T Clark, 1993.
———. "Judgment in the Book of Revelation." *ExAud* 10 (2004) 1–24.
———. *2 Peter, Jude*. WBC 50. Dallas: Word, 1998.
———. *The Theology of the Book of Revelation*. Cambridge: Cambridge University Press, 1993.
Bauer, H. "Die Gottheiten von Ras Schamra." *ZAW* 51 (1933) 94–96.
Bautch, Richard. "The Formulary of Atonement (Lev 16:21) in Penitential Prayers of the Second Temple Period." In *The Day of Atonement: Its Interpretations in Early Jewish and Christian Traditions*, edited by Thomas Hieke and Tobias Nicklas, 33–45. TBN 15. Leiden: Brill, 2012.
Beal, Timothy. *The Book of Revelation: A Biography*. Princeton: Princeton University Press, 2018.
Beale, Gregory K. *Handbook on the New Testament Use of the Old Testament*. Grand Rapids: Baker Academic, 2012.
———. *The Book of Revelation: A Commentary on the Greek Text*. NIGTC. Grand Rapids: Eerdmans, 1999.

———. "The Descent of the Eschatological Temple. Part 1: The Clearest Evidence." *TynBul* 56/1 (2005) 73–102.

———. *John's Use of the Old Testament in Revelation*. JSNTSup 166. Sheffield: Sheffield Academic Press, 1998.

———. *A New Testament Biblical Theology: the Unfolding of the Old Testament in the New*. Grand Rapids: Baker Academic, 2011.

———. "Questions of Authorial Intent, Epistemology and Presuppositions and Their Bearing on the Study of the Old Testament in the New: A Rejoinder to Steve Moyise." *IBS* 21 (1999) 151–180.

———. "A Response to Jon Paulien on the Use of the Old Testament in Revelation." *AUSS* 39/1 (2002) 23–34.

———. "Revelation." In *It Is Written: Scripture Citing Scripture. Essays in Honour of Barnabas Lindars*, edited by D. A. Carson and H. G. Williamson, 318–336. Cambridge: Cambridge University Press, 1988.

———, ed. *Right Doctrine from the Wrong Texts: Essays on the Use of the Old Testament in the New*. Grand Rapids: Baker Academic, 1994.

———. "Solecisms in the Apocalypse as Signals for the Presence of Old Testament Allusions: A Selective Analysis of Revelation 1–22." In *Early Christian Interpretation of the Scriptures of Israel*, edited by Craig A. Evans and J. A. Sanders, 42–146. JSNTSup 148. Sheffield: Sheffield Academic, 1997.

———. *The Use of Daniel in Jewish Apocalyptic Literature and in the Revelation of St. John*. Lanham: University Press of America, 1984.

Bebis, George S. "Influence of Jewish Worship on Orthodox Christian Worship." *GOTR* 22 (1977) 136–42.

Bechmann, U. "Duft im Alten Testament." In *Die Macht der Nase*, edited by Joachim Kügler, 49–98. Stuttgarter Bibelstudien 187. Stuttgart: Katholisches Bibelwerk, 2000.

Beetham, Christopher A. *Echoes of Scripture in the Letter of Paul to the Colossians*. BIS 96. Leiden: Brill, 2008.

Begg, Christopher T. "Yom Kippur in Josephus." In *The Day of Atonement: Its Interpretations in Early Jewish and Christian Traditions*, edited by Thomas Hieke and Tobias Nicklas, 97–120. TBN 15. Leiden: Brill, 2012.

Bell, Albert A. "Date of John's Apocalypse: The Evidence of Some Roman Historians Reconsidered." *NTS* 25/1 (1978) 93–102.

Ben-Daniel, John and Gloria Ben-Daniel. *The Apocalypse in the Light of the Temple*. Jerusalem: Beit Yochanan, 2003.

Ben Ezra, Daniel Stökl. "'Christians' Observing 'Jewish' Festivals of Autumn." In *The Image of the Judaeo-Christians in Ancient Jewish and Christian Literature*, edited by Peter J. Tomson and Doris Lambers-Petry, 53–72. WUNT 158. Tübingen: Mohr Siebeck, 2003.

———. "Fasting with Jews, Thinking with Scapegoats on Yom Kippur in Early Judaism and Christianity, in Particular 4Q541, Barnabas 7, Matthew 27 and Acts 27." In *The Day of Atonement: Its Interpretation in Early Jewish and Christian Traditions*, edited by Thomas Hieke and Tobias Niklas, 165–188. TBN 15. Leiden: Brill, 2012.

———. *The Impact of Yom Kippur on Early Christianity: The Day of Atonement from Second Temple Judaism to the Fifth Century*. WUNT, 2nd ser. 163. Tübingen: Mohr Siebeck, 2003.

———. "Yom Kippur in the Apocalyptic *Imaginaire* and the Roots of Jesus' High Priesthood: Yom Kippur in Zechariah 3, 1 Enoch 10, 11QMelkizedeq, Hebrews and the Apocalypse of Abraham 13." In *Transformations of the Inner Self in Ancient Religions*, edited by Jan Assmann and Gary Stroumsa, 349–366. SHR 83. Leiden: Brill, 1999.

———. "Whose Fast is It? The Ember Day and Yom Kippur." In *The Ways that Never Parted: Jews and Christians in Antiquity and the Early Middle Ages*, edited by Adam H. Becker and Annette Y. Reed, 259–282. TSAJ 95. Tübingen: Mohr Siebeck, 2003.

Berger, Klaus. *Die Apokalypse des Johannes*. 2 vols. Freiburg: Herder, 2017.

Bergsma, John S. *The Jubilee from Leviticus to Qumran: A History of Interpretation*. VTSup 115. Leiden: Brill, 2007.

Bernardakis, Gregorius N., ed. Vol. 4 of *Plutarchus Moralia*. Leipzig: Teubner, 1892.

Bibb, Bryan D. *Ritual Words and Narrative Worlds in the Book of Leviticus*. LHBOTS, 480. London: T&T Clark: 2009.

Black, Matthew, ed. *Apocalypsis Henochi Graece*. PVTG 3. Leiden: Brill, 1970.

Blair, Judit M. *De-Demonising the Old Testament: An Investigation of Azazel, Lilith, Deber, Qeteb and Reshef in the Hebrew Bible*. Tübingen: Mohr Siebeck, 2009.

Blount, Brian K. *Revelation: A Commentary*. Louisville: Westminster John Knox, 2009.

Böcher, Otto. "Die Johannes-Apokalypse in der neueren Forschung." *ANRW* II.25.5:3850–93.

———. "Das Verhältnis der Apokalypse des Johannes zum Evangelium des Johannes." In *L'Apocalypse Johannique et l'Apocalyptique dans le Nouveau Testament*, edited by J. Lambrecht, 289–301. Duculot: Leuven University Press, 1980.

Bock, Darrell L. "Dating the Parables of Enoch: A Forschungsbericht." In *Parables of Enoch: A Paradigm Shift*, edited by Darrell Bock and James H. Charlesworth, 58–113. London: Bloomsbury, 2013.

Boda, Mark J. *A Severe Mercy: Sin and Its Remedies in the Old Testament*. Winona Lake: Eisenbrauns, 2009.

Boring, M. Eugene. *Revelation: Interpretation: A Bible Commentary for Teaching and Preaching*. Louisville: John Knox, 1989.

Boyce, Richard. *Leviticus and Numbers*. Louisville; London: Westminster John Knox, 2008.

Bremmer, Jan N. "Scapegoat Rituals in Ancient Greece." In *Oxford Readings in Greek Religion*, edited by Richard Buxton, 271–293. Oxford: Oxford University Press, 2000.

Breu, Clarissa. *Autorschaft in der Johannesoffenbarung: Eine postmoderne Lektüre*. WUNT, 2nd ser. 541. Tübingen: Mohr Siebeck, 2020.

Briggs, Robert A. *Jewish Temple Imagery in the Book of Revelation*. New York: Peter Lang, 1999.

Brodie, Frederick. *The Revelation Viewed by the Light of the Old Testament Scriptures and Thus Criticizing Many of the Commonly Received Opinions Regarding the Meaning of its Prophecies*. London: Partridge & Co, 1880.

Brown, Francis, Samuel Rolles Driver, and Charles Augustus Briggs. *Enhanced Brown-Driver-Briggs Hebrew and English Lexicon*. Oxford: Clarendon, 1977.

Brown, Raymond E. *The Death of the Messiah: From Gethsemane to the Grave*, 2 vols. New York: Doubleday, 1994.

———. *An Introduction to the New Testament*. ABRL. New York: Doubleday, 1997.

Brownlee, W. H. "The Priestly Character of the Church in the Apocalypse." *NTS* 5 (1959) 224–225.
Bruce, F. F. *The Epistle to the Hebrews*. NICNT. Grand Rapids: Eerdmans, 1990.
Brueggemann, Walter. *Theology of the Old Testament: Testimony, Dispute, Advocacy*. Minneapolis: Fortress, 1997.
Buchanan, George W. "The Day of Atonement and Paul's Doctrine of Redemption." *NovT* 32 (1990) 236–249.
———. "Worship, Feasts and Ceremonies in the Early Jewish-Christian Church." *NTS* 26 (1980) 279–297.
Büchsel, Friedrich and Johannes Herrmann. "ἵλεως, ἱλάσκομαι, ἱλασμός, ἱλαστήριον." *TDNT* 3:300–323.
Burkert, Walter. *Structure and History in Greek Mythology and Ritual*. SCL 47. Berkeley: University of California Press, 1979.
Burtchaell, James T. *From Synagogue to Church: Public Services and Offices in the Earliest Christian Communities*. Cambridge: Cambridge University Press, 1992.
Calaway, Jared G. *The Sabbath and the Sanctuary Access to God in the Letter to the Hebrews and its Priestly Context*. Tübingen: Mohr Siebeck, 2013.
Caldwell, William. "The Doctrine of Satan: I. In the Old Testament." *BW* 41/1 (1913) 29–33.
Campbell, W. Gordon. "Findings, Seals, Trumpets, and Bowls: Variations Upon the Theme of Covenant Rupture and Restoration in the Book of Revelation." *WTJ* 66/1 (2004) 71–96.
———. *Reading Revelation: A Thematic Approach*. Cambridge: James Clark, 2012.
Carmichael, Calum M. "The Origin of the Scapegoat Ritual." *VT* 50 (2000) 167–182.
Carrington, P. *The Meaning of Revelation*. London; New York; Toronto: Society for Promoting Christian Knowledge, 1931.
———. *The Primitive Christian Calendar*. Cambridge: Cambridge University Press, 1952.
Caird, George B. *New Testament Theology*. Oxford: Clarendon, 1994.
———. *The Revelation of Saint John*. London: Adam & Charles Black, 1966.
Carroll, James. *Constantine's Sword. The Church and the Jews: A History*. Boston; New York: Houghton Mifflin, 2002.
Cazelles, Henri. "La question du 'lamed auctoris'." *RB* 56 (1949) 93–101.
Charles, R. H. *The Book of Enoch or 1 Enoch*. Oxford: Clarendon, 1912.
———. *A Critical and Exegetical Commentary of the Revelation of St. John*. 2 vols. ICC. New York: Scribner's Sons, 1920.
———, ed. *Pseudepigrapha of the Old Testament*. 2 vols. Bellingham: Logos, 2004.
Charlesworth, James. H. "The Date and Provenience of the Parables of Enoch." In *Parables of Enoch: A Paradigm Shift*, edited by Darrell Bock and James H. Charlesworth, 37–57. London: Bloomsbury, 2013.
Chesterton, G. K. *Orthodoxy*. New York: John Lane, 1908.
Cheyne, T. K. "The Date and Origin of the Ritual of the "Scapegoat." *ZAW* 15/1 (1895) 153–156.
Chronis, Harry L. "The Torn Veil: Cultus and Christology in Mark 15:37–39." *JBL* 101/1 (1982) 97–114.
Clarke, E. G. et al. *Targum Pseudo-Jonathan of the Pentateuch: Text and Concordance*. Hoboken: Ktav, 1984.

Cohn, Naftali S. *The Memory of the Temple and the Making of the Rabbis.* Philadelphia: University of Pennsylvania Press, 2013.

Collins, Adela Yarbro. *Crisis and Catharsis: The Power of the Apocalypse.* Philadelphia: Westminster, 1984.

———. "Finding Meaning in the Death of Jesus." *JR* 78/2 (1998) 175–196.

———. "Insiders and Outsiders in the Book of Revelation and its Social Context." In *To See Ourselves as Others See Us: Christians, Jews, and "Others" in Late Antiquity,* edited by J. Neusner and E. S. Frerichs, 187–218. Chico: Scholars, 1985.

——— and John J. Collins, eds. *King and Messiah as Son of God.* Grand Rapids: Eerdmans, 2008.

———. "Mark's Interpretation of the Death of Jesus." *JBL* 128 (2009) 545–554.

———. "Reading the Book of Revelation in the 20th Century." *Int* 40 (1986) 229–242.

Collins, John J. *The Apocalyptic Imagination: An Introduction to Jewish Apocalyptic Literature.* BRS. Grand Rapids: Eerdmans, 1998.

———. "Eschatological Dynamics and Utopian Ideals in Early Judaism." In *Imagining the End: Visions of Apocalypse from the Ancient Middle East to Modern America,* edited by Abbas Amanat and Magnus T. Bernardson, 69–89. London: Taurus, 2002.

———. "The Morphology of a Genre: Introduction." *Semeia* 14 (1979) 1–20.

Congar, Yves M. J. "Church, Kingdom, and the Eschatological Temple." *LS* 4 (2008) 289–317.

Cortez, Felix H. "Atonement and inauguration at the Heavenly Sanctuary: A wider perspective to Jesus's ascension in Hebrews." In *Earthly Shadows, Heavenly Realities: Temple/Sanctuary Cosmology in Ancient Near Eastern, Biblical, and Early Jewish Literature,* edited by Kim Papaiouannou and Ioannis Giantzaklidis, 175–188. Berrien Springs: Andrews University Press, 2017.

———. "From the Holy to the Most Holy Place: The Period of Hebrews 9:6–10 and the Day of Atonement as a Metaphor of Transition." *JBL* 125 (2006) 527–547.

Crossan, John Dominic. *The Cross That Spoke: The Origins of the Passion Narrative.* San Francisco: Harper and Row, 1988.

Crüsemann, Frank. *The Torah: Theology and Social History of Old Testament Law.* Trans. A. W. Mahnke. Minneapolis: Fortress, 1996.

Culler, Jonathan. *The Pursuit of Signs: Semiotics, Literature and Deconstruction.* Ithaca: Cornell University Press, 1976.

Cullmann, Oscar. *The Christology of the New Testament.* London: SCM, 1959.

Davidson, Richard M. "Christ's Entry 'Within the Veil' in Hebrews 6:19–20: The Old Testament Background." *AUSS* 39 (2001) 176–190.

———. "The Divine Covenant Lawsuit Motif in Canonical Perspective." *JATS* 21 (2010) 45–84.

———. "Inauguration or Day of Atonement? A Response to Norman Young's 'Old Testament Background to Hebrews 6:19–20 Revisited.'" *AUSS* 40 (2002) 69–88.

———. "Sanctuary Typology." In *Symposium on Revelation, Book 1: Introductory and Exegetical Issues,* edited by Frank B. Holbrook, 99–130. DARCOM 6. Silver Spring: Biblical Research Institute of Seventh-Day Adventists, 1992.

Davies, Douglas. "An Interpretation of Sacrifice in Leviticus." *ZAW* 89 (1977) 387–399.

Davies, Philip R. "Sons of Cain" In *A Word in Season: Essays in Honour of William McKane*, edited by J. D. Martin and Philip R. Davies, 35–56. JSOTSup 42. Sheffield: Sheffield Academic, 1986.
Davies, W. D. "Reflections on Archbishop Carrington's "The Primitive Christian Calendar." In *The Background of the New Testament and its Eschatology: Studies in Honor of C. H. Dodd*, edited by W. D. Davies and David Daube, 124–152. Cambridge: Cambridge University Press, 1956.
Davis, Carl Judson. "Acts 2 and the Old Testament: The Pentecost Event in Light of Sinai, Babel, and the Table of Nations." *CTR* 7/1 (2009) 29–48.
Davis, Robert Dean. *The Heavenly Court Judgment of Revelation 4–5*. Lanham: University Press of America, 1992.
Dawson, David. *Flesh Becomes Word: A Lexicography of the Scapegoat or, the History of an Idea*. East Lansing: Michigan State University Press, 2013.
———. *Studies in Violence, Mimesis and Culture: Flesh Becomes Word: A Lexicography of the Scapegoat or, the History of an Idea*. East Lansing: Michigan State University Press, 2013.
Decock, Paul B. "The Symbol of Blood in the Apocalypse of John." *Neo* 38 (2004) 157–82.
Deiana, Giovanni. "Azazel in Lv. 16." *Lat* 54 (1988) 16–33.
———. "Il giorno del *Kippur* in Filone di Alessandria." In vol. 2 of *Sangue e Antropologia Riti e Culto*, edited by Francisco Vattioni, 891–905. Rome: Pia Unione, 1987.
Deissmann, G. Adolf. *Bible Studies: Contributions Chiefly from Papyri and Inscriptions to the History of the Language, the Literature, and the Religion of Hellenistic Judaism and Primitive Christianity*. 2nd ed. Translated by Alexander Grieve. Edinburgh, 1909.
DeMaris, Richard E. "Jesus Jettisoned." In *The New Testament in Its Ritual World*, edited by Richard E. DeMaris, 91–111. London: Routledge, 2008.
DeSilva, David A. *Discovering Revelation: Content, Interpretation, Reception*. Grand Rapids: Eerdmans, 2021.
Dimant, Devorah. "1 Enoch 6–11: A Methodological Perspective." SBLSP (1978) 323–339.
———. "Use and Interpretation of Mikra in the Apocrypha and Pseudepigrapha." Vol. 1 of *Mikra: Text, Translation, Reading and Interpretation of the Hebrew Bible in Ancient Judaism and Early Christianity*, edited by Martin Jan Mulder, 379–419. Philadelphia: Fortress, 1988.
Do, Joseph Toan. "Jesus Death as Hilasmos According to 1 John: Expiation of Propitiation – 'ΕΞΙΛΑΣΚΟΜΑΙ in the Septuagint." In *The Death of Jesus in the Fourth Gospel*, edited by G. Van Belle, 561–577. Leuven: Leuven University Press, 2007.
Dodd, C. H. "*Hilaskesthai*, Its Cognates, Derivatives, and Synonyms in the Septuagint." *JTS* 32 (1931) 352–360.
Dorman, Anke. "Commit Injustice and Shed Innocent Blood. Motives Behind the Institution of the Day of Atonement in the Book of Jubilees." In *The Day of Atonement: Its Interpretation in Early Jewish and Christian Traditions*, edited by Thomas Hieke and Tobias Nicklas, 49–61. TBN 15. Leiden: Brill, 2012.
Douglas, Mary. "The Go-Away Goat." In *The Book of Leviticus: Composition and Reception*, edited by Rolf Rendtorff and Robert A. Kugler, 121–141. Leiden: Brill, 2003.

Draper, Jonathan A. "The Heavenly Feast of Tabernacles: Revelation 7:1–17." *JSNT* 19 (1983) 133–147.

Driver, G. R. "Three Technical Terms in the Pentateuch." *JSS* 1 (1956) 97–105.

Duhm, Hans. *Die bösen Geister im Alten Testament*. Tübingen: Mohr Siebeck, 1904.

Dumbrell, William J. *The End of the Beginning: Revelation 21–22 and the Old* Testament. Grand Rapids: Baker, 1985.

Dunn, James D. G. *The Acts of the Apostles*. Grand Rapids: Eerdmans, 1996.

———. "Paul's Epistle to the Romans: An Analysis of Structure and Argument." *ANRW* II.25.4:2842–2889.

———. *Romans 1–8*. World Biblical Commentary 38A. Dallas: Word, 1988.

———. *Romans 9–16*. World Biblical Commentary 38B. Dallas: Word, 1988.

Eberhart, Christian A. "To Atone or Not to Atone: Remarks on the Day of Atonement and the Meaning of Atonement." In *Sacrifice, Cult, and Atonement in Early Judaism and Christianity*, edited by Henrietta L. Wiley and Christian A. Eberhart, 197–231. Atlanta: Society of Biblical Literature, 2017.

———. "Characteristics of Sacrificial Metaphors in Hebrews." In *Hebrews: Contemporary Methods-New Insights*, edited by Gabriella Gelardini, 37–64. Leiden: Brill, 2005.

———. *The Sacrifice of Jesus: Understanding Atonement Biblically*. Eugene: Wipf & Stock, 2018.

Eissfeldt, O. "Zur Deutung von Motiven auf den 1937 gefundenen Elfenbeinarbeiten von Megiddo." *FF* 26 (1950) 1–4.

Ellingworth, Paul. *The Epistle to the Hebrews: A Commentary on the Greek Text*. NIGTC. Grand Rapids: Eerdmans, 1993.

Ellul, Jacques. *L'Apocalypse: Architecture en Mouvement*. Genève: Labor et Fides, 1977.

Emerton, J. A. "'The High Places of the Gates' in 2 Kings XXIII 8." *VT* 44 (1994) 455–67.

England, Breck. *The Day of Atonement: A Novel of the End*. Coral Gables: Mango Media, 2018.

Enns, Peter. *Exodus*. NIVAC. Grand Rapids: Zondervan, 2000.

Erho, Ted. M. "The Ahistorical Nature of 1 Enoch 56:5–8 and Its Ramifications upon the *Opinio Communis* on the Dating of the *Similitudes of Enoch*." *JSJ* 40 (2009) 23–54.

———. "Historical-Allusional Dating and the Similitudes of Enoch." *JBL* 130 (2011) 493–511.

———. "Internal Dating Methodologies and the Problem Posed by the *Similitudes of Enoch*." *JSPS* 20 (2010) 83–103.

Eslinger, Lyle. "Inner-Biblical Exegesis and Inner-Biblical Allusion: The Question of Category." *VT* 42 (1992) 45–58.

Evans, Craig A. "Barnabas Lindars and the Semitic Context of Scripture." *Bulletin of the John Rylands Library* (2004) 125–140.

Ezell, M. Douglas. *Revelations on Revelation*. Waco: Word, 1977.

Falk, D. K. "Scriptural Inspiration for Penitential Prayer in the Dead Sea Scrolls." In vol. 2 of *Seeking the Favor of God: The Development of Penitential Prayer in Second Temple Judaism*, edited by Mark J. Boda, D. K. Falk, R. A. Werline, 127–157. Atlanta: Society of Biblical Literature, 2007.

Fitzmyer, J. A. "The Ascension of Christ and Pentecost." *TS* 45 (1984) 409–440.

Farrer, Austin. *A Rebirth of Images: The Making of St John's Apocalypse*. 1949. Reprint, Albany: State University of New York Press, 1986.

Fauth, Wolfgang. "Auf den Spuren des biblischen Azazel (Lev 16): Einige Residuen der Gestalt oder des Namens in jüdisch-aramäischen, griechischen, koptischen, äthiopischen, syrischen und mandäischen Texten." *ZAW* 110/4 (1998) 514–534.

Feinberg, Charles L. "The Scapegoat of Leviticus Sixteen." *BibSac* 115 (1958) 320–333.

Fekkes, Jan. *Isaiah and Prophetic Traditions in the Book of Revelation: Visionary Antecedents and their Development*. JSNTSup 93. Sheffield: Sheffield Academic, 1994.

Ferguson, David. "'I Never Did an Evil Thing': An Examination of Hittite Sin and Religious Sensibility." *SA* 8/1 (2010) 55–60.

Fishbane, Michael A. *Biblical Interpretation in Ancient Israel*. Oxford: Oxford University Press, 1985.

———. "The Hebrew Bible and Exegetical Tradition." In *Intertextuality in Ugarit and Israel*, edited by Johannes C. De Moor, 15–30. OSt 40. Leiden: Brill, 1998.

———. "Revelation and Tradition: Aspects of Inner-Biblical Exegesis." *JBL* 99/3 (1980) 343–361.

Flint, Peter W. "The Book of Leviticus in the Dead Sea Scrolls." In *The Book of Leviticus: Composition and Reception*, edited by Rolf Rendtorff and Robert A. Kugler, 323–339. FIOTL 3; VTSup 93. Leiden: Brill, 2003.

Ford, Desmond. *Daniel 8:14, the Day of Atonement and the Investigative Judgment*. Casselberry: Euangelion, 1980.

Ford, J. Massyngberde. *Revelation: Introduction, Translation and Commentary*. AB 38. Garden City: Doubleday, 1975.

Fransen, I. "Cahier de Bible: Jésus, le Témoin Fidèle (Apocalypse)." *BVC* 16 (1956–7) 66–79.

Frazer, Sir James G. *The Golden Bough*. London: Macmillan, 1914.

Frei, Hans W. *The Eclipse of Biblical Narrative: A Study in Eighteenth-and Nineteenth-Century Hermeneutics*. Yale University Press, 1974.

Friesen, Steven J. *Imperial Cults and the Apocalypse of John: Reading Revelation in the Ruins*. New York: Oxford University Press, 2001.

Frilingos, Christopher A. *Spectacles of Empire: Monsters, Martyrs, and the Book of Revelation*. Philadelphia: University of Pennsylvania Press, 2004.

Fuller, R. H. Review of *The Cross That Spoke: The Origins of the Passion Narrative* by John Dominic Crossan. *Int* 45 (1991) 71–73.

Gane, Roy. *Cult and Character: Purification Offerings, Day of Atonement and Theodicy*. Winona Lake: Eisenbrauns, 2005.

———. *Leviticus and Numbers*. NIVAC. Grand Rapids: Zondervan, 2004.

———. "Re-Opening Katapetasma ("Veil") In Hebrews 6:19." *AUSS* 38 (2000) 5–8.

———. "Schedules for Deities: Macrostructure of Israelite, Babylonian, and Hittite Sancta Purification Days." *AUSS* 36 (1998) 231–44.

Gardiner, F. "On Heb. 10:20." *JBL* 8 (1888) 142–146.

Gaustad, Edwin, ed. *The Rise of Adventism: Religion and Society in Mid-nineteenth-century America*. New York: Harper & Row, 1974.

Gelardini, Gabriella. "The Inauguration of Yom Kippur According to the LXX and its Cessation or Perpetuation According to the Book of Hebrews." In *The Day of Atonement: Its Interpretations in Early Jewish and Christian Traditions,* edited by Thomas Hieke and Tobias Nicklas, 225–254. TBN 15. Leiden: Brill, 2011.

———. "Verhärtet eure Herzen nicht:' Der Hebräer, eine Synagogenhomilie zu Tischa be–Aw. BIS 83. Leiden: Brill, 2007.

Gesenius, Wilhelm and Samuel Prideaux Tregelles. *Gesenius Hebrew and Chaldee Lexicon to the Old Testament Scriptures.* Bellingham: Logos, 2003.

Gentry, K. L. *Before Jerusalem Fell. Dating the Book of Revelation. An Exegetical and Historical Argument for a Pre-A.D. 70 Composition.* Tyler: Institute for Christian Economics, 1989.

Gerstenberger, Erhard. *Leviticus: A Commentary.* Louisville: Westminster John Knox, 1996.

Gieschen, Charles Arthur. "Angelomorphic Christology: Antecedents and Early Evidence." PhD dissertation, University of Michigan, 1995.

Gilchrest, Eric J. *Revelation 21–22 in Light of Jewish and Greco-Roman Utopianism.* BIS 118. Leiden: Brill, 2013.

Gilders, William K. "Blood as Purificant in Priestly Torah: What Do We Know and How Do We Know It?" In *Pespectives on Purity and Purification in the Bible,* edited by Naphtali S. Meshel, Jeffrey Stackert, David P. Wright, and Baruch J. Schwartz, 77–83. LHBOTS 474. New York; London: T&T Clark, 2008.

Ginsburskaya, Mila. "Leviticus in the Light of the Dead Sea Scrolls: Atonement and Purification of Sin." In vol. 1 of *The Dead Sea Scrolls in Context,* edited by Armin Lange, Emanuel Tov and Matthias Weigold, 265–277. VTSup 140. Leiden: Brill, 2011.

Glassius, Salomon. *Philologiae sacrae qua totius sacrosanctae Veteris & Novi Testamenti, scripturae, tum stylus & Literatura, tum sensus & genuinae interpretationis ratio expenditure.* 5th ed. 5 vols. Frankfurt: 1686.

Goetze, Albrecht. "Hittite Rituals, Incantations and Description of Festival." In *Ancient Near Eastern Texts Relating to the Old Testament,* edited by James B. Pritchard, 346–364. Princeton: Princeton University Press, 1969.

Görg, M. "Asasel." NBL 1 (1991) 181–182.

———. "Eine neue Deutung für kapporet." *ZAW* 89 (1977) 115–118.

———. "Beobachtungen zum sogenannten Azazel-Ritus." *BN* 33 (1986) 10–16.

Gorman, Michael J. *Reading Revelation Responsibly: Uncivil Worship and Witness: Following the Lamb Into the New Creation.* Eugene: Cascade, 2011.

Grabbe, Lester L. "The Scapegoat Tradition: A Study in Early Jewish Interpretation." *JSJ* 18 (1987) 152–167.

Gradwohl, Roland. "Das 'fremde Feuer' von Nadab und Abihu." *ZAW* 75 (1963) 288–96.

Gray, Timothy C. *The Temple in the Gospel of Mark: A Study in Its Narrative Role.* Grand Rapids: Baker Academic, 2010.

Green, Joel B. "The Gospel of Peter: Source for a Pre-Canonical Passion Narrative?" *ZAW* 78 (1987) 293–301

Greenberg, James A. *A New Look at Atonement in Leviticus: The Meaning and Purpose of Kipper Revisited.* University Park: Pennsylvania State University Press, 2019.

Greenfield, J. C. and M. E. Stone. "The Enochic Pentateuch and the Date of the Similitudes." *HTR* 70 (1977) 51–65.

Gruenwald, Ithamar. *Rituals and Ritual Theory in Ancient Israel.* Leiden: Brill, 2003.

Guilding, Aileen. *The Fourth Gospel and Jewish Worship: A Study of the Relations of St. John's Gospel to the Ancient Jewish Lectionary System*. Oxford: Clarendon, 1960.

Guinot, Jean Noël. "L'Exégèse du bouc emissaire chez Cyrille d'Alexandrie et Theodore de Cyr." *Aug* 28 (1988) 16–33.

Gulley, Norman R. "Revelation 4 and 5: Judgment or Inauguration?" *JATS* 8 (1997) 59–81.

Gundry, Robert. "Angelomorphic Christology in the Book of Revelation." In *The Old Is Better: New Testament Essays in Support of Traditional Interpretations*, 377–398. WUNT 178. Tübingen: Mohr Siebeck, 2005.

———. "Angelomorphic Christology in the Book of Revelation." In *Society of Biblical Literature 1994 Seminar Papers*, edited by Eugene H. Lovering, Jr., 662–78. SBLSP Series 33. Atlanta: Scholars, 1994.

Gurney, O. R. *Babylonian Prophylactic Figures and Their Rituals*. AAA 22. Liverpool: University Press, 1935.

Gurtner, Daniel M. "The 'House of the Veil' in Sirach 50." *JSPS* 14 (2005) 187–200.

———. "Καταπέτασμα: Lexicographical and Etymological Considerations on the Biblical Text." *AUSS* 42/1 (2004) 105–111.

———. "LXX Syntax and the Identity of the New Testament Veil." *NovT* 47/4 (2005) 344–353.

———. "The Rending of the Veil and Markan Christology: 'Unveiling' the 'ΥΙΟΣ ΘΕΟΥ (Mark 15:38–39)." *BibInt* 15 (2007) 292–306.

———. "The Rending of the Veil (Matt. 27:51a Par): A Look Back and a Way Forward." *Them* 29 (2004) 4–14.

———. *The Torn Veil: Matthew's Exposition of the Death of Jesus*. SNTSMS 139. Cambridge: Cambridge University Press, 2007.

———. "The Veil of the Temple in History and Legend." *JETS* 49/1 (2006) 97–114.

Hagner, Donald A. *Encountering the Book of Hebrews (Encountering Biblical Studies): An Exposition*. Grand Rapids: Baker Academic, 2002.

———. *Matthew 14–28*. WBC 33b. Dallas: Word, 1998.

Hahm, Clement Taek. "The Priestly Influence upon Daniel 7–12." PhD dissertation, The Claremont Graduate University, 2008.

Hahn, Ferdinand. "Die Offenbarung des Johannes als Geschichtsdeutung und Trostbuch." *KuD* 51/1 (2005) 55–70.

Hall, Robert G. "The 'Christian Interpolation' in the Apocalypse of Abraham." *JBL* 107 (1988) 107–112.

Hamilton, Catherine Sider. *The Death of Jesus in Matthew Innocent Blood and the End of Exile*. Tübingen: Mohr Siebeck, 2017.

Hamilton, Victor P. "מְעַל." *TWOT* 519.

Hangyas, Laszlo I. "The Use and Abuse of Authority: An Investigation of the ΕΞΟΥΣΙΑ Passages in Revelation." PhD dissertation, Andrews University, 1997.

Hannah, Darrell D. "The Throne of His Glory: The Divine Throne and Heavenly Mediators in Revelation and the Similitudes of Enoch." *ZNW* 94 (2003) 68–96.

Hanson, Paul D. *The Dawn of Apocalyptic*. Philadelphia, PA: Fortress Press, 1979.

———. "Rebellion in Heaven, Azazel, and Euhemeristic Heroes in 1 Enoch 6–11." *JBL* 96 (1977) 195–233.

Haran, Menahem. *Temples and Temple Service in Ancient Israel: An Inquiry into Biblical Cult Phenomena and the Historical Setting of the Priestly School*. Oxford: Clarendon, 1978.

———. "The Uses of Incense in the Ancient Israelite Ritual." *VT* 10 (1960) 113–29.
Harrington, Willfrid J. *Revelation*. SP 16. Collegeville: Liturgical, 1993.
Harris, Murray J. *The Second Epistle to the Corinthians: A Commentary on the Greek Text*. NIGTC. Grand Rapids, MI; Milton Keynes: Eerdmans Pub. Co.; Paternoster, 2005.
Harrison, Jane E. "The Pharmakos." *Folklore* 27/3 (1916) 298–99.
———. *Prolegomena to the Study of Greek Religion*. 1903. Reprint, Cleveland: Meridian,1966.
Harrison, R. K. *Leviticus: An Introduction and Commentary*. TOTC. Downers Grove: InterVarsity, 1980.
Hartley, John E. *Leviticus*. WBC 4. Nashville: Thomas Nelson, 1992.
Hatina, Thomas R. "Intertextuality and Historical Criticism in New Testament Studies: Is There a Relationship?" *BibInt* 7/1 (1999) 28–43.
Hayman, Henry. "The Book of Enoch in Reference to the New Testament and Early Christian Antiquity." *BW* 12 (1898) 37–46.
Hayward, C. T. R. "Understandings of the Temple Service in the Pentateuch Septuagint." In *Temple Worship in Biblical Israel*, edited by John Day, 385–400. London: T&T Clark, 2007.
Hayes, John H. "Atonement in the Book of Leviticus." *Int* 52/1 (1998) 5–15.
Hays, Richard B. *Echoes of Scripture in the Gospels*. Waco: Baylor University Press, 2016.
———. *Echoes of Scripture in the Letters of Paul*. New Haven: Yale University Press, 1989.
———. *Reading Backwards: Figural Christology and the Fourfold Gospel Witness*. Waco: Baylor University Press, 2014.
———. *The Conversion of the Imagination: Paul As Interpreter of Israel's Scripture*. Grand Rapids: Eerdmans, 2005.
Heger, P. *The Development of Incense Cult in Israel*. BZAW 245. Berlin: de Gruyter, 1997.
Heil, John Paul. "Jesus as Unique High Priest in the Gospel of John." *CBQ* 57 (1995) 729–745.
Hellholm, David. "The Problem of Apocalyptic Genre and the Apocalypse of John." *Semeia* 36 (1986) 13–64.
Helm, R. "Azazel in Early Jewish Literature." *AUSS* 32 (1994) 217–26.
Henderson, Timothy P. *The Gospel of Peter and Early Christian Apologetics: Rewriting the Story of Jesus' Death, Burial and Resurrection*. Tübingen: Mohr Siebeck, 2011.
Hertz, J. H. *Leviticus*. London: Oxford University Press, 1932.
Hieke, Thomas. *Levitikus*. Zweiter Teilband 16–27. Freiburg: Herder, 2014.
——— and Tobias Niklas, eds. *The Day of Atonement: Its Interpretation in Early Jewish and Christian Traditions*. TBN 15. Leiden: Brill, 2012.
———. "Participation and Abstraction in Yom Kippur Ritual According to Leviticus 16." In *Writing a Commentary on Leviticus: Hermeneutics – Methodology – Themes*, edited by Christian A. Eberhart and Thomas Hieke, 151–158. Göttingen: Vandenhoeck & Ruprecht, 2019.
Hill, David. *Greek Words and Hebrew Meanings: Studies in the Semantics of Soteriological Terms*. Cambridge: Cambridge University Press, 1967.
———. David Hill, "Prophecy and Prophets in the Revelation of St. John." *NTS* 18 (1971–72) 406–11.

Himmelfarb, Martha. *Ascent to Heaven in Jewish and Christian Apocalypses*. Oxford: Oxford University Press, 1993.

Hindley, J. C. "Towards a Date for the Similitudes of Enoch." *NTS* 14 (1968) 551–65.

Hodge, Zane D. "A Historical and Grammatical Examination of Azazel in Biblical and Extra-biblical Sources with Special Emphasis Given to its Meaning with the Hebrew Preposition ל." PhD dissertation, Mid-America Baptist Theological Seminary, 2004.

Hoenig, Sidney B. "The New Pesher on Azazel." *JQR* 56/3 (1966) 248–253.

Hoffmann, H. "Kleinigkeiten." *ZAW* 2 (1882) 175.

Hoffmann, Matthias Reinhard. *The Destroyer and the Lamb. The Relationship Between Angelomorphic and Lamb Christology in the Book of Revelation*. WUNT 203. Tübingen: Mohr Siebeck, 2005.

Hofius, Ottfried. "Inkarnation und Opfertod Jesu nach Hebr 10, 19f." In *Der Ruf und die Antwort der Gemeinde: Festschrift Joachim Jeremias*, edited by E. Lohse, 132–43. Göttingen: Vandenhoeck & Ruprecht, 1970.

Holladay, William Lee and Ludwig Köhler. *A Concise Hebrew and Aramaic Lexicon of the Old Testament*. Leiden: Brill, 2000.

Hollander, John. *The Figure of Echo: A Mode of Allusion in Milton and After*. Berkeley: University of California Press, 1981.

Homer. *The Odyssey, with an English Translation by A.T. Murray, Ph.D.* 2 vols. Cambridge: Harvard University Press; London: William Heinemann, 1919.

Hongisto, Leif. *Experiencing the Apocalypse at the Limits of Alterity*. Leiden: Brill, 2010.

Horbury, W. "The Aaronic Priesthood in the Epistle to the Hebrews." *JSNT* 9 (1983) 43–71.

Houtman, C. "On the Function of the Holy Incense (Exodus xxx 34–8) and the Sacred Anointing Oil (Exodus xxx 22–33)." *VT* 42 (1992) 458–65.

Hubbard Jr., Robert L. "Reading through the Rearview Mirror Inner-Biblical Exegesis and the New Testament." In *Doing Theology for the Church: Essays in Honor of Klyne Snodgrass*, edited by Rebekah A. Eklund and John E. Phelan Jr., 125–139. Eugene: Wipf and Stock, 2014.

Hughes, David D. *Human Sacrifice in Ancient Greece*. London: Routledge, 1991.

Hundley, Michael B. *Keeping Heaven on Earth: Safeguarding the Divine Presence in the Priestly Tabernacle*. FAT, 2nd ser. 50. Tübingen: Mohr Siebeck, 2011.

Hunter, Erica D. "Who Are Demons?" *SEL* 15 (1998) 95–115.

Hurtado, Larry. "Revelation 4–5 in the Light of Jewish Apocalyptic Analogies." *JSNT* 25(1985) 105–124.

Isaac, Marie. "Priesthood and the Epistle to the Hebrews." *HeytJ* 38 (1997) 51–62.

Jackson, Howard M. "The Death of Jesus in Mark and the Miracle from the Cross" *NTS* 33 (1987) 16–37.

Janowski, Bernd. "Azazel." *DDD* 128–131. Grand Rapids: Eerdmans, 1999.

———. "Azazel." In *Iconography of Deities and Demons in the Ancient Near East*, edited by Jürg Eggler. http://www.religionswissenschaft.unizh.ch/idd/prepublications/e_idd_azazel.pdf. Accessed Feb 28, 2013.

———. "Das Geschenck der Versöhnhung." In *The Day of Atonement: Its Interpretation in Early Jewish and Christian Traditions*, edited by Thomas Hieke and Tobias Niklas, 3–31. TBN 15. Leiden: Brill, 2012.

——— and G. Wilhelm, "Der Bock, der die Sünden hinausträgt: zur Religionsgeschichte des Azazel-Ritus Lev 16,10, 21f." In *Religionsgeschichtliche Beziehungen zwischen Kleinasien, Nordsyrien und dem Alten Testament*, edited by K. Koch and G. Wilhelm, 109–169. Göttingen: Vandenhoeck & Ruprecht, 1993.

Jastrow, Marcus. "כַּפֹּרֶת." In *A Dictionary of the Targumim, the Talmud Babli and Yerushalmi, and the Midrashic Literature*, compiled by Marcus Jastrow, 1:658. 1903. Reprint, Brooklyn: P. Shalom, 1967.

Jenkins, Ferrell. *The Old Testament in the Book of Revelation*. Marion: Cogdill, 1972.

Jenks, Gregory C. *The Origins and Early Development of the Antichrist Myth*. Berlin; New York: de Gruyter, 2011.

Jeremias, J. "Hebräer 10:20 τοῦτ' ἔστιν τῆς σαρκὸς αὐτοῦ." *ZNW* 62 (1971) 131.

Johns, Loren. "Atonement and Sacrifice in the Book of Revelation." In *The Work of Jesus Christ in Anabaptist Perspective: Essays in Honor of J. Denny Weaver*, edited by Alain Epp Weaver and Gerald J. Mast, 124–46. Telford: Cascadia, 2008.

———. "Jesus in the Book of Revelation." In *The Oxford Handbook of the Book of Revelation*, edited by Craig R. Koester, 223–239. Oxford: Oxford University Press, 2020.

———. *The Lamb Christology of the Apocalypse of John: An Investigation into Its Origins and Rhetorical Force*. WUNT, 2nd ser. 167. Tübingen: Mohr Siebeck, 2003.

Johnsson, A. F. "Revelation." *The Expositor's Bible Commentary*, edited by F. E. Gabelein, 758–59. Grand Rapids: Zondervan, 2006.

Johnsson, Luke Timothy. *Hebrews*. NTL. Louisville: Westminster John Knox, 2006.

Johnsson, William G. "Defilement and Purgation in the Book of Hebrews." PhD. Dissertation, Vanderbilt University, 1973.

Jürgens, B. *Heiligkeit und Versöhnung: Levitikus 16 in seinem literarischen Kontext*. HBS 28. Freiburg: Herder, 2001.

Kaiser, Walter C. "לִילִית." *TWOT* 479.

Kalimi, Isaac. "The Day of Atonement in the Late Second Temple Period: Sadducees' High Priests, Pharisees' Norms, and Qumranites' Calendar(s)." *RRJ* 14 (2011) 71–91.

Kapelrud, A. S. "The Number Seven in Ugaritic Texts." *VT* 18 (1968) 494–499.

Kaufmann, Yehezkel. *The Religion of Israel, from Its Beginnings to the Babylonian Exile*. Chicago: University of Chicago Press, 1960.

Keil, C. F. and F. Delitzsch. *The Pentateuch*. In vol. 2 of *Biblical Commentary on the Old Testament*. 1864. Reprint, Grand Rapids: Eerdmans, 1951.

Kellogg, S. *The Book of Leviticus*. New York: Funk & Wagnalls, 1900.

Kibbe, Michael. "'Is it Finished? When Did it Start? Hebrews, Priesthood, and Atonement in Biblical, Systematic, and Historical Perspective.'" *JTS* 65/1 (2014) 25-61.

Kistemaker, Simon J. *Revelation*. NTC. Grand Rapids: Baker Academic, 2001.

Kiuchi, Nobuyoshi. *Leviticus*. AOTC. Nottingham; Downers Grove: InterVarsity, 2007.

———. *The Purification Offering in the Priestly Literature*. JSOTSup 56. Sheffield: Sheffield Academic, 1987.

Klaassen, William. "The Ascetic Way: Reflections on Peace, Justice and Vengeance in the Apocalypse of John." In *Asceticism and the New Testament*, edited by Leif E. Vaage and Vincent L. Wimbush. 393–410. New York; London: Rutledge, 1999.

Klawans, Jonathan. *Impurity and Sin in Ancient Judaism*. Oxford: Oxford University Press, 2000.

Klingbeil, Gerald A. *Bridging the Gap Between Ritual and Ritual Texts*. BBRSup 1. Winona Lake: Eisenbrauns, 2007.

Klostermann, August. *Der Pentateuch: Beiträge zu Seinem Verständnis und Seiner Entstehungsgeschichte.* Leipzig: A. Deichart, 1893.
Knibb, Michael A. "The Date of the Parables of Enoch: A Critical Review." *NTS* 25/3 (1979) 345–359.
———. *Essays on the Book of Enoch and Other Early Jewish Texts and Traditions.* SVTP 22. Leiden: Brill, 2008.
———. Review of *Der auserwählte Richter: Untersuchungen zum traditionsgeschichtlichen Ort der Menschensohnsgestalt der Bilderreden des Äthiopischen Henoch* by Johannes Theisohn. *JSS* 21 (1976) 197–200.
Koehler, Ludwig and W. Baumgartner, eds. *Lexicon in Veteris Testamenti Libros.* Leiden: Brill, 1958.
Koester, Craig R. *Hebrews: A New Translation with Introduction and Commentary.* New York: Doubleday, 2001.
———, ed. *The Oxford Handbook of the Book of Revelation.* Oxford: Oxford University Press, 2020.
———. *Revelation: A New Translation with Introduction and Commentary,* edited by John J. Collins. AYB 38A. New Haven; London: Yale University Press, 2014.
Koester, Helmut. *Ancient Christian Gospels. Their History and Development.* Philadelphia and London: SCM, 1990.
Körting, Corinna. "Theology of Atonement in the Feast Calendar of the Temple Scroll: Some Observations." *SJOT* 18/2 (2004) 232–247
Kowalski, Beate. *Die Rezeption des Propheten Ezechiel in der Offenbarung des Johannes.* SBB 52. Stuttgart: Katholisches Bibelwerk, 2004.
Kraybill, J. Nelson. *Apocalypse and Allegiance: Worship, Politics, and Devotion in the Book of Revelation.* Grand Rapids: Brazos, 2010.
Kristeva, Julia. *Desire in Language.* New York: Columbia University Press, 1980.
———. *Sèméiotiké: Recherches Pour Une Sémanalyse.* Paris: Le Sevil, 1969.
———. "Word, Dialogue and Novel." In *The Kristeva Reader,* edited by Toril Moi. New York: Columbia University Press, 1986.
Kügler, J., ed. *Die Macht der Nase. Zur religiösen Bedeutung des Duftes.* Stuttgarter Bibelstudien 187. Stuttgart: Katholisches Bibelwerk, 2000.
Kugler, Robert and Kyung S. Baek. *Leviticus at Qumran: Text and Interpretation.* Leiden: Brill, 2016.
Kulik, Alexander. *Retroverting Slavonic Pseudepigrapha: Toward the Original of the Apocalypse of Abraham.* TCSt 3. Atlanta: Society of Biblical Literature, 2004.
Kurtz, J. H. *Sacrificial Worship of the Old Testament.* Minneapolis: Klock & Klock, 1980.
Kuykendall, Robert Michael. "The Literary Genre of the Book of Revelation: A Study of the History of Apocalyptic Research and its Relationship to John's Apocalypse." PhD dissertation, Southwestern Baptist Theological Seminary, 1986.
Ladd, George Eldon. *A Commentary on the Revelation of John.* Grand Rapids: Eerdmans, 1972.
———. *A Theology of the New Testament.* Rev. ed. Grand Rapids: Eerdmans, 1993.
Landersdorfer, Simon K. *Studien zum biblischen Versöhnungstag.* Münster: Aschendorff, 1924.
Landgraf, Paul David. "The Structure of Hebrews: A Word of Exhortation in Light of the Day of Atonement." In *A Cloud of Witness: The Theology of Hebrews in its Ancient Contexts,* edited by Richard Bauckham, Daniel Driver, Trevor Hart, Nathan McDonald, 19–27. LNTS 387. London: T&T Clark, 2008.

Lane, William L. *Hebrews 1–8*. WBC, vol. 47A. Dallas: Word, 1991.
———. *Hebrews 9–13*. WBC, vol. 47B. Dallas: Word, 1991.
Lang, B. "כִּפֶּר." *TDOT* 7:288–303.
Langenhoven, Hanno et al. "The Day of Atonement as a Hermeneutical Key to the Understanding of Christology in Hebrews." *JECH* 1 (2011) 85–97.
Laughlin, John C. H. "The 'Strange Fire' of Nadab and Abihu." *JBL* 95 (1976) 559–65.
Laughlin, Cowden T. *The Solecisms of the Apocalypse*. Princeton: University Printers, 1902.
Leonard, Jeffery M. "Identifying Inner-Biblical Allusions: Psalm 78 as a Test Case." *JBL* 127 (2008) 241–265.
Lestringant, Pierre. Essai sur l'unité de la révelation biblique. Paris: Editions Je Sers, 1942.
Levine, Baruch A. "The Descriptive Tabernacle Texts of the Pentateuch." *JAOS* 85 (1965) 307–318.
———. *The JPS Torah Commentary: Leviticus*. Philadelphia; New York; Jerusalem: JPS, 1989.
———. "Kippurim." *EI* 9 (1969) 88–95
———. *In the Presence of the Lord: A Study of Cult and Some Cultic Terms in Ancient Israel*. SJLA 5. Leiden: Brill, 1974.
Lightfoot, Joseph B. *Saint Paul's Epistles to the Colossians and to Philemon*. ZCS. Grand Rapids: Zondervan, 1979.
——— and J. R. Harmer. *The Apostolic Fathers*. London: Macmillan, 1891.
Lindars, Barnabas. Review of *The Apocalypse and Semitic Syntax*. *JSS* 30/2 (1985) 289–291.
———. "The Place of the Old Testament in the Formation of New Testament Theology: Prolegomena." *NTS* 23 (1976–7) 59–66.
Lindeskog, Gösta. "Der Prozess Jesu im Jüdisch-Christlichen Religionsgespräch." In *Abraham unser Vater: Juden und Christen in Gespräch Über die Bibel: Festschrift für Otto Michel zum 60 Geburtstag*, edited by Ott Betz and Martin Hengel, 325–36. Leiden: Brill, 1963.
———. "The Veil of the Temple." In *In Honorem Antonii Fridrichsen sexagenarii. Edenda curavit Seminarium Neotestamenticum Upsaliense*, 132–37. ConNT 11. Lund: Gleerup, 1947.
Link, Hans-Georg. "ἱλάσκομαι." *NIDNTT* 3:149. Grand Rapids: Zondervan, 1975–.
Litwak, K. D. *Echoes of Scripture in Luke-Acts: Telling the History of God's People Intertextually*. Journal for the Study of the New Testament Supplement Series 282. London: T&T Clark, 2005.
Loader, William R. G. *Sohn und Hoherpriester: Eine traditionsgeschichtliche Untersuchung zur Christologie des Hebräerbriefes*. WMANT 53. Neukirchen-Vluyn: Neukirchener, 1981.
Lockshin, Martin I. *Rashbam's Commentary on Leviticus and Numbers*, edited by Martin I. Lockshin. BJS. Providence: Brown Judaic Studies, 2001.
Longenecker, Richard N. *The Christology of Early Jewish Christianity*. SBT 17. Naperville: Alec R. Allenson, 1970.
Loretz, O. Leberschau. *Sündenbock, Asasel in Ugarit und Israel*. Altenberge: CIS, 1985.

Louw, Johannes P. and Eugene A. Nida. *Greek-English Lexicon of the New Testament: Based on Semantic Domains*. New York: United Bible Societies, 1996.
Lunn, Nicholas P. "Jesus, the Ark and the Day of Atonement: Intertextual Echoes in John 19:38–20:18." *JETS* 52/4 (2009) 731–746.
Macaskill, Grant. "Matthew and the Parables of Enoch." In *Parables of Enoch: A Paradigm Shift*, edited by Darrell Bock and James H. Charlesworth, 219–230. London: Bloomsbury, 2013.
Maclean, Jennifer K. Berenson. "Barabbas, the Scapegoat Ritual, and the Development of the Passion Narrative." *HTR* 110 (2007) 309–34.
Maccoby, Hyam. *Ritual and Morality: The Ritual Purity System and its Place in Judaism*. Cambridge: Cambridge University Press, 1999.
Maier, Harry O. *Apocalypse Recalled: The Book of Revelation after Christendom*. Minneapolis: Fortress, 2002.
Maier, Johann. *The Temple Scroll: An Introduction, Translation & Commentary*. JSOTSup 34. Sheffield: Sheffield Academic, 1985.
Malina, B. *Christian Origins and Cultural Anthropology: Practical Models for Biblical Interpretation*. Atlanta: John Knox, 1986.
Manning, Jr., Gary T. *Echoes of a Prophet: The Use of Ezekiel in the Gospel of John and in Literature of the Second Temple Period*. London: T&T Clark, 2004.
Manson, T. W. "Hilasterion." *JTS* 46 (1945) 1–10.
Marshall, John W. *Parables of War: Reading John's Jewish Apocalypse*. Studies in Christianity and Judaism 10. Waterloo: Wilfrid Laurier University Press, 2001.
Martin, Troy. "Pagan and Judeo-Christian Time-Keeping Schemes in Gal 4.10 and Col 2.16." *NTS* 42/1 (1996) 105–119.
Martínez, Florentino García and E. J. C. Tigchelaar. *The Dead Sea Scrolls, Study Edition*. 2 vols. Leiden: Brill, 1997.
Marx, Alfred. *Les systèmes sacrificiels de l'Ancien Testament*. VTSup 105. Leiden: Brill, 2005.
———. "The Theology of Sacrifice According to Leviticus 1–7." In *The Book of Leviticus: Composition and Reception*, edited by Rolf Rendtorff and Robert. A. Kugler, 103–120. VTSup 93. Leiden: Brill, 2003.
Mason, Eric F. *You Are a Priest Forever*. Leiden: Brill, 2008.
Matera, Frank. "The Theology of the Epistle to the Hebrews." In *Reading the Epistle to the Hebrews*, edited by Eric F. Mason and Kevin B. McCruden, 189–208. Atlanta: Society of Biblical Literature, 2011.
Mathewson, David. *A New Heaven and a New Earth: The Meaning and Function of the Old Testament in Revelation 21:1–22:5*. JSNTSup 238. Sheffield: Sheffield Academic, 2003.
Mazzaferri, Frederick David. *The Genre of the Book of Revelation from a Source-critical Perspective*. BZNW 54. Berlin: de Gruyter, 1989.
Mays, James Luther. *The Book of Leviticus. The Book of Numbers*. LBC. Atlanta: John Knox, 1977.
Mbamalu, A. "Jesus the Interceding High Priest: A Fresh Look at Hebrews 7:25." *HTS Teologiese Studies* 71(1) (2015).
McKnight, Edgar V. and Christopher Church. *Hebrews-James*. Macon: Smyth & Helwys, 2004.
McLean, B. H. *The Cursed Christ: Mediterranean Expulsion Rituals and Pauline Soteriology*. JSNTSup 126. Sheffield: Sheffield Academic, 1996.

McLean, Bradley. "On the Revision of Scapegoat Terminology." *Numen* 37/2 (1990) 168–73.
McNamara, Martin and Michael Maher, eds. *Targum Pseudo-Jonathan Leviticus*. Vol. 3 of *The Aramaic Bible*, 168–169. Collegeville: Liturgical, 1994.
McRay, John. "Atonement and Apocalyptic in the Book of Hebrews." *ResQ* 23/1 (1980) 1–9.
Meeks, Wayne A. *In Search of the Early Christians*. New Haven: Yale University Press, 2002.
Michel, Otto. *Der Brief and die Hebräer*, 12th ed. KEK 13. Göttingen: Vandenhoeck & Ruprecht, 1966.
Milgrom, Jacob and Roy Gane. "פָּרֹכֶת." *TDOT* 12:95–97.
———. *Cult and Conscience: The Asham and the Priestly Doctrine of Repentance*. SJLA. Leiden: Brill, 1976.
———. "Day of Atonement." *EncJud* 5:1384–1387.
———. "Day of Atonement." *IDBSup* 82–83.
———. *The JPS Commentary to Numbers*. Jerusalem: JPS, 1990.
———. "Israel's Sanctuary: The Priestly 'Picture of Dorian Gray'." *RB* 83 (1983): 390–99.
———. *Leviticus: A Book of Ritual and Ethics*. CC Series. Minneapolis: Fortress, 2004.
———. *Leviticus 1–16: A New Translation with Introduction and Commentary*, 1st ed. AB. New York: Doubleday, 1991.
———. *Leviticus 17–22: A New Translation with Introduction and Commentary*, 1st ed. AB. New York: Doubleday, 2000.
———. *Leviticus 23–27: A New Translation with Introduction and Commentary*, 1st ed. AB. New York: Doubleday, 2001.
———. "Sin-offering or Purification-offering?" *VT* 21 (1971): 237–239.
———. *Studies in Cultic Theology and Terminology*. SJLA. Leiden: Brill, 1983.
———. *Studies in Levitical Terminology*. NES 14. Berkeley: University of California Press, 1970.
———. "The Changing Concept of Holiness in the Pentateuchal Codes with Emphasis on Leviticus 19." In *Reading Leviticus: A Conversation with Mary Douglas*, edited by John F. A. Sawyer, 65–75. JSOTSup 227. Sheffield: Sheffield Academic, 1996.
Matson, Mark A. "The Historical Plausibility of John's Passion Dating." In *John, Jesus and History 2: Aspects of Historicity in the Fourth Gospel*, edited by Paul N. Anderson, Felix Just, and S. J. Tom Thatcher, 291–312. Atlanta: Society of Biblical Literature, 2009.
Metzger, Bruce M. *Breaking the Code: Understanding the Book of Revelation*. Nashville: Abingdon, 1993.
Excerpt From: Michael J. Gorman. "Reading Revelation Responsibly: Uncivil Worship and Witness: Following the Lamb Into the New Creation." Apple Books.
Milik, J. T. *The Books of Enoch: Aramaic Fragments from Qumrân Cave* 4. Oxford: Clarendon, 1976.
Miller, Merrill P. "The Social Logic of the Gospel of Mark: Cultural Persistence and Social Escape in a Postwar Time." In *Redescribing the Gospel of Mark*, edited by Barry S. Crawford and Merrill P. Miller, 207–399. Atlanta: Society of Biblical Literature, 2017.
Mills, Kevin. *Approaching the Apocalypse: Unveiling Revelation in Victorian Writing*. Cranbury: Associated University Presses, 2007.

Miscall, Peter D. "Isaiah: New Heavens, New Earth, New Book." In *Reading Between Texts: Intertextuality and the Hebrew Bible*, edited by Donna N. Fewell, 41–56. Louisville: Westminster John Knox, 1992.
Moberly, Robert B. "When Was Revelation Conceived?" *Bib* 73 (1992) 376–393.
Moffitt, David M. "Blood, Life, and Atonement: Reassessing Hebrews' Christological Appropriation of Yom Kippur." In *The Day of Atonement: Its Interpretation in Early Jewish and Christian Traditions*, edited by Thomas Hieke and Tobias Niklas, 211–224. TBN 15. Leiden: Brill, 2012.
Mojola, Aloo Osotsi. "The Chagga Scapegoat Purification Ritual and Another Rereading of the Goat of Azazel in Leviticus 16." *MelT* 50 (1999) 57–83.
Mollaun, Romuald A. *St. Paul's Concept of* ΙΛΑΣΤΗΡΙΟΝ*: a Historico-Exegetical Investigation*. Washington, DC, n.p., 1923.
Möller, Wilhelm. "Azazel." *ISBE* 1:343. Grand Rapids: Eerdmans, 1939.
Monroe, Lauren A. S. "A 'Holiness' Substratum in the Deuteronomistic Account of Josiah's Reform." *JHS* 7 (2011) 45–49.
Montefiore, H. W. *The Epistle to the Hebrews*. BNTC. London: Adam & Charles Black, 1964.
Moore, Nicholas J. "'Not to Offer Himself Again and Again': An Exegetical and Theological Study of Repetition in the Letter to the Hebrews." PhD dissertation, University of Oxford, 2014.
Morris, Leon. *The Apostolic Preaching of the Cross*. Grand Rapids: Eerdmans, 1965.
———. "The Meaning of 'ΙΛΑΣΤΗΡΙΟΝ in Romans iii. 25." *NTS* 2/1 (1955) 33–43.
———. "The Use of Hilaskesthai etc., in Biblical Greek." *ET* 62 (1950–51) 227–233.
Moscicke, Hans M. *The New Day of Atonement: A Matthean Typology*. Tübingen: Mohr Siebeck, 2020.
Mot, Laurentiu Florentin. "The Measurement Motif in Revelation 11:1–2." In *Earthly Shadows, Heavenly Realities: Temple/Sanctuary Cosmology in Ancient Near Eastern, Biblical, and Early Jewish Literature*, edited by Kim Papaiouannou and Ioannis Giantzaklidis, 229–248. Berrien Springs: Andrews University Press, 2017.
Motyer, S. "The Rending of the Veil: A Markan Pentecost." *NTS* 33 (1987) 155–157.
Mounce, Robert H. *The Book of Revelation*, rev. ed. NICNT. Grand Rapids: Eerdmans, 1998.
———. *Romans*. NAC 27. Nashville: Broadman & Holman, 1995.
Moyise, Steve. "Authorial Intention and the Book of Revelation." *AUSS* 39 (2002) 35–40.
———. "Dialogical Intertextuality." In *Exploring Intertextuality*, edited by B. J. Oropeza and Steve Moyise, 3–15. Eugene: Cascade Books, 2016.
———. *Evoking Scripture: Seeing the Old Testament in the New*. New York; London: T&T Clark, 2008.
———. *The Old Testament in the Book of Revelation*. JSNTSup 115. Sheffield: Sheffield Academic, 1995.
———. *The Old Testament in the New*. London: T&T Clark, 2001.
———. "Recent Developments in the Study of the Book of Revelation." *AUSS* 26 (1988) 159–170.
Murphy, Frederick J. *Fallen is Babylon. The Revelation to John*. Harrisburg: Trinity, 1998.

Musvosvi, Joel. "The Issue of Genre and Apocalyptic Prophecy." *AASS* 5 (2002) 43–60.
Nelson, Richard D. "'He Offered Himself': Sacrifice in Hebrews." *Int* 57 (2003) 251–65.
Nestle, E. "Azazel." *Encyclopedia of Religion and Ethics*, edited by J. Hastings, 282–283. New York: Charles Scribner's Sons, 1916.
Neufeld, Dietmar. "Under the Cover of Clothing: Scripted Clothing Performances in the Apocalypse of John." *BTB* 35 (2005) 67–76.
Neusner, Jacob. *The Mishnah: A New Translation*. New Haven; London: Yale University Press, 1988.
Newport, Kenneth G. C. *Apocalypse and Millennium: Studies in Biblical Eisegesis*. Cambridge: Cambridge University Press, 2000.
Nibley, Hugh. *Temple and Cosmos: Beyond This Ignorant Present*. Salt Lake City: Deseret Book, 1992.
Nickelsburg, G. W. E. *Jewish Literature Between the Bible and the Mishnah*. London: SCM, 2005.
Nicole, Roger R. "C. H. Dodd and the Doctrine of Propitiation." *WTJ* 17 (1955) 117–157.
Nielsen, K. *Incense in Ancient Israel*. VTSup 38. Leiden: Brill, 1986.
Niese, B. *Flavius Josephus. Flavii Iosephi Opera*. Berlin: Weidmann, 1892.
Noë, John. "An Exegetical Basis for a Preterist-Idealist Understanding of the Book of Revelation." *JETS* 49/4 (2006) 767–96.
Nolland, John. *The Gospel of Matthew: A Commentary on the Greek Text*. NIGTC. Grand Rapids: Eerdmans, 2005.
Norton, T. C. G. "The Meaning of *kai peri hamartias* in Romans viii.3." *JTS* 22 (1971) 515–517.
Noth, Martin. *Leviticus*. Philadelphia: Westminster, 1977.
Nusca, A. Robert. *The Christ of the Apocalypse: Contemplating the Faces of Jesus in the Book of Revelation*. Steubenville: Emmaus Road, 2018.
Odek, Rabach. "The Heavenly Sanctuary in Revelation: Context and Significance." In *Earthly Shadows, Heavenly Realities: Temple/Sanctuary Cosmology in Ancient Near Eastern, Biblical, and Early Jewish Literature*, edited by Kim Papaiouannou and Ioannis Giantzaklidis, 217–227. Berrien Springs: Andrews University Press, 2017.
Orlov, Andrei A. *The Atoning Dyad: The Two Goats of Yom Kippur in the Apocalypse of Abraham*. Leiden: Brill, 2016.
———. *Dark Mirrors: Azazel and Satanael in Early Jewish Demonology*. Albany: State University Press, 2011.
———. *Divine Scapegoats: Demonic Mimesis in Early Jewish Mysticism*. New York: State University Press, 2015.
———. "The Eschatological Yom Kippur in the Apocalypse of Abraham: Part I: The Scapegoat Ritual." In *Symbola Caelestis. Le symbolisme liturgique et paraliturgique dans le monde Chrétien*, edited by A. Orlov and B. Lourié, 3–35. Scrinium 5. Piscataway: Gorgias, 2009.
———. *Heavenly Priesthood in the Apocalypse of Abraham*. New York: Cambridge University Press, 2013.
———. "The Likeness of Heaven: The *Kavod* of Azazel in the *Apocalypse of Abraham*." In *With Letters of Light*, edited by Daphna V. Arbel and Andrei A. Orlov, 232–253. Berlin: de Gruyter, 2011.

———. "The Pteromorphic Angelology of the Apocalypse of Abraham." *CBQ* 71/4 (2009) 830–42.

———. *Yahoel and Metatron: Aural Apocalypticism and the Origins of Early Jewish Mysticism*. Tübingen: Mohr Siebeck, 2017.

Osborne, Grant R. *Revelation*. BECNT. Grand Rapids: Baker Academic, 2002.

———. *Romans Verse by Verse*. Bellingham: Lexham, 2017.

Ounsworth, Richard. *Joshua Typology in the New Testament*. WUNT 328. Tübingen: Mohr Siebeck, 2012.

Parker, Robert. *On Greek Religion*. Ithaca: Cornell University Press, 2011.

Parry, Donald W. and Emanuel Tov. *Exegetical Texts*. DSSR, Part 2. Leiden: Brill, 2004.

Paul, Ian. *Revelation*. TNTC 20. Downers Grove: Intervarsity, 2018.

Paulien, Jon. "Criteria and the Assessment of Allusions to the Old Testament in the Book of Revelation." In *Studies in Revelation*, edited by Steve Moyise, 113–129. Edinburgh: T&T Clark, 2001.

———. *Decoding Revelation's Trumpets: Allusions and the Interpretation of Revelation 8:7–12*. AUSDDS 11. Berrien Springs: Andrews University Press, 1988.

———. "Dreading the Whirlwind: Intertextuality and the Use of the Old Testament in Revelation." *AUSS* 29 (2001) 5–22.

———. "Elusive Allusions: The Problematic Use of the Old Testament in Revelation." *BibR* 33 (1988) 37–53.

———. "New Testament Use of the Old Testament." In *Hermeneutic, Intertextuality and the Contemporary Meaning of Scripture*, edited by Ross Cole and Paul Petersen, 29–49. Cooranbong: Avondale Academic Press, 2014.

———. Review of *Die Rezeption des Propheten Ezechiel in der Offenbarung des Johannes* by Beate Kowalski. *JBL* 124/4 (2005) 782–785.

———. "The Role of the Hebrew Cultus, Sanctuary, and Temple in the Plot and Structure of the Book of Revelation." *AUSS* 33 (1995) 245–264.

———. "Seals and Trumpets: Some Current Discussions." In vol. 1 of *Symposium on Revelation*, edited by Frank B. Holbrook, 183–198. Hagerstown: Review and Herald, 1992.

———. "The Seven Seals." In vol. 1 of *Symposium on Revelation*, edited by Frank B. Holbrook, 199–229. Hagerstown: Review and Herald, 1992.

Paxy, Alumkal Jacob. *Death and Resurrection of Jesus Christ Implied in the Image of the Paschal Lamb in 1 Cor 5:7*. Bern: Peter Lang, 2014.

Pfochen, Sebastien. *Diatribe de linguae graecae Novi Testamenti puritate*. Amsterdam: Janson, 1629.

Philip, Mayjee. *Leviticus in Hebrews*. New York: Peter Lang, 2011.

Pietersma, Albert. "Greek Jeremiah and the Land of Azazel." In *Studies in the Hebrew Bible, Qumran, and the Septuagint. Presented to Eugene Ulrich*, edited by Peter W. Flint, Emanuel Tov and James C. VanderKam, 403–413. VTSup 101. Leiden: Brill, 2006.

Pinker, Aron. "A Goat to Go to Azazel." *JHS* 7 (2007) 1–25.

Piper, Otto A. "The Apocalypse of John and the Liturgy of the Ancient Church." *CH* 20 (1951) 10–22.

Pippin, Tina. *Death and Desire: The Rhetoric of Gender in the Apocalypse of John*. Louisville: Westminster John Knox, 1992.

Plummer, Robert L. "Something Awry In The Temple? The Rending of the Temple Veil And Early Jewish Sources That Report Unusual Phenomena In The Temple Around AD 30." *JETS* 48/2 (2005) 301–16.

Polhill, John B. *Acts*. NAC 26. Nashville: Broadman & Holman, 1992.
Porter, Stanley E. "Allusions and Echoes." In *As It Is Written: Studying Paul's Use of Scripture*, edited by Stanley E. Porter and Christopher D. Stanley, 29–40. Atlanta: Society of Biblical Literature, 2008.
———. "Further Comments on the Use of the Old Testament in the New Testament." In *Intertextuality of the Epistles: Explorations of Theory and Practice*, edited by Thomas L. Brodie, Dennis R. MacDonald, and Stanley E. Porter, 98–110. NTM 6. Sheffield: Sheffield Phoenix, 2007.
———. *Hearing the Old Testament in the New Testament*. Grand Rapids: Eerdmans, 2006.
———. "The Language of the Apocalypse in Recent Discussion." *NTS* 35 (1989) 582–603.
———. *The Letter to the Romans: Linguistic and Literary Commentary*. NTM 37. Sheffield: Sheffield Phoenix, 2015.
Prashker, David. *The Day of Atonement: A Guide to the History, Liturgy and Nature of the Jewish Festival of Yom Kippur*. Argaman, 2014.
Priest, Tammy L. *Rending the Curtain*. Tammy L. Priest, 2018.
Prigent, Pierre. *Flash sur l'Apocalypse*. Paris: Collection Flèches, 1974.
Punt, Jeremy. "Inhabiting the World in Front of the Text: The New Testament and Reception Studies." *Neo* 34/1 (2000) 207–24.
Radner, Ephraim. *Leviticus*. BTCB. Grand Rapids: Brazos, 2008.
Reis, André. Review of *Apocalypse of Empire: Imperial Eschatology in Late Antiquity and Early Islam* by Stephen J. Shoemaker. *AUSS* 57/1 (2019) 239–242.
———. Review of *Nebuchadnezzar's Dream: The Crusades, Apocalyptic Prophecy, and the End of History* by Jay Rubenstein. *AUSS* 58/ (2020) 320–325.
———. "Robert Sloan Donnell: From Righteousness by Faith to Sinless Perfection." *Spes Christiana* 31/2 (2020) 47–84.
———. *The Figure of Typological Echo in the New Testament: The Abomination of Desolation as a Case Study*, forthcoming.
Rendtorff, Rolf. "Leviticus 16 als Mitte der Tora." *BibInt* 11 (2003) 252–258.
———. *The Old Testament: An Introduction*. Philadelphia: Fortress, 1985.
———. *Studien zur Geschichte des Opfers im Alten Israel*. Neukirchen-Vluyn: Neukirchener, 1967.
———. *Theologie des Alten Testaments: Ein kanonischer Entwurf*. 2 vols. Neukirchen-Vluyn: Neukirchener, 2001.
Resseguie, James L. *Revelation Unsealed: A Narrative Critical Approach to John's Apocalypse*. Leiden: Brill, 1998.
Rhyder, Julia. *Centralizing the Cult: The Holiness Legislation in Leviticus 17–26*. FAT 134. Tübingen: Mohr Siebeck, 2019.
Ridderbos, H. *Paul: An Outline of His Theology*. Grand Rapids: Eerdmans, 1975.
Rissi, M. *Time and History: A Study on the Revelation*. Richmond: John Knox, 1966.
Ritchie, Ian D. "The Nose Knows: Bodily Knowing in Isaiah 11.3." *JSOT* 87 (2000) 59–73.
Robins, Ellen. "The Pleiades, the Flood and the Jewish New Year." In *Ki Baruch Hu: Ancient Near Eastern, Biblical and Judaic Studies in Honor of Baruch A. Levine*, edited by Robert Chazan, William W. Hallo and Lawrence Schiffman, 341–344. Winona Lake: Eisenbrauns, 1999.
Roberts, Morley. "The Pharmakos." *Folklore* 27 (1916) 218–24.
Robinson, John A. T. *Redating the New Testament*. Eugene: Wipf and Stock, 2000.

Rodríguez, Ángel M. *Substitution in the Hebrew Cultus.* AUSDDS 3. Berrien Springs: Andrews University Press, 1979.
Rojas-Flores, Gonzalo. "The Book of Revelation and the First Years of Nero's Reign." *Bib* 85/3 (2004) 375–392.
Rooke, Deborah W. "The Day of Atonement as a Ritual of Validation for the High Priest." In *Temple Worship in Biblical Israel,* edited by John Day, 342–364. London: T&T Clark, 2007.
Rooker, Mark F. *Leviticus.* NAC 3a. Nashville: Broadman & Holman, 2000.
Rothstein, Eric. "Diversity and Change and Literary Histories." In *Influence and Intertextuality in Literary History,* edited by Jay Clayton and Eric Rothstein, 114–145. Madison: University of Wisconsin Press, 1991.
Rowland, Christopher. "A Man Clothed in Linen: Daniel 10.6ff. and Jewish Angelology." *JSNT* 24 (1985) 99–110.
———. "The Temple in the New Testament." In *Temple Worship in Biblical Israel,* edited by John Day, 489–483. London: T&T Clark, 2007.
Royalty, Jr., Robert M. "Don't Touch *This* Book! Revelation 22:18–19 and the Rhetoric of Reading (In) the Apocalypse of John." *BibInt* 12/3 (2004) 282–299.
Rubinkiewicz, Ryszard. "Abraham, Apocalypse of." *AYBD* 1:41–43.
———. "Apocalypse of Abraham." *OTP* 1:681–705.
———. *L'Apocalypse d'Abraham en vieux slave.* Édition critique du texte, introduction, traduction et commentaire. Lublin: Katolickiego, 1987.
Rudman, Dominic. "A Note on Azazel." *ZAW* (2004) 396–401.
Ruiz, Jean-Pierre. *Ezekiel in the Apocalypse: The Transformation of Prophetic Language in Revelation 16, 17–19,10.* EUS Series 23; 376. Frankfurt am Main: Peter Lang, 1989.
Rylaarsdam, J. C. "Atonement, Day of." *IDB* 1:313–316.
Sacchi, Paolo. *Jewish Apocalyptic and its History.* JSPSup 20. Sheffield: Sheffield Academic, 1990.
Safren, Jonathan D. "Jubilee and the Day of Atonement." In *Proceedings of the 12th World Congress of Jewish Studies, Division A: The Bible and Its World,* edited by Ron Margolin, 107–113. Jerusalem: World Union of Jewish Studies, 1999.
Sampley, J. Paul. "The Weak and the Strong: Paul's Careful and Crafty Rhetorical Strategy in Romans 14:1–15:13." In *The Social World of the First Christians: Essays in Honor of Wayne A. Meeks,* edited by L. Michael White and O. Larry Yarbrough, 40–52. Minneapolis: Fortress, 1995.
Sanders, E. P. *Judaism: Practice & Belief 63BCE–66CE.* London: SCM, 1992.
Schenck, Kenneth. "Hebrews as the Re-Presentation of a Story: A Narrative Approach to Hebrews." In *Reading the Epistle to the Hebrews,* edited by Eric F. Mason and Kevin B. McCruden, 171–188. Atlanta: Society of Biblical Literature, 2011.
Schiffman, Lawrence H. "The Case of the Day of Atonement Ritual." In *Biblical Perspectives: Early Use & Interpretation of the Bible in Light of the Dead Sea Scrolls.* Proceedings from the First International Symposium of the Orion Center, 12–14 May 1996, edited by Michael E. Stone & Esther G. Chazon, 181–188. Leiden: Brill, 1998.
Schreiber, S. "Das Weihegeschenk Gottes; Eine Deutung des Todes Jesu in Rom 3,25." *ZNW* 97 (2006) 88–110.
Scullion, J. P. "A Traditio-Historical Study of the Day of Atonement." PhD dissertation, Catholic University of America, Washington, DC, 1990.

Schabow, Stefanie. *Gemacht zu einem Königreich und Priestern für Gott*. WMANT 147. Neukirchen-Vluyn: Neukirchener, 2016.

Schenker, Adrian. "Das Zeichen des Blutes und die Gewißheit der Vergebung im Alten Testament: die sühnende Funktion des Blutes auf dem Altar nach Lev 17.10–12." *MTZ* 34 (1983) 195–213.

Schlatter, A. *Das Alte Testament in der johanneischen Apokalypse*. BFCT 6. Gütersloh: C. Bertelsmann, 1912.

Schneider, Carl. "καταπέτασμα." *TDNT* 3:629–630.

Schoenberg, Devorah. "A Good Argument to Penitents: Sin and Forgiveness in Midrashic Interpretations of the Golden Calf." In *Golden Calf Traditions in Early Judaism, Christianity, and Islam*, edited by Eric F. Mason and Edmondo F. Lupieri, 176–193. TBN 23. Leiden: Brill, 2019.

Schreiner, Patrick. *The Ascension of Christ: Recovering a Neglected Doctrine*. Bellingham: Lexham, 2020.

Schreiner, Thomas R. *Romans*. BECNT. Grand Rapids: Baker Academic, 2018.

Schur, Israel. *Versöhnungstag und Sündenbock: Jom-ha-kippurim und Sair-la-'zazel*. Helsingfors: Societas Scientiarum Fennica, 1933.

Schüssler Fiorenza, Elisabeth. Priester für Gott*: Studien zum Herrschafts- und Priestermotiv in der Apokalypse*. NTA 7. Münster: Aschendorff, 1972.

———. *Revelation: Justice and Judgment*. Philadelphia: Fortress, 1985.

———. *Revelation: Vision of a Just World*. Minneapolis: Augsburger, 1998.

Schwartz, Baruch J. "The Bearing of Sin in the Priestly Literature." In *Pomegranates and Golden Bells: Studies in Biblical, Jewish, and Near Eastern Ritual, Law, and Literature in Honor of Jacob Milgrom*, edited by David P. Wright, D. N. Freedman, and A. Hurvitz, 3–21. Winona Lake: Eisenbrauns, 1995.

———. "Prohibitions Concerning the 'Eating' of Blood." In *Priesthood and Cult in Ancient Israel*, edited by Gary A. Anderson and Saul M. Olyan, 34–66. JSOTSup 125. Sheffield: Sheffield Academic, 1991.

———. Review of *Cult and Character* by Roy Gane. *AUSS* 45 (2007) 267–272.

Schwartz, Daniel R. "Two Pauline Allusions to the Redemptive Mechanism of the Crucifixion." *JBL* 102/2 (1983) 259–268.

Segal J. B. and E. C. D. Hunter. *Aramaic and Mandaic Incantation Bowls in the British Museum*. London: British Museum, 2000.

Segal, M. H. *The Pentateuch: Its Composition and Its Authorship and Other Biblical Studies*. Jerusalem: Magnes, 1967.

———. "The Religion of Israel before Sinai." *JQR* 53 (1962/63) 226–256.

Shearman, Susan Lee and John Briggs Curtis. "Divine-Human Conflicts in the Old Testament." *JNES* 28/4 (1969) 231–242.

Shelton, L. "A Covenant Concept of Atonement." *WTJ* 19 (1984) 92–96.

Shepherd Jr., Massey H. *The Paschal Liturgy and the Apocalypse*. Richmond: John Knox, 1960.

Shevel, H. D, ed. *Ramban's Commentary on the Pentateuch*. Jerusalem: Mossad HaRav Kook, 1969.

Sim, D. C. "The Man without the Wedding Garment (Matthew 22:11–13)." *HeytJ* 31 (1990) 165–78.

Sklar, Jay. *Leviticus: An Introduction and Commentary*. TOTC 3. Downers Grove: Intervarsity, 2014.

———. "Sin and Impurity: Atoned or Purified? Yes!" In *Perspectives on Purity and Purification in the Bible*, edited by Baruch J. Schwartz et al., 18–31. LHBOTS 464. London: T&T Clark, 2008.

———. *Sin, Impurity, Sacrifice, Atonement: The Priestly Conceptions*. Sheffield: Sheffield Phoenix, 2005.

Slater, Thomas B. "Dating the Apocalypse to John." *Bib* 84 (2003) 252–258.

Sleeman, Matthew. *Geography and the Ascension Narrative in Acts*. SNTSMS 146. Cambridge: Cambridge University Press.

Smalley, Stephen S. *The Revelation to John: A Commentary on the Greek Text of the Apocalypse*. Downers Grove: Intervarsity, 2005.

Snaith, N. "The meaning of שׂערים." *VT* 25 (1975) 115–118.

Spatafora, Andrea. *From the Temple of God to God as the Temple: A Biblical Theological Study of the Temple in the Book of Revelation*. Rome: Pontificia Università Gregoriana, 1997.

Speiser, E. A. "A Vision of the Nether World." In *Ancient Near Eastern Texts Relating to the Old Testament*, edited by James B. Pritchard, 109–111. Princeton: Princeton University Press, 1969.

Spence-Jones, H. D. M., ed. *Hebrews*. PC. London: Funk & Wagnalls, 1909.

Spencer, John R. "Aaron (Person)." *AYBD* 1:5.

Stanley, Steve. "Hebrews 9:6–10: The 'Parable' of the Tabernacle." *NovT* 37/4 (1995) 385–399.

Stegemann, Ekkehard W. and Wolfgang Stegemann. "Does The Cultic Language In Hebrews Represent Sacrificial Metaphors? Reflections On Some Basic Problems." In *Hebrews: Contemporary Methods, New Insights*, edited by Gabriella Gelardini, 13–24. BIS 75. Leiden: Brill, 2005.

Steiner, Deborah. "Diverting Demons: Ritual, Poetic Mockery and the Odysseus-Iros Encounter." *Classical Antiquity* 28/1 (2009) 71–100.

Stefanović, Ranko. "The Angel at the Altar (Revelation 8:3–5). A Case Study on Intercalations in Revelation." *AUSS* 44 (2006) 79–94.

———. "The Background and Meaning of the Sealed Book of Revelation 5." PhD dissertation, Andrews University, 1995.

———. *Revelation of Jesus Christ: Commentary on the Book of Revelation*. Berrien Springs: Andrews University Press, 2002.

Stemberger, Günter. "Yom Kippur in Mishnah Yoma." In *Day of Atonement: Its Interpretation in Early Jewish and Christian Traditions*, edited by Thomas Hieke, Tobias Nicklas, 121–137. TBN 15. Leiden: Brill, 2012.

Stern, Jacob. "Scapegoat Narratives in Herodotus." *Hermes* 119/3 (1991) 304–11.

Stevenson, Gregory. *Power and Place: Temple and Identity in the Book of Revelation*. Berlin: de Gruyter, 2001.

Stott, Wilfrid. "A Note on the Word ΚΥΡΙΑΚΗ in Rev. i. 10." *NTS* 12 (1965) 70–75.

Stökl, Daniel J. "The Christian Exegesis of the Scapegoat Between Jews and Pagans." In *Sacrifice in Religious Experience*, edited by Albert I. Baumgarten, 207–232. SHR 93. Leiden: Brill, 2002.

Strand, Kenneth A. "Another Look at the 'Lord's Day' in the Early Church." *NTS* 13 (1967) 174–181.

———. *Interpreting the Book of Revelation: Hermeneutical Guidelines with Brief Introduction to Literary Analysis*. Naples: Ann Arbor, 1976.

———. "An Overlooked Old-Testament Background to Revelation 11:1." *AUSS* 22 (1984) 317–325.

Stramara, Daniel F. *God's Timetable: The Book of Revelation and the Feast of Seven Weeks*. Eugene: Pickwick, 2011.

Stuckenbruck, Loren T. *The Myth of Rebellious Angels: Studies in Second Temple Judaism and New Testament Texts*. Grand Rapids: Eerdmans, 2017.

Sturdy, J. V. M. *Redrawing the Boundaries: The Date of Early Christian Literature*. Oakville: Equinox, 2007.

Suleiman, Susan R. "Introduction: Varieties of Audience-Oriented Criticism." In *The Reader in the Text: Essays on Audience and Interpretation*, edited by Susan R. Suleiman and I. Crossman, 1–45. Princeton: Princeton University Press, 1980.

Sun, Henry T. C. "Holiness Code." *AYBD* 3:254–258.

Surridge, Robert. "Seventh-day Adventism: Self-Appointed Laodicea." In *Studies in the Book of Revelation*, edited by Steve Moyise, 21–42. London: T&T Clark, 2001.

Sutter, David W. "Weighed in the Balance: The Similitudes of Enoch in Recent Discussion." *RSR* 7 (1981) 217–21.

Swanson, James. "תְּכֵלֶת." In *Dictionary of Biblical Languages with Semantic Domains: Hebrew (Old Testament)*. Oak Harbor: Logos, 1997.

Sweeney, Marvin A. "Ezekiel: Zadokite Priest and Visionary Prophet of the Exile." In *Form and Intertextuality in Prophetic and Apocalyptic Literature*. FAT 45. Tübingen: Mohr Siebeck, 2005.

Swartz, Michael D. "The Semiotics of the Priestly Vestments." In *Sacrifice in Religious Experience*, edited by Albert I. Baumgarten, 57–80. SHR 93. Leiden: Brill, 2002.

Sweet, J. P. M. *Revelation*. PNTC. London: SCM, 1979.

Swete, Henry Barclay. *The Apocalypse of John*. London: Macmillan, 1906.

Tabberne, William. *Prophets and Gravestones: An Imaginative History of Montanists and Other Early Christians*. Peabody: Hendrickson, 2009.

Talbert, Charles H. *The Apocalypse: A Reading of the Revelation of John*. Louisville: Westminster John Knox, 1994.

Tavo, Felise. *Woman, Mother and the Bride: An Exegetical Investigation into the Ecclesial Notion of the Apocalypse*. Leuven: Peeters, 2007.

Tawil, H. "Azazel the Prince of the Steepe: A Comparative Study." *ZAW* 92 (1980) 43–59.

Tenney, Merrill C. *Interpreting Revelation*. Grand Rapids: Eerdmans, 1957.

Thiselton, Anthony C. *The First Epistle to the Corinthians: A Commentary on the Greek Text*. NIGTC. Grand Rapids: Eerdmans, 2000.

———. *The Hermeneutics of Doctrine*. Grand Rapids: Eerdmans, 2007.

Tiwald, Markus. "Christ as Hilasterion (Rom 3:25) Pauline Theology on the Day of Atonement in the Mirror of Early Jewish Thought." In *The Day of Atonement: Its Interpretation in Early Jewish and Christian Traditions*, edited by Thomas Hieke and Tobias Niklas, 189–20. TBN 15. Leiden: Brill, 2012.

Theisohn, Johannes. *Der auserwählte Richter: Untersuchungen zum traditionsgeschichtlichen Ort der Menschensohnsgestalt der Bilderreden des Äthiopischen Henoch*. SUNT 12. Göttingen: Vandenhoeck & Ruprecht, 1975.

Thompson, Leonard. *The Book of Revelation: Apocalypse and Empire*. Oxford: Oxford University Press, 1990.

Thompson, Steven. *Apocalypse and Semitic Syntax*. Cambridge: Cambridge University Press, 1985.

———. "The End of Satan." *AUSS* 37/2 (1999) 257–268.

Tonstad, Sigve K. *Revelation*. PCNT. Grand Rapids: Baker Academic, 2019.

———. *Saving God's Reputation: The Theological Function of Pistis Iesou in the Cosmic Narratives of Revelation*. London: T&T Clark, 2006.

Trench, Richard Chenevix. *Synonyms of the New Testament*. London: Macmillan, 1880.

Trudinger, Paul. "The Apocalypse and the Palestinian Targum." *BTB* 16 (1986) 78–79.

———. " 'O AMHN' (Rev III:14) and the Case for a Semitic Original of the Apocalypse." *NovT* 14 (1972) 227–279.

Ulfgard, Håkan. *Feast and Future: Revelation 7:9-17 and the Feast of Tabernacles*. Stockholm: Almqvist & Wiksell, 1989.

Ulansey, David. "The Heavenly Veil Torn: Mark's Cosmic Inclusio." *JBL* 110 (1991) 123–25.

Unger, Merrill Frederick. *The Hodder Bible Handbook*. London: Hodder and Stoughton, 1984.

Haloviak Valentine, Kendra. *Worlds at War, Nations in Song: Dialogic Imagination and Moral Vision in the Hymns of the Book of Revelation*. Eugene: Wipf & Stock, 2015.

VanderKam, James C. *The Book of Jubilees: A Critical Text*. Leuven: Peeters, 1989.

———. *A Commentary on the Book of Jubilees* 1–21. Minneapolis: Fortress, 2018.

———. *A Commentary on the Book of Jubilees* 22–50. Minneapolis: Fortress, 2018.

———. "1 Enochic, Enochic Motifs and Enoch in Early Christian Literature." In *The Jewish Apocalyptic Heritage in Early Christianity*, edited by James C. VanderKam and W. Adler, 33–101. CRINT 4. Minneapolis: Fortress, 1996.

———. "Moses Trumping Moses: Making the Book of Jubilees." In *The Dead Sea Scrolls: Transmission of Traditions and Production of Texts*, edited by Sarianna Metso, Hindy Najman and Eileen Schuller, 25–44. Leiden: Brill, 2010.

Vlach, Michael J. *Has the Church Replaced Israel: A Theological Evaluation*. Nashville: B&H Academic, 2010.

Voelz, James W. "The Language of the New Testament." *ANRW* II.25.2:894–977.

Vogel, Winfried. *Cultic Motif in the Book of Daniel*. New York: Peter Lang, 2009.

Vogelgesang, Jeffrey Marshall. "The Interpretation of Ezekiel in the Book of Revelation." PhD dissertation, Harvard University, 1985.

Volgger, David. "The Day of Atonement According to the Temple Scroll." *Bib* 87/2 (2006) 251–260.

von Rad, Gerhard. *Old Testament Theology*, vol. I. Edinburgh; London: Oliver & Boyd, 1962.

Vorster, Willem S. "1 Enoch and the Jewish Literary Setting of the New Testament: A Study in Text Types." *Neo* 17 (1983) 1–14.

———. "Genre and the Revelation of John: A Study in Text, Context and Intertext." *Neo* 22 (1998) 103–23.

———. "Intertextuality and Redaktionsgeschichte." In *Intertextuality in Biblical Writings: Essays in Honour of Bas van Iersel* edited by S. Draisma, 15–26. Kampen: Kok, 1989.

Vos, L. H. *The Synoptic Traditions in the Apocalypse*. Kampen: Kok, 1965.

Walck, Leslie. "The Parables of Enoch and the Synoptic Gospels." In *Parables of Enoch: A Paradigm Shift*, edited by Darrell Bock and James H. Charlesworth, 231–268. London: Bloomsbury, 2013.

Warning, Wilfried. *Literary Artistry in Leviticus*. BIS 35. Leiden: Brill, 1999.

Watts, James. *Leviticus 1–10.* HCOT. Leuven: Peeters, 2013.

———. *Ritual and Rhetoric in Leviticus: From Sacrifice to Scripture.* Cambridge: Cambridge University Press, 207.

Wellhausen, J. *Die Composition des Hexateuchs und der historischen Bücher des Alten Testaments.* Berlin: de Gruyter, 1963.

Wenham, Gordon J. *The Book of Leviticus.* Grand Rapids: Eerdmans, 1979.

Westbrook, Raymond. "Who Led the Scapegoat in Leviticus 16:21?" *JBL* 127 (2008) 417–422.

Weyde, Karl William. *The Appointed Feasts of Yahweh: The Festival Calendar in Leviticus 23 and the Sukkot Festival in Other Biblical Texts.* Tübingen: Mohr Siebeck, 2004.

Whiston, William, ed. *The Works of Josephus: Complete and Unabridged.* 1895. Reprint, Peabody: Hendrickson, 1987.

Wilcox, Max. "Semitisms in the New Testament." *ANRW* II.25.2:977–1029.

Wiencke, G. *Paulus über Jesu Tod: Die Deutung des Todes Jesu bei Paulus und ihre Herkunft.* BFCT 2/42. Gütersloh: Bertelsmann, 1939.

Williams-Tinajero, Lace Marie. *The Reshaped Mind.* Leiden: Brill, 2010.

Winer, Georg Benedict. *Grammatik des neutestamentlichen Sprachidioms als sichere Grundlage der neutestamentlichen Exegese.* 6th ed. Leipzig: 1855.

Wilson, B. *Systems, Concepts, Methodologies, and Applications.* New York: Wiley, 1984.

Wilson, J. Christian. "The Problem of the Domitianic Date of Revelation." *NTS* 39 (1993) 587–605.

Wilson, Mark. "The Early Christians in Ephesus and the Date of Revelation, Again." *Neo* 39/1 (2005) 163–93.

Winkle, Ross E. "Clothes Make the (One Like a Son of) Man: Dress Imagery in Revelation 1 as an Indicator of High-priestly Status." PhD dissertation, Andrews University, 2012.

Wise, Michael Owen. *A Critical Study of the Temple Scroll from Qumran Cave 11.* SAOC 49. Chicago: University of Chicago Press, 1990.

Witherup, R. D. "The Death of Jesus and the Raising of the Saints: Matthew 27:51–54 in Context." SBLSP (1987) 574–85.

Wolf, Herbert. "אָזַל." *TWOT* 28.

Wolff, Christian "Die Gemeinde des Christus in der Apokalypse des Johannes." *NTS* 27 (1981) 186–197.

Wratislaw, A. H. "The Scapegoat-Barrabas." *ExpTim* 3 (1891/92) 400–403.

Wright, David P. "Day of Atonement." *AYBD* 2:72–76.

———. *The Disposal of the Impurity: Elimination Rites in the Bible and in Hittite and Mesopotamian Literature.* SBLDS 101. Atlanta: Society of Biblical Literature, 1987.

———. "The Gesture of Hand-Placement in the Hebrew Bible and in Hittite Literature." *JAOS* 106 (1986) 433–446.

———. "The Spectrum of Priestly Impurity." In *Priesthood and Cult in Ancient Israel,* edited by Gary A. Anderson and Saul M. Olyan, 155–181. JSOTSup 125. Sheffield: JSOT, 1991.

——— et al. *Pomegranates and Golden Bells: Studies in Biblical, Jewish, and Near Eastern Ritual, Law, and Literature in Honor of Jacob Milgrom.* Winona Lake: Eisenbrauns, 1995.

Wright, N. T. *Paul: A Biography.* New York: HarperOne, 2018.

———. *The Climax of the Covenant.* London: T&T Clark, 1991.

———. "The Meaning of περὶ ἁμαρτίας in Romans 8:3." In *Papers on Paul and Other New Testament Authors*, edited by E. A. Livingstone, 453–459. JSOTSup 3. Sheffield: University of Sheffield Press, 1980.

Wyatt, N. "Atonement Theology in Ugarit and Israel." *UF* 8 (1976) 415–430.

Yamauchi, Edwin. "טָהֵר." *TWOT* 343–345.

Yasser, Joseph. "The Magrepha of the Herodian Temple: A Five-Fold Hypothesis." *JAMS* 13 (1960) 24–42.

Yee, Gale A. *Jewish Feasts in the Gospel of John*. Eugene: Wipf & Stock, 1989.

Yonge, Charles Duke. *The Works of Philo: Complete and Unabridged*. 1854. Reprint, Peabody: Hendrickson, 1995.

Young, Norman H. "C. H. Dodd, 'Hilaskesthai' and his Critics." *EQ* 48 (1976) 67–78.

———. "The Day of Dedication of the Day of Atonement? The Old Testament Background to Hebrews 6:19–20 Revisited." *AUSS* 40 (2002) 61–68.

———. "Did St. Paul Compose Rom iii:24f?" *ABR* 22 (1974) 23–32.

———. "The Gospel According to Hebrews 9." *NTS* 27 (1981) 198–210.

———. "Hilaskesthai and Related Words in the New Testament." *EQ* 55 (1983) 169–176.

———. "The Impact of the Jewish Day of Atonement Upon the Thought of the New Testament." PhD dissertation, Manchester University, 1973.

———. "Romans 14:5–6 in Its Social Setting." *AUSS* 54/1 (2016) 51–70.

———. "ΤΟΥΤ' ΕΣΤΙΝ ΤΗΣ ΣΑΡΚΟΣ ΑΥΤΟΥ (Heb. X.20): Apposition, Dependent or Explicative." *NTS* 20 (1974) 100–104.

———. "Where Jesus Has Gone as a Forerunner on Our Behalf (Hebrews 6:20)." *AUSS* 39 (2001) 165–173.

Youngblood, Ronald F. "תִּכְלֶת." *TWOT* 968–969.

Zatelli, Ida. "The Origin of the Biblical Scapegoat Ritual: The Evidence of the Two Eblaite Texts." *VT* 48 (1998) 254–263.

Zohar, Noam. "Repentance and Purification: The Significance and Semantics of חטאת in the Pentateuch." *JBL* 107 (1988) 609–618.